Democracy and the
New Religious Pluralism

Democracy and the New Religious Pluralism

EDITED BY
THOMAS BANCHOFF

UNIVERSITY PRESS

2007

OXFORD
UNIVERSITY PRESS

Oxford University Press, Inc., publishes works that further
Oxford University's objective of excellence
in research, scholarship, and education.

Oxford   New York
Auckland   Cape Town   Dar es Salaam   Hong Kong   Karachi
Kuala Lumpur   Madrid   Melbourne   Mexico City   Nairobi
New Delhi   Shanghai   Taipei   Toronto

With offices in
Argentina   Austria   Brazil   Chile   Czech Republic   France   Greece
Guatemala   Hungary   Italy   Japan   Poland   Portugal   Singapore
South Korea   Switzerland   Thailand   Turkey   Ukraine   Vietnam

Copyright © 2007 by Oxford University Press, Inc.

Published by Oxford University Press, Inc.
198 Madison Avenue, New York, New York 10016
www.oup.com

Oxford is a registered trademark of Oxford University Press

Library of Congress Cataloging-in-Publication Data
Democracy and the new religious pluralism / edited by Thomas Banchoff.
    p. cm
Includes bibliographical references and index.
ISBN-13: 978-0-19-530722-1; 978-0-19-530729-0 (pbk.)
    1. Democracy—Religious aspects—Congresses.   2. Religious pluralism—Political aspects—
Congresses.   I. Banchoff, Thomas F., 1964–
BL65P7D465   2007
201'.5—dc22   2006016702

9 8 7 6 5 4 3 2 1

Printed in the United States of America
on acid-free paper

Acknowledgments

This book grew out of a conference entitled "The New Religious Pluralism and Democracy" held at Georgetown University in April 2005. The Initiative on Religion, Politics, and Peace, a university-wide effort to advance the interdisciplinary study of religion and promote interreligious understanding, was its main sponsor. In March 2006 the initiative led to the creation of the Berkley Center for Religion, Peace, and World Affairs at Georgetown University.

The editor would like to thank the contributors for revising their conference papers in a timely fashion for publication in this volume. The open and productive exchanges that characterized the conference are reproduced here. Our group was very diverse. It included scholars from the disciplines of philosophy, political science, religious studies, sociology, and theology. We share the conviction that religious pluralism poses both challenges and opportunities for democratic societies on both sides of the Atlantic. The book analyzes those challenges and points some ways forward. It is intended as a contribution both to scholarship and to an ongoing society-wide and international debate.

The book was made possible through the generous collaboration of many people and organizations. For their help and support, the editor would like to thank members of the faculty steering committee of the Initiative on Religion, Politics, and Peace, as well as John J. DeGioia, president of Georgetown University, and Jane McAuliffe, dean of the College of Arts and Sciences. Conference cosponsors at Georgetown included the BMW Center for German and European Studies, the Center for Democracy and Civil Society, the Prince Al-waleed Bin Talal Center for Muslim-Christian Understanding, the Department of Government, the Department of Theology, and the

Program for Jewish Civilization. Dafina Nikolova and Nicholas Ingaciola proved expert assistants in the preparation of both the conference and the manuscript. Susan Frost, Michael Kessler, and Chris Vukicevich provided invaluable support and encouragement. Theo Calderara of Oxford University Press shepherded the volume expertly to publication.

Contents

Contributors

Thomas Banchoff is associate professor in the Department of Government and the Edmund A. Walsh School of Foreign Service and director of the Berkley Center for Religion, Peace, and World Affairs at Georgetown University.

Peter L. Berger is emeritus professor of sociology at Boston University and director of its Institute on Culture, Religion and World Affairs.

José Casanova is professor of sociology and a member of the graduate faculty of political and social science at the New School for Social Research.

Sam Cherribi is senior lecturer in sociology at Emory University.

Grace Davie is a professor in the sociology of religion at Exeter University.

Diana L. Eck is professor of comparative religion and Indian studies and a member of the faculty of divinity at Harvard University.

John L. Esposito is university professor and founding director of the Prince Alwaleed Bin Talal Center for Muslim-Christian Understanding at Georgetown University.

Stanley Hauerwas is the Gilbert T. Rowe Professor of Theological Ethics at the Divinity School of Duke University.

Danièle Hervieu-Léger is professor of sociology and president of the École des Hautes Études en Sciences Sociales.

Ronald Inglehart is professor of political science and program director at the Center for Political Studies at the Institute for Social Research at the University of Michigan.

Pippa Norris is the McGuire Lecturer in Comparative Politics at the John F. Kennedy School of Government at Harvard University.

Martha C. Nussbaum is the Ernst Freund Distinguished Service Professor of Law and Ethics in Philosophy, Law, and Divinity at the University of Chicago.

Yossi Shain is professor in the Department of Government, Georgetown University, and the Department of Political Science, Tel Aviv University.

Miroslav Volf is Henry B. Wright Professor of Theology at Yale Divinity School and director of Yale's Center for Faith and Culture.

Robert Wuthnow is Gerhard R. Andlinger Professor of Sociology and director of the Center for the Study of Religion at Princeton University.

Democracy and the
New Religious Pluralism

I

Introduction

Thomas Banchoff

A new religious pluralism is shaking up Atlantic democracies. In the United States, controversies surrounding the "under God" clause of the Pledge of Allegiance and the display of the Ten Commandments are part of a long-running constitutional struggle. But such controversies are now also colored by the concerns of Hindus, Buddhists, and other religious citizens who reject monotheism. In France, the recent ban on headscarves and other prominent religious symbols in public schools is a dramatic reaffirmation of the tradition of *laïcité*—the exclusion of religion from the public sphere. At the same time, it is a political response to greater religious diversity and to the growth of Islam in particular. In the United Kingdom, controversy surrounding the blasphemy laws is part of an old debate about the institutional prerogatives of the Church of England. But it also raises questions about whether and how to protect the sensibilities of minority faith traditions.

These and other controversies are occasions to rethink the relationship between religion and politics in Atlantic democracies. Entrenched arguments center on whether religion is increasing or decreasing as a social and political force.[1] This familiar secularization debate should not deflect attention from a striking development of the last several decades: the emergence of a more diverse religious landscape with new political implications. In both Western Europe and North America, that diversity encompasses dominant Christian and long-established Jewish groups, a growing Muslim population, and increasing adherents of non-Abrahamic traditions, ranging from Hinduism and Buddhism to New Age spiritualities. Religious diversity is nothing new. But it has increased in scope since the 1980s and 1990s, sparking greater interaction among religious groups and challenges for democratic governance. That interaction and those challenges constitute a new religious pluralism.

What is at stake? For some observers, nothing less than the survival of democracy hangs in the balance. Samuel Huntington, for example, sees Hispanic immigration eroding the Anglo-Protestant culture that has sustained democratic institutions for more than two centuries. Religious diversity, in his view, threatens to undercut moral order and national identity and endanger the American experiment with democracy. In the Western European context, Oriana Fallaci articulates a parallel argument about Muslim immigration. Islam, she argues, is inimical to democracy and human rights. Europe must rediscover and reassert its Christian and Enlightenment identity against a hostile outsider now on the inside. If not, Fallaci opines, European civilization faces a crisis. Huntington and Fallaci are not isolated voices. Their notoriety attests to broad anxiety about the social and political implications of greater religious pluralism on both sides of the Atlantic.[2]

This book rejects such alarmism. The contributors acknowledge the challenges posed by the new religious pluralism. Because it involves beliefs and practices suffused with ultimate meaning, religion is a deep-seated marker of collective identity. When diverse religious communities clash in the political arena, two of democracy's core pillars can begin to falter: minority rights and majority rule. Dominant traditions may seek to constrain minority groups, and religious tensions may undermine effective government by majority. While aware of these challenges, the contributors do not see them as threats to the social bases of democracy or the stability of its institutions. Rising faith communities, and Islam in particular, are engaging the democratic process on both sides of the Atlantic. And established religious groups and secular majorities are accommodating—and not just resisting—the new cultural and political landscape. A multiplicity of faith traditions presents not just challenges for social cohesion and governance but also opportunities for a more vibrant civil society and political culture.

As an interdisciplinary, multinational undertaking, this volume breaks with studies of religious pluralism that begin within defined scholarly communities and geographical spaces.[3] The disciplines of theology and religious studies center their attention on the implications of pluralism for individual belief and shared practices, while social theorists, sociologists, and political scientists more often address its impact on civil society and democratic politics. Scholars of the United States situate religious pluralism within broad social and historical currents of cultural pluralism. For scholars of Western Europe, the confrontation of secular political cultures and majority faith traditions with Islam demands more attention. By juxtaposing disciplinary and national approaches, this book illuminates the phenomenon of religious pluralism from different perspectives and underscores its distinctive and convergent characteristics on both sides of the Atlantic.

The book goes beyond mere juxtaposition. It is also a structured conversation about the social and political implications of the new religious pluralism. Its starting point is broad agreement on what religious pluralism does and

R-Pluralism = belief + social practice interaction with civil/state society, institutions.

does not mean. If the term is here to stay—and there is every reason to expect that it is—it must be defined carefully. In his essay, Stanley Hauerwas raises two red flags. First, the term *religion* often connotes a narrow form of privatized belief that arose within the modern constitutional state. It tends to abstract faith from community and, as others point out, marginalize traditions less centered on beliefs and more on social practices. Second, the term *pluralism* has problematic normative associations. For Hauerwas the theologian, it evokes the idea that religions are so many paths to the same truth. For many other observers, it suggests an affirmation of U.S.-style interest group politics over the corporatist or statist alternatives more prevalent in other democracies.[4]

If religious pluralism is to be redeemed, it must be defined carefully. It refers here to the interaction among religious groups in society and politics. *Religion* is understood broadly to include not only individual and shared beliefs but also social practices and institutions that bind groups. *Pluralism* denotes group interaction in civil society and state institutions. As deployed throughout the volume, the term *religious pluralism* describes a social and political phenomenon and does not imply a variety of ways to one truth or the superiority of the American polity over other forms of social and political organization. If a normative undertone remains, it concerns the view that religious pluralism should be *peaceful*. A preference for nonviolence, as Miroslav Volf points out in his essay, is shared in principle across religious faiths and institutionalized in democratic orders. It is also shared by all of the contributors to this volume. Concern about the potential for social conflict and violence, heightened in the years since September 11, 2001, gives the problem of religious pluralism much of its urgency.

If the contributors agree on a working definition of religious pluralism and a normative commitment to its peaceful management, they take different approaches to the two questions that organize the volume: What are the contours of the new religious pluralism? And how does it challenge democratic governance? The first half of the volume explores the contours of the transatlantic religious landscape. It examines the differential impact of demographic and cultural shifts and points to salient differences between the United States and Western Europe. The second half of the volume addresses the response of democratic civil societies and states to the new religious pluralism. It centers on the twin challenges of protecting minority rights and forging stable majorities, and it brings in philosophical and theological, as well as social science, perspectives. Here the volume goes beyond analysis to prescription: it explores how Atlantic polities can and should engage difference in a shifting religious and secular constellation.

Contours of the New Religious Pluralism

The new religious pluralism is, in part, an outgrowth of a more fluid demographic and cultural landscape. Migration flows generate greater demographic diversity, while modernization tends to loosen social attachments and generate more fluid and multiple possibilities for religious identification and belonging. The contributors give due attention to changes in the religious landscape. But they do not allow the landscape metaphor, with its suggestion of a level playing field upon which religions interact, to obscure the hierarchical dimension of the new pluralism. There are majority religious traditions and majority political cultures—different on both sides of the Atlantic—within which diversity is articulated. Pluralism is about the responses of minorities to majorities and vice versa. Only by viewing the interaction among religious groups on an uneven playing field can one specify distinctive contours of the new religious pluralism.

The demographic characteristics of the new religious pluralism on both sides of the Atlantic are anchored in migration patterns and differential birth rates. In the United States, the 1965 Immigration Act generated more diverse migration flows; Muslim, Buddhist, and Hindu groups have expanded their presence alongside established Christian and Jewish communities. At the same time, those established communities have been transformed by immigration from Asia, the former Soviet bloc, and Latin America. In the European context, Muslim immigration is the most striking phenomenon of the past several decades. In the case of Britain, France, and the Netherlands—three countries treated in the most depth in this volume—Muslim migration from former colonies in Asia and North Africa has been significant. In Germany, a large Turkish community that originated with postwar guest workers and their families has diversified the religious landscape. With Muslims in Europe, as with Hispanics in the United States, higher than average birth rates have contributed to growing numbers and reinforced the diversifying effects of migration. Even without Turkey, Europe's Muslims now number 15–20 million.

The new religious pluralism has a cultural as well as a demographic dynamic. It is not only about population shifts, but also about a shifting array of religious choices and forms of association. Cross-border flows of ideas and commerce have accelerated the drive toward greater individualism that characterizes modernity as a whole. In the context of globalization, individuals face a plural array of choices, including religious choices. "All that is solid melts into air," Marx and Engels argued in *The Communist Manifesto*, pointing to capitalism's relentless erosion of traditional cultural and social attachments. "All that is sacred is profaned," they continued, clearly overstating their case. In industrialized and increasingly globalized societies, religion is alive and well, if more loosely configured. People take on and put down religious identities with greater frequency. They combine elements of different traditions to form a "bricolage" (Hervieu-Léger) or a kind of "patchwork quilt" (Wuthnow). The new religious pluralism, then, is not just about demographics. It is also about more diverse patterns of individual belief.[5]

Different patterns of belief go hand in hand with different kinds of religious practice and association. Religion is lived with and through others. In the context of globalization and modernity, individuals constitute and reconstitute religious groups on a more fluid basis. As Peter Berger points out in his essay, this dynamic can feed fundamentalism, as people seek to reestablish lost certainties and reorder their lives under the shadow of charismatic leadership. But individualization can also reshape patterns of interaction among traditional religious groups. Berger sees a "voluntary principle" at work—the tendency of religious organizations to become voluntary associations, responsive to the shifting preferences of discriminating religious consumers. The American phenomenon of denominationalism, traditionally applied to Protestant churches, now increasingly extends to other traditional and nontraditional religious groups. Berger further argues that this trend of "Protestantization" is evident outside the United States as well. In Western Europe, historically dominant churches, uneasily embedded within a secular political culture, face competition from a range of religious newcomers, both Christian and non-Christian.

In their essay, Pippa Norris and Ronald Inglehart focus on the differential impact of modernization on religion in Western Europe and the United States. Drawing on an impressive array of survey data, they show that identification with established religious communities has declined on both sides of the Atlantic, but much more precipitously in Western Europe. They see an overarching economic, social, and cultural process of secularization at work, a process evident in correlations between rising levels of social and economic well-being, on the one hand, and declining church affiliation and attendance, on the other. Yes, they acknowledge, the United States is a nation both prosperous and pious, but levels of religious identification and practice within the country vary with socioeconomic position. Norris and Inglehart are agnostic on a crucial point: whether modernization drives not only a decline in traditional religious identities and communities, but also a collapse of religious sensibilities altogether. Evidence suggests that the search for ultimate meaning goes on, even in affluent settings. Modernization may drive both a more secular culture and a more fluid and ambiguous religious landscape.

The fact of a changing landscape should not overstate the demographic and cultural changes of the last several decades. In absolute numbers, the current wave of immigration pales alongside that of the late nineteenth and early twentieth centuries. As José Casanova points out in his essay, this wave is more diverse, going beyond the predominantly Christian and transatlantic flows of the earlier era to encompass more Asians, Africans, and Latin Americans from more religious traditions. But it has not fundamentally shifted the religious makeup on either side of the Atlantic. In the United States, more than 80% of the citizens profess Christianity, while in Western Europe, where church attendance is much lower and attitudes more secular, majorities still identify broadly with the Catholic and Protestant traditions. Jews have always been a small minority. In France, the Muslim population has grown, but still accounts for only about 5–7% of the total population. As these numbers suggest, cultural shifts—the individualization of belief and more fluid forms of religious association—have not transformed the overall constellation.

Numbers tell only part of the story. The new religious pluralism consists not only of greater diversity, but of *perceptions* of that diversity and new patterns of *interaction* among religious groups. The media have discovered the theme of religious pluralism in the years since 9/11. Simultaneously, religious groups have begun to interact with one another more in the public sphere. And here, the metaphor of a landscape with its suggestion of a level playing field fails, for the interaction is among unequals. The reaction of minority groups to majority groups—and the other way around—gives religious pluralism its particular cast on each side of the Atlantic. The United States is a majority Christian culture with a well-established Jewish population, coming to terms with Islam and other faith traditions. As Casanova points out, American political culture encourages the cultivation of religious difference, while encouraging cultural assimilation to the norms of an individualist and capitalist society. Western Europe has less experience with immigration and, with its more secular political culture, appears to be less comfortable with religious pluralism. Majorities respect religious freedom but must grapple with Muslim traditions that incorporate different views of personal responsibility and social obligation— some at odds with the dominant secular ones.

The American Jewish experience provides an example of a flourishing religious minority in the face of a predominantly Christian culture. As Yossi Shain demonstrates, the American Jewish community has thrived not just by adapting to (and shaping) dominant norms of American society but also by maintaining strong transnational ties. While the Jewish community has fragmented along religious and cultural lines, an overarching sense of Jewish identity has been preserved—and in some sense strengthened—through its relationship with Israel. Not only has the American Jewish community emerged as a crucial influence on Israeli debates about Jewish identity, favoring a more inclusive understanding, but the maintenance of a transnational identity has also helped to shore up cohesive group identity in the United States. The American Jewish experience suggests the importance of transnational ties for minority groups in diaspora. Shain's analysis further underscores the importance of placing the new religious pluralism, and the emerging role of new and rising groups, in an international context.

The case of Islam in Atlantic democracies, while very different, also points to the importance of international ties for national religious minorities. Islam often has a transnational thrust and self-understanding, even if it is expressed differently in diverse national and local communities. Some Muslims see themselves first as members of an international community of the faithful, or umma, and second as citizens of particular countries. Muslim religious identity can set barriers against assimilation to majority national cultures, whether Christian or secular, and has sometimes served as a source of tension with both. International terrorism has made things much worse. The acts of violent extremists in New York and Washington on September 11, 2001, in Madrid on March 11, 2004, and in London on July 7, 2005, have placed Muslim communities in the United States and Europe in a precarious position. On many occasions, fear and ignorance have fed anti-Muslim prejudice and produced louder calls for cultural integration, challenging Muslims to organize more effectively within civil society in response.

The particular constraints faced by Muslim communities—and their responses to them—are different in Western Europe and the United States. For Europe, with its more secular political cultures, Islam represents not just a minority religious tradition but a challenge to secularism altogether. As Sam Cherribi argues in his essay, public anxieties about extremist violence, on the one hand, and about a creeping "Islamization" of Europe, on the other, color the social and political debate. Elites and publics are committed to the principle of religious freedom and civil rights for all. At the same time, most express the expectation that immigrants will adapt to the culture of their host countries. These patterns hold across the political spectrum, with conservatives only slightly more likely to be insistent about cultural integration. There are important differences of emphasis. Pressure for assimilation is strongest in France's secular political culture, while the United Kingdom has more experience with, and is more tolerant of, religious diversity. Germany and Italy occupy a middle ground. Cherribi's native Netherlands now represents a crucial case. Historically tolerant of cultural difference, its political elites responded to the murder of Theo van Gogh by a Muslim extremist in 2004 with a flurry of measures designed to integrate Muslims more fully into Dutch society.

The situation of Muslims in the United States is different—and in many ways less difficult. The United States has a long history of religious and ethnic minorities organizing effectively at the level of civil society. And while the Muslim population hails from many different countries, about a third consists of American converts and their descendants, mainly African Americans. Islam, while overshadowed by Christianity in American culture, has less of an outsider status than in much of Europe. 9/11 certainly made it more difficult to be a Muslim in the United States. But as John Esposito notes in his essay, it also had a catalytic effect in mobilizing Muslims against prejudice, in defense of their civil rights, and in favor of greater political participation. For Esposito, the interplay between Islam and American culture is giving rise to understanding of Islam more in tune with dominant American values, such as religious tolerance, individualism, and multiculturalism. There is still sharp division within the Muslim community and considerable ambivalence about the individualist ethos of the wider culture. But American society, more accustomed to religious expression and religious difference than the European, presents greater opportunities for effective organization and engagement.

If the United States is viewed as a country rife with religious minorities and a supportive pluralist culture, religious pluralism would appear to pose few problems. But if one focuses on the attitudes of the *majority*, the picture is less reassuring. Robert Wuthnow's essay shows how American conceptions of a "Christian nation" coexist uneasily with a growing awareness of religious difference. More and more Americans claim to have encountered people of other religious faiths in the workplace and in their neighborhoods. While their knowledge of non-Christian traditions is limited, they profess tolerance for other traditions in general and acknowledge, in the abstract, that they contain much that is truthful. When asked about specific traditions, however, the tenor of responses changes. Islam, Hinduism, Buddhism, and other faiths are often derided as strange. The superiority of Christianity is routinely asserted. An intolerant streak comes to the fore. One in five Americans, Wuthnow notes, favors a ban on Muslim worship. In view of such attitudes, it is far from clear whether religious pluralism poses more of a challenge to secular Europe than it does to a religious America. Much depends on how that pluralism is articulated in the public sphere and translates into politics. The response of democratic institutions is the focus of the second half of the volume.

Democratic Responses to the New Religious Pluralism

The new religious pluralism poses difficult challenges to two basic democratic principles—minority protection and majority rule. Potential threats to minorities can take two main forms. First, dominant traditions can respond to diversity by using the state to privilege their own communities over perceived competitors. In the American context, some critics see an attachment to the "under God" clause of the Pledge of Allegiance or government support for predominantly Christian faith-based organizations in this light. Neither practice establishes anything like a theocracy, but each represents state support—symbolic in one case, financial in the other—for majority religious communities not equally available to religious minorities. Second, governments can define religion narrowly, so as to constrain the practices of particular minority groups. Here, some point to the French headscarf ban in public schools. In this case, a secular state confronted with the growth of a minority tradition, Islam, defines the bounds of religious freedom so narrowly as to curtail a practice central to the identities of some Muslims.

The potential threats that religious pluralism poses to majority rule can also be divided into two categories. First, clashing religious groups may undermine democratic institutions. Where diverse religious and cultural communities are sharply divided, it is more difficult to foster shared identification with and support for central democratic institutions. The legacy of sectarian division and violence in Northern Ireland provides a salient example. Second, a greater variety of religious voices may impede the formation of workable political majorites on salient public policy issues. Here, "culture wars" over abortion and stem cell research in the United States spring to mind. Polarized public policy debates marked by a multiplicity of voices can undercut effective democratic governance, particularly around value-driven issues.

The first set of issues, concerning the protection of religious minorities, is far from new. From the early modern period onward, theorizing about liberal democracy has centered on safeguarding freedoms of speech, association, and conscience. Contemporary ideas about the freedom of religion were slow to evolve. John Locke, for example, was against civil rights for Roman Catholics. And dominant Catholic political theory did not fully acknowledge the principle of religious freedom until the Second Vatican Council. By the mid-twentieth century, however, the twin principles of nonestablishment and free exercise of religion were well entrenched in Atlantic democracies. Nonestablishment meant the abolition of state churches or, as in the Church of England, a drastic reduction of their power and privileges. Free exercise meant the rights of religious minorities to profess and practice their faith. During the postwar decades, both the predominance of Christianity and the low political salience of religion kept the issue of protections for religious minorities low on national political agendas. With the new religious pluralism, it is back.

Martha Nussbaum's essay places the problem of protecting cultural and religious minorities within a broader philosophical and historical context. Nussbaum tackles the problem of radical evil identified by Kant—the human tendency to respond to plurality with competitive and aggressive behavior. She argues that classical liberal theory from Locke through Kant and Rousseau does not provide a satisfactory account of how to address radical evil and the intolerance it generates. The problem cannot be resolved without careful thought about how a liberal state can cultivate emotions that support equal respect and a toleration that is more than grudging obedience to law. Here public education to tolerance is important. But so too is the deployment of cultural resources. Nussbaum gives the examples of the poetry of Walt Whitman and the rhetoric of Martin Luther King, which powerfully evoke a nation respectful of difference. She sees the cultivation of tolerance as especially vital at a time when the Bush administration is privileging the majority Christian tradition in its rhetoric and public policy.

The challenge posed by religious diversity for governance in Europe is a different one. It is less about the power of majority faith traditions than about the state's response to Islam. Here, as Grace Davie argues, the underlying problem is cultural: a dominant conception of what religion should be—a private affair—confronts a Muslim tradition less supportive of a public/private distinction. Within European society, this tension was evident in the United Kingdom and the Netherlands in controversies surrounding Salman Rushdie's *Satanic Verses* and Theo van Gogh's *Submission: Part I*. What a majority saw as the free artistic expression of an individual was, for many Muslims, an illicit attack on an entire faith community. Such cultural dissonances are increasingly finding their way into the political sphere. The French law on religious symbols, passed by a cross-party majority, was an effort to draw the private/ public distinction in a way that prohibited the wearing of Muslim headscarves in public schools, but allowed for less obtrusive crucifixes or Stars of David. Davie notes that the British state, while less democratic than the French in certain respects, has proven more tolerant of religious difference in the public sphere. She cites the Queen's 2004 Christmas Address for its insistence that religious diversity was something not just to be tolerated but to be welcomed in the United Kingdom.

Danièle Hervieu-Léger takes up the French case from a different perspective. The French dilemma, she argues, is not fundamentally about tolerance or solely about Islam. It is rather about how the secular state should relate to greater religious diversity. Given the strict separation of church and state incorporated into French law in 1905, the key problem is not how to protect religious freedom or advance tolerance—undisputed norms in the French constitution and educational system. Nor is it any purported antidemocratic character of Islam, for recent sociological work has explored a variety of ways of being Muslim in France, many compatible with the secular and democratic order. The key problem is rather how a secular state should interact with a religious community as fluid and fragmented as the Muslim one. Islam in France lacks a clear corporate structure through which it might relate to the secular state on the model of the Catholic, Protestant, and Jewish communities. The challenge of Islam is part of a larger challenge to the French model of *laïcité*: how, in the context of greater religious diversity, the state should grapple with plural forms of religious identification and association.

Subsequent essays deal not only with the state's response to religious minorities but also with the problem of creating and sustaining majorities under conditions of religious pluralism. The concern here is an old one—that religious claims are exclusive in their essence, brook no compromise, and therefore can lead to conflict and violence. The post-Reformation wars serve as a historical point of reference. Whether the "religious wars" were less about religion than about state power—Hauerwas restates the latter view in his essay— they left an enduring legacy for subsequent liberal political theory. A long series of liberal thinkers has cautioned against injecting religious language into the public sphere in order to preserve civil peace and allow for political compromise and public policy on the broadest possible foundation. Over the past decade, Rawls, Jürgen Habermas, and other thinkers in this tradition, impressed by the resilience and depth of religious identities in contemporary democracies, have moderated their positions somewhat. But the anxiety about religious claims in politics remains.[6]

Greater religious pluralism makes it more and more difficult to exclude religious claims from the public sphere.[7] As voices become varied and more assertive over time, the possibility of cultural divisions and social conflict may grow correspondingly. One way to address the problem, set out by Diana Eck in her essay, is to distinguish between civic and theological language in the public sphere. Under conditions of increasing religious diversity, she argues, the encounter of different theological perspectives is both public and inevitable. Engagement across faith traditions that acknowledges both commonalities and differences can contribute to a vibrant political culture. In the context of democratic politics, however, where believers engage one another as citizens, theological language is unproductive. Where politicians seek to build majorities and broker compromise, the assertion of faith claims can create division and foster hostility. Echoing Rawls's idea of public reason, she calls for a civic language oriented toward the public good rather than a theological language anchored in the identity of a particular religious community. Not to nurture such a civic language under conditions of growing religious diversity could prove divisive and dangerous.

Miroslav Volf differs on this key point. Like Eck, he sees religion as a core component of personal and collective identity. But in contrast to her, drawing on the work of Nicholas Wolterstorff, he insists that religion can and should be expressed not just in the public sphere in general, but also in the context of democratic politics. Not to bring religious reasons to bear in public policy disputes, he argues, is to cede the field to secularism—an all-encompassing belief system with its own ultimate truth claims that bears a family resemblance to religion itself. Volf, who has written extensively on ethnic and religious conflict and worked to promote reconciliation in the former Yugoslavia, acknowledges the danger of confrontation or even violence as religious voices are heard more loudly and more often. But he insists that the response to that danger must come from within religious communities themselves. Drawing on his own Christian tradition, Volf argues that the idea of permeable identities and for-giving love provides a foundation for engaging other religious traditions in society and politics. Other traditions can draw on their own resources to pro-mote the peaceful engagement of difference.

Stanley Hauerwas is less concerned than either Eck or Volf about religious language placing strains on democratic institutions. For him, faith and com-munity come first. If their open articulation and practice is incompatible with certain conceptions of democracy, so be it. Hauerwas rejects the idea that a civic language, or what he calls a "third language," might mediate between different religious traditions. Such a language is never neutral but always embodies a particular set of ethical claims—"rights talk," for example, enthrones the ideal of the autonomous individual. Though less concerned than either Eck or Volf about the fate of democracy, Hauerwas is more sanguine about an open con-frontation of religious perspectives in the public sphere and in democratic politics. Traditions, he argues, are made up of different parts that can overlap and connect in surprising ways. One can grasp those overlaps and connections only through the process of debate and engagement. Honesty is nothing to fear. And open engagement with other faith traditions may even deepen one's un-derstanding of one's own faith.

Eck, Volf, and Hauerwas revisit old theoretical debates about religion in the public sphere in the context of the new religious pluralism, and they reach different conclusions. Thomas Banchoff explores the question from the bot-tom up. His essay takes up a public policy issue, stem cell research, and ex-amines the intersection of religious and secular claims in the American and French controversies. Neither case fits popular constructions of the issue as a confrontation between religious forces protective of the embryo and secular forces pressing scientific breakthroughs. In the United States, religious voices are increasingly proliferating on both sides of the issue: not just for embryo protection but also for biomedical advances to promote an ethic of healing. And in France, where religious reasoning plays almost no role in the public controversy, the dominant secular arguments have until recently tended to oppose the destruction of embryos for research as the illicit instrumentaliza-tion of human life. The case of stem cell politics reveals a multiplicity of public policy views *within* religious traditions and points of overlap between religious and secular perspectives.

Challenges Ahead

The new religious pluralism, this book argues, is less a threat than an oppor-tunity for democracy. Its contours—both demographic and cultural—represent new challenges for Atlantic societies, but none that is insurmountable. Religious traditions are a powerful and persistent foundation for collective identity and shared ethical commitments. They are a source of solace and solidarity, on the one hand, and of enmity and—potentially—violence, on the other. In Europe and the United States, new religious minorities, and Muslims in particular, are engaging the wider society and adapting their identities and practices in different ways. Majority cultures, whether Christian or secular in inflection, are grappling with a new pluralism that tests received commitments to cultural and religious tolerance. Atlantic societies have managed to channel these tensions peacefully thus far. Religious pluralism has provoked believers and nonbelievers to reengage their own traditions through more active engagement with others—to reaffirm but also to rethink. On balance, it has been more productive than destructive.

When one adopts a more global perspective, there is less reason for optimism. While democratic regimes worldwide have successfully institutionalized religious freedom and other civil liberties, adapting peacefully to growing religious diversity and its articulation in society and politics, autocracies and failed democracies often have not. The Mohammed Cartoon Controversy of 2006 illustrates the contrast. The publication of negative depictions of Mohammed in Denmark sparked outrage among many Muslims around the world. Public officials on both sides of the Atlantic, while generally critical of the decision to publish, defended freedom of the press as an inviolable norm. With few exceptions, protests within democracies remained peaceful. In Pakistan, Syria, and Lebanon, by contrast, countries marked by autocratic rule or unstable democratic institutions, violent demonstrations took place. State elites either encouraged the violence or were powerless to prevent it. The Cartoon Controversy showed how, in the absence of democracy and stable constitutional order, religious difference can contribute to division and bloodshed. Religious pluralism is possible without democracy. But the peaceful interaction of religious communities in politics is best secured in a democratic setting.

NOTES

1. The literature includes David Martin, *A General Theory of Secularization* (New York: Harper & Row, 1978); José Casanova, *Public Religions in the Modern World* (Chicago: University of Chicago Press, 1994); Peter L. Berger, ed., *The Desecularization of the World: Resurgent Religion and World Politics* (Washington, DC: Ethics and Public Policy Center/Grand Rapids: Eerdmans, 1999); and Ronald Inglehart and Pippa Norris, *The Sacred and the Secular: Religion and Politics Worldwide* (Cambridge: Cambridge University Press, 2004).

2. Samuel P. Huntington, *Who Are We? The Challenges to America's National Identity* (New York: Simon & Schuster, 2004); and Oriana Fallaci, *The Rage and the Pride* (New York: Rizzoli, 2002).

3. See, for example, Diana L. Eck, *A New Religious America: How a "Christian Country" Has Become the World's Most Religiously Diverse Nation* (San Francisco: Harper, 2002); Kenneth Wald, *Religion and Politics in the United States* (Lanham, MD: Rowman & Littlefield, 2003); Grace Davie, *Religion in Modern Europe: A Memory*

Mutates (Oxford: Oxford University Press, 2000); and John Madeley and Zsolt Enyedi, eds., *Church and State in Contemporary Europe* (London: Cass, 2003). The transatlantic comparison emerges out of Ted Jelen and Clyde Wilcox, eds., *Religion and Politics in Comparative Perspective: The One, the Few, and the Many* (New York: Cambridge University Press, 2002).

4. American political scientist Harold Laski first developed "pluralism" as an analytical category in 1919. See Harold Laski, *Authority and the Modern State* (New Haven: Yale University Press, 1919); and Robert Dahl, *On Democracy* (New Haven: Yale University Press, 1998). John Hick is the most influential representative of the pluralist approach in theology. See, for example, John Hick, *An Interpretation of Religion: Human Responses to the Transcendent* (New Haven: Yale University Press, 2004).

5. Danièle Hervieu-Léger, *Religion en mouvement: Le pelerin et le converti* (Paris: Flammarion, 1999); and Robert Wuthnow, *After Heaven: Spirituality in America since the 1950s* (Berkeley: University of California Press, 1998).

6. John Rawls, *Political Liberalism* (New York: Columbia University Press, 1996); and Jürgen Habermas and Jan Philipp Reemtsma, *Glauben und Wissen: Friedenspreis des deutschen Buchhandels 2001* (Frankfurt am Main: Suhrkamp, 2001). See also Robert Audi and Nicholas Wolterstorff, *Religion in the Public Square: The Place of Religious Convictions in Political Debate* (Lanham, MD: Rowman & Littlefield, 1997).

7. For an analysis of debates about the changing relationship between religious traditions and democratic institutions, see Jeffrey Stout, *Democracy and Tradition* (Princeton: Princeton University Press, 2003).

BIBLIOGRAPHY

Audi, Robert, and Nicholas Wolterstorff. *Religion in the Public Square: The Place of Religious Convictions in Political Debate*. Lanham, MD: Rowman & Littlefield, 1997.
Berger, Peter L., ed. *The Desecularization of the World: Resurgent Religion and World Politics*. Washington, DC: Ethics and Public Policy Center/Grand Rapids: Eerdmans, 1999.
Casanova, José. *Public Religions in the Modern World*. Chicago: University of Chicago Press, 1994.
Dahl, Robert. *On Democracy*. New Haven: Yale University Press, 1998.
Davie, Grace. *Religion in Modern Europe: A Memory Mutates*. Oxford: Oxford University Press, 2000.
Eck, Diana L. *A New Religious America: How a "Christian Country" Has Become the World's Most Religiously Diverse Nation*. San Francisco: Harper, 2002.
Fallaci, Oriana. *The Rage and the Pride*. New York: Rizzoli, 2002.
Habermas, Jürgen, and Jan Philipp Reemtsma. *Glauben und Wissen: Friedenspreis des deutschen Buchhandels 2001*. Frankfurt am Main: Suhrkamp, 2001.
Hervieu-Léger, Danièle. *Religion en mouvement: le pelerin et le converti*. Paris: Flammarion, 1999.
Hick, John. *An Interpretation of Religion: Human Responses to the Transcendent*. New Haven: Yale University Press, 2004.
Huntington, Samuel P. *Who Are We? The Challenges to America's National Identity*. New York: Simon & Schuster, 2004.
Inglehart, Ronald, and Pippa Norris. *The Sacred and the Secular: Religion and Politics Worldwide*. Cambridge: Cambridge University Press, 2004.
Jelen, Ted, and Clyde Wilcox, eds. *Religion and Politics in Comparative Perspective: The One, the Few, and the Many*. New York: Cambridge University Press, 2002.

Laski, Harold. *Authority and the Modern State*. New Haven: Yale University Press, 1919.

Madeley, John, and Zsolt Enyedi, eds. *Church and State in Contemporary Europe*. London: Cass, 2003.

Martin, David. *A General Theory of Secularization*. New York: Harper & Row, 1978.

Rawls, John. *Political Liberalism*. New York: Columbia University Press, 1996.

Stout, Jeffrey. *Democracy and Tradition*. Princeton: Princeton University Press, 2003.

Wald, Kenneth. *Religion and Politics in the United States*. Lanham, MD: Rowman & Littlefield, 2003.

Wuthnow, Robert. *After Heaven: Spirituality in America since the 1950s*. Berkeley: University of California Press, 1998.

PART I

Contours of the New Religious Pluralism

2

Pluralism, Protestantization, and the Voluntary Principle

Peter L. Berger

The relation between pluralism and religion has never been un-ambiguous. On the one hand, as has been argued especially for the American case, pluralism in religion can encourage political plural-ism and thus democracy. On the other hand, pluralism tests the limits of what religious people find tolerable in the society and thus tests their acceptance of democracy if a democratically constituted regime legislates religiously unacceptable behavior. The current furor in American churches over abortion and same-sex marriage sharply il-luminates this problem. (In other words, one does not have to go to the Middle East to find cases of tension between a religious code and democracy.) Also, religious and moral pluralism raises the question of how a democratic regime can ultimately be legitimated. Again, the American case is instructive: the republic was first legitimated in Prot-estant terms, then in Christian terms, then in Judeo-Christian terms. We now have the interesting legitimation of a putative "Abrahamic faith" (Judeo-Christian-Muslim), which is not comforting to the ad-herents of nonmonotheistic traditions, not to mention the religiously unaffiliated who have long been uncomfortable with religious rhetoric of any sort in American political discourse.

The "new pluralism," of course, is the result of globalization. Almost all societies are today inevitably pluralistic. Globalization has meant an enormous increase in intercultural communication. Reli-gion has not been immune to this process of intercontinental chatter. The present essay will look at the institutional and personal implica-tions of globalized religion and then at the relation of these to de-mocracy.[1]

Arguably the two most dynamic religious movements in the contemporary world are resurgent Islam and popular Protestantism, the latter principally in the form of the Pentecostal movement. Both are truly global phenomena. Not only are Islamic movements interacting throughout the huge region from the Atlantic Ocean to the South China Sea, but the Muslim diaspora in Europe and North America has become a powerful presence. In England, for example, more people every week attend services in mosques than in Anglican churches. For understandable reasons, attention has focused on the most aggressive versions of this globalizing Islam, but it is moderate Muslims as well as practitioners of jihad who talk to each other on the Internet and on cell phones and who gather for both clandestine and public conferences. As to Pentecostalism, it has been spreading like wildfire through Latin America, sub-Saharan Africa, parts of east Asia, and to such unlikely groups as European gypsies and hill tribes in India. David Martin, the British sociologist who pioneered in the study of cross-national Pentecostalism, estimates that there are at least 250 million Pentecostals worldwide and possibly many more. (A crucial case is China, where we know that the movement is spreading, but which is difficult to study because it is mostly illegal and therefore underground.)[2]

However, globalizing religion is by no means limited to Islam and Protestantism. The Roman Catholic Church has always been a global institution, but globalization is profoundly altering its international profile: increasingly its areas of strength are outside its traditional European heartland, with the interesting consequence that precisely those of its features that trouble progressive Catholics in, say, the Netherlands are an attraction in the Philippines or in Africa. (The Vatican is well aware of this phenomenon, which explains many of its policies.) The Russian Orthodox Church, presiding over a strong religious revival in the post-Soviet era and enjoying the favor of the Putin government, is flexing its muscles in the Balkans and the Middle East, not to mention what the Russians call the "near abroad."

Hasidic movements with headquarters in Brooklyn, New York, are sending missionaries to Israel and to Jewish communities in Eastern Europe. The so-called Jesus Movie, a film produced by an American evangelical organization and synchronized in well over a hundred languages, is being screened by aggressive missionaries in villages throughout India, despite the outrage of pious Brahmins and the opposition of the Indian government. But Hinduism is returning the compliment. Devotees dance and chant in praise of Krishna in major American and European cities. Hindu missionary organizations (ranging from the sedate Vedanta Society to the exuberant Sai Baba movement) are busily evangelizing wherever they can. Similarly, Buddhist groups with headquarters in Japan, Taiwan, and Southeast Asia are attracting sizable numbers of converts in Western countries.

If one is to get an intellectual handle on these developments, it is important to put away a view which, despite massive evidence to the contrary, is still very widespread (not least among Christian theologians): often called the "secularization theory," this view holds that modernity brings about a decline of religion. Simply put, this view has been empirically falsified. This is not the place to enlarge upon the debates that have ranged over the secularization theory in recent years. Suffice it to say that, contrary to the theory, the contemporary world, far from being secularized, is characterized by a veritable explosion of passionate religion. (There are two exceptions to this statement—western and central Europe—and a thin but influential class of "progressive" intellectuals in most countries. Again, the reasons for these exceptions cannot be discussed here.)[3]

Modernity does not necessarily lead to a decline of religion. What it does lead to, more or less necessarily, is religious pluralism. Modern developments—mass migration and travel, urbanization, literacy, and, most important, the new technology of communication—have brought about a situation in which different religious traditions are present to each other in a historically unprecedented manner. For obvious reasons this interaction is facilitated under conditions of legally protected religious liberty. But even where governments, in various degrees, try to limit or suppress religious pluralism (as is the case in China, India, and Russia), this is difficult to do under contemporary conditions.

A personal example illustrates this: a couple of years ago I visited Buenos Aires for the first time. I had long been enamored of the writings of Borges, and I was anticipating a rather romantic encounter with the world of the tango. As my taxi left the airport, the first sight that greeted me was a huge Mormon church, with a gilded Angel Moroni sitting atop its steeple. Here was an outpost of a religion born in upstate New York, which until recently had barely spread beyond Utah and certainly not beyond the United States. Today Mormonism has been experiencing impressive growth in many countries, notably in the South Pacific and Siberia. There are now large numbers of people throughout the world whose spiritual, intellectual, and social center is Salt Lake City.

Implications of Religious Pluralism

Religious pluralism has both institutional and cognitive implications. It is important to understand both. Institutionally it means that something like a religious market is established. This does not mean that concepts of market economics can be unambiguously applied to the study of religion (as has been done, very interestingly, by Rodney Stark and other American sociologists, with the use of so-called rational choice theory).[4] But what it does mean is that religious institutions must *compete* for the allegiance of their putative clientele. This competition naturally becomes more intense under a regime of religious liberty, when the state can no longer be relied upon to fill the pews. This situation inevitably affects the behavior of religious institutions, even if their theological self-understanding is averse to such changed behavior.

The clergy (using this term broadly for the officials of religious institutions) now face a rather inconvenient fact: since their authority is no longer a social given, they must seek to reestablish it by means of *persuasion*. This gives a new social role to the laity. No longer a subject population, the laity becomes a community of consumers whose notions, however objectionable on theological grounds, must be seriously addressed.

The Roman Catholic case is paradigmatic in this respect. It is fair to say that, of all Christian churches, the Roman church has the most impressive hierarchical structure, which in many ways is at the core of its self-understanding. As far as the relevant doctrine is concerned, this has not fundamentally changed, though it has been modified by the pronouncements of the Second Vatican Council and subsequent papal encyclicals. Yet the *behavior* of the church toward its lay members has changed significantly. Some Catholics have gone so far as to describe the present time as the era of the laity in the church. This may be an exaggeration, but clearly the laity has become more assertive. The past few years have offered an impressive example of this in Boston (once called the "holy city" of American Catholicism). The archdiocese, under severe financial pressure because of the huge payments made to alleged victims of clerical sexual abuse, decided to close a number of parishes. The laypeople of the parishes rose in rebellion in a way not seen before, respectfully but firmly opposing the archbishop.

The pluralistic situation also changes the relations of religious institutions with each other. Participants in a market, religious or other, not only compete but are frequently engaged in efforts to reduce or regulate the competition. Obviously attempts are made in the educational activities of religious institutions to discourage their members from going over to competitors. For example, American Judaism has made great efforts to immunize Jews against Christian missionary activities. But competing religious institutions also negotiate with each other to regulate the competition. This helps to clarify at least some of the phenomenon known as "ecumenicity": ecumenical amity among Christian churches means, at least in part, explicit or implicit agreements not to poach on each other's territory.

Until a few decades ago such a negotiating process among American Protestant churches was known as "comity." Protestant denominations portioned out certain areas for their outreach activities, allocating a particular area to, say, the Presbyterians; the others then promised to stay out of this area. This reached a somewhat bizarre climax in Puerto Rico, where the mainline denominations divided up the entire island in this way. If you knew that someone was, say, a Presbyterian, you could guess which town he or she came from. Some evangelical Protestants did not participate in this comity, much to the annoyance of other Protestants. The term has fallen into disuse, but it is still a very significant reality and now goes beyond the Protestant fold. Mainline Protestants and Catholics do not actively proselytize each other, and neither seek to proselytize Jews. Indeed, the very word *proselytization* has acquired a pejorative meaning in American religious discourse, and those who continue to practice it are looked at askance. Thus there was an outpouring of protests when not long ago the Southern Baptist Convention (the largest evangelical denomination in the United States) announced that it would continue its program to convert Jews. Sociologically speaking, one could say that today comity is informally extended to every religious group in the United States that does not engage in blatantly illegal behavior.[5]

Religious pluralism also has important implications for the subjective consciousness of individuals. This can be stated in one sentence: religion loses its taken-for-granted status in consciousness. No society can function without some ideas and behavior patterns being taken for granted. For most of history, religion was part and parcel of what was taken for granted. Social psychology has given us a good idea of how taken-for-grantedness is maintained in consciousness: it is the result of social consensus in an individual's environment. And for most of history, most individuals lived in such environments. Pluralism undermines this sort of homogeneity. Individuals are continually confronted with others who do *not* take for granted what was so taken traditionally in their community. They must now *reflect about* the cognitive and normative assumptions of their tradition, and consequently they must *make choices*. A religion that is chosen, on whatever level of intellectual sophistication, is different from a religion that is taken for granted. It is not necessarily less passionate, nor do its doctrinal propositions necessarily change. It is not so much the *what* as the *how* of religious belief that changes. Thus modern Catholics may affirm the same doctrines and engage in the same practices as their ancestors in a traditional Catholic village. But they have decided, and must continue to decide, to so believe and behave. This makes their religion both more personal and more vulnerable. Put differently, religion is subjectivized, and religious certitude is more difficult to come by.

In one of my books I described this process as the "heretical imperative" (from the Greek word *hairesis*, which means, precisely, "choice").[6] This process occurs not only in liberal or progressive religious groups. It also occurs in the most militantly conservative groups, for there too individuals have *chosen* to be militantly conservative. In other words, there is a mountain of difference between traditional and *neo*traditional religion. Psychologically, the former can be very relaxed and tolerant; the latter is necessarily tense and has at least an inclination toward intolerance.

Needless to say, these developments are not unique to religion. They affect all cognitive and normative definitions of reality and their behavioral consequences. I have long argued that modernity leads to a profound change in the human condition, *from fate to choice*. Religion participates in this change. Just as modernity inevitably leads to greater individuation, so modern religion is characterized by individuals who reflect upon, modify, pick, and choose from the religious resources available to them. French sociologist Danièle Hervieu-Léger calls this phenomenon *bricolage* (loosely translatable as "tinkering," as in putting together the pieces of a Lego game); her American colleague Robert Wuthnow uses the term *patchwork religion*. The American language has a wonderfully apt term for this—"religious preference"—tellingly a term derived from the world of consumption, carrying the implication that the individual decided upon this particular religious identity and that in the future he or she might make a different decision.

Putting together the institutional and the subjective dimensions of pluralism, we can arrive at a far-reaching proposition: under conditions of pluralism all religious institutions, sooner or later, become voluntary associations—and they become so whether they like it or not.

Max Weber and Ernst Troeltsch classically analyzed two prototypical social forms of religion—the "church," into which one is born, and the "sect," which one decides to join. Richard Niebuhr suggested that American religion invented a third type, the "denomination," which he defined as a church that recognizes the right of other churches to exist, be it de jure or de facto. One could then say that, in the course of American religious history, all religious groups have become "denominationalized." Even Judaism, despite its distinctive merging of religious and ethnic identity, split into at least three denominations in America (and, depending on how one counts, several more). But the process of denominationalization is no longer limited to the United States. As pluralism spreads globally, all religious groups become in fact voluntary associations, even if they have to be dragged into this social form kicking and screaming. Not surprisingly, some of them will perceive pluralism as a lethal threat and will mobilize all available resources to resist it.

A simple conclusion follows from the preceding considerations: the capacity of a religious institution to adapt successfully to a pluralist environment will be closely linked to its capacity to take on the social form of the voluntary association. And that, of course, will be greatly influenced by its preceding history. If this is understood, then Protestantism clearly has what may be called a comparative advantage over other religious traditions (Christian or not). Both the Lutheran and the Calvinist Reformations, in their emphasis on the conscience of the individual, have an a priori affinity with modern individuation and thus with the pluralist dynamic. But not all Protestant groups have had the same capacity to organize themselves as voluntary associations.

David Martin recently suggested that three types of relations between religion and society developed in the postmedieval history of Western Christianity (the case of Eastern Orthodoxy is different).[7] The first type he calls the "baroque counter-Reformation," which sought to maintain or reestablish a harmonious unity between church, state, and society. It flourished in the *ancien régime* of Catholic Europe and, following the French Revolution, morphed into the republic understood as a sort of secular (*laique*) church. In both its sacred and secular versions, this type has great difficulties with pluralism. The second type he calls "enlightened absolutism," characteristic of Lutheran northern Europe and the Anglican establishment. It became gradually more tolerant of pluralist diversity and eventually morphed into the north European welfare state. The third type is what Martin nicely labels "the Amsterdam-London-Boston bourgeois axis," which may be seen as the matrix of religious pluralism. But, again, not all three points on this axis have been equally hospitable to voluntary association. Dutch pluralism flourished under a famously tolerant regime, but its diverse religious groups (Calvinist, Arminian, Catholic) became rather rigidly solidified as "pillars" (*verzuiling*) of an overarching political establishment. In England there occurred a more ample flourishing of diverse religious groups—the wide spectrum of so-called Nonconformity—but, as already indicated by this name, it did so under the shadow of the Anglican state church. It was in the English-speaking colonies in what became the United States that religious pluralism attained its most unconstrained and exuberant version, giving birth to the denomination as the religious voluntary association par excellence. Naturally enough, American society has ever since been the vanguard of both religious and secular pluralism.

The comparative advantage of Protestantism continues today. The amazing cross-national success of Pentecostalism and other forms of popular Protestantism can in no small measure be explained by a distinctive capacity to operate as voluntary associations. But a religious group need not be Protestant to be able to reorganize itself denominationally, even if, so to speak, it does help to be Protestant. I have already mentioned post–Vatican II Catholicism and American Judaism as cases in point. Other cases can be found far from the Judeo-Christian world. The upsurge of Buddhist and other religious movements in Japan since the 1950s (one author calls it "the rush hour of the gods")[8] has been largely carried by voluntary lay organizations. Hinduism has generated similar organizations since the reform movements of the nineteenth century. The largest Muslim organizations in the world, Nadhatul-Ulama and Muhammadiyah in Indonesia, are also voluntary lay movements, and there are similar organizations in other Islamic countries.

Pluralism and the "Voluntary Imperative"

I have mentioned the "heretical imperative." Perhaps we could use another concept—the "voluntary imperative." It imposes itself wherever religious pluralism comes to predominate. Catholic observers have coined the term *Protestantization* to refer, usually pejoratively, to recent changes in their church. Stripped of its pejorative undertone, it is rather an apt term. Sometimes it describes doctrinal changes, most of which need not concern us here. But the term is most apt in describing social changes within the church—to wit, the role of an increasingly assertive laity, the transformation of the church into a de facto denomination, and one doctrinal change that is definitely relevant here—the theological undergirding of the norm of religious liberty. It is notable that the two individuals who were most influential in the affirmation of this norm by the Second Vatican Council came from the two homelands of modern democracy—Jacques Maritain from France and John Courtney Murray from the United States.

Americans in particular are prone to view the aforementioned developments as inexorable and irreversible—modernity generates pluralism, which generates the voluntary association, which then functions as a school for democracy. Eventually something like the New England town meeting will become a universal social and political norm. Alas, the empirical reality is more complicated. There are indeed pressures toward such a sociological trajectory. But the outcome of these pressures is not a foregone conclusion. There are possibilities of resistance, and under the right circumstances the pressures can be defeated and the trajectory reversed.

Resistances to pluralism have been conventionally subsumed under the category of "fundamentalism." I am uneasy about this term; it comes from a particular episode in the history of American Protestantism and is awkward when applied to other religious traditions (such as Islam). I will use it, because it has attained such wide currency, but I will define it more sharply: fundamentalism is any project to restore taken-for-grantedness in the individual's consciousness and therefore, necessarily, in his or her social and/or political environment. Such a project can have both religious and secular forms; the former concerns us here.

Religious fundamentalism can be more or less ambitious. In its more ambitious form it seeks to reshape the entire society in its image. In recent history the last (so far) Christian version of this was the ideal of the Nationalists in the Spanish civil war—the ideal of a Catholic *reconquista* of Spain from the supposedly anti-Christian secularism of the republic. It was the last flowering of the "counter-Reformation baroque." It collapsed with the Franco regime, which intended to realize it, and today it is inconceivable that the Roman Catholic Church would again give its blessing to any comparable project. Nor are there other Christian analogues. (The notion, current in progressive circles today, that the Christian right in America has such intentions has little basis in the facts. No politically significant group in American evangelicalism intends to set up a theocratic regime, and fundamentalism as I define it has its adherents both on the left and on the right of the political spectrum in the United States.) But fundamentalist projects abound in the non-Western world.

There are sizable groupings in Russia who would like to set up a regime in which, once again, there would be a unity between church and state (a radical version of what in Orthodox political thought has been called *sinfonia*). Influential groups in Israel would reshape that society, with its entire political structure based on religious law, as a halachic state. Even more influential groups in India would replace its secular constitution with Hindutva, understood as a coercive Hinduism imposed on all citizens, including the large Muslim minority. And most importantly today, Islamist ideology seeks a theocratic state based on Islamic law, a *sharia* state imposed on the entire society. In its most ambitious version, this is the jihadist dream of a renewed caliphate embracing the entire Muslim world (and conceivably also lands that were once Muslim, notably the Balkans and "Al Andalus").

The chances for success of such projects vary from country to country. But it is possible to formulate one necessary condition for a successful realization: to convert an entire society into a support structure (what I would call a "plausibility structure") for a renewed taken-for-granted consensus, it will be necessary to establish a totalitarian regime. That is, the theocratic state will have to fully control all institutions in the society and, crucially, all channels of interaction and communication with the outside world. Under modern conditions this is very difficult, unless one wants to pay the price of catastrophic economic stagnation. The developments in Iran since the establishment of the Islamist regime clearly demonstrate the difficulty. It would be mistaken, though, to conclude that any project of religious totalitarianism is impossible.

A regime willing to use ruthless and continuous repression, and indifferent to the material misery of its subjects, could yet pull such a project off.

The less ambitious form of religious fundamentalism is the sectarian one. It seeks to restore taken-for-grantedness in a subculture under its control, while the rest of society is, as it were, abandoned to the enemy. It is within the subculture that the individual can find the social consensus needed for cognitive and normative certainty. This, of course, has always been characteristic of sects. But in a society marked by pluralism the controls over interaction and communication with the outside have to be very rigorous indeed. The slightest relaxation of these controls can breach the protective dam against the pluralistic infection, alternative definitions of reality will then flood in, and the precariously maintained taken-for-grantedness can collapse overnight. Therefore, the denizens of the subculture must limit contacts with outsiders to a minimum, avoid all unnecessary conversation, and equally avoid all media of communication originating in the pluralistic world outside. In other words, what must be established and maintained is a kind of minitotalitarianism.

The sectarian project is thus not without its own serious difficulties, but these are less onerous than those confronting a project of *reconquista*. There are a good number of successful cases, in different religious traditions. Ideally for success, the fundamentalist group must have a territory, however small, under its control. This can be an isolated community (such as the Davidic compound in Waco, Texas), a circumscribed urban community (such as the ultra-Orthodox communities in Brooklyn or Mea Shearim in Jerusalem), a monastic or quasimonastic center (there are, of course, many of these in the Christian orbit), or an even larger geographical base (such as areas of northern Nigeria under Islamist control). But sectarian subcultures can also function without a territorial location, as long as the controls over interaction and communication are rigorously maintained. There are numerous examples of this in every major religious tradition—from Opus Dei to Sokka Gakkai, from the Lubavitcher Chabad to the Muslim Brotherhood (I cite these as sociological cases in point, without necessarily suggesting that they are morally equivalent).

Both society-wide totalitarianism and sectarian minitotalitarianism constitute difficult projects under modern conditions. The second is a better bet in terms of possible success. *Reconquista* totalitarianism is incompatible with pluralism, indeed must be implacably hostile to it. Minitotalitarianism is compatible with pluralism, but only to the extent that it accepts the pluralistic dominance in the larger society as long as its own subsociety is kept intact.

What follows from the argument of this essay is that the relation between pluralism (be it old or new) to democracy is complex. One cannot simply say that pluralism is either good or bad for democracy. It will be either, depending on the response to it by both religious and political institutions. As far as the latter is concerned, the distinction between liberal and illiberal democracy is very important here. A democratically elected regime can be intolerant of religious minorities (such as the difficulties of evangelical Protestants in Russia, in the Muslim world, and in India). Conversely, there have been tolerant authoritarian regimes (such as Prussia under Frederick the Great, Austria under Joseph II, and the Ottoman Empire on its better days).

Looking at any particular case, one must ask two key questions: how have the relevant religious traditions responded to the pluralistic challenge? I have argued here that acceptance (openly or de facto) of the voluntary principle will be decisive in this matter. One must then ask: what political interests have an affinity to this or that response, and what is the power of these interests to influence the course of events? For both historical and ideational reasons, Protestantism has had a comparative advantage in a positive adaptation to pluralism. This advantage continues today, notably in the global expansion of Pentecostalism and other versions of popular Protestantism. But there is also Protestantization in other religious traditions, even in that old adversary of Protestantism, the Roman Catholic Church. Thus both Protestant and non-Protestant religious institutions can, today, serve to bring about and solidify democracy. The most direct threat to democracy obviously comes from movements and regimes with an interest in establishing a totalitarian unity based on a reconquest (*reconquista*) of society in the name of this or that religious ideology. It would be a mistake to understand this threat exclusively in terms of radical Islam.

NOTES

1. On globalization, see Peter L. Berger and Samuel P. Huntington, eds., *Many Globalizations: Cultural Diversity in the Contemporary World* (Oxford: Oxford University Press, 2003). On religious pluralism in the American context, see Robert Wuthnow, *America and the Challenges of Religious Diversity* (Princeton: Princeton University Press, 2005); and Diana L. Eck, *A New Religious America: How a "Christian Country" Has Become the World's Most Religiously Diverse Nation* (New York: Harper, 2001).

2. David Martin, *Pentecostalism: The World Their Parish* (Oxford: Blackwell, 2001). See also Harvey Cox, *Fire from Heaven: The Rise of Pentecostal Spirituality and the Reshaping of Religion in the 21st Century* (Cambridge, MA: Da Capo, 2001).

3. Peter L. Berger, ed., *The Desecularization of the World: Resurgent Religion and World Politics* (Washington, DC: Ethics and Public Policy Center/Grand Rapids: Eerdmans, 1999).

4. See, for example, Rodney Stark, *One True God: Historical Consequences of Monotheism* (Princeton: Princeton University Press, 2003).

5. "Baptists' Ardor for Evangelism Angers Some Jews and Hindus," *New York Times*, Dec. 4, 1999, A10.

6. Peter L. Berger, *The Heretical Imperative: Contemporary Possibilities of Religious Affirmation* (New York: Anchor, 1980).

7. David Martin, "Integration und Fragmentierung: Religionsmuster in Europa," *Transit* 26 (Winter 2003–2004): 120–43.

8. H. Neil McFarlane, *Rush Hour of the Gods* (New York: Macmillan, 1967).

BIBLIOGRAPHY

Berger, Peter L., ed. *The Desecularization of the World: Resurgent Religion and World Politics.* Washington, DC: Ethics and Public Policy Center/Grand Rapids: Eerdmans, 1999.

———. *The Heretical Imperative: Contemporary Possibilities of Religious Affirmation*. New York: Anchor, 1980.

Berger, Peter L., and Samuel P. Huntington, eds. *Many Globalizations: Cultural Diversity in the Contemporary World*. Oxford: Oxford University Press, 2003.

Cox, Harvey. *Fire from Heaven: The Rise of Pentecostal Spirituality and the Reshaping of Religion in the 21st Century*. Cambridge, MA: Da Capo, 2001.

Eck, Diana L. *A New Religious America: How a "Christian Country" Has Become the World's Most Religiously Diverse Nation*. New York: Harper, 2001.

Martin, David. *Pentecostalism: The World Their Parish*. Oxford: Blackwell, 2001.

McFarlane, H. Neil. *Rush Hour of the Gods*. New York: Macmillan, 1967.

Stark, Rodney. *One True God: Historical Consequences of Monotheism*. Princeton: Princeton University Press, 2003.

Wuthnow, Robert. *America and the Challenges of Religious Diversity*. Princeton: Princeton University Press, 2005.

3

Uneven Secularization in the United States and Western Europe

Pippa Norris and Ronald Inglehart

After the September 11, 2001, terrorist attacks and their aftermath in Afghanistan and Iraq, public interest in religious pluralism has grown tremendously on both sides of the Atlantic. Religious diversity has become more visible, and religious issues have grown more salient. Centuries-old differences among Protestant and Catholic churches, Orthodox Christians, and long-established Jewish groups have combined with growing multiculturalism from immigrant populations adhering to Muslim, Hindu, Buddhist, and other faiths, as well as those adhering to none. New Age spiritualities and the development of more individualized practices outside of organized religion complete a varied picture. Within this new context, some traditional political conflicts between religious communities have become more muted, notably among Protestants and Catholics in northern Ireland. At the same time, new forms of identity politics have become more salient, compounded by events such as the assassination of Theo van Gogh in the Netherlands and the bombings by radical Muslim groups in Madrid and London.

In the context of this new religious pluralism, the long-running academic debate about secularization has greater contemporary relevance. Religion has definitely moved up the political agenda in Western Europe, in the United States, and around the world. One should be careful, however, not to confuse the increasing political salience of religion with any overall growth in religiosity. This essay argues that secularization is proceeding apace on both sides of the Atlantic—at different speeds and at different levels. It describes a cultural landscape marked not just by religious diversity but also by the coexistence and interaction of religious and secular beliefs and practices. A structured comparison of the United States and Europe provides a window on this uneven process of secularization and the underlying social, political, and economic forces that are driving it forward.

The idea of secularization has a long and distinguished history in the social sciences, with many seminal thinkers arguing that religiosity was declining throughout Western societies. Key leaders in the incipient social sciences of the nineteenth and early twentieth centuries—Auguste Comte, Herbert Spencer, Émile Durkheim, Max Weber, Karl Marx, and Sigmund Freud—generally held that religion would gradually fade in importance and cease to be significant with the advent of industrial society.[1] Their views were not new. Ever since the Enlightenment, leading thinkers in the European tradition have held that theological superstitions, symbolic liturgical rituals, and sacred practices are the product of the past that will be outgrown in the modern era. The death of religion was the conventional wisdom in the social sciences during most of the twentieth century. Many have regarded secularization as *the* master model of sociological inquiry, one closely related to bureaucratization, rationalization, and urbanization as the key historical revolutions transforming medieval agrarian societies into modern industrial nations. "Once the world was filled with the sacred—in thought, practice, and institutional form," C. Wright Mills argued, echoing the dominant view during the postwar decades. "After the Reformation and the Renaissance, the forces of modernization swept across the globe and secularization, a corollary historical process, loosened the dominance of the sacred." He concluded: "In due course, the sacred shall disappear altogether except, possibly, in the private realm."[2]

Over the past decade this thesis of the slow and steady death of religion has come under growing criticism. Indeed, secularization theory is currently experiencing the most sustained challenge in its long history. Critics point to multiple indicators of religious health and vitality today, ranging from the continued popularity of churchgoing in the United States to the emergence of New Age spirituality in Western Europe, the growth in fundamentalist[3] movements and religious parties in the Muslim world, the evangelical revival sweeping through Latin America, and the upsurge of ethnoreligious conflict in international affairs. After reviewing these developments, Peter L. Berger, one of the foremost advocates of secularization during the 1960s, recanted his earlier claims. "The world today, with some exceptions, . . . is as furiously religious as it ever was, and in some places more so than ever," Berger argued in the late 1990s; "this means that a whole body of literature by historians and social scientists loosely labeled 'secularization theory' is essentially mistaken."[4] Rodney Stark and Roger Finke, leading critics of the secularization thesis, reach a similar conclusion: "After nearly three centuries of utterly failed prophesies and misrepresentations of both present and past, it seems time to carry the secularization doctrine to the graveyard of failed theories."[5]

Were Comte, Durkheim, Weber, and Marx completely misled in their beliefs about religious decline in industrialized societies? Was the predominant sociological view during the twentieth century totally misguided? Has the debate been settled? We think not. Talk of burying the secularization theory is premature. The critique relies too heavily on selected anomalies and focuses too heavily on the United States (which happens to be a striking deviant case) rather than comparing systematic evidence across a broad range of rich and poor societies.[6] We need to move beyond studies of Catholic and Protestant church attendance in Europe (where attendance is falling) and the United States (where attendance remains stable) if we are to understand broader trends in religious vitality in a diverse religious landscape populated by churches, mosques, shrines, synagogues, and temples. Evidence indicates that the overall trend in the United States and Western Europe remains one of an increasing secularization of beliefs and practices—a process that has unfolded unevenly in different countries, but broadly in the same direction.[7]

This study is divided into three parts. Part one describes systematic and consistent evidence establishing the variations in religiosity among postindustrial nations, in particular, contrasts between America and Western Europe. The analysis focuses upon similar postindustrial nations, all affluent countries and established democracies, most (but not all) sharing a cultural heritage of Christendom, even as they confront greater religious diversity. Against the backdrop of this structural similarity, our essay examines whether the United States is indeed exceptional among rich nations in the vitality of its spiritual life, as conventional wisdom has long suggested, or whether, as Berger proposes, Western Europe is exceptional in its secularization.[8] The evidence suggests different levels of religious belief and engagement—a more religious America and a more secular Europe—but highlights the overall trend toward secularization on both sides of the Atlantic.

Parts two and three compare and contrast two alternative explanations for transatlantic differences. *Religious market theory* postulates a link between levels of religious competition and levels of religious observance. It draws causal linkages between the patterns of religious supply (the number of denominations competing for adherents and kinds of state regulation) and religious demand (strength of belief and practice). The theory provides one possible explanation for exceptionally high levels of religious observance in the United States, linking it back to the plural and competitive religious landscape. But it is plagued by both conceptual and empirical problems.

Part three puts forward an alternative theory of *secure secularization*—the view that levels of societal modernization, human development, and economic inequality drive levels of religious belief and activity. The theory of secure secularization builds on key elements of traditional sociological accounts while revising others. We argue that feelings of vulnerability to physical, societal, and personal risks are a key factor driving religiosity, and we demonstrate that the process of secularization—a systematic erosion of religious practices, values, and beliefs—has occurred most clearly among the most prosperous social sectors living in affluent and secure postindustrial nations. We believe that the importance of religiosity persists most strongly among vulnerable populations, especially those living in poorer nations, facing personal survival-threatening risks. Variation between the United States and Western Europe, from this perspective, is partly a function of different levels of social protection and economic inequality on both sides of the Atlantic. In combination with other historical and institutional factors, greater economic and social insecurity accounts for greater overall religiosity within the United States and for much of the variation of belief and practice within the country.

Comparing Religiosity in Postindustrial Nations

We can start by considering the cross-national evidence of religiosity in post-industrial nations. Figure 3.1 shows different patterns of religious behavior, highlighting the substantial contrasts between the cluster of countries which prove by far the most religious in this comparison, including the United States, Ireland, and Italy. At the other extreme, the most secular nations include France, Denmark, and Britain. There is a fairly similar pattern across both indicators of religious behavior—attendance at religious services and prayer—suggesting that both collective and individual forms of participation are fairly consistent in each society. Although religion in the United States is distinctive among rich nations, it would still be misleading to refer to American "exceptionalism," as so many emphasize, as though it were a deviant case from *all* other postindustrial nations. Ireland and Italy also fall outside the mainstream.

The existing evidence in Western Europe consistently and unequivocally shows two things: traditional religious beliefs and involvement in institutionalized religion (1) vary considerably from one country to another and (2) have steadily declined throughout Western Europe, particularly since the 1960s. Studies have often reported that many Western Europeans have ceased to be regular churchgoers today outside of special occasions such as Christmas and Easter, weddings and funerals, a pattern especially evident among the young.[9] One important study compared the proportion of regular (weekly) churchgoers in seven European countries from 1970 to 1991, based on the Eurobarometer surveys, and documented a dramatic fall in congregations during this period in countries with large Catholic populations (Belgium, France, the Netherlands, and West Germany). Overall levels of church disengagement had advanced furthest in France, Britain, and the Netherlands: "Although the timing and pace differ from one country to the next," the authors concluded, echoing many colleagues, "the general tendency is quite stable: in the long run, the percentage of unaffiliated is increasing."[10]

Figure 3.2 illustrates other evidence for the erosion of regular church attendance that has occurred throughout Western Europe since the early 1970s. The fall is steepest and most significant in many Catholic societies, notably Belgium, France, Ireland, Luxembourg, the Netherlands, Portugal, and Spain. To conclude, as Andrew Greeley does, that religion is "still relatively unchanged" in the traditional Catholic nations of Europe seems a triumph of hope over experience and sharply at odds with the evidence.[11] Marked contrasts in the strength of churchgoing habits remain clear, say, between contemporary rates of religious participation in Ireland and Denmark. Nevertheless all the

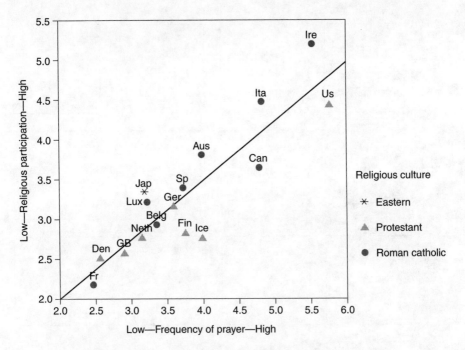

FIGURE 3.1 Religious Behavior in Cross-national Perspective

Notes: Religious participation, Question 185: "Apart from weddings, funerals and christenings, about how often do you attend religious services these days? More than once a week, once a week, once a month, only on special holy days, once a year, less often, never or practically never" (number = mean frequency of attendance at religious services). Frequency of prayer, Question 199: "How often do you pray to God outside of religious services? Would you say ... Every day (7), more than once a week (6), once a week (5), at least once a month (4), several times a year (3), less often (2), never (1)" (number = mean frequency per society).

Source: World Values Survey, pooled 1981–2001.

trends point consistently downward. Moreover the erosion of religiosity is not exclusive to Western European nations. Regular churchgoing also dropped during the last two decades in affluent English-speaking nations such as Canada and Australia.[12]

An interpretation of these patterns that resists the concept of secularization is the view that religiosity has evolved and reinvented itself today as diverse forms of personal "spirituality." In the American context, Wade Clark Roof and other observers suggest that collective engagement with religion in public life has eroded in America among the younger generation. Reasons for this are thought to include the declining status and authority of traditional church institutions and clergy, the individualization of the quest for spirituality, and the rise of multiple New Age movements concerned with "lived religion."[13] These developments are exemplified by a revival of alternative spiritual practices such as astrology, meditation, and atypical therapies, involving a diverse bricolage of personal beliefs. If similar developments are also evident in Europe, public engagement with churches could have been replaced by a "private" or "personal"

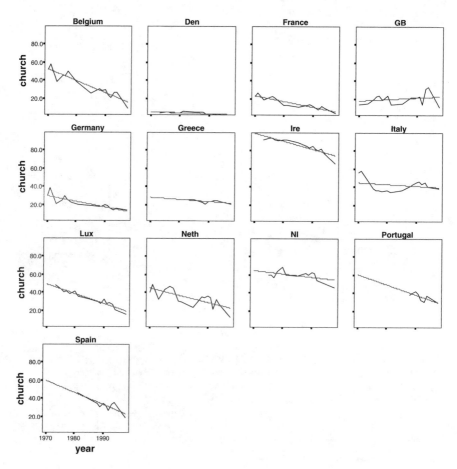

FIGURE 3.2 Religious Participation in Western Europe, 1970–2000

Notes: Number = the percentage of population who said they attended a religious service "at least once a week" and the regression line of the trend.

Source: Mannheim Eurobarometer Trend File, 1970–99.

search for spirituality and meaning in life, making the practices, beliefs, and symbols of religiosity less visible.[14] Along these lines, Greeley suggests that indicators of subjective beliefs in Europe, exemplified by faith in God or in life after death, display a mixed picture during the last two decades, rather than a simple uniform decline.[15]

This objection to the secularization thesis does not hold up well, however. Evidence suggests that one reason for the decline in religious participation during the late twentieth century actually lies in the gradual erosion of common spiritual belief. Greeley's results are based primarily upon analysis of the International Social Survey Program, which conducted opinion polls on religion in 1991 and 1998. Unfortunately this provides too limited a time period to detect long-term change. Instead, here we monitor trends in religious beliefs in God and in life after death during the last fifty years by matching survey data in the Gallup polls starting in 1947 to the more recent data, where the same questions were replicated in the World Values Surveys.

Table 3.1 shows that in 1947 eight out of ten people believed in God, with the highest levels of belief expressed in Australia, Canada, the United States, and Brazil. Over subsequent decades, belief in God fell significantly in all but

TABLE 3.1. Belief in God, 1947–2001

Nation	1947	1968	1975	1981	1990	1995	2001	Change
Sweden	80	60		52	38	48	46	−34
Netherlands	80	79		64	61		58	−22
Australia	95		80	79		75	75	−20
Norway	84	73		68	58	65		−19
Denmark	80			53	59		62	−18
Britain		77	76	73	72		61	−16
Greece		96					84	−12
West Germany		81	72	68	63	71	69	−12
Belgium			78	76	65		67	−11
Finland	83	83			61	73	72	−11
France	66	73	72	59	57		56	−10
Canada	95		89	91	85		88	−7
Switzerland		84			77	77		−7
India			98		93	94		−4
Japan			38	39	37	44	35	−3
Austria		85			78		83	−2
Italy			88	82	82		88	0
United States	94	98	94	96	93	94	94	0
Brazil	96				98	99		+3
Average 1947–2001	85						72	−13

Notes: The percentage of the public who express belief in God in nineteen societies, listed in order of decreasing change in belief between 1947 and 2001. Numbers represent the percentage of respondents who answered "yes." "Change" is the percentage difference between the first and last observation in the series. "Average 1947–2001" indicates the average for the eight nations with observations in both 1947 and 2001. Percentages based on the following questions and answers:

Year	Source	Question	Possible Answers
1947	Gallup Opinion Index	Do you, personally, believe in God?	yes/no/don't know
1968	Gallup Opinion Index	Do you believe in God?	yes/no/don't know
1975	Gallup Opinion Index	Do you believe in God or a universal spirit?	yes/no/don't know
1981–2001	World Values Survey/European Values Survey	Do you believe in God?	yes/no/don't know

Source for Gallup polls: Lee Sigelman, "Review of the Polls: Multination Surveys of Religious Beliefs," Journal for the Scientific Study of Religion 16.3 (1977): 289–94.

two countries, the United States and Brazil. The decline proved sharpest in the Scandinavian nations, the Netherlands, Australia, and Britain. Table 3.2 illustrates very similar patterns for belief in life after death, where an erosion of subjective religiosity occurred in thirteen of the nineteen countries where evidence is available. The greatest falls during the last fifty years took place in northern Europe, Canada, and Brazil, and the only exceptions to this pattern were the United States, Japan, and Italy. These results show that declines in church attendance went hand in hand with a decline in certain core spiritual beliefs. One cannot separate the public and private dimensions of religiosity.

In the light of these European patterns, many have regarded the United States as the religious exception, although in fact the evidence remains somewhat ambiguous. At least until the late 1980s, analysis of trends in church

TABLE 3.2. Belief in Life after Death, 1947–2001

Country	1947	1968	1975	1981	1990	2001	Change
Norway	71	54		41	36		−35
Finland	69	55			44	44	−25
Denmark	55			25	29	32	−23
Netherlands	68	50		41	39	47	−21
France	58	35	39	35	38	39	−19
Australia	63		48	49			−14
Canada	78		54	61	61	67	−11
Sweden	49	38		28	31	39	−10
Greece		57				47	−10
Brazil	78				70		−8
Belgium			48	36	37	40	−8
Britain	49	38	43	46	44	45	−4
West Germany		41	33	36	38	38	−3
Switzerland		50			52		+2
United States	68	73	69	70	70	76	+8
Japan			18	33	30	32	+14
Italy			46	46	53	61	+15
Average 1947–2001	68					46	−22

Notes: The percentage of the public who express belief in life after death in seventeen societies, listed in order of decreasing change in belief between 1947 and 2001. Numbers represent the percentage of respondents who answered "yes." "Change" is the percentage difference between the first and last observation in the series. "Average 1947–2001" indicates the average for the eight nations with observations in both 1947 and 2001. Percentages based on the following questions and answers:

Year	Source	Question	Possible Answers
1947–75	Gallup Opinion Index	Do you believe in life after death?	yes/no/don't know
1981–2001	World Values Survey/European Values Survey	Do you believe in life after death?	yes/no/don't know

Source for Gallup polls: Lee Sigelman, "Review of the Polls: Multination Surveys of Religious Beliefs," Journal for the Scientific Study of Religion 16.3 (1977): 289–94.

attendance derived from historical records and from representative surveys commonly reported that the size of congregations in the United States had remained stable over decades. Protestant church attendance had not declined significantly, and Catholic attendance, while falling rapidly from 1968 to 1975, did not erode further in subsequent years.[16] The first benchmark from the Gallup organization measuring religiosity found that in March 1939 40% of American adults reported attending church the previous week, exactly the same figure given by Gallup more than sixty years later in 2003.[17]

Yet there are serious difficulties in obtaining reliable estimates of churchgoing from survey data. Studies suggest that the Gallup organization's procedures may systematically exaggerate attendance rates; some respondents claim to go to church because of the perceived social expectation that they should do so.[18] Other data confirm that these estimates may be inflated. The American National Election Survey, conducted every two years since the late 1950s, suggests that weekly church attendance never rises much above 25% in the United States. Moreover, when the National Election Survey modified the question sequence to reduce any perception that attendance might be the norm, the proportion reporting that they never attend church jumped from 12% to 33% and has stayed at that level in subsequent surveys.[19] The U.S. General Social Survey, conducted annually by the National Opinion Research Center during the last three decades, also indicates that weekly church attendance in America hovers around the 25%–30% range, with a significant fall in church attendance occurring during the last decade. According to the General Social Survey, the proportion of Americans reporting that they attended church at least weekly fell to one quarter in the most recent poll, while at the same time the proportion saying that they never attended church doubled to one fifth of all Americans (see figure 3.3).[20]

Other indicators also suggest that traditional religious participation may have eroded in the United States, parallel to the long-term trends experienced throughout Europe. For example, Gallup polls registered a modest decline in the proportion of Americans who are *members* of a church or synagogue, down from about three-quarters (73%) of the population in 1937 to about two-thirds (65%) in 2001. The General Social Survey monitored religious identities annually during the last three decades. It found that the proportion of Americans who are secularists, reporting that they have *no* religious preference or identity, climbed steadily from 5% in 1972 to just under 15% thirty years later. During these decades, the main erosion occurred among American Protestants at a time when patterns of adherence were changing within that community. Many studies report that congregations for newer evangelical churches have expanded their membership at the expense of mainline Protestant denominations such as the Methodists, Presbyterians, and Episcopalians, in part due to changes in the American population and also patterns of immigration from Latin America and Asia. Meanwhile, the proportion of Catholics in the population has remained fairly steady, in part due to a substantial influx of Hispanic immigrants with large families. The picture is one of greater religious diversity within the Christian fold and still high levels of identification and participation—even if the overall trend has been slightly downward.[21]

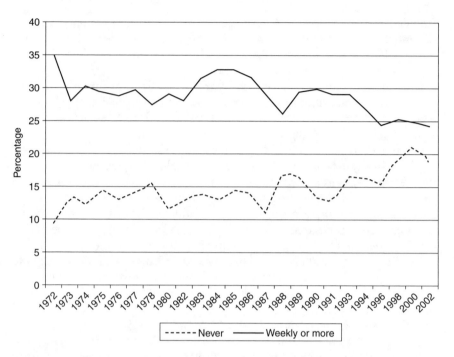

FIGURE 3.3 Religious Participation in the United States, 1972–2002

Notes: Question: "How often do you attend religious services?" Answers: never/at least once a week or more often.

Source: U.S. General Social Survey, 1972–2002 N.43, 204.

We can conclude that the United States remains one of the most religious in the club of rich countries, alongside Ireland and Italy, and indeed as observed earlier this makes America one of the most religious countries in the world. The pervasive importance of these religious values is apparent in many American practices, especially in public life—even prior to the Bush administration and 9/11—despite the strict division of church and state that characterizes much of the legal system. Nevertheless the accumulated evidence suggests that that secular tendencies in the United States may have strengthened, at least during the last decade, narrowing the gap with the less religious societies that dominate Western Europe. Public displays of religiosity by politicians and the salience of religious issues in an increasingly diverse population should not be confused with a broad-based religious revival within society. There is little evidence of the latter.

Explaining Variations in Religiosity: The Religious Market Model

What explains the cross-national variations in religiosity particularly evident in the transatlantic context? Religious market theory suggests that supply-side factors, notably denominational competition and state regulation of religious institutions, shape levels of religious participation in the United States and Europe and beyond. During the last decade many American commentators have enthusiastically advanced this account, and the principle proponents include Roger Finke, Rodney Stark, Lawrence R. Iannaccone, William Sims Bainbridge, and R. Stephen Warner.[22] Market-based theories in the sociology of religion assume that the demand for religious products is relatively constant, based on the otherworldly rewards of life after death promised by most (although not all) faiths.[23] Dissimilar levels of spiritual behavior evident in various countries are believed to result less from "bottom up" demand than from variance in "top down" religious supply. Religious groups compete for congregations with different degrees of vigor. Established churches are thought to be complacent monopolies taking their congregations for granted, with a fixed market share due to state regulation and subsidy for one particular faith that enjoys special status and privileges. By contrast, where a free religious marketplace exists, energetic competition between churches expands the supply of religious "products," thereby mobilizing religious activism among the public.

The theory claims to be a universal generalization applicable to all faiths, although the evidence to support this argument is drawn largely from the United States and Western Europe. The proliferation of diverse churches in the United States, such as Methodist, Lutheran, Presbyterian, and Episcopalian mainline churches, as well as the Southern Baptist Convention, the Assemblies of God, Pentecostal, and Holiness churches among conservative denominations, is claimed to have maximized choice and competition among faiths, thereby mobilizing the American public. American churches are subject to market forces. Their survival and success depends upon their ability to attract clergy and volunteers, as well as the financial resources from their membership. Competition is thought to generate certain benefits, producing diversity, stimulating innovation, and compelling churches to actively recruit congregations by responding to public demands. For example, the National Congregations Study found that American churches commonly seek to attract new adherents by offering multiple social activities beyond worship, including religious education, cultural and arts groups, engagement in community politics, and welfare services such as soup kitchens.[24]

Proponents of religious market theory point to very different conditions in Europe. Stark and Finke argue that many European countries sustain what they term "a *socialized* religious economy," with state subsidies for established churches restricting the free competition that creates more religious demand in the U.S. context. Religious monopolies are believed to be less innovative, responsive, and efficient. Where clergy enjoy secure incomes and tenure regardless of their performance, such as in Germany and Sweden, priests and ministers are thought to grow complacent, slothful, and lax. "When people have little need or motive to work, they tend not to work," Stark and Finke argue. "Subsidized churches will therefore be lazy."[25] If the "supply" of churches were expanded in Europe through disestablishment and deregulation, they suggest, and if clerics just made more effort, a resurgence of religious behavior among the public might take place. "To the extent that organizations work harder," they conclude, "they are more successful. What could be more obvious?"[26]

What indeed? Yet, after considerable debate during the last decade, the evidence that religious competition provides a plausible explanation of religious participation remains controversial.[27] Criticisms have been both theoretical and empirical. Conceptually Joseph Bryant questions the appropriateness of the cost-benefit model and the use of metaphors such as "markets," "products," "commodities," and "capital" in the analysis of religion.[28] In terms of the evidence, commentators note serious flaws with the measures commonly used to gauge the degree of religious competition. Mark Chaves and Philip Gorski conducted a thorough metareview of the literature by examining the results of 193 tests of the evidence, drawn from different geographical and historical settings, from a series of twenty-six articles published on this subject. They conclude that the theory lacked consistent support, as some studies found a significant correlation between religious pluralism and religious participation, while others failed to confirm any linkage.[29] The most critical analysis by David Voas, Daniel Olson, and Alasdair Crockett concludes that any observed relationships are spurious and that a purely mathematical association between the leading pluralism index and religious participation rates can explain any positive or negative correlations. The study concludes that there is no compelling evidence from *any* of the existing studies that religious pluralism influences church participation rates.[30]

The appropriate geographic unit of analysis is also problematic. The original supply-side theory conceived of religious competition as rivalry between different churches within a particular local community, typified by the role of Baptist, Episcopalian, and Catholic churches in the United States. Once we extend the comparison more broadly cross-nationally, however, it becomes unclear how competition should be gauged, for example, whether the key comparison should be competition among different denominations and sects, or whether we should focus on rivalry between and among multiple churches, temples, mosques, synagogues, and shrines representing all the major world religions. There is still no compelling way to extend a theory grounded in the U.S. experience in an international direction.

What other empirical evidence could be mustered to support the argument that greater religious competition leads to more churchgoing in the United States than in Western Europe? Stark and Finke provide numerous examples of specific limitations experienced by particular denominations and faiths in Western European countries. They include incidents of limited religious freedoms, such as harassment experienced by Jehovah's Witnesses in Portugal, Germany, and France, and legal regulations such as tax-free status with positive fiscal benefits for established churches.[31] Yet this approach, centered on particular examples, is unsystematic, and bias may arise from the particular selection of cases. It is true that the United States displays a diverse range of churches and temples and relatively high rates of churchgoing and subjective religiosity. This fits the theory. But clear anomalies to this relationship also exist, most notably high levels of churchgoing evident in Ireland and Italy, despite the fact that the Catholic Church predominates as a virtual monopoly in these nations.[32]

More systematic cross-national evidence is provided in a study by Lawrence Iannaccone comparing church attendance in eight Western European nations (excluding six predominantly Catholic cultures) plus four Anglo-American democracies. Regression analysis found a significant and very strong relationship between the degree of denominational pluralism in these countries and levels of religious participation (rates of weekly church attendance).[33] It remains unclear, however, why the six predominantly Catholic cultures in southern and western Europe are excluded from this comparison—countries with dominant churches and relatively high participation. Their incorporation would have challenged the model. Ian Smith, John Sawkins, and Paul Seaman compared eighteen societies based on the 1991 International Social Survey Program religion survey and reported that religious pluralism was significantly related to regular religious participation.[34] Other cross-national studies have reported results inconsistent with the supply-side thesis. For example, Johan Verweij, Peter Ester, and Rein Nauta conducted a cross-national comparison using the 1990 European Values Survey in sixteen countries. They found that irrespective of the model specification, religious pluralism in any particular country was an insignificant predictor of levels of religious participation, whether measured against rates of church attendance or church membership. By contrast, the degree of state regulation was important, along with the predominant religious culture and the overall level of societal modernization.[35] Research by Steve Bruce, comparing religiosity in the Nordic and Baltic states, also concludes that trends in religious observance contradicted a number of core supply-side propositions.[36] The empirical evidence supporting the supply-side thesis has come under serious attack, as the conclusions of most of the studies by Stark and Finke were contaminated by a coding error and the index most often used to measure religious pluralism was flawed in certain respects.[37]

In defense of the religious market approach, it should be noted that it is a viable theory that is open to testing. It should not be dismissed because of methodological and measurement problems that have arisen. When the best available methods and data are applied, however, it ultimately fails to demonstrate a link between religious competition and religious behavior. If the supply-side theory is correct, both religious pluralism and state regulation of religion should be important in predicting rates of churchgoing in postindustrial societies. In particular, countries with great competition among multiple pluralist religious churches, denominations, and faiths should have the highest religious participation.[38]

Contrary to the predictions of supply-side theory, the correlation between religious pluralism and religious behavior all prove insignificant in postindustrial societies. The results *lend no support to the claim of a significant link between religious pluralism and participation*, and this is true irrespective of whether the comparison focuses on frequency of attendance at services of worship or the frequency of prayer.[39] Among postindustrial societies, the United States is exceptional in its combination of high rates of religious pluralism *and* participation: the theory does indeed fit the American case, but the problem is that it fails to work elsewhere. Other English-speaking nations share similar levels of religious pluralism. In these countries, however, far fewer people regularly attend church. Moreover, in Catholic postindustrial societies the relationship is actually *reversed*, with the highest participation evident in Ireland and Italy, where the church enjoys a virtual religious monopoly, compared with more pluralist Netherlands and France, where churchgoing habits are far weaker. Nor is this merely due to the comparison of postindustrial societies: the global comparison in all nations confirms that there is no significant relationship between participation and pluralism across the broader distribution of societies worldwide.[40]

Of course, the theory might be revived by arguing that what matters is less competition among the major faiths, since people rarely convert directly, but rather competition among or within specific denominations, since people are more likely to switch particular churches within closely related families. This proposition would require testing at community level with other forms of data, at a finer level of denominational detail than is available in most social surveys, and indeed even in most census data. It should be recalled, though, that if the claims of the original theory were modified in this direction, its applicability for cross-national research would become limited outside the U.S. context, with its denominational configuration. If one looks at major religious communities, not their subdivisions, and at a range of different countries, religious market theory centered on levels of religious competition does not hold up well at all.

An alternative version of religious market theory predicts that participation will also be maximized where there is a strong constitutional division between church and state, protecting religious freedom of worship and toleration of different denominations, without hindrance to particular sects and faiths. This is one of the explanations for American exceptionalism advanced by Seymour Martin Lipset, who argues that the long-standing separation of church and state in the United States has given the churches greater autonomy and allowed varied opportunities for people to participate in religion.[41] Three indicators have been deployed to analyze this relationship: (1) A six-point scale measuring levels of state regulation of religion developed by Mark Chaves and David E. Cann in the context of eighteen postindustrial nations; (2) the Norris and Inglehart Freedom of Religion Index constructed by coding twenty indicators such as the role of the state in subsidizing churches, constitutional recognition of freedom of religion, and restrictions of certain denominations, cults, or sects; and (3) the summary analysis of religious freedom generated every year by a leading nongovernmental organization, Freedom House.[42]

Contrary to the expectations of religious market theory, the results of the simple correlations using these data sources suggest that no significant relationship exists between any of these indicators of religious freedom and levels of religious behavior. This is true in a comparison of postindustrial nations that encompasses the United States and Europe, as well as in the global comparison of all countries where data were available.[43] There are many reasons why one might imagine that the spread of greater tolerance and freedom of worship, by facilitating religious competition, might prove conducive to greater religious activity among the public. But so far the range of evidence using multiple indicators fails to support the supply-side claims.

Religious market theory therefore provides only limited insights into the diversity of religious participation found in rich nations. In postindustrial nations no empirical support that we examined could explain the puzzle why some rich nations are far more religious than others, and there is no significant link between patterns of religious behavior and the indicators of religious pluralism, religious freedom, and state-church relations. But, of course, this still leaves us with the question posed at the outset: Why are some societies such as the United States more religious in their habits and beliefs than most comparable Western nations sharing a Christian cultural heritage?

Secure Secularization Thesis

Our answer to this question centers on patterns of human security and, in particular, conditions of socioeconomic inequality. Where there is less societal vulnerability, insecurity, and risk, we argue that people generally have less recourse to religion. Historically, the growth of the welfare state in industrialized nations has insured large sectors of the public against the worst risks of ill health and old age, penury, and destitution. The work of nonprofit charitable foundations, private insurance, and financial institutions have also increased human security in postindustrial nations. These developments, taken together, have reduced the vital role of religion in people's lives, both as a source of comfort and meaning and as a reservoir of community support. Of course, affluent nations have multiple pockets of long-term poverty, whether afflicting unemployed African Americans living in the inner cities of Los Angeles and Detroit; farm laborers in Sicily; or Bangladeshi, Pakistani, and Indian émigrés in Leicester and Birmingham. Populations typically most at risk in industrialized nations, capable of falling through the welfare safety net, include the elderly and children; single-parent female-headed households; the long-term disabled, homeless, and unemployed; and ethnic minorities. If we are correct that feelings of vulnerability are key drivers of religiosity, even in rich nations, one should be able to discern patterns linking levels of economic inequality across societies with levels of religious belief and engagement.

We can analyze the distribution of economic resources in postindustrial societies by comparing the extent to which the distribution of income among households within a society deviates from a perfectly equal distribution. It turns out that the level of economic inequality proves strongly and significantly related to both attendance at religious services and prayer, and the latter in particular. Figure 3.4 illustrates this relationship. The United States is exceptionally high in religiosity in large part, we believe, because it is also one of the most unequal postindustrial societies under comparison. Despite private affluence for the well-off, many American families, even in the professional middle classes, face serious risks of loss of paid work by the main breadwinner, the dangers of sudden ill heath without adequate private medical insurance, vulnerability to becoming a victim of crime, as well as the problems of paying for long-term care of the elderly. Americans face greater anxieties than citizens in other advanced industrialized countries about whether they will be covered by medical insurance, whether they will be fired arbitrarily, or whether they will be forced to choose between losing their job and devoting themselves to their newborn child.[44] The entrepreneurial culture and the emphasis on personal responsibility has generated conditions of individual freedom and delivered considerable societal affluence, and yet one trade-off is that the United States has greater income inequality than any other advanced industrial democracy.[45] By comparison, despite recent pressures on restructuring, the secular Scandinavian and Western European states remain some of the most egalitarian societies, with relatively high levels of personal taxation, but also an expansive array of welfare services in the public sector, including comprehensive health care, social services, and pensions.[46]

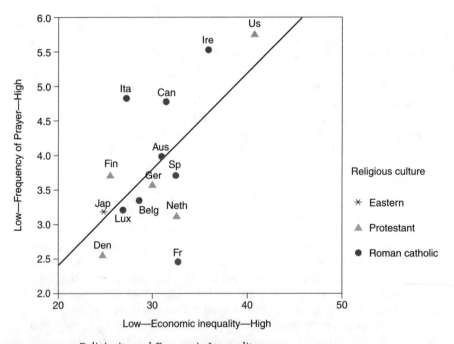

FIGURE 3.4 Religiosity and Economic Inequality

Notes: Question 199: "How often do you pray to God outside of religious services? Would you say ... Every day (7), more than once a week (6), once a week (5), at least once a month (4), several times a year (3), less often (2), never (1)" (number = mean frequency per society). Economic inequality is gauged by the Gini coefficient (latest year: World Bank, 2002).

Source: World Values Survey, pooled 1981–2001.

If this argument rested only on the cross-national comparisons then, of course, it would be too limited, as multiple other characteristics distinguish Western Europe and the United States. But evidence can also be examined at the individual level by looking at how far the distribution of income relates to religious behavior. The patterns in figure 3.5 show that religiosity is systematically related at the individual level to the distribution of income groups in postindustrial societies. Generally speaking, *the poor are almost twice as religious as the rich*. Similar patterns can be found in the United States (see figure 3.6). For example, two-thirds (66%) of the least well-off income group pray daily, compared with 47% of the highest income group.

The range of evidence presented here in postindustrial societies serves to confirm a broader pattern. Secularization is not a deterministic process but it is still one that is largely predictable, based on knowing just a few facts about levels of human development and socioeconomic equality in each country. Growing up in societies in which survival is uncertain is conducive to a strong emphasis on religion; conversely, experiencing high levels of existential security throughout one's formative years reduces the subjective importance of religion in people's lives. The religious market assumption that demand for religion is constant does not hold in practice. Globally, the evidence suggests that as a society moves past the early stages of industrialization and life becomes less nasty, less brutish, and longer, people tend to become more secular in their orientations. The most crucial explanatory variables are those that differentiate between vulnerable societies and societies in which human security is so robust so as to be taken for granted by most of the population.

If the levels of societal and individual security in any society seem to provide the most persuasive and parsimonious explanation for variations in religiosity, a number of other possible explanatory factors could be brought into the picture as well—from institutional structures to state restrictions on freedom of worship, the historical role of church-state relations, and patterns of denominational and church competition. Although rising levels of existential security are conducive to secularization, cultural change is path dependent: the historically predominant religious tradition of a given society tends to leave a lasting impact on religious beliefs and other social norms, ranging from approval of divorce to gender roles, tolerance of homosexuality, and work orientations. Where a society started from continues to influence where it is at later points in time, so that the citizens of historically Protestant societies continue to show values that are distinct from those prevailing in historically Catholic or Hindu or Orthodox or Confucian societies. These cross-national differences do not reflect the influence of the religious authorities today—they persist even in societies where the vast majority no longer attends church. They reflect historical influences that shaped given national cultures and today affect the entire population. Within the Netherlands, for example, those who have left the church tend to share a common national value system that is very distinctive in global perspective.

A society's historical heritage leaves a lasting imprint, but the process of secularization tends to bring systematic cultural changes that move in a predictable direction, diminishing the importance of religion in people's lives and

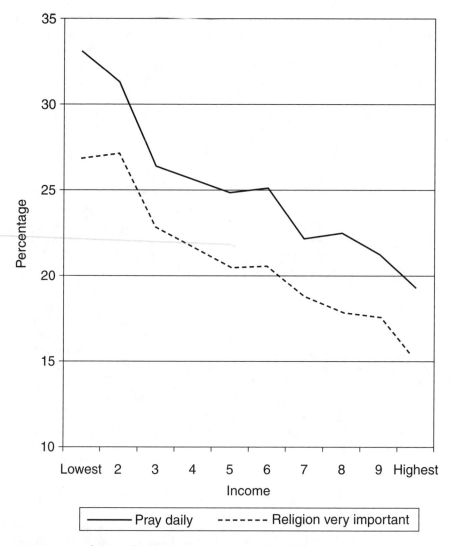

FIGURE 3.5 Religiosity by Income in Postindustrial Societies

Notes: The percentage of the public who pray daily and who regard religion as very important by decile household income group (counting all wages, salaries, pensions, and other incomes, before taxes and other deduction) in postindustrial societies.

Source: World Values Study, pooled 1981–2001.

weakening allegiance to traditional cultural norms, making people more tolerant of divorce, abortion, homosexuality, and cultural change in general. It may seem paradoxical to claim that economic development brings systematic changes *and* that a society's cultural heritage continues to have an impact, but it is not. If every society in the world were moving in the same direction, at the

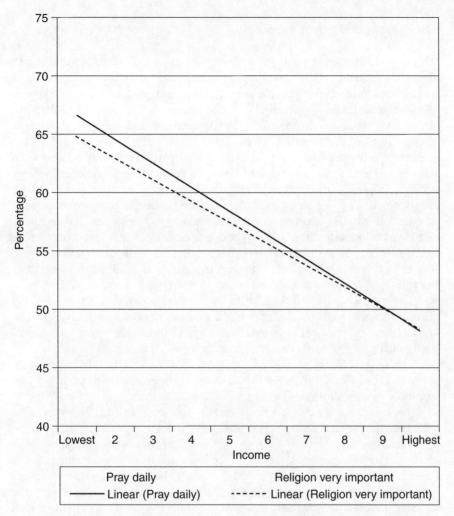

FIGURE 3.6 Religiosity by Income in the United States

Notes: Linear trends in the percentage of the American public who pray daily and who regard religion as very important by decile household income group (counting all wages, salaries, pensions, and other incomes, before taxes and other deduction).

Source: World Values Study, pooled 1981–2001.

same speed, they would remain as far apart as ever and would never converge. The reality is not that simple. Secularization started earliest and has moved farthest in the most economically developed countries; and little or no secularization has taken place in the low-income countries. This means that the cultural differences linked with economic development not only are not shrinking, they are growing *larger*. Secularization and the persistence of cultural differences are perfectly compatible.

Conclusions and Implications

This essay addressed the dynamics of religious pluralism, understood both as a diversity of beliefs, values, and practices among communities of different faiths, as well as patterns of competition among religious organizations for adherents. We described the divergent religious landscapes on both sides of the Atlantic—the greater religiosity in the United States compared with most of Western Europe. Against this backdrop we made two claims. The first is that despite the greater visibility of religion in the public sphere, particularly evident since 9/11, the overall trend at the societal level is toward greater secularization. No single indicator is ever sufficient by itself to confirm or refute the secularization thesis, since the specific choice of measures and concepts always remain open to question. Studies use alternative time periods and cross-national comparative frameworks, and often we lack good long-term evidence. The most persuasive evidence about secularization in rich nations concerns values and behavior. The critical test is what people say is important to their lives and what they actually *do*. During the twentieth century in nearly all postindustrial nations—ranging from Canada and Sweden to France, Britain, and Australia—official church records report that where once the public flocked to worship services, the pews are now almost deserted. The surveys monitoring European churchgoing during the last fifty years confirm this phenomenon.

The United States remains exceptional. The strongest challenge to secularization theory arises from American observers who commonly point out that claims of steadily diminishing congregations in Western Europe are sharply at odds with U.S. trends, at least until the early 1990s.[47] In fact, the evidence is very mixed. The best data suggest that religious identification and behavior have declined considerably in the United States, if not as precipitously as Europe. The United States should not be excluded from any consideration of the dynamics of secularization in today's world. A vibrant religious pluralism now encompassing a greater diversity of faith traditions characterizes the country, and religious issues find their way into the media and politics with great frequency. But the salience of religion should not be confused with its resurgence at a societal level. Transatlantic differences in levels of religiosity are stark and important, but should not be exaggerated beyond their actual extent.

The second part of the essay presented and critiqued one major effort to explain these transatlantic differences—religious market theory. The view that the religious supply creates its own demand—that competition among churches is what explains the general higher level of religiosity in the United States—does not survive analytical scrutiny. An alternative approach, based on different levels of existential security, was put forward. Evidence suggests that the more that basic existential economic and social needs are met, the more religiosity declines. One can easily think of striking exceptions, such as Osama bin Laden, someone both extremely rich and fanatically religious. But when we go beyond anecdotal evidence such as this, we find that the overwhelming bulk of evidence points in the opposite direction: people who experience ego-tropic risks during their formative years (posing direct threats to themselves and their families) or socio-tropic risks (threatening their community) tend to be far more religious than those who grow up under safer, comfortable, and more pre- dictable conditions. In relatively secure societies, the remnants of religion have not died away; in surveys most Europeans still express formal belief in God or identify themselves as Protestants or Catholics on official forms. But in these societies the importance and vitality of religion, its ever-present influence on how people live their daily lives, has gradually eroded. In the United States, with its lower levels of social cohesion and higher levels of existential uncer- tainty, religious belief and practice are higher. And within the United States, the more secure economically and socially tend to be less religious. There is no question that the traditional secularization thesis needs updating. It is obvious that religion has not disappeared from the world, nor does it seem likely to do so. Nevertheless, the concept of secularization captures an important part of what is going on.

When this argument about Atlantic democracies is placed within a global context, a different picture emerges. Despite trends in secularization occurring in rich nations, the world as a whole has not become less religious. The most recent research supports two broad conclusions: (1) the publics of virtually all advanced industrial societies have been moving toward more secular orienta- tions during the past fifty years; and (2) the world as a whole now has more people with traditional religious views than ever before—and they constitute a growing proportion of the world's population. Though these two propositions may initially seem contradictory, they are not. In fact, that the first proposition is true helps account for the second—because secularization and human de- velopment have a powerful negative impact on human fertility rates. Practically all of the countries in which secularization is most advanced show fertility rates far below the replacement level—while societies with traditional religious ori- entations have fertility rates that are two or three times the replacement level. They contain a growing share of the world's population. This expanding gap between sacred and secular societies around the globe has important consequences for the future of religious pluralism, cultural change, and world politics.

NOTES

1. For a discussion, see Steve Bruce, ed., *Religion and Modernization: Sociologists and Historians Debate the Secularization Thesis* (Oxford: Clarendon, 1992), 170–94; and Alan Aldridge, *Religion in the Contemporary World* (Cambridge: Polity Press, 2000), chap. 4.

2. C. Wright Mills, *The Sociological Imagination* (Oxford: Oxford University Press, 1959), 32–33.

3. The term *fundamentalist* is used in a neutral way to refer to those with an absolute conviction in the fundamental principles of their faith to the exclusion of other beliefs.

4. See, for example, Peter L. Berger, ed., *The Desecularization of the World: Re-surgent Religion and World Politics* (Washington, DC: Ethics and Public Policy Center/ Grand Rapids: Eerdmans, 1999), 2. Compare this statement with the arguments in idem, *The Sacred Canopy* (Garden City, NY: Doubleday, 1967).

5. Rodney Stark and Roger Finke, *Acts of Faith: Explaining the Human Side of Religion* (Berkeley: University of California Press, 2000), 79. See also Rodney Stark, "Secularization, RIP," *Sociology of Religion* 60.3 (1990): 270.

6. As Roger Finke puts it, "The vibrancy and growth of American religious in-stitutions presents the most open defiance of the secularization model"; "An Unsec-ular America," in *Religion and Modernization: Sociologists and Historians Debate the Secularization Thesis*, ed. Steve Bruce (Oxford: Clarendon, 1992), 148.

7. Further discussion of related issues can be found in Pippa Norris and Ronald Inglehart, *Sacred and Secular: Religion and Politics Worldwide* (New York: Cambridge University Press, 2004).

8. Berger, *Desecularization of the World*.

9. See, for example, Sabino Samele Acquaviva, *The Decline of the Sacred in Industrial Society* (Oxford: Blackwell, 1979); Steve Bruce, *Religion in the Modern World: From Cathedrals to Cults* (Oxford: Oxford University Press, 1996); and idem, *God Is Dead* (Oxford: Blackwell, 2002). For a challenge to this view, see Rodney Stark and Lawrence Iannaccone, "A Supply-side Reinterpretation of the 'Secularization' of Europe," *Journal for the Scientific Study of Religion* 33 (1985): 230–52.

10. Wolfgang Jagodzinski and Karel Dobbelaere, "Secularization and Church Religiosity," in *The Impact of Values*, ed. Jan W. van Deth and Elinor Scarbrough (Oxford: Oxford University Press, 1995), 105.

11. Andrew M. Greeley, *Religion in Europe at the End of the Second Millennium* (New Brunswick, NJ: Transaction, 2003), xi.

12. Reginald W. Bibby, "The State of Collective Religiosity in Canada: An Em-pirical Analysis," *Canadian Review of Sociology and Anthropology* 16.1 (1979): 105–16; and Ian McAllister, "Religious Change and Secularization: The Transmission of Re-ligious Values in Australia," *Sociological Analysis* 49.3 (1988): 249–63.

13. Wade Clark Roof, *Spiritual Marketplace: Baby Boomers and the Remaking of American Religion* (Princeton: Princeton University Press, 2001). See also Robert C. Fuller, *Spiritual, But Not Religious: Understanding Unchurched America* (New York: Oxford University Press, 2002).

14. Grace Davie, *Religion in Britain since 1945: Believing without Belonging* (Oxford: Blackwell, 1994); and Danièle Hervieu-Léger, "The Case for a Sociology of 'Multiple Religious Modernities': A Different Approach to the 'Invisible Religion' of European Societies," *Social Compass* 50.3 (2003): 287–95.

15. Greeley, *Religion in Europe*.

16. Andrew M. Greeley, *Religious Change in America* (Cambridge: Harvard Uni-versity Press, 1980).

17. The March 1939 Gallup–AIPO poll asked, "Did you happen to go to church last Sunday?" (answers: 40% yes, 60% no). The March 14, 2003, Gallup–CNN/*USA Today* poll asked (with percentages in brackets), "How often do you attend church or synagogue—at least once a week [31%], almost every week [9%], about once a month [16%], seldom [28%], or never [16%]?" Kirk Hadaway points out that self-reported church attendance figures may well contain systematic bias toward overreporting, compared with records of the actual size of congregations; C. Kirk Hadaway, Penny L. Marler, and Mark Chaves, "What the Polls Don't Show: A Closer Look at Church Attendance," *American Sociological Review* 58.6 (1993): 741–52. For more details about

the Gallup organization's time-series tracking religion in America, see D. Michael Lindsay, *Surveying the Religious Landscape: Trends in U.S. Beliefs* (New York: Moorhouse, 2000).

18. See, for example, Robert D. Woodberry, "When Surveys Lie and People Tell the Truth: How Surveys Oversample Church Attenders," *American Sociological Review* 63.1 (1998): 119–22.

19. See details of the National Election Survey series at www.umich.edu/~NES.

20. See also C. Kirk Hadaway, Penny L. Marler, and Mark Chaves, "Over-reporting Church Attendance in America: Evidence That Demands the Same Verdict," *American Sociological Review* 63.1 (1998): 122–30.

21. Robert Wuthnow, *The Restructuring of American Religion* (Princeton: Princeton University Press, 1988); and Michael Hout, Andrew M. Greeley, and Melissa J. Wilde, "The Demographic Imperative in Religious Change in the United States," *American Journal of Sociology* 107.2 (2001): 468–500.

22. Stark and Iannaccone, "Supply-side Reinterpretation"; Rodney Stark and William Sims Bainbridge, *A Theory of Religion* (New York: Peter Lang, 1987); Roger Finke and Rodney Stark, *The Churching of America* (New Brunswick: Rutgers University Press, 1992); Roger Finke and Lawrence R. Iannaccone, "The Illusion of Shifting Demand: Supply-side Explanations for Trends and Change in the American Religious Market Place," *Annals of the American Association of Political and Social Science* 527 (1993): 27–39.

23. Stark and Finke, *Acts of Faith*, 88. It should be noted that the assumed universal rationality in the supply-side theory has been criticized as inapplicable to religions such as Confucianism and Judaism that do not believe that behavior in this life generates otherworldly rewards in any afterlife. See Mark Chaves and Philip S. Gorski, "Religious Pluralism and Religious Participation," *Annual Review of Sociology* 27 (2001): 261–81; and Stephen Sharot, "Beyond Christianity: A Critique of the Rational Choice Theory of Religion from a Weberian and Comparative Religions Perspective," *Sociology of Religion* 63.4 (2002): 427–54.

24. Mark Chaves, "The National Congregations Study: Background, Methods, and Selected Results," *Journal for the Scientific Study of Religion* 38.4 (1999): 458–76.

25. Stark and Finke, *Acts of Faith*, 230.

26. Ibid., 237–38, 257.

27. Chaves and Gorski, "Religious Pluralism and Religious Participation."

28. Joseph M. Bryant, "Cost-benefit Accounting and the Piety Business: Is *Homo Religious*, at bottom, a *Homo Economicus*?" *Methods and Theory in the Study of Religion* 12 (2000): 520–48.

29. Chaves and Gorski, "Religious Pluralism and Religious Participation."

30. David Voas, Daniel V. A. Olson, and Alasdair Crockett, "Religious Pluralism and Participation: Why Previous Research Is Wrong," *American Sociological Review* 67.2 (2002): 212–30.

31. See also Stark and Iannaccone, "Supply-side Reinterpretation."

32. For an attempt to explain the Italian case as the result of internal competition within Catholicism, see Luca Diotallevi, "Internal Competition in a National Religious Monopoly: The Catholic Effect and the Italian Case," *Sociology of Religion* 63.2 (2002): 137–55.

33. Lawrence R. Iannaccone, "The Consequences of Religious Market Structure," *Rationality and Society* 3 (1991): 156–77.

34. Ian Smith, John W. Sawkins, and Paul T. Seaman, "The Economics of Religious Participation: A Cross-country Study," *Kyklos* 51.1 (1998): 25–43.

35. Johan Verweij, Peter Ester, and Rein Nauta, "Secularization as an Economic and Cultural Phenomenon: A Cross-national Analysis," *Journal for the Scientific Study of Religion* 36.2 (1997): 309–24.

36. Steve Bruce, "The Supply-side Model of Religion: The Nordic and Baltic States," *Journal for the Scientific Study of Religion* 39.1 (2000): 32–46. See also Peter Beyer's related argument that the privatization of religion in Canada led toward greater secularization; "Religious Vitality in Canada: The Complimentarity of Religious Market and Secularization Perspectives," *Journal for the Scientific Study of Religion* 36.2 (1997): 272–88.

37. Chaves and Gorski, "Religious Pluralism and Religious Participation"; and Voas, Olson, and Crockett, "Religious Pluralism and Participation."

38. This argument finds parallels in the debate about the relative importance of changes in the mass political culture and in society, or in the strength of party organizations, for explaining patterns of social and partisan dealignment. See the discussion in Pippa Norris, *Electoral Engineering* (Cambridge: Cambridge University Press, 2003).

39. It should be noted that the proportion of adherents to the majority religion in each country was also compared as an alternative measure of religious diversity or homogeneity, but this measure also proved an insignificant predictor of religious participation, whether the comparison was restricted to postindustrial societies or broadened to all nations worldwide.

40. Norris and Inglehart, *Sacred and Secular*.

41. Seymour Martin Lipset, *Continental Divide: The Values and Institutions of Canada and the United States* (New York: Routledge, 1990).

42. Mark Chaves and David E. Cann, "Regulation, Pluralism, and Religious Market Structure," *Rationality and Society* 4 (1992): 272–90; Norris and Inglehart, *Sacred and Secular*; and Paul Marshall, "Religious Freedom in the World," www .freedomhouse.org.

43. For a full discussion, see Norris and Inglehart, *Sacred and Secular*, 99.

44. For a discussion of the comparative evidence, see, for example, Derek Bok, *The State of the Nation: Government and the Quest for a Better Society* (Cambridge: Harvard University Press, 1996).

45. For example, a recent detailed study comparing the levels of household income after government redistribution through tax and welfare transfers, based on the Luxembourg Income Study database, found that the Gini coefficient for income inequality was greatest in the United States compared with thirteen other advanced industrial democracies. See David Bradley et al., "Distribution and Redistribution in Postindustrial Democracies," *World Politics* 55.1 (2003): 193–228.

46. Katherine McFate, Roger Lawson, and William Julius Wilson, eds., *Poverty, Inequality, and the Future of Social Policy: Western States in the New World Order* (New York: Russell Sage Foundation, 1995); Alexander Hicks, *Social Democracy and Welfare Capitalism: A Century of Income Security Policies* (Ithaca: Cornell University Press, 1999); and Gosta Esping-Andersen, *Social Foundations of Postindustrial Economies* (Oxford: Oxford University Press, 1999).

47. Berger, *Desecularization of the World*; and Greeley, *Religion in Europe*.

BIBLIOGRAPHY

Acquaviva, Sabino Samele. *The Decline of the Sacred in Industrial Society*. Oxford: Blackwell, 1998.

Aldridge, Alan. *Religion in the Contemporary World*. Cambridge: Polity Press, 2000.

Berger, Peter L., ed. *The Desecularization of the World: Resurgent Religion and World Politics*. Washington, DC: Ethics and Public Policy Center/Grand Rapids: Eerdmans, 1999.

———. *The Sacred Canopy*. Garden City, NY: Doubleday, 1967.

Beyer, Peter. "Religious Vitality in Canada: The Complimentarity of Religious Market and Secularization Perspectives." *Journal for the Scientific Study of Religion* 36.2 (1997): 272–88.

Bibby, Reginald W. "The State of Collective Religiosity in Canada: An Empirical Analysis." *Canadian Review of Sociology and Anthropology* 16.1 (1979): 105–16.

Bok, Derek. *The State of the Nation: Government and the Quest for a Better Society*. Cambridge: Harvard University Press, 1996.

Bradley, David, et al. "Distribution and Redistribution in Postindustrial Democracies." *World Politics* 55.1 (2003): 193–228.

Bruce, Steve. *God Is Dead*. Oxford: Blackwell, 2002.

———, ed. *Religion and Modernization: Sociologists and Historians Debate the Secularization Thesis*. Oxford: Clarendon, 1992.

———. *Religion in the Modern World: From Cathedrals to Cults*. Oxford: Oxford University Press, 1996.

———. "The Supply-side Model of Religion: The Nordic and Baltic States." *Journal for the Scientific Study of Religion* 39.1 (2000): 32–46.

Bryant, Joseph M. "Cost-benefit Accounting and the Piety Business: Is *Homo Religious*, at Bottom, a *Homo Economicus?*" *Methods and Theory in the Study of Religion* 12 (2000): 520–48.

Chaves, Mark. "The National Congregations Study: Background, Methods, and Selected Results." *Journal for the Scientific Study of Religion* 38.4 (1999): 458–76.

Chaves, Mark, and David E. Cann. "Regulation, Pluralism, and Religious Market Structure." *Rationality and Society* 4 (1992): 272–90.

Chaves, Mark, and Philip S. Gorski. "Religious Pluralism and Religious Participation." *Annual Review of Sociology* 27 (2001): 261–81.

Davie, Grace. *Religion in Britain since 1945: Believing without Belonging*. Oxford: Blackwell, 1994.

Diotallevi, Luca. "Internal Competition in a National Religious Monopoly: The Catholic Effect and the Italian Case." *Sociology of Religion* 63.2 (2002): 137–55.

Esping-Andersen, Gosta. *Social Foundations of Postindustrial Economies*. Oxford: Oxford University Press, 1999.

Finke, Roger. "An Unsecular America." In *Religion and Modernization: Sociologists and Historians Debate the Secularization Thesis*. Edited by Steve Bruce. Oxford: Clarendon, 1992.

Finke, Roger, and Lawrence R. Iannaccone. "The Illusion of Shifting Demand: Supply-side Explanations for Trends and Change in the American Religious Market Place." *Annals of the American Association of Political and Social Science* 527 (1993): 27–39.

Finke, Roger, and Rodney Stark. *The Churching of America*. New Brunswick: Rutgers University Press, 1992.

Fuller, Robert C. *Spiritual, but Not Religious: Understanding Unchurched America*. New York: Oxford University Press, 2002.

Gallup–AIPO Poll. "Did You Happen to Go to Church Last Sunday?" March 1939. http://poll.gallup.com/.

Gallup–CNN/*USA Today* Poll. "How Often Do You Attend Church or Synagogue?" March 14, 2003. http://poll.gallup.com/.

Greeley, Andrew M. *Religion in Europe at the End of the Second Millennium*. New Brunswick, NJ: Transaction, 2003.

———. *Religious Change in America*. Cambridge: Harvard University Press, 1980.

Hadaway, C. Kirk, and Penny L. Marler. "Did You Really Go to Church This Week? Behind the Poll Data." *Christian Century*, May 6, 1998, 472–75.

Hadaway, C. Kirk, Penny L. Marler, and Mark Chaves. "Over-reporting Church Attendance in America: Evidence That Demands the Same Verdict." *American Sociological Review* 63.1 (1998): 122–30.

———. "What the Polls Don't Show: A Closer Look at Church Attendance," *American Sociological Review* 58.6 (1993): 741–52.

Hervieu-Léger, Danièle. "The Case for a Sociology of 'Multiple Religious Modernities': A Different Approach to the 'Invisible Religion' of European Societies." *Social Compass* 50.3 (2003): 287–95.

Hicks, Alexander. *Social Democracy and Welfare Capitalism: A Century of Income Security Policies*. Ithaca: Cornell University Press, 1999.

Hout, Michael, and Andrew M. Greeley. "What Church Officials' Reports Don't Show: Another Look at Church Attendance Data." *American Sociological Review* 63.1 (1998): 113–19.

Hout, Michael, Andrew M. Greeley, and Melissa J. Wilde. "The Demographic Imperative in Religious Change in the United States." *American Journal of Sociology* 107.2 (2001): 468–500.

Iannaccone, Lawrence R. "The Consequences of Religious Market Structure." *Rationality and Society* 3 (1991): 156–77.

Jagodzinski, Wolfgang, and Karel Dobbelaere. "Secularization and Church Religiosity." In *The Impact of Values*. Edited by Jan W. van Deth and Elinor Scarbrough. Oxford: Oxford University Press, 1995.

Lindsay, D. Michael. *Surveying the Religious Landscape: Trends in U.S. Beliefs*. New York: Moorhouse, 2000.

Lipset, Seymor Martin. *Continental Divide: The Values and Institutions of Canada and the United States*. New York: Routledge, 1990.

Marshall, Paul. "Religious Freedom in the World." www.freedomhouse.org.

McAllister, Ian. "Religious Change and Secularization: The Transmission of Religious Values in Australia." *Sociological Analysis* 49.3 (1988): 249–63.

McFate, Katherine, Roger Lawson, and William Julius Wilson, eds. *Poverty, Inequality, and the Future of Social Policy: Western States in the New World Order*. New York: Russell Sage Foundation, 1995.

Mills, C. Wright. *The Sociological Imagination*. Oxford: Oxford University Press, 1959.

National Election Survey series. www.umich.edu/~NES.

Norris, Pippa. *Electoral Engineering*. Cambridge: Cambridge University Press, 2003.

Norris, Pippa, and Ronald Inglehart. *Sacred and Secular: Religion and Politics Worldwide*. New York: Cambridge University Press, 2004.

Roof, Wade Clark. *Spiritual Marketplace: Baby Boomers and the Remaking of American Religion*. Princeton: Princeton University Press, 2001.

Sharot, Stephen. "Beyond Christianity: A Critique of the Rational Choice Theory of Religion from a Weberian and Comparative Religions Perspective." *Sociology of Religion* 63.4 (2002): 427–54.

Sigelman, Lee. "Review of the Polls: Multination Surveys of Religious Beliefs." *Journal for the Scientific Study of Religion* 16.3 (1977): 289–94.

Smith, Ian, John W. Sawkins, and Paul T. Seaman. "The Economics of Religious Participation: A Cross-country Study." *Kyklos* 51.1 (1998): 25–43.

Stark, Rodney. "Secularization, RIP." *Sociology of Religion* 60.3 (1990): 270.

Stark, Rodney, and William Sims Bainbridge. *A Theory of Religion.* New York: Peter Lang, 1987.

Stark, Rodney, and Roger Finke. *Acts of Faith: Explaining the Human Side of Religion.* Berkeley: University of California Press, 2000.

Stark, Rodney, and Lawrence Iannaccone. "A Supply-side Reinterpretation of the 'Secularization' of Europe." *Journal for the Scientific Study of Religion* 33 (1994): 230–52.

Verweij, Johan, Peter Ester, and Rein Nauta. "Secularization as an Economic and Cultural Phenomenon: A Cross-national Analysis." *Journal for the Scientific Study of Religion* 36.2 (1997): 309–24.

Voas, David, Daniel V. A. Olson, and Alasdair Crockett. "Religious Pluralism and Participation: Why Previous Research Is Wrong." *American Sociological Review* 67.2 (2002): 212–30.

Woodberry, Robert D. "When Surveys Lie and People Tell the Truth: How Surveys Oversample Church Attenders." *American Sociological Review* 63.1 (1998): 119–22.

Wuthnow, Robert. *The Restructuring of American Religion.* Princeton: Princeton University Press, 1988.

4

Immigration and the New Religious Pluralism: A European Union/United States Comparison

José Casanova

In the last four decades the United States and Western European societies have become the main destinations of new global migration flows. In the case of the United States, the 1965 new immigration law overturned the draconian anti-immigration laws of the 1920s and brought a resumption of a long tradition of immigration. Unlike the nineteenth-century immigrants, however, who came mainly from Europe, the new immigrants originate primarily from the Americas and Asia and increasingly from all regions of the world. In the case of Western Europe, the new immigration has meant a radical reversal of a long history of European emigration to the rest of the world.[1]

Throughout the modern era, Western European societies had been the primary source of immigration in the world. During the colonial phase, European colonists and colonizers, indentured servants and penal laborers, missionaries and entrepreneurs, settled all the corners of the globe. During the age of industrialization, from the 1800s to the 1920s, it is estimated that around 85 million Europeans emigrated to the new world and to the Southern Hemisphere, 60% of them to the United States alone. In the last decades, however, the migration flows have reversed and Western European societies have become instead centers of global immigration.

It began in the 1950s with guest worker programs attracting migrant labor from the less developed southern European countries (Italy, Spain, Portugal, Yugoslavia, Greece, and Turkey). Decolonization brought former colonial subjects from North and West Africa, South and Southeast Asia, and the Caribbean to the colonial metropolises (France, Great Britain, and Holland). Economic disruptions, famines, political violence, wars, and global smuggling rings added refugees, asylum seekers, and illegal migrants from less privileged regions, long after the post–World War II economic boom had come to an end in the 1970s, bringing also a stop to the regulated labor migration programs. The fall of communism in 1989 opened the gates to new immigrants from Eastern Europe and the former Soviet Union. Most of the initial guest workers from poorer neighboring European countries either returned home or have been successfully integrated into the host countries. But the policies of voluntary repatriation of non-European immigrants have proved less successful, as the guest workers not only overstayed their welcome but have settled permanently with their reunited families. In 2004 Spain and Italy, which only three decades earlier had been immigrant-sending countries, received the largest number of legal immigrants in Europe, around 500,000 and 400,000 respectively, while traditional immigrant-receiving countries such as Germany, France, and Great Britain were able to reduce drastically their legal immigration to 100,000 entries or less.

Although the proportion of foreign immigrants in many European countries (United Kingdom, France, Holland, or West Germany before reunification), at approximately 10%, is similar to the proportion of foreign born in the United States today, most European countries still have difficulty viewing themselves as permanent immigrant societies, or viewing the foreign born, and even the native second and third generation, as nationals, irrespective of their legal status. The United States, by contrast, tends to view itself as the paradigmatic immigrant society, and the distinction between native citizen, naturalized immigrant, immigrant alien, and undocumented alien, while legally clear, is not immediately evident in ordinary social encounters or relevant in most social contexts.[2]

The Challenge of the New Religious Diversity in Secular Europe

One of the most significant consequences of the new immigration has been a dramatic growth in religious diversity on both sides of the Atlantic. But while in the United States the new immigrant religions have mainly contributed to the further expansion of an already vibrant American religious pluralism, in the case of Europe, immigrant religions present a greater challenge to local patterns of limited religious pluralism and, even more importantly, to recent European trends of drastic secularization. It is true that European societies distinguish themselves not only from the United States but also from one another, in the different ways in which they try to accommodate and regulate immigrant religions, particularly Islam. European societies have markedly different institutional and legal structures regarding religious associations; very diverse policies of state recognition, of state regulation, and of state aid to religious groups; as well as diverse norms concerning when and where one may publicly express religious beliefs and practices.[3]

In their dealing with immigrant religions, European countries, like the United States, tend to replicate their particular model of separation of church and state and the patterns of regulation of their own religious minorities.[4] France's etatist secularist model and the political culture of *laïcité* require the strict privatization of religion, eliminating religion from any public forum, while at the same time pressuring religious groups to organize themselves into a single centralized churchlike institutional structure that can be regulated by and can serve as interlocutor to the state, following the traditional model of the concordat with the Catholic Church. Great Britain, by contrast, while maintaining the established Church of England, has historically accommodated a much greater religious pluralism and today allows greater freedom of religious associations, which deal directly with local authorities and school boards to press for changes in religious education, diet, and so on, with little direct appeal to the central government. Germany, following the multiestablishment model, has tried to organize a quasiofficial Islamic institution, at times in conjunction with parallel strivings on the part of the Turkish state to regulate its diaspora. But the internal divisions among immigrants from Turkey and the public expression and mobilization of competing identities (secular and Muslim, Alevi and Kurd) in the German democratic context have undermined any project of institutionalization from above. Holland, following its traditional pattern of pillarization, seemed, until very recently at least, bent on establishing a state-regulated but self-organized separate Muslim pillar. Lately, however, even liberal, tolerant Holland is expressing second thoughts and seems ready to pass more restrictive legislation, setting clear limits to the kinds of un-European, unmodern norms and habits it is ready to tolerate.

Looking at Western Europe as a whole, however, there are two fundamental differences with the situation in the United States. In the first place, in continental Europe at least, immigration and Islam are almost synonymous. Except for the United Kingdom, where one finds a much greater diversity of immigrants from former colonies of the British Empire, until very recently a majority of immigrants in most European countries have been Muslims. Moreover, despite the symbolic presence of small groups of European converts to Islam, the overwhelming majority of Western European Muslims are immigrants. This identification of immigration and Islam appears even more pronounced in those cases, where the majority of Muslim immigrants tend to come predominantly from a single region of origin (e.g., Turkey in the case of Germany, the Maghreb in the case of France). This entails a superimposition of different dimensions of otherness that exacerbates issues of boundaries, accommodation, and incorporation. The immigrant, the religious, the racial, and the socioeconomic disprivileged other all tend to coincide.[5]

In the United States, by contrast, Muslims constitute at most 10% of all new immigrants, a figure that is likely to decrease, if the strict restrictions to Arab and Muslim immigration imposed after September 11, 2001, continue. Since the U.S. Census Bureau, the Immigration and Naturalization Service, and other government agencies are not allowed to gather information on religion, there are no reliable estimates on the number of Muslims in the United States. Available but self-interested estimates range widely between 2.8 million and 8 million. It is safe to assume that the actual number lies somewhere in the middle—between 4 and 6 million. More reliable is the estimate that from 30% to 42% of all Muslims in the United States are African American converts to Islam, making more difficult the characterization of Islam as a foreign, un-American religion. Furthermore, the Muslim immigrant communities in the United States are extremely diverse in terms of geographic region of origin from all over the Muslim world, in terms of discursive Islamic traditions, and in terms of socio-economic characteristics. As a result, the dynamics of interaction with other Muslim immigrants, with African American Muslims, with non-Muslim immigrants from the same regions of origin, and with their immediate American hosts, depending upon socioeconomic characteristics and residential patterns, are much more complex and diverse than anything one finds in Europe.[6]

The second main difference between Western Europe and United States has to do with the role of religion and religious group identities in public life and in the organization of civil society. Internal differences notwithstanding, Western European societies are deeply secular societies, shaped by the hegemonic knowledge regime of secularism.[7] The progressive, though highly uneven, secularization of Europe is an undeniable social fact.[8] It is true that the rates of religiosity vary significantly across Europe. East Germany is by far the least religious country of Europe by any measure, followed at a long distance by the Czech Republic and the Scandinavian countries. At the other extreme, Ireland and Poland are by far the most religious countries of Europe, with rates comparable to those of the United States. In general, with the significant exception of France and the Czech Republic, Catholic countries tend to be more religious than Protestant or mixed countries (West Germany, the Netherlands), although Switzerland (a mixed and traditionally pillarized country comparable to Holland) stands at the high end of the European religious scale, with rates similar to those of Catholic Austria and Spain, both of which, however, have been undergoing drastic rates of decline.

In any case, across Europe since the 1960s an increasing majority of the population has ceased participating in traditional religious practices, at least on a regular basis, while still maintaining relatively high levels of private individual religious belief. In this respect, one should perhaps talk of the *unchurching* of the European population and of religious individualization, rather than of secularization. Grace Davie characterizes this general European situation as "believing without belonging."[9] At the same time, however, large numbers of Europeans, even in the most secular countries, still identify themselves as Christian, pointing to an implicit, diffused, and submerged Christian cultural identity. In this sense, Danièle Hervieu-Léger is also correct, when she offers the reverse characterization of the European situation as "belonging without believing."[10] From France to Sweden and from England to Scotland, the historical churches (Catholic, Lutheran, Anglican, or Calvinist), although emptied of active membership, still function, vicariously as it were, as public carriers of the national religion. In this respect, "secular" and "Christian" cultural identities are intertwined in complex and rarely verbalized modes among most Europeans.

Indeed, the most interesting issue sociologically is not the fact of progressive religious decline among the European population since the 1950s, but the fact that this decline is interpreted through the lenses of the secularization paradigm and is therefore accompanied by a secularist self-understanding that interprets the decline as normal and progressive, that is, as a quasinormative consequence of being a modern and enlightened European. We need to entertain seriously the proposition that secularization became a self-fulfilling prophecy in Europe, once large sectors of the population of Western European societies, including the Christian churches, accepted the basic premises of the theory of secularization: that secularization is a teleological process of modern social change; that the more modern a society, the more secular it becomes; and that secularity is "a *sign of the times*." If such a proposition is correct, then the secularization of Western European societies can be explained better in terms of the triumph of the knowledge regime of secularism than in terms of structural processes of socioeconomic development, such as urbanization, education, rationalization, and so on. The internal variations within Europe, moreover, can be explained better in terms of historical patterns of church-state and church-nation relations, as well as in terms of different paths of secularization among the different branches of Christianity, than in terms of levels of modernization.

It is the secular identity shared by European elites and ordinary people alike that paradoxically turns religion and the barely submerged Christian European identity into a thorny and perplexing issue, when it comes to delimiting the external geographic boundaries and to defining the internal cultural identity of a European Union in the process of being constituted. The contentious debates over the potential integration of Muslim Turkey into the European Union are superimposed on the debates over the failure to integrate second- and third-generation Muslim immigrants into Europe—all contributing to the specter of Islam as the other of the modern, liberal, secular West. Moreover, the debates over textual references to God or to the Christian heritage in the preamble to the new European constitution have shown that Europe, rather than Turkey, is actually the "torn country," deeply divided over its cultural identity, unable to answer the question whether European unity, and therefore its external and internal boundaries, should be defined by the common heritage of Christianity and Western civilization or by its modern, secular values of liberalism, universal human rights, political democracy, and tolerant and inclusive multiculturalism. Publicly, of course, European liberal, secular elites could not share the pope's definition of European civilization as essentially Christian. But they also could not verbalize the unspoken cultural requirements that make the integration of Turkey into Europe such a difficult issue. The specter of millions of Turkish citizens already in Europe but not of Europe, many of them second-generation immigrants, caught between an old country they have left behind and their European host societies, unable or unwilling to fully assimilate them, makes the problem only more visible. Guest workers can be successfully incorporated economically. They may even gain voting rights, at least on the local level, and prove to be model or at least ordinary citizens. But can they pass the unwritten rules of cultural European membership or are they to remain "strangers"? Can the European Union open new conditions for the kind of multiculturalism that its constituent national societies find so difficult to accept? Contemporary debates across Europe illustrate a fundamental tension between cosmopolitan secularism and the kind of multiculturalism that could bring public recognition of the mores, customs, and lifeworlds of Muslim and other immigrant religious communities.[11]

As liberal, democratic polities, all European societies respect and protect constitutionally the private exercise of religion, including Islam, as an individual human right. It is the public and collective free exercise of Islam as an immigrant religion that most European societies find difficult to tolerate, precisely on the grounds that Islam is perceived as an essentially un-European religion. The stated rationales for considering Islam un-European vary significantly across Europe and among social and political groups. For the anti-immigrant, xenophobic, nationalist right, represented by Jean-Marie Le Pen's discourse in France and by Jörg Haider in Austria, the message is straightforward. Islam is unwelcome and unassimilable simply because it is a "foreign" immigrant religion. Such a nativist and usually racist attitude can be differentiated clearly from the conservative Catholic position, paradigmatically expressed by the Cardinal of Bologna, when he declared that Italy should welcome immigrants of all races and regions of the world, but should particularly select Catholic immigrants in order to preserve the Catholic identity of the country. Christian democratic parties have in fact become the cultural defenders of a narrow, nativist, and territorial definition of European Christianity, at a time when the millennial identification of Christianity and European civilization has come to an end, due to a dual process of advanced secularization in post-Christian Europe and increasing globalization of a deterritorialized and decentered non-European Christianity.

Liberal, secular Europeans tend to look askance at such blatant expressions of racist bigotry and religious intolerance coming from nationalists and religious conservatives. But when it comes to Islam, secular Europeans also tend to reveal the limits and prejudices of modern, secularist toleration. One is not likely to hear among liberal politicians and secular intellectuals explicitly xenophobic or antireligious statements. The politically correct formulation tends to run along such lines as "we welcome each and all immigrants irrespective of race or religion as long as they are willing to respect and accept our modern, liberal, secular European norms." The explicit articulation of those norms may vary from country to country. The controversies over the Muslim veil in so many European societies and the overwhelming support among the French citizenry, including apparently among a majority of French Muslims, for the restrictive legislation prohibiting the wearing of Muslim veils and other ostensibly religious symbols in public schools, as "a threat to national cohesion," may be an extreme example of illiberal secularism.[12] But in fact one sees similar trends of restrictive legislation directed at immigrant Muslims in liberal Holland, precisely in the name of protecting its liberal, tolerant traditions from the threat of illiberal, fundamentalist, patriarchal customs, reproduced and transmitted to the younger generation by Muslim immigrants.

Revealingly enough, Prime Minister Jean-Pierre Raffarin, in his address to the French legislature, defending the banning of ostensibly religious symbols in public schools, made reference in the same breath to France as "the old land of Christianity" and to the inviolable principle of laïcité, exhorting Islam to adapt itself to the principle of secularism as all other religions of France have done before: "For the most recently arrived, I'm speaking here of Islam, secularism is a chance, the chance to be a religion of France."[13] The Islamic veil and other religious signs are justifiably banned from public schools, he added, because "they are taking on a political meaning," while according to the secularist principle of privatization of religion, "religion cannot be a political project." Time will tell whether the restrictive legislation will have the intended effect of stopping the spread of "radical Islam," or whether it is likely to bring forth the opposite result of radicalizing further an already alienated and maladjusted immigrant community.

The positive rationale one hears among liberals, in support of such illiberal restriction of the free exercise of religion, is usually put in terms of the desirable enforced emancipation of young girls, if necessary against their expressed will, from gender discrimination and from patriarchal control. This was the discourse on which the assassinated Dutch politician Pim Fortuyn built his electorally successful anti-immigrant platform in liberal Holland, a campaign that is now bearing fruit in new restrictive legislation and in further violence. While conservative religious people are expected to tolerate behavior they may consider morally abhorrent, such as homosexuality, liberal, secular Europeans are openly stating that European societies ought not to tolerate religious behavior or cultural customs that are morally abhorrent, insofar as they are contrary to modern, liberal, secular European norms. What makes the intolerant tyranny of the secular, liberal majority justifiable in principle is not just the democratic principle of majority rule, but rather the secularist teleological assumption built into theories of modernization that one set of norms is reactionary, fundamentalist, and antimodern, while the other set is progressive, liberal, and modern.

Anti-immigrant xenophobic nativism, secularist antireligious prejudices, liberal-feminist critiques of Muslim patriarchal fundamentalism, and the fear of Islamist terrorist networks are being fused indiscriminately throughout Europe into a uniform anti-Muslim discourse, which practically precludes the kind of mutual accommodation between immigrant groups and host societies that is necessary for successful immigrant incorporation.[14] The parallels with Protestant-republican anti-Catholic nativism in mid-nineteenth-century America are indeed striking. Today's totalizing discourse on Islam as an essentially antimodern, fundamentalist, illiberal, and undemocratic religion and culture echoes the nineteenth-century discourse on Catholicism.[15]

European societies tend to tolerate and respect individual religious freedom. But due to the pressure toward the privatization of religion, which among European societies has become a taken-for-granted characteristic of the self-definition of a modern, secular society, those societies have a much greater difficulty in recognizing some legitimate role for religion in public life and in the organization and mobilization of collective group identities. Muslim-organized collective identities and their public representations become a source of anxiety, not only because of their religious otherness as a non-Christian and non-European religion, but more importantly because of their religiousness itself as the other of European secularity. In this context, the temptation to identify Islam and fundamentalism becomes the more pronounced. Islam, by definition, becomes the other of Western secular modernity, an identification that becomes superimposed upon the older image of Islam as the other of European Christianity. Therefore, the problems posed by the incorporation of Muslim immigrants become consciously or unconsciously associated with seemingly related and vexatious issues concerning the role of religion in the public sphere, which European societies assumed they had already solved according to the liberal, secular norm of privatization of religion.[16]

Immigrant Religions and the Expansion of American Denominationalism

The structural conditions that immigrants encounter in the United States are substantially different.[17] It is not only that Americans are demonstrably more religious than the Europeans and therefore there is a certain pressure for immigrants to conform to American religious norms. Even more significantly, today, as in the past, religion and public religious denominational identities play an important role in the process of incorporation of the new immigrants. Thus, the paradox observed again and again by students of immigrant communities that, in the words of Raymond Williams, "immigrants are religious—by all counts more religious than they were before they left home."[18]

It is important to realize, therefore, that immigrant religiosity is not simply a traditional residue, an old world survival likely to disappear with adaptation to the new context, but rather an adaptive response to the new world. I find unconvincing, however, Timothy Smith's explanation that it is the immigration experience per se that calls forth such a religious response, because immigration itself is a "theologizing" experience, because the uprootedness it entails from traditional ways, the uncertainty of the journey, and the anomic experience of being strangers in a new land calls forth a religious response.[19]

It is often the case that phenomenologically many immigrant groups, in trying to express and verbalize the experience of the immigrant journey, resort to religious language and draw upon available discursive archetypes from various religious traditions, framing it in terms of a pilgrimage (Christians and Hindus), an exodus to a promised land (Puritans, Jews, and African Americans), or a new hegira (Muslims). The problem begins when this particular phenomenological observation is turned into a neo-Durkheimian general explanation, in terms of reactive responses to the cultural strains and anomic disintegration associated with the uprooting experience of immigration. Such a general explanation is not convincing, because one actually finds an enormous range in the religious responses of contemporary immigrant groups in

America, from Korean Americans, who are arguably more religious than any other ethnic group in America, immigrant or native, to Soviet Jews, who are as little religious as they were in the old country. But more importantly, it is not plausible as a general explanation, because it is not confirmed by the comparative evidence from other immigrant societies, today or in the past.[20]

It is not the general context of immigration but the particular context of immigration to America and the structural and institutional context of American society that provokes this particular religious response. The thesis of Will Herberg concerning the old European immigrant, that "not only was he expected to retain his old religion, as he was not expected to retain his old language or nationality, but such was the shape of America that it was largely in and through religion that he, or rather his children and grandchildren, found an identifiable place in American life," is still operative with the new immigrants.[21] The thesis implies not only that immigrants tend to be religious because of a certain social pressure to conform to American religious norms. More importantly, the thesis implies that collective religious identities have been one of the primary ways of structuring internal societal pluralism in American history.

Since Americans in general tend to be religious, more religious probably than most people in other modern societies, immigrants in America will tend to conform to the American norm. "When in Rome do as the Romans." About the pressure to conform to American standards of religiosity, there can be little doubt. Ask any political candidate whether they can afford to confess that they have "no religion." What is relevant is the "definition of the situation." Since Americans define themselves as a religious people, they think and act accordingly. Even more striking is the fact that they tend to lie to the pollsters and to inflate their rates of church attendance and to exaggerate the depth and seriousness of their religious beliefs.[22] Indeed, the very tendency of the Americans to exaggerate their religiousness, in contrast to the opposite tendency of the Europeans to discount and undercount their own persistent religiosity— tendencies which are evident among ordinary people, as well as among scholars on both sides of the Atlantic—are themselves part of the very different and consequential definitions of the situation in both places. Obviously, Americans think that they are supposed to be religious, while Europeans think that they are supposed to be irreligious. This would explain, at least in part, the reason why the same groups of immigrants tend to be more religious and to carry their religious identity more openly in public in the United States than in most European countries.

But more important than the diffuse social pressure to conform to American religious norms are, in my view, the structural conditions shaping American religious pluralism. The fact that religion, religious institutions, and religious identities played a central role in the process of incorporation of the old European immigrants has been amply documented. Rather than decreasing, as one would expect from conventional theories of modernization and secularization, religious identities tended to gain salience in the particular context of immigration to America. Herberg's thesis implied that collective religious identities have been one of the primary ways of structuring internal societal pluralism in American history, the reason being that "almost from the beginning, the structure of American society presupposed diversity and substantial equality of religious associations."[23]

The particular pattern of separation of church and state codified in the dual clause of the First Amendment, "free exercise of religion" and "no establishment," served to structure this diversity and substantial equality. After independence, the establishment of any particular church at the federal/national level was probably precluded by the territorial distribution and the relative equal strength of the three colonial churches: Congregational, Presbyterian, and Anglican. However, either multiple establishment or the establishment of a generalized Christian (i.e., Protestant) religion could have been likely outcomes, had it not been for the active coalition of Jefferson, Madison, and dissenting Baptists in Virginia.

The American constitutional formula challenged the notion, taken for granted and shared at the time by religionists and secularists (deists) alike, that the state or the political community of citizens needed a religion, ecclesiastical or civil, as the base of its normative integration and that, moreover, it was the business of the sovereign to regulate the religious sphere. The First Amendment raised not only a "wall of separation" protecting the state from religion (no establishment) and religion from the state (free exercise), but actually established a principle of differentiation between the political community of citizens and any and all religious communities. Eventually, all religions in America, churches as well as sects, irrespective of their origins, doctrinal claims, and ecclesiastical identities, would turn into "denominations," formally equal under the Constitution and competing in a relatively free, pluralistic, and voluntaristic religious market. As the organizational form and principle of such a religious system, denominationalism constitutes the great American religious invention.[24]

At first, this diversity and substantial equality was institutionalized only as internal denominational religious pluralism within American Protestantism. America was defined as a "Christian" nation and Christian meant solely "Protestant." But eventually, after prolonged outbursts of Protestant nativism, directed primarily at Catholic immigrants, the pattern allowed for the incorporation of the religious others, Catholics and Jews, into the system of American religious pluralism.[25] A process of dual accommodation took place, whereby Catholicism and Judaism became American religions, while American religion and the nation were equally transformed in the process. America became a "Judeo-Christian" nation, and Protestant, Catholic, and Jew became the three denominations of the American civil religion. It is this final outcome—the assimilation of immigrant European Catholics and Jews into the American mainstream—that Herberg's book celebrates.[26] And it is worth remembering that it is this same self-congratulatory context and the inaugural speech of the first Catholic president that serve as the background for Robert Bellah's thesis of civil religion in America a decade later.[27]

Herberg's thesis of American ethnoreligious pluralism has serious shortcomings. The most blatant is the fact that Herberg is absolutely blind to issues of race, and thus *Protestant-Catholic-Jew* examines only the process of incorporation of European immigrants, while being absolutely silent about non-European immigrants. The crucial problem is not that Herberg ignores other non-European immigrant minorities and their non-Judeo-Christian religions, such as Japanese Buddhists or Chinese Daoists or Arab Muslims—groups that were already part of the old immigration. Though a serious oversight, one could still argue defensively that those were at the time relatively small minorities. The real problem is that Herberg ignores the truly relevant racial minorities among the religious groups he is studying, the Christian others: black Protestants and Hispanic Catholics. After all, Herberg wrote his study in the 1950s, at the high point of the great internal migration of African Americans from the rural South to the Northern urban industrial centers and of the Puerto Rican migration to New York, leaving aside for the moment the other relevant Hispanic Catholics, the "Chicanos" from the Southwest, who were themselves mostly, with the exception of the braceros, not migrants.[28] As in the case of Puerto Rico, it was the U.S. borders that had migrated to their ancestral territories. Strictly speaking, of course, African Americans and Hispanics were not immigrant aliens. But it is the fact that Herberg constructs Protestant, Catholic, and Jew as the three imagined religious communities making up the imagined community of the American nation that makes the omission of African Americans and Hispanics the more problematic and revealing. What the omission of black Protestants and Hispanic Catholics reveals is that in the 1950s those groups remained the invisible racial alien at a time when European immigrants, Catholics and Jews, had been incorporated into the imagined community of the American nation.

Rightly, the new immigration studies literature has placed issues of race, racialization, and racial identities at the very center of the analysis of processes of immigrant incorporation. Blacks and Hispanics have become, indeed, the truly relevant *tertium comparationis* in all comparative studies of the old and the new immigration. At least implicitly, the three terms of comparison in all contemporary debates are (a) European white ethnics (the old immigrants), (b) American racial minorities (African American and Hispanic), and (c) the new immigrants from all over the world (Asian, Caribbean, Latin American, African, etc.). Once the comparative framework is constructed in such a way, it becomes immediately obvious that race matters and that matters of race are crucial in the process of immigrant incorporation. But what Herberg's study shows is that religion matters also and that matters of religion may be equally relevant in processes of immigrant incorporation in America. Not religion alone, as Herberg's study would seem to imply, and not race alone, as contemporary immigration studies would seem to imply, but religion and race and their complex entanglements have served to structure the American experience of immigrant incorporation and indeed are the keys to "American exceptionalism."[29]

Simplifying a complex story, one could say that assimilation into the American mainstream meant at first becoming WASP or WASP-like. Of the four markers of American identity—White, Anglo, Saxon, Protestant—the truly relevant ones, however, were the first and the last, race and religion.[30] One could be as white as it gets, but if one was not Protestant, it was hard to pass as an American. Irish Protestants (and do not forget that the majority of Americans of Irish descent are of Protestant origin, descendants of the Scottish-Irish) never had a problem passing as white. It was the Irish Catholics and other Catholics (Italian, Slavs, etc.) that were racialized as the other. Becoming as devoutly Protestant as most African Americans did was also not enough. If one was not white, one could not be fully American.[31] Today, religion and race are becoming, once again, the two critical markers identifying the new immigrants either as assimilable or as suspiciously alien. In this respect, religious and racial self-identifications and ascriptions represent parallel and at times alternative ways of organizing American multiculturalism.[32]

Immigration as a Context for United States Religious Pluralism

The United States has become an immigrant society again. During the past decade alone, approximately one million immigrants annually entered the United States, the largest wave in the nation's history, even outnumbering the nine million immigrants who came during the first decade of the twentieth century. Moreover, the trend may have slowed down slightly after 9/11, but there are no clear indications that it is likely to be reversed in the near future. More important than the increase in numbers, however, are the changes in the regions of origin and in the characteristics of the new immigrants. In comparison with the old immigrants, two characteristics of the new immigrants are most relevant: (a) they are primarily non-European, increasingly from all regions of the world, but predominantly from Asia and the Americas, and (b) in addition to the tremendous range in all forms of human diversity (racial, ethnic, religious, cultural, linguistic) which they bring, the new immigrants are also extremely diverse, almost bifurcated, in the levels of human and social capital, skills, and resources which they bring.[33]

From the particular perspective of this essay, the most important characteristic is the extraordinary religious pluralism and diversity that they bring to a country that was already the most religiously diverse and pluralistic in the world.[34] Since U.S. government agencies cannot gather information on the religious makeup of the population, we do not have reliable data even on the denominational religious affiliation of the new immigrants.[35] Attempts to extrapolate from the religious composition of the country of origin have to be sensitive to the fact that today, as always, religious minorities tend to immigrate to America in disproportionate numbers. Arab Christians and Russian Jews in the past, Korean Christians and Latino Protestants today, would be obvious examples. Moreover, one has to be aware of the intrinsic difficulties in applying Western categories of religious affiliation to non-Western religions. Nominal affiliation is in any case problematic as a measure of individual religiosity, since it does not tell how truly religious the nominally affiliated are, that is, whether, how, and how often they practice their religion. Much less, of course, can denominational affiliation categories, or "religious preference," measure the religion of the unaffiliated, namely those religious practices and forms of religion which are not defined by membership or affiliation in an organized religious institution, congregation, or community.

In any case, it is safe to assume that the immense majority of all new immigrants are Christian, Protestant, and Catholic in various proportions, with small numbers of Eastern Orthodox, depending upon the port of entry. In the case of New York, our own very rough estimate from the RIINY (Religion and Immigrant Incorporation in New York) project, is that close to 50% of all new immigrants are nominally Catholic, while approximately 25% of the new immigrants are nominally Protestant. Protestants and Catholics together, therefore, constitute around 75% of all new immigrants to New York. For the United States as a whole the proportion of Christians among the new immigrants is likely to be slightly lower, somewhere between two-thirds and three-fourths.[36] In this respect, the most significant religious impact of the new immigrants is likely to be the replenishing and renovation of American Christianity. But since they bring non-European versions of Christianity, the new immigrants are also going to contribute to the de-Europeanization of American Protestantism and American Catholicism. The Hispanization or Latin Americanization of American Catholicism is one of the most obvious and relevant trends. But it is accompanied by the no less significant trend of Protestantification of Latin America and of Latino Americans.[37]

But the most striking new development with extraordinary potential repercussions, both national and global, is the arrival of increasing numbers of Muslims, Hindus, Buddhists, indeed of representatives of all world religions. The numbers may not yet be as large as the exaggerated estimates of 6–7 million Muslims, 2.8–4 million Buddhists, and 1.2–2 million Hindus that one sees floating around. But the battle over numbers and the attempts by the National Opinion Research Center and the American Jewish Committee to deflate those exaggerated estimates in order to prove that, as a *Chicago Tribune* headline put it, "Christians, Jews still predominate" misses the point.[38]

In terms of numbers, American Jews never presented a real challenge to Christian predominance, but the incorporation of Judaism as an American religion radically transformed the American religious landscape and the self-definition of the American nation. It is true that unlike the deeply seated Protestant anti-Catholic nativism, Judaism in America did not encounter similarly religiously based anti-Semitism, and in general American Protestantism has tended to maintain a philo-Hebraic attitude. But the addition of Catholicism and Judaism as American denominations altered the very system of American denominationalism. The perceived threat posed by immigrant Catholicism was not primarily due to its size, but rather to the fact that it was viewed as an un-American religion, insofar as Republicanism and Romanism were defined as being incompatible.

American religious pluralism is expanding and incorporating all the world religions in the same way as it previously incorporated the religions of the old immigrants.[39] A complex process of mutual accommodation is taking place.

Like Catholicism and Judaism before, other world religions (Islam, Hinduism, Buddhism) are being Americanized, and in the process they are transforming American religion, while the religious diasporas in America are simultaneously serving as catalysts for the transformation of the old religions in their civilizational homes, in the same way as American Catholicism had an impact upon the transformation of world Catholicism and as American Judaism had transformed world Judaism.[40]

A similar story and similar patterns of conflictive incorporation and mutual accommodation are being repeated today. It is true that the models of immigrant incorporation have been radically altered by the expanding multiculturalism at home and by the proliferation of global transnational networks. The increasing global migration in turn leads to a spiraling acceleration of multiculturalism and religious pluralism, now encompassing all world religions. We have entered a new phase in the American experiment. The United States is called to become not just "the first new nation," made up primarily of all the European nations. The traditional model of assimilation, turning European nationals into American "ethnics," can no longer serve as a model of incorporation now that immigration is literally worldwide. America is bound to become "the first new global society," made up of all world religions and civilizations, at a time when religious civilizational identities are regaining prominence in the global stage.[41]

It is due to the corrosive logic of racialization, so prominent and pervasive in American society, that the dynamics of religious identity formation assume a double positive form in the process of immigrant incorporation. Due to the institutionalized acceptance of religious pluralism and religious identities, for the structural reasons mentioned above, it is not surprising that the affirmation of religious identities is enhanced among the new immigrants. This positive affirmation of religious identities is reinforced further by what appears to be a common defensive reaction by most immigrant groups against ascribed racialization, particularly against the stigma of racial darkness. If anything, the new patterns of global migration are turning our absurd binary racial categories ever more confusing and untenable. In this context, the positive affirmation of religious identities by Hindus from India and the Caribbean, by Muslims from West Africa, or by Creole Catholics from Haiti is adding a dimension of resistance to the dynamics of racialization. In this respect, religious and racial self-identifications and ascriptions represent alternative ways of organizing American (and global) multiculturalism.[42] One of the obvious advantages of religious pluralism over racial pluralism is that under proper constitutional institutionalization it is more reconcilable with principled equality and nonhierarchic diversity and therefore with genuine multiculturalism.

American denominationalism functions at three different levels, each affecting diversely the transformation of immigrant religions in America. The first is the basic "congregational" level of the local religious community. This is the most important level in which the fundamental process of Americanization takes place. As Stephen Warner rightly points out, all immigrant religions in America, irrespective of their institutional form in their traditional civilizational settings, tend to adopt a typically Protestant congregational form.[43] It happened to the old immigrants, Catholics and Jews, and it is happening to the new immigrants, irrespective of whether they already had a quasicongregational form, like the Muslims, or have no congregational tradition, like Buddhists or Hindus. All religious communities in America tend to assume a voluntary associational form and become incorporated as a nonprofit organization, led by the laity. Churches, synagogues, temples, masjids, and so on tend to become more than houses of worship or prayer and become authentic community centers with different kinds of educational and social services, fellowship and recreational activities, and task-specific associational networks. Indeed, they become, as Tocqueville already pointed out, schools of democracy and the centers of associational life of the immigrant communities.

This is the fundamental difference between the American denominations and the European churches, which never made the full transition to congregational voluntary associations and remained anchored in the territorially based national church and local parish. Structurally significant is the fact that at least for some groups the American experience of immigration seems to call forth the reflexive affirmation of religious identities. The key is the reflexive affirmation of a religious identity, that is to say, naming oneself and being named by others according to some religious denomination. This active, achieved, and reflexive denomination, moreover, is very different from the passive, ascribed, and nominal affiliation to a religion into which one is born. This was, of course, the experience of immigrant Catholic and Jew in America. They could not simply maintain the nominal affiliation, at least not if they wanted to pass on the same affiliation to their children. They had to become voluntary members of an association and actively maintain and pass on their family traditions.

The second level is the denominational proper, in the sense in which it originally emerged as doctrinally, organizationally, or ethnoracially differentiated plural denominations within American Protestantism. While the hierarchically organized Roman Catholic Church was able to incorporate all Catholics immigrants (with the exception of the Polish National Church) into a single American Catholic Church through the ethnic parish system, American Judaism also became differentiated into three main denominations (Reform, Conservative, and Orthodox). It is still unclear whether various branches or traditions of the other world religions (Islam, Hinduism, and Buddhism) will become institutionalized as separate denominations in America, or whether other denominational divisions will emerge.

Finally, there is the national level of "imagined community" in the sense in which Herberg talks of Protestant, Catholic, and Jew as the three denominational forms of the American civil religion. This is also the level at which the immigrant religions gain symbolic recognition and are thus incorporated into the nation as "American," irrespective of whether they also develop unified national organizations.

The Particular Challenge of American Islam

Of all the new immigrant religions, Islam represents the most interesting testing ground and challenge to the pattern of immigrant incorporation. Due to geopolitical rationales and the common portrayal of Islam as fundamentalist, Islam today, as Catholicism before, is often represented as the other and therefore as un-American. Tragically, these debates have only exacerbated in the wake of the 9/11 terrorist attacks by Muslim militants and the U.S. military response. Paradoxically, however, these developments are forcing not only a debate about the alleged civilizational clash between Islam and the West, but also a recognition that Islam has taken roots in America and is becoming a major American religion.[44]

Certainly, one can observe striking similarities between today's discourse on Islam as a fundamentalist, antimodern religion incompatible with democracy and yesterday's discourse on Catholicism. From the 1830s to the 1950s anti-Catholic Protestant nativism in America was based on the alleged incompatibility between Republicanism and Romanism. In his portrayal of Catholics in America, Tocqueville had already tried to refute this thesis, as well as the widely held perception on both sides of the French Republican-laicist and monarchist-Catholic divide that Catholicism was incompatible with modern democracy and with individual freedoms.

As in the case of Catholicism before, the internal and external debates over the compatibility between Islam and democracy and modern individual freedoms is taking place at three separate yet interrelated levels: debates over the proper articulation of a Muslim *umma* in diasporic contexts outside of *Dar al-Islam*; debates over the democratic legitimacy of Muslim political parties in Turkey and elsewhere, which like their, at first equally suspect, Catholic counterparts may establish new forms of Muslim democracy, akin to Christian democracy; and debates over the alleged clash of civilizations between Islam and the West at the geopolitical level, with clear parallels with earlier debates on the clash between Republicanism and Romanism. Under conditions of globalization, all three issues become ever more entangled.[45]

One can also witness, however, an ambiguous and tortuous process of public symbolic recognition of Islam as an American religion that resembles the processes of incorporation of Catholicism and Judaism. The self-defining discourse of America that had changed from that of a "Christian" to a "Judeo-Christian" nation was lately assuming the new denominational characterization of "Abrahamic," symbolically incorporating all three monotheistic religions claiming descent from the first covenant between God and Abraham. The presence of a Muslim imam along with a Protestant minister, a Catholic priest, and a Jewish rabbi in public ceremonies in Washington, in state capitals, and in large urban centers has become routine. Among symbolic milestones in the process of public recognition one could mention the following: the first commissioned Islamic chaplain in the U.S. Army was established in 1993 and in the U.S. Navy in 1996; a Muslim symbol was displayed on the White House

Ellipse in 1997; the Pentagon hosted its first Ramadan meal for Muslims in 1998; on the first day of Ramadan in November 2000 the New Jersey legislature opened with a reading of the Qur'an by an imam. The Muslim public presence in official ceremonies and in interfaith encounters has become even more prominent after the 9/11 terrorist attacks.[46] But simultaneously, one can also witness a mainly Protestant nativist backlash against Islam, which had actually begun before 9/11, but became exacerbated thereafter.[47]

The new anti-Muslim evangelical discourse has three main sources: (1) the militant premillennial Zionism among American evangelicals, who after the fall of the Soviet Union transferred the role, which the communist "hordes" of the north and their Arab secular nationalist allies in the Middle East were supposed to play in their apocalyptic visions of the impending Armageddon, to all Muslim countries as enemies of Israel; (2) the missionary competition between Muslims and Christians (evangelicals and Pentecostals) throughout sub-Saharan Africa and in other parts of the world where one finds ethnoreligious conflicts between Muslims and Christians, which adds to the evangelical frustration of being unable to preach openly the gospel of Jesus Christ in Muslim countries, and (3) the global "war on terror" after 9/11, which, notwithstanding the carefully phrased official disclaimers coming from the White House, prominent evangelical leaders such as Pat Robertson, Franklin Graham, and Jerry Falwell have not hesitated to characterize openly as a "crusade" and as an inevitable conflict between an essentially "violent" Islam and the Christian West.[48]

The most alarming manifestation of the emerging nativist Protestant anti-Muslim discourse is the series of blasphemous, defamatory tracts one finds in Christian bookstores, often written by Muslim converts to Christianity and resembling the old antipopish tracts, which slander the Prophet Muhammad as a depraved sinner and discredit Islam as a false monotheistic and Abrahamic religion which has pagan roots in the pre-Islamic worship of Kaaba.

The challenge confronting Islam in America is how to transform diverse immigrants from South Asia, which today constitute the largest and fastest growing group of Muslim immigrants, from Arab countries, and from West Africa into a single American Muslim *umma*. In this respect, the process of incorporation is not unlike that of different Catholic national groups into a single American Catholic church. The two options being debated today within Islamic communities across America, often put in terms of the Nation of Islam model versus the model of an assertive and powerful Jewish minority, reiterate some of the debates in nineteenth-century American Catholicism. At issue is whether Islam in America should be constructed as a segregated defensive subculture, protecting itself from corrosive Americanization, or whether it should organize itself as a public self-assertive cultural option within American competitive multiculturalism. The threat of the Americanization of Islam this would entail would be balanced by the opportunity of the Islamization of America, which many Muslims view as an actualization of Islam's universalism.

Due to the still-growing Islamization of the African American community, in a process which African American Muslims often depict not as conversion, but rather as reversion to a preslavery African Islam, the often contentious dialogue and dynamic interaction between African American and immigrant Muslims is bound to have a dramatic impact upon the transformation of American culture. It is still an open question which kind of internal denominational structure Islam in America is going to assume: whether it will succumb to what H. Richard Niebuhr called "the evil of denominationalism," which he saw grounded in socioeconomic and ethnoracial divisions, or if it will organize itself into a national churchlike *umma*, able to bridge its internal ethnolinguistic and juridical-doctrinal divisions. American Protestantism, Catholicism, and Judaism represent in this respect alternative denominational models. American Islam is likely to develop its own distinct denominational pattern, while sharing some elements with all three. But if it is able to overcome in any way the pattern of congregational racial segregation which has plagued American Christianity and to bridge the divide between immigrant and African American Muslims, it will have a significant impact upon American race relations.

The process of the Americanization of Islam is already taking place, despite all the difficulties presented by internal debates, nativist resistance, and geopolitical conflicts. Islam is becoming not just a fast growing religion *in* America, but an American religion, one of the denominational alternatives of being religiously American. Moreover, Islam is destined to become, like Catholicism, an important public religion, which is likely to play a relevant role in American public debates in the future.

Conclusion

This essay has tried to show that one of the most significant consequences of the new global patterns of transnational migration has been a dramatic growth in religious diversity on both sides of the Atlantic. The new immigrant religions, however, present significantly different challenges of integration in Christian/Secular Europe and in Judeo-Christian/Secular America due to the different histories of immigration and modes of immigrant incorporation, the different patterns of religious pluralism and the different types of secularism in both regions. Ultimately, religion in the United States constitutes a positive resource insofar as today as in the past religious associations and religious collective identities constitute one of the accepted avenues for immigrant incorporation and for mutual group recognition in the public sphere of American civil society. In Europe, by contrast, secularist world views and very different institutional patterns of public recognition through different forms of church-state relations make the incorporation of immigrant religions in the public sphere of European civil societies a more contentious issue.

NOTES

1. Charles Hirschman, Philip Kasinitz, and Josh de Wind, eds., *The Handbook of International Migration: The American Experience* (New York: Russell Sage Foundation,

1999); Leslie Page Moch, *Moving Europeans: Migration in Western Europe since 1650,* 2nd ed. (Bloomington: Indiana University Press, 2003); and Robin Cohen, ed., *The Cambridge Survey of World Migration* (Cambridge: Cambridge University Press, 1995).

2. Rainer Bauböck, ed., *From Aliens to Citizens: Redefining the Status of Immigrants in Europe* (Aldershot: Ashgate, 1994); Rainer Bauböck, Agnes Heller, and Aristide R. Zolberg, eds., *The Challenges of Diversity: Integration and Pluralism in Societies of Immigration* (Aldershot: Ashgate, 1996); and Rainer Bauböck and John Rundell, eds., *Blurred Boundaries: Migration, Ethnicity, Citizenship* (Aldershot: Ashgate, 1998).

3. Silvio Ferrari and Anthony Bradney, eds., *Islam and European Legal Systems* (Aldershot: Ashgate, 2000).

4. John Madeley and Zsolt Enyedi, eds., *Church and State in Contemporary Europe* (London: Cass, 2003); and Ted Jelen and Clyde Wilcox, eds., *Religion and Politics in Comparative Perspective: The One, the Few and the Many* (New York: Cambridge University Press, 2002).

5. Jocelyne Cesari, *When Islam and Democracy Meet: Muslims in Europe and in the United States* (New York: Palgrave Macmillan, 2004); Steve Vertovec and Ceri Peach, eds., *Islam in Europe: The Politics of Religion and Community* (Basingstoke: Macmillan, 1997); and Brigitte Maréchal, Stefano Allievi, Felice Dassetto, and Jørgen Nielsen, eds., *Muslims in the Enlarged Europe* (Leiden: Brill, 2003).

6. Karen Isaksen Leonard, *Muslims in the United States: The State of Research* (New York: Russell Sage Foundation, 2003); and Yvonne Yazbeck Haddad, ed., *Muslims in the West: From Sojourners to Citizens* (New York: Oxford University Press, 2002).

7. The following section draws upon an argument developed more extensively in José Casanova, "Religion, Secular Identities, and European Integration," in *Religion and European Integration*, ed. Timothy Byrnes and Peter Katzenstein (Cambridge: Cambridge University Press, 2006).

8. David Martin, *A General Theory of Secularization* (New York: Harper & Row, 1978); and Andrew M. Greeley, *Religion in Europe at the End of the Second Millennium: A Sociological Profile* (New Brunswick, NJ: Transaction, 2003).

9. Grace Davie, *Religion in Britain since 1945: Believing without Belonging* (Oxford: Blackwell, 1994); and idem, *Religion in Modern Europe: A Memory Mutates* (Oxford: Oxford University Press, 2000).

10. Danièle Hervieu-Léger, "Religion und Sozialer Zusammenhalt," *Transit: Europäische Review* 26 (Summer 2004).

11. Tariq Modood, *Multicultural Politics: Racism, Ethnicity, and Muslims in Britain* (Minneapolis: University of Minnesota Press, 2005).

12. John Bowen, "Muslims and Citizens: France's Headscarf Controversy," *Boston Review*, Feb./March 2004; and Talal Asad, "Trying to Understand French Secularism," in *Political Theologies*, ed. Hent de Vries (New York: Fordham University Press, 2006).

13. Elaine Sciolino, "Debate Begins in France on Religion in the Schools," *New York Times*, Feb. 4, 2004.

14. For a notorious expression of Islamophobia, see Oriana Fallaci, *The Rage and the Pride* (New York: Rizzoli, 2002). On the issue, see Runnymede Trust, *Islamophobia: A Challenge for Us All* (London: Runnymede Trust, 1997); and B. Said, *A Fundamental Fear: Eurocentrism and the Emergence of Islamism* (London: Zed, 1997).

15. José Casanova, "Civil Society and Religion: Retrospective Reflections on Catholicism and Prospective Reflections on Islam," *Social Research* 68.4 (Winter 2001).

16. José Casanova, *Public Religions in the Modern World* (Chicago: University of Chicago Press, 1994).

17. The following section draws substantially upon the still-unpublished findings of the RIINY research project, "Religion and Immigrant Incorporation in New York," led by José Casanova and Aristide Zolberg at the International Center for Migration, Ethnicity, and Citizenship at the New School for Social Research in New York. RIINY (1999–2002) was one of seven "Gateway Cities" projects financed by the Pew Charitable Trusts.

18. Raymond Brady Williams, *Religion of Immigrants from India and Pakistan: New Threads in the American Tapestry* (New York: Cambridge University Press, 1988), 29. The claim that immigrants become more religious as they become more American was central to Will Herberg's thesis in his classic study *Protestant-Catholic-Jew* (Garden City, NY: Doubleday, 1960). The same claim has been restated by most contemporary studies of immigrant religions in America. See, for example, R. Stephen Warner and Judith G. Wittner, eds., *Gatherings in Diaspora: Religious Communities and the New Immigration* (Philadelphia: Temple University Press, 1998); and Helen Rose Ebaugh and Janet Saltzman Chafetz, eds., *Religion and the New Immigrants* (Walnut Creek, CA: AltaMira, 2000).

19. Timothy L. Smith, "Religion and Ethnicity in America," *American Historical Review* 83 (1978).

20. Rural Italian immigrants from the south at the turn of the twentieth century, for instance, tended to adopt anticlerical socialist and anarchist identities when they migrated to urban industrial centers in northern Italy or to Catholic Argentina, while they tended to become "better" practicing Catholics when they migrated to urban industrial centers in the United States. One could make similar comparisons in the present between Hindu immigrants in London and New York or between francophone West African Muslims in Paris and New York.

21. Herberg, *Protestant-Catholic-Jew*, 27–28.

22. Kirk Hadaway, Penny Long Marler, and Mark Chaves, "What the Polls Don't Show: A Closer Look at U.S. Church Attendance," *American Sociological Review* 58 (1993).

23. Herberg, *Protestant-Catholic-Jew*, 27.

24. Sydney E. Mead, "Denominationalism: The Shape of Protestantism in America," in *The Lively Experiment: The Shaping of Christianity in America* (New York: Harper & Row, 1976); and Andrew M. Greeley, *The Denominational Society: A Sociological Approach to Religion in America* (Glenview, IL: Scott, Foresman, 1972). In Western Europe, by contrast, the model has remained that of one single church which claims to be coextensive with the nation or that of two (Catholic and Protestant) competing but territorially based national churches along with an indefinite number of religious minorities, which tend to assume the structural position of sects vis-à-vis the national church or churches. Postindependence Ukraine may be the only European society that resembles the denominational model. See José Casanova, "Between Nation and Civil Society: Ethno-Linguistic and Religious Pluralism in Ukraine," in *Democratic Civility*, ed. Robert Heffner (New Brunswick, NJ: Transaction, 1998).

25. Ray A. Billington, *The Protestant Crusade, 1800–1860: A Study of the Origins of American Nativism* (New York: Macmillan, 1938); David Brion Davis, "Some Themes of Countersubversion: An Analysis of Anti-Masonic, Anti-Catholic, and Anti-Mormon Literature," *Mississippi Valley Historical Review* 47 (1960); John Higham, *Strangers in the Land: Patterns of American Nativism, 1860–1925*, 2nd ed. (New Brunswick: Rutgers University Press, 1988); and idem, "Instead of a Sequel; or, How I Lost My Subject," in *Handbook of International Migration: The American Experience*, ed. Charles Hirschman, Philip Kasinitz, and Josh de Wind (New York: Russell Sage Foundation, 1999).

26. Actually, on theological monotheistic grounds, Herberg himself was personally highly critical of the idolatrous immanent character of the American or any national civil religion.

27. Robert Bellah, "Civil Religion in America," *Daedalus* 96.1 (1967).

28. Nicholas Lemann, *The Promised Land: The Great Black Migration and How It Changed America* (New York: Vintage, 1996); Nathan Glazer and Daniel Patrick Moynihan, *Beyond the Melting Pot: The Negroes, Puerto Ricans, Jews, Italians, and Irish of New York City* (Cambridge: MIT Press, 1963); and Jay P. Dolan and Jaime R. Vidal, eds., *Puerto Rican and Cuban Catholics in the United States, 1900–65* (Notre Dame: Notre Dame University Press, 1994).

29. Eric C. Lincoln, *Race, Religion, and the Continuing American Dilemma* (New York: Hill & Wang, 1984); and Forrest G. Wood, *The Arrogance of Faith: Christianity and Race in America from the Colonial Era to the Twentieth Century* (New York: Knopf, 1990). Until recently the new field of immigration studies had paid little attention to religion, but this situation has been radically altered in the last decade.

30. For a prominent voice of Anglo-Protestant nativism directed at the threat of Hispanic Catholics, see Samuel P. Huntington, *Who Are We? The Challenges to America's National Identity* (New York: Simon & Schuster, 2004).

31. Desmond S. King, *Making Americans: Immigration, Race, and the Origins of the Diverse Democracy* (Cambridge: Harvard University Press, 2000).

32. Bruce B. Lawrence, *New Faiths, Old Fears: Muslims and Other Asian Immigrants in American Religious Life* (New York: Columbia University Press, 2002).

33. Alejandro Portes and Rubén G. Rumbaut, *Immigrant America: A Portrait*, 2nd ed. (Berkeley: University of California Press, 1996).

34. Diana L. Eck, *A New Religious America: How a "Christian Country" Has Become the World's Most Religiously Diverse Nation* (San Francisco: Harper, 2002).

35. The New Immigrant Survey is fortunately going to remedy this situation. See http://nis.princeton.edu and note 36 below.

36. According to the New Immigrant Survey Pilot (NIS-P 1996), almost two-thirds of new immigrants are nominally Christian (Catholic 41.9%; Protestant 18.6%; Orthodox 4.2%), 2.6% denominated themselves Jewish, while close to 17% chose non-Judeo-Christian religions as their denomination (Muslim 8%; Buddhist 4%; Hindu 3.4%; other 1.4%), and 15% chose "no religion" as their "religious preference." One has to treat these data with some caution given the very small sample (976) of respondents. The adult sample of the new NIS-2003 (to be released in early 2006) is much larger (8,573), and therefore its data on the religious preference or nominal affiliation of the new immigrants will be more conclusive. See Guillermina Jasso, Douglas S. Massey, Mark R. Rosenzweig, and James P. Smith, "Exploring the Religious Preferences of Recent Immigrants to the United Sates: Evidence from the New Immigrant Survey Pilot," in *Religion and Immigration: Christian, Jewish, and Muslim Experiences in the United States*, ed. Yvonne Yazbeck Haddad, Jane I. Smith, and John L. Esposito (Walnut Creek, CA: AltaMira, 2003).

37. On the Hispanization of American Catholicism and Protestantism and the parallel Protestantification of Latin America, see Jay P. Dolan and Allan Figueroa Deck, eds., *Hispanic Catholic Culture in the United States* (Notre Dame: University of Notre Dame Press, 1994); and Ana Maria Diaz-Stevens and Anthony M. Stevens-Arroyo, *Recognizing the Latino Resurgence in U.S. Religion* (Boulder, CO: Westview, 1998).

38. "Christians, Jews Still Predominate," *Chicago Tribune*, Jan. 29, 2002, 8; and Tom W. Smith, *Estimating the Muslim Population in the United States* (New York: American Jewish Committee, 2001).

39. See the Pluralism Project CD-Rom, *On Common Ground: World Religions in America* (New York: Columbia University Press, 1997).

40. Jay P. Dolan, *The American Catholic Experience* (Garden City, NY: Doubleday, 1985); Arthur Hertzberg, *The Jews in America: Four Centuries of an Uneasy Encounter* (New York: Simon & Schuster, 1989); and Laurence R. Moore, *Religious Outsiders and the Making of Americans* (New York: Oxford University Press, 1986).

41. Stephen Protero, ed., *A Nation of Religions: The Politics of Pluralism in Multi-religious America* (Chapel Hill: University of North Carolina Press, 2005).

42. For a poignant illustration, see Prema Kurien, "Being Young, Brown, and Hindu: The Identity Struggles of Second Generation Indian Americans," *Journal of Contemporary Ethnography* (forthcoming).

43. R. Stephen Warner, *A Church of Our Own: Disestablishment and Diversity in American Religion* (New Brunswick: Rutgers University Press, 2005).

44. See John Esposito's essay in this volume.

45. Olivier Roy, *Globalised Islam: The Search for a New Umma* (London: Hurst, 2004).

46. See Jane Smith, *Islam in America* (New York: Columbia University Press, 1999).

47. Richard Cimino, "Evangelical Discourse on Islam after 9/11," paper presented at the annual meeting of the Association for the Sociology of Religion, Atlanta, Aug. 15–17, 2003. Beyond this paper, the following material draws heavily and freely upon personal conversations with Richard Cimino at the New School for Social Research.

48. Sonja Barisic, "Pat Roberson Describes Islam as a Violent Religion That Wants to Dominate," *Associated Press*, Feb. 22, 2002.

BIBLIOGRAPHY

Asad, Talal. "Trying to Understand French Secularism." In *Political Theologies*. Edited by Hent de Vries. New York: Fordham University Press, 2006.

Bauböck, Rainer, ed. *From Aliens to Citizens: Redefining the Status of Immigrants in Europe*. Aldershot: Ashgate, 1994.

Bauböck, Rainer, Agnes Heller, and Aristide R. Zolberg, eds. *The Challenges of Diversity: Integration and Pluralism in Societies of Immigration*. Aldershot: Ashgate, 1996.

Bauböck, Rainer, and John Rundell, eds. *Blurred Boundaries: Migration, Ethnicity, Citizenship*. Aldershot: Ashgate, 1998.

Bellah, Robert. "Civil Religion in America." *Daedalus* 96.1 (1967).

Billington, Ray A. *The Protestant Crusade, 1800–1860: A Study of the Origins of American Nativism*. New York: Macmillan, 1938.

Bowen, John. "Muslims and Citizens: France's Headscarf Controversy." *Boston Review*, Feb./March 2004.

Casanova, José. "Between Nation and Civil Society: Ethno-Linguistic and Religious Pluralism in Ukraine." In *Democratic Civility*. Edited by Robert Heffner. New Brunswick, NJ: Transaction, 1998.

———. *Public Religions in the Modern World*. Chicago: University of Chicago Press, 1994.

———. "Religion, Secular Identities, and European Integration." In *Religion and European Integration*. Edited by Timothy Byrnes and Peter Katzenstein. Cambridge: Cambridge University Press, 2006.

Cesari, Jocelyne. *When Islam and Democracy Meet: Muslims in Europe and in the United States.* New York: Palgrave Macmillan, 2004.
Cimino, Richard. "Evangelical Discourse on Islam after 9/11." Paper presented at the Association for the Sociology of Religion annual meeting, Atlanta, Aug. 2003.
Davie, Grace. *Religion in Britain since 1945: Believing without Belonging.* Oxford: Blackwell, 1994.
———. *Religion in Modern Europe: A Memory Mutates.* Oxford: Oxford University Press, 2000.
Davis, David Brion. "Some Themes of Countersubversion: An Analysis of Anti-Masonic, Anti-Catholic, and Anti-Mormon Literature." *Mississippi Valley Historical Review* 47 (1960).
Diaz-Stevens, Ana Maria, and Anthony M. Stevens-Arroyo. *Recognizing the Latino Resurgence in U.S. Religion.* Boulder, CO: Westview, 1998.
Dolan, Jay P. *The American Catholic Experience.* Garden City, NY: Doubleday, 1985.
Dolan, Jay P., and Allan Figueroa Deck, eds. *Hispanic Catholic Culture in the United States.* Notre Dame: University of Notre Dame Press, 1994.
Dolan, Jay P., and Jaime R. Vidal, eds. *Puerto Rican and Cuban Catholics in the United States, 1900–65.* Notre Dame: Notre Dame University Press, 1994.
Ebaugh, Helen Rose, and Janet Saltzman Chafetz, eds. *Religion and the New Immigrants.* Walnut Creek, CA: AltaMira, 2000.
Eck, Diana L. *A New Religious America: How a "Christian Country" Has Become the World's Most Religiously Diverse Nation.* San Francisco: Harper, 2002.
Fallaci, Oriana. *The Rage and the Pride.* New York: Rizzoli, 2002.
Ferrari, Silvio, and Anthony Bradney, eds. *Islam and European Legal Systems.* Aldershot: Ashgate, 2000.
Glazer, Nathan, and Daniel Patrick Moynihan. *Beyond the Melting Pot: The Negroes, Puerto Ricans, Jews, Italians, and Irish of New York City.* Cambridge: MIT Press, 1963.
Greeley, Andrew M. *The Denominational Society: A Sociological Approach to Religion in America.* Glenview, IL: Scott, Foresman, 1972.
———. *Religion in Europe at the End of the Second Millennium: A Sociological Profile.* New Brunswick, NJ: Transaction, 2003.
Hadaway, Kirk, Penny Long Marler, and Mark Chaves. "What the Polls Don't Show: A Closer Look at U.S. Church Attendance." *American Sociological Review* 58 (1993).
Haddad, Yvonne Yazbeck, ed. *Muslims in the West: From Sojourners to Citizens.* New York: Oxford University Press, 2002.
Herberg, Will. *Protestant-Catholic-Jew.* Garden City, NY: Doubleday, 1960.
Hervieu-Léger, Danièle. "Religion und Sozialer Zusammenhalt." *Transit: Europäische Review* 26 (Summer 2004).
Higham, John. "Instead of a Sequel; or, How I Lost My Subject." In *Handbook of International Migration: The American Experience.* Edited by Charles Hirschman, Philip Kasinitz, and Josh de Wind. New York: Russell Sage Foundation, 1999.
———. *Strangers in the Land: Patterns of American Nativism, 1860–1925.* 2nd ed. New Brunswick: Rutgers University Press, 1988.
Hirschman, Charles, Philip Kasinitz, and Josh de Wind, eds. *Handbook of International Migration: The American Experience.* New York: Russell Sage Foundation, 1999.
Huntington, Samuel P. *Who Are We? The Challenges to America's National Identity.* New York: Simon & Schuster, 2004.
Jasso, Guillermina, Douglas S. Massey, Mark R. Rosenzweig, and James P. Smith. "Exploring the Religious Preferences of Recent Immigrants to the United Sates:

Evidence from the New Immigrant Survey Pilot." In *Religion and Immigration: Christian, Jewish, and Muslim Experiences in the United States*. Edited by Yvonne Yazbeck Haddad, Jane I. Smith, and John L. Esposito. Walnut Creek, CA: AltaMira, 2003.

Jelen, Ted, and Clyde Wilcox, eds. *Religion and Politics in Comparative Perspective: The One, the Few and the Many*. New York: Cambridge University Press, 2002.

King, Desmond S. *Making Americans: Immigration, Race, and the Origins of the Diverse Democracy*. Cambridge: Harvard University Press, 2000.

Kurien, Prema. "Being Young, Brown, and Hindu: The Identity Struggles of Second Generation Indian Americans." *Journal of Contemporary Ethnography* (forthcoming).

Lawrence, Bruce B. *New Faiths, Old Fears: Muslims and Other Asian Immigrants in American Religious Life*. New York: Columbia University Press, 2002.

Lemann, Nicholas. *The Promised Land: The Great Black Migration and How It Changed America*. New York: Vintage, 1996.

Leonard, Karen Isaksen. *Muslims in the United States: The State of Research*. New York: Russell Sage Foundation, 2003.

Lincoln, Eric C. *Race, Religion, and the Continuing American Dilemma*. New York: Hill & Wang, 1984.

Madeley, John, and Zsolt Enyedi, eds. *Church and State in Contemporary Europe*. London: Cass, 2003.

Maréchal, Brigitte, Stefano Allievi, Felice Dassetto, and Jørgen Nielsen, eds. *Muslims in the Enlarged Europe*. Leiden: Brill, 2003.

Martin, David. *A General Theory of Secularization*. New York: Harper & Row, 1978.

Mead, Sydney E. "Denominationalism: The Shape of Protestantism in America." In *The Lively Experiment: The Shaping of Christianity in America*. New York: Harper & Row, 1976.

Moch, Leslie Page. *Moving Europeans: Migration in Western Europe since 1650*. 2nd ed. Bloomington: Indiana University Press, 2003.

Modood, Tariq. *Multicultural Politics: Racism, Ethnicity, and Muslims in Britain*. Minneapolis: University of Minnesota Press, 2005.

New Immigrant Survey. http://nis.princeton.edu.

Pluralism Project CD-ROM. *On Common Ground: World Religions in America*. New York: Columbia University Press, 1997.

Portes, Alejandro, and Rubén G. Rumbaut. *Immigrant America: A Portrait*. 2nd. ed. Berkeley: University of California Press, 1996.

Protero, Stephen, ed. *A Nation of Religions: The Politics of Pluralism in Multireligious America*. Chapel Hill: University of North Carolina Press, 2005.

Roy, Olivier. *Globalised Islam: The Search for a New Umma*. London: Hurst, 2004.

Runnymede Trust. *Islamophobia: A Challenge for Us All*. London: Runnymede Trust, 1997.

Smith, Jane. *Islam in America*. New York: Columbia University Press, 1999.

Smith, Timothy L. "Religion and Ethnicity in America." *American Historical Review* 83 (1978).

Smith, Tom W. *Estimating the Muslim Population in the United States*. New York: American Jewish Committee, 2001.

Vertovec, Steve, and Ceri Peach, eds. *Islam in Europe: The Politics of Religion and Community*. Basingstoke: Macmillan, 1997.

Warner, R. Stephen. *A Church of Our Own: Disestablishment and Diversity in American Religion*. New Brunswick: Rutgers University Press, 2005.

Warner, R. Stephen, and Judith G. Wittner, eds. *Gatherings in Diaspora: Religious Communities and the New Immigration.* Philadelphia: Temple University Press, 1998.

Williams, Raymond Brady. *Religion of Immigrants from India and Pakistan: New Threads in the American Tapestry.* New York: Cambridge University Press, 1988.

Wood, Forrest G. *The Arrogance of Faith: Christianity and Race in America from the Colonial Era to the Twentieth Century.* New York: Knopf, 1990.

5

The Transnational Struggle for Jewish Pluralism

Yossi Shain

On March 31, 2005, after six years of debates, Israel's Supreme Court—sitting as the High Court of Justice—ruled that non-Orthodox conversions in which the study process was conducted in Israel but was finalized in the United States by Reform or Conservative rabbis will be recognized. This ruling broke the monopoly of the Orthodoxy over recognized conversions inside Israel. The court accepted the petition filed by the Religious Action Center, the extension arm of the U.S.-based Reform movement, and allowed for the first time in the state's history non-Orthodox converts to be fully recognized by Israel as Jews deserving Israeli citizenship based on Israel's law of return. The ruling, which drew harsh criticism from Orthodox leaders, was the latest manifestation of a culture war over Jewish identity inside and outside Israel. Part of the debate is over the dilemma of who is a Jew and the question of who has the ultimate religious authority among Jews to determine membership. Israel and Diaspora Jewry also involve dilemmas of Jewish politics and geography—including who speaks on behalf of the Jews and where the boundaries of the state of Israel or the Jewish homeland end.

This essay examines the relationship between the American Jewish community and Israel from the perspective of a transnational struggle over Jewish pluralism. The question of Jewish identity in Israel and in the United States, the continuing insistence of many Jewish Americans on perceiving Israel as a critical source of their own identity—and therefore as a crucial target of their influence—and Israel's direct or indirect involvement in the lives of all Jewish communities create a dynamic in which reciprocal influences mutually constitute Jewish identity. The new modes of Jewish American participation in Israeli affairs—domestic and international, on the one hand, and Israeli rethinking of its own position vis-à-vis the Diaspora in terms of legitimacy, status, power, and identity, on the other—has opened the way for greater negotiation over, and coordination of, the meaning and purpose of Judaism in our time.

At a time when many speak of the widening "gulf between the two centers of world Jewry" due to divergence of identities or of "the waning of the American Jewish love affairs with Israel," I argue the opposite.[1] Today, Jewish Americans influence the nature of Jewish identity in Israel more than ever before, and Israel is reaching out to diasporic voices in an unprecedented manner. This mutual reinforcement draws the two communities closer together, reinvigorating Jewish identity in both countries. Indeed, American Jews, from those most deeply and directly involved with Jewish communal life and with Israel to those who habitually shunned synagogues and other Jewish institutions and eschewed involvement with anything Israeli, found themselves by the beginning of the twenty-first century confronted by myriad issues, ranging from identity to physical security, that were catalyzed or radically intensified by the Middle East's newest war of attrition and further exacerbated by the terror attacks of September 11, 2001, and their aftermath. The new conflict raised uncomfortable questions for American Jews, not least for the unaffiliated. These questions included, among others, the direct and personal meaning to themselves of an existential crisis in Israel and among threatened Jewish communities elsewhere; the moral component of war and their responsibility for it, if any; and, based on these two dilemmas, what they owed their country—or countries—and how would it be possible to navigate their several obligations.

Judaism and the Homeland Dimension

Throughout the 1990s the Israeli-Diaspora relationship had been evolving in different directions. For almost a decade, many Israelis and Diaspora Jews believed that a comprehensive Middle East peace would alter fundamentally both Israel's Jewish character and relations between the sovereign Jewish state and Jewish existence in the West. Peace would have enabled Israel to achieve a level of normalization that would have loosened the bonds of involvement with and responsibility for the Diaspora, while releasing the Diaspora from burdensome entanglements with Israeli security issues that had overshadowed their lives in their countries of domicile for over a generation. As late as summer 2000 the prevailing sense among observers of Jewish American affairs was that "the Israel agenda" of American Jews and Jewish advocacy groups "has changed radically. Whatever the serious problems and deep pitfalls in the peace process, the issues that have come to the fore are related more to the relationship between Israel and America's Jews than with the physical security of Israel."[2]

The 1990s were marked by a growing involvement of Jewish American liberal movements in the backlash against and coercion by Israel's religious establishment, which led many Israelis to shed their religious identities even beyond their secular Zionist socialization. In 1999 U.S.-based Reform and Conservative movements funded a public campaign on Israeli billboards and in the media, calling on secular Israelis to embrace religious pluralism under the slogan, "There is more than one way to be a Jew." The campaign, financed by a grant from a Jewish family foundation in San Francisco, met with a harsh response from the Israeli ultra-Orthodox sector. This campaign was part of a growing Jewish American involvement in the battle over Israel's Jewish identity. This battle, often described in general terms as the struggle between secular and religious Jews, or between "Israeliness" and "Jewishness," was the most controversial domestic theme in Israeli politics and civic culture in the 1990s, with far-reaching political, economic, and legal ramifications.[3] Only the al-Aqsa *intifada*, which erupted in late September 2000, and the ensuing wave of Palestinian terrorism that brought security back to the center of the Jewish agenda were able to stem this rupture that threatened Israeli society from within.[4] Ari Shavit, one of Israel's famous writers, said that

> today the Jewish people is waging two existential wars simultaneously. One for the body, against the Arabs, and a second war for the soul, against itself. The identification of Judaism with a religion from which people are trying to dissociate themselves is creating a very serious vacuum [in Israel]. That is why there is a deep recoil from everything Jewish. But without Jewish identity, we will not be able to exist.[5]

As Asher Arian notes, since the 1980s "there has been a parallel growth of both secularism and religion in the country, decreasing the spirit of coexistence and pluralism, and increasing the anxieties and fears of a 'war of cultures'—or worse—among the Jews of Israel."[6] Certainly by the mid-1990s violence has become a common feature of the Israeli *Kulturkampf*, most dramatically expressed in the assassination of Prime Minister Yitzhak Rabin. Religious ultranationalists saw Rabin's willingness to trade Jewish land for peace with the Palestinians as a sin against divine law.[7] Indeed, the religious aspects of the Israeli *Kulturkampf* link dilemmas of Jewish identity boundaries with attachments and commitments to the physical ancient and modern boundaries of the Jewish state. On June 24, 2000, with secular-religious tensions rising, religious extremists set a Conservative synagogue in the heart of Jerusalem on fire. Former Prime Minister Ehud Barak declared the attack "shocking...a horrible act that chills the souls of all Jews."[8] Yet, just months later, after the apparent collapse of the Oslo peace process and as the identity issues among Jews were pushed to the side in the face of a renewed Arab-Jewish conflict, Israeli President Moshe Katsav said that the violent clashes between Jews and Arabs helped reduce the divisions which exist in Israeli society.[9]

Before the eruption of violence between Israeli and Palestinians in autumn 2000, the struggle over Israel's Jewish character also had been considered the most contentious issue within the Jewish American Diaspora, which has been grappling with its own identity. True, internal Jewish American debates regarding the standards for gauging Jewish identity are mostly informed by the reality of Jewish life in the United States and are thus somewhat distant from internal Israeli debates. Yet, the American and Israeli contexts are closely interconnected in principle and in practice. Jewish American positions on matters of politics and society in the United States, including on Judaism and the interest of the Jewish people, are often fashioned according to perceptions about Israel, U.S.-Israeli relations, and Israeli domestic and international behavior. Israeli politics and society, in turn, have been highly dependent on the government and the Jewish community of the United States and must take into consideration the views of the Diaspora regarding Israel's disposition on matters of war and peace, as well as Israel's Jewish and democratic character.

Certainly the efforts of non-Orthodox denominations to influence the homeland's Jewish identity are not new.[10] Yet, until the 1980s their intervention in Israeli affairs was sporadic and not vigorous. In 1977 Charles Liebman wrote that "because Israel is a symbol, its particular policies are not very important to [non-Orthodox] American Jews . . . fall[ing] outside the boundaries of [their] legitimate activity." The Orthodox, however, are the only ones who "have a clear image of what Israel should be like and a sense of religious obligation to translate the image into specific policies."[11] Liebman could envisage only Jewish American Orthodox interventions to restrain Israeli Zionist attempts to erode the state's "Jewish content." The assertion that Israeli Jewish content is more relevant to the Diaspora Orthodoxy than to non-Orthodox denominations was thus built on the assumption that the latter's version of Judaism is loose and ephemeral.

Regardless of the validity of this argument, then, this is certainly not the case today, with the Reform and Conservative now increasingly embracing more traditional Jewish religious practices as a way of combating complete secularization and the impact interrelations marriages. A corollary of this indigenously American trend is the heightened attention toward Jewish identity in Israel. There are many answers to the question of why Reform and Conservative Jews in the United States, who have always considered the United States their chosen country, are so invested in shaping Jewish identity inside Israel at this juncture. Many emphasize the comfort of having a place to which one can always move should conditions in the United States become unfriendly. Periodic episodes of anti-Semitism are seen as reminders to older generations of Jewish Americans of the precariousness of being a Jew in a Christian-majority culture. Others argue that it is not danger, but rather the absence thereof, that drives the current attention of Jewish Americans to Israel. As they achieve full integration and great triumphs in all aspects of American life, American Jews, qua Jews, have become victims of their own success.[12] From the point of view of Jewish identity, some argue that the community faces a demographic peril as half of its members marry non-Jews, assimilate, or drift.[13]

In *American Jewish Identity Survey, 2001*, a study of American Jewry, Egon Mayer et al. portray mutually reinforcing trends of increasing secularity, decreasing attachment to Jewish religious and communal institutions, decreasing commitment to and involvement with Israel, and a weakening sense of Jewish identity among large parts of American Jewry. Heightened divisions among American Jews over the nature and future of Jewish identity and affiliation were accompanied by increased assimilation in the forms of inter-marriage and religious and philosophical syncretism, conversion, and indiffer-ence. The primary fault line was Jewish religious observance, a line pressed further into the ground by issues such as membership in other Jewish organi-zations, general social milieu, and attachment to Israel, with largely the same individuals falling on either side of the line.

Mayer describes the ongoing exodus of Jews from organized Jewish life, shedding both the form and the substance of Jewish affiliation. Jews who became more secular found Jewish organizations less accommodating and less fulfilling. This process fed on itself, pushing these individuals further away not only from Jewish organizations, but from Jewish social attachments and other potential reinforcements of Jewish identity, eventually placing many altogether outside any kind of Jewish identity or affiliation. Among the ever-larger portion of American Jews who described themselves as secular but retained con-sciousness of Jewish identity, many searched for something substantive upon which to base this identity and develop effective vehicles for belonging and community and did not find it in the larger Jewish community's existing frameworks. In the conclusion to Mayer's study, Jewish philanthropist Felix Posen writes that since so many American Jews do not identify with the main religious streams of Judaism, "Jewish secularism" must be given serious at-tention and new resources in order to become "a potent source of identification and motivation."[14]

Notwithstanding the debate regarding the content of Jewish secularism—especially outside the state of Israel—it is clear that with Jewish American ethnicity (as a cultural trait) no longer enough to sustain Jewish existence in the United States, and with the fading of traditional Jewish neighborhoods, Jews in America have lost many of their distinctive ethnic markers. Not sur-prisingly, other survey data show that religion is the most distinctive attribute of most Jewish Americans.[15] Today, even the most liberal streams in American Jewry acknowledge that "without the synagogue Jewish life in the U.S. cannot endure."[16] Reform Jews—as part of the movement's "worship revolution"—are now searching for new meaning in old religious rituals which were dis-posed of as part of their grandparents' desire to assimilate.[17] Likewise Con-servative Jews also experienced renewed interest in ritual observance. A 1995 survey of Conservative synagogue members found that "younger Conservative Jewish adults are . . . more Jewishly active than their older counterparts, even when taking family life stage and presence of children into account." The younger Conservative Jews were also proved "more ritually active than older congregants despite having been raised by less observant parents."[18]

Certainly, the memory of the Holocaust has become a major source of communal identity and mobilization and to a large extent is "a primary vehicle not only of invoking unity among Jews . . . but also of connection between the Jewish and non-Jewish communities."[19] However, given the fact that the Ho-locaust is gradually becoming what Daniel Levy and Natan Sznaider call a uni-versalized "cosmopolitan memory"—the outcome of its dissemination in the United States and worldwide—even this memory is no longer sufficient in and of itself to foster and retain Jewish identity (especially as the generation of survivors leaves the historical stage).[20] These trends further heighten the importance of religion in the ongoing formation of American-Jewish identity.

In the mid-1950s many Jews were satisfied with the legitimization and normalization of Judaism as part of a larger Americanized Judeo-Christian framework that downplayed religious differences with Christians, best articulated in Will Herberg's famous American "Tripartite Settlement": *Protestant-Catholic-Jew.*[21] Yet a generation later, the resurgence of religious exclusivity, rather than the process of religious blending, was the desirable goal. The fact that Jews do not have to hide their religion, but rather celebrate it as part of their American identity, was made evident most strikingly by the landmark selection of modern Orthodox Jewish Senator Joseph Lieberman as Al Gore's running mate in 2000. His candidacy symbolized, perhaps more than anything else, that accentuating one's Jewish religious life is, in itself, a part of normal American life. Even inside Israel, Lieberman's selection seemed to challenge some of the fundamental assumptions of modern Zionism regarding the alleged anomaly of Diaspora life. It also presented many Israelis with an attractive model of reconciling religion and state.[22]

Among the major religions, Jewish theology is distinctive with its stress that religious membership is tied to a particular homeland, "the land of Israel" (*Eretz Yisrael*). From biblical times, Jewish nationalism has been indistinguishable from religion, as "God chose a particular people and promised them a particular land."[23] The fact that Jewish kinship is territorially related makes the character of the Jewish Diaspora quite unique, since living outside the land is theologically a sign of failing to fulfill God's plan. The vision of returning to the holy homeland is built into the very definition of all Jewish diasporic communities, at least symbolically. Thus, while most religions do not define themselves according to "political maps" and are not bound by membership in states, nations, or homelands, Judaism lends itself more to nationalism than to transnationalism.

Interesting enough, even though traditional Zionism and many Israelis have long rejected the theological significance of the land of Israel as the *holy homeland* (emphasizing instead the creation of the state of as a political/secular undertaking to ensure a safe haven for Jews—like all other "normal" nations), the very existence of a Jewish state has great theological implications for many non-Jews (Christians and Muslims). Joseph Dan writes that secular "Israelis would do well to note the vast differences between their understanding of the state as secular, and the perception by others that it is a theological phenomenon par excellence."[24]

For fundamentally religious Jews, whose religious self precedes their other identities, the halachic decree of dwelling in the land of Israel implies that life in the United States is only a temporary sojourn, at least conceptually. Those religious Jews who consider exilic life (*galut*) as a punishment from God may suspend their move to *Eretz Yisrael* until the coming of the Messiah. In fact, at least until 1945, "most Orthodox Jewish authorities opposed Zionism as a blasphemous anticipation of the divine eschatological plan. And on this point they found common cause with most early (modernist) leaders of Reform Judaism—though the two groups would have shrunk with horror from any thought of commonality."[25] Yet the founding of Israel in 1948 presented all streams of American Jews with a constant dilemma of whether the modern nation-state of Israel and its policies, both internal and external, reflect their aspirations of a true Jewish state.

In the mid-1950s Rabbi Joseph B. Soloveitchik, representing the most important voice of centrist modern Orthodox rabbis in the United States, urged members of his community to commit themselves fully to the project of secular Zionists in Israel. He argued that the unifying fate of the Jewish people—regardless of the degree of their religious observance, economic status, or place of residence—obliges religious Jews to have a feeling of solidarity, kinship, and responsibility for all secular Jews. Hence, when religious Jews overlook the critical importance in the creation of the state of Israel they ignore God's "knocking." Soloveitchik, who decried the failure of American Jews to utilize their resources during the Holocaust, reminded his Orthodox followers that the security and destiny of the new state of Israel was in their hands. Israel's very existence in his view was entangled with the fate of the Diaspora. Other religious Orthodox Zionists in the United States, like their counterparts in Israel, considered the creation of Israel as the "beginning of the flowering of Jewish redemption [geula]," a messianic doctrine which became the ideological hallmark of many American Orthodox after the Six Day War.[26]

Indeed, a disproportionate number of Jewish American immigrants to Israel are Orthodox.[27] A 1998 survey indicates that while 81% of Orthodox Jews in America visited Israel, only 38% of Reform Jews visited the country, and only 25% of Reform Jews think that a visit to Israel is important for maintaining their Jewish identity. Still, 91% of Conservative Jews and 73% of Reform Jews agree that "caring about Israel is a very important part of my being a Jew."[28] To be sure, the centrality of the state of Israel as the spiritual and cultural center of world Jewry is now recognized even by the Reform movement, which has undergone a dramatic shift from its early anti-Zionist position toward endorsing Zionism. In its 1999 Pittsburgh Convention, the Reform movement embraced "religious and cultural pluralism as an expression of the vitality of Jewish communal life in Israel and the Diaspora," affirming the unique qualities of living in Eretz Yisrael and encouraging aliyah (moving to Israel).[29]

Perhaps even more critical is the growing understanding of Reform and Conservative rabbis in the United States that their ability to develop and disseminate their creed of Judaism in the context of modernity and democracy inside Israel is the "ultimate test of Jewish authenticity for Progressive Judaism" in the Diaspora. These sentiments were expressed by Rabbi Richard Hirsch, executive director of the World Union of Progressive Judaism, in his keynote address to the 29th International Convention of the movement, held notably in Jerusalem in March 1999.[30] Similarly, Ismar Schorsch, chancellor of the Jewish Theological Seminary of the American Conservative movement, acknowledges that building a strong presence of the Conservative (Masorti) stream inside Israel is essential for "revitalizing the Conservative movement in North America."[31] Thus, the question of how to strengthen the ties between Jewish Americans and Israel preoccupies the leadership of the more liberal Jewish American religious streams, who consider Israel to be indispensable to their Jewish identity in the United States.

The Israeli *Kulturkampf* and Jewish Americans

In its first three decades the state of Israel was able to contain the strain between secularism and religion by turning the Zionist ideology and institutions into Israel's civil religion. To begin with, Israel was established as the state of all Jews. Israel's famous 1950 law of return is not only "the concrete expression of the prophetic vision of the 'ingathering of exiles,'"[32] but also a statutory expression of its commitment to its Jewish character. The state's legal system distinguishes between personal status laws, which are based on the religious Jewish legal code (halacha), and all other laws (criminal and civil), which are based on the Napoleonic codex and Western universalistic orientations. The state was set at the center of a belief system (*mamlachtiyut* or statism) that provided the base for an eclectic Zionist identity. It gave Jewish content to the national project by building on the ideas of a divinely chosen nation (*am nivchar*) or "light unto the nations [or *lagoyim*]."[33] The state often used religious symbols in order to build the national narrative, enhance nationalist conformity and collaboration among the nationalist religious community, and co-opt the newly arrived religious Mizrahim (or oriental Jews). Zionism, in turn, was slowly accepted by the nationalist religious community as a modern theology that perceived the establishment of the state as a divine intervention in Jewish history.[34]

In the last two decades and especially during the years of the Oslo peace process, however, Zionism has been in decline, some argue under assault, inside Israel. This attrition was the result of a general perception that the Zionist vision had reached its triumphant realization—a secure sovereign state with a large Jewish majority. The decline of traditional Zionism was also a result of a confluence of factors in the rapidly changing context of Israeli politics and society. In the words of Peter Berkowitz, the forces of market capitalism and globalization pushed large segments of the Israeli public to embrace "hedonism over heroism and modern consumerism over piety."[35] These tendencies, coupled with growing public sentiment that peace with the Arabs was imminent, further exacerbated Jewish-Israeli disunity. Within this context, several ideological and political camps challenged the core values of mainstream Zionism. The ultra-Orthodox envisioned Israel as a Jewish state ruled by Orthodox precepts. This camp includes the ultra-Orthodox Ashkenazim of European origin and a growing voting bloc of Mizrahim represented by the Shas Party, which "seeks to replace secular Zionism with religious Judaism as the hegemonic ideology in Israeli society and presents this as the remedy for both the socio-economic and the cultural grievances [of Mizrahim]."[36] The secular universalistic forces, on the other hand, advocate transforming Israel into a liberal and secular state for both its Jewish and Arab citizens. While the more extreme among the ultra-Orthodox veer toward Jewish theocracy, radicals in the secularist community see post-Zionism as an opportunity to "de-Judaize" the country. Israel's internal cultural debate has also been compounded by conflicting visions over peace with the Arabs and Palestinians and the future of the occupied territories. During the late 1990s these factors ruptured the alliance between religious and secular Zionists, culminating in fundamentalist nationalism and a growing blurring of the distinctions between religious Zionists and the ultra-Orthodox (haredim).

For years, many believed that the internal Israeli Kulturkampf between the religious and secular communities was "fought out against the background of a general agreement on the value and importance of the Jewish tradition to Israel's cultural identity."[37] This was also the prevailing opinion among Jewish Americans, many of whom adopted idealized images of Israel after its 1967 victory in the Six Day War. Yet by early 2000 many in Israel and in the United States were no longer certain about the unassailable nature of Israel's Jewish-Zionist character, let alone satisfied with its conflicting directions—the insularity and perceived backwardness of Israeli ultra-Orthodoxy or the weakening sense of Jewish identity among secular Israelis. Many now fear that Israeli religious forces will continue to gain power and erode Israel's liberal democracy or, alternatively, that the secularism of the West, which Israel has adopted as its own, will obliterate Israel's distinctly Jewish identity. The debates are complicated by the large influx of about one million post-Soviet immigrants, about a quarter of whom are not Jewish by halacha. This wave of newcomers introduced a large bloc of nonreligious citizens into Israeli society who may be seeking non-Orthodox options.

In this complex reality, the American Reform and Conservative movements have appeared in Israel as one of the main groups trying to confront the religious establishment in the battleground over Israeli Jewish identity. They have mainly targeted Israelis who have been exposed to Jewish alternatives in America and want similar religious choice at home and those who wish to register protest against the ultra-Orthodox political, legal, and religious stronghold. These movements also appeal to secular Israeli values, such as egalitarianism.[38] In other words, these movements are trying to provide a middle-ground Jewish option and put special emphasis on outreach programs for the new post-Soviet immigrants.[39] The movement toward pluralistic Judaism has grown inside Israel, with the Reform and Conservatives establishing synagogue centers, educational programs, rabbinic schools, youth movements, and other outreach institutions. They attract a significant number of the new Russian immigrants, whose secular upbringing made liberal Judaism a natural fit to their needs and orientation in the process of becoming Israeli citizens.[40] These movements are also instrumental in the legal struggles to alter the Orthodox monopoly over Jewish marriage and conversion, to loosen Orthodox domination of religious councils, and to allow burial in nondenominational cemeteries. These Jewish American movements and their Israeli kindred organizations have also played a role in the Israeli High Court ruling to allow women to hold religious services at the Western Wall, Judaism's holiest site. Finally, they led in redirecting diasporic funds from general fundraising for Israel to educational institutions and sociopolitical programs aimed at promoting tolerance, democracy, and religious pluralism.[41] This new pattern in financial flows has greatly affected the sums, structure, and destination within Israel of Jewish American philanthropy.

Since the early 1990s, targeted American-Jewish giving to Israel has quadrupled, reaching approximately two billion dollars in 2000.[42] The campaign for pluralist Judaism further made the Reform and Conservative movements the nemesis of much of Israel's religious establishment, which has, at various times, denounced them as nonreligious, antireligious "enemies of Judaism and the Jewish State," and even "more dangerous to the Jewish nation than the Holocaust." The last statement, made in 1999 by Israel's Sephardi Chief Rabbi Bakshi-Doron, was described by leaders of the Reform movement in Israel as an "incitement to bloodshed and civil war."[43] Ultra-Orthodox leaders also charged that these movements represent a foreign, American phenomenon.

As they have become more cognizant of the centrality of Israel to their own Jewish American identity, liberal American Jews have decided to engage directly in a struggle to redefine Israel's identity in their own image. The assumption of many Jewish Americans, writes Jack Wertheimer, provost of the Jewish Theological Seminary of America, is that the Diaspora

> has much to teach its benighted Israeli cousins. Living in a hetero-
> geneous environment, American Jews . . . have learned the blessings
> of diversity, and accept the legitimacy of many different forms of
> religious Jewish expression. Moreover, thanks to constitutional guar-
> antees of church/state separation, American Judaism is not demeaned
> by the kinds of electoral horse-trading to which Israeli religious parties
> inevitably must stoop. In short, American Jews and American Juda-
> ism have grown in an atmosphere of pluralism and tolerance, and
> Israeli Jews would do well to learn from their example.[44]

The Controversy over "Who Is a Jew?"

The involvement of Conservative and Reform Jewish Americans in Israeli affairs was rejuvenated in 1988 when the religious parties moved to redefine who is a Jew in a manner that invalidated Reform and Conservative rabbis in the United States. Subsequently, leaders of the vast majority of American organized Jewry declared "open revolt against Israel."[45] It was the first time that the bitter hostility between American non-Orthodox leaders and the New York–based Lubavitch Hasidic movement—led by the late Rabbi Menachem Mendel Schneerson—was injected into the Israeli arena with such ferocity. The Lubavitchers' ardor and money ignited Israeli religious zealousness and the move to change Israel's legal definition of who is a Jew.[46] It left an indelible

mark on the future direction of Israeli politics and society. Schorsch commented at the time:

> This is not an Israeli affair. This is a personal affair of the Lubavitcher
> Rebbe. He is trying to use the Law of Return in order to discomfit
> Conservative and Reform Judaism. His concern is not the purity of
> immigrants to Israel, but rather the strength of Conservative and Re-
> form in America. This is an American affair which the Lubavitcher
> Rebbe is forcing upon Israel. . . . Israel is the battlefield; but the war is
> in America. . . . If the State of Israel declares that [our] conversion is no
> conversion, that means that [our] rabbis are no rabbis. This is the
> instrument through which the Lubavitcher Rebbe proposes to declare
> that Conservative and Reform Judaism in America are not authentic
> Judaism.[47]

Such debates signaled the rise of diasporic intervention in Israeli domestic and
foreign affairs and brought into the open the divergence between Diaspora
"hawks" and "doves" regarding the Oslo peace process.[48] Diaspora activists
fueled the sharp divide within Israel over the peace process, even to the point of
American ultra-Orthodox rabbis issuing rulings that sanctioned Israeli soldiers' insubordination and the assassination of Prime Minister Rabin in 1995.

Although the initial impetus for political battle over the legitimacy of non-
Orthodox Judaism came from the Diaspora, these issues took on a life of
their own in Israel, raised again under the Netanyahu government (1996–99),
which comprised an unprecedented number of religious party representatives.
In 1997 the Israeli religious establishment sought once again to enact a conversion law "designed to formalize and institutionalize the prevailing norm,
according to which the only acceptable conversions in Israel would be those
performed by Orthodox rabbinical authorities" and "delegitimize Reform and
Conservative rabbis."[49] This brought Israeli-Diaspora relations to their lowest
point. Although the conversion law was eventually suspended, the storm left a
lasting mark on Israel-Diaspora relations. It eroded further the posture of automatic Jewish American support of Israel in U.S. foreign policy. Thus, with
the increasing involvement of Jewish Americans, the Israeli *Kulturkampf* took
on an ever more complex international dimension.

Confronting the religious establishment inside Israel with outright
secularism—which denies Israel's Jewish character as a sine qua non of the
state's identity—seems unrealistic even to secularized and staunchly antireligious sectors of Israeli society. Thus when leading Israeli writers, like Amos
Oz, A. B. Yehoshua, Yehuda Amichai, and David Grossman, criticized what
they saw as the ultra-Orthodox attack on Israeli liberal-democratic institutions,
they called on Israelis to join the Reform and Conservative movements in order
to "save Judaism from the enemies of democracy" and to "generate a new dynamic which will renew Israel's spiritual and cultural landscape."[50] Yehoshua
added that "to stand with the Reform and Conservative movements is to defend ourselves."[51] Capping these trends, in 1999 Prime Minister Ehud Barak

appointed Israel's first Minister for Diaspora Affairs. When in November of that year the new Diaspora Minister Michael Melchior addressed the Jewish American General Assembly, he said that "the future of the Jewish people requires a new definition of the partnership between all Jews and finding common ground on the question of Jewish pluralism."[52]

In sum, when ultra-Orthodox and more liberal Jewish denominations in the United States and in Israel clash over the central question of who is a Jew, they are fighting not only to decide the character of the modern Jewish homeland but also over the right to claim and determine religious and national identity for Jews wherever they reside. It was at this juncture that a semantic change began to appear in the discourse over Israeli-Diaspora relations, with terms such as the negative *galut* (exile) and the more neutral *tfutzot* (Diaspora) being replaced by references to partnership with *ha'am hayehudi* (the Jewish people). This new approach was also behind the unprecedented financial backing (seventy million dollars) that the Israeli government provided to the Birthright Israel program. This program was initiated by diasporic philanthropists and is also supported by North American Jewry's communal institutions as an outreach effort to young people in the Diaspora "who have not been drawn into existing Jewish frameworks and may therefore soon be lost to the Jewish people."[53]

Jewish American Identity and Its Israeli Component

Given the complex ties between Israel and American Jewry that developed over the last two decades, it should be recalled that Israel was not always the main focus of American Jewish life. Although Zionism captured the imagination of many Jews in America, until World War II major Jewish groups—Reform, Orthodox, and socialists—were very hesitant or hostile regarding the idea Jewish nationalism. Moreover, even American Zionists rejected the idea that life in America is exilic or temporary; they held a new vision of a dual Jewish existence in two promised homelands that coexist and nurture each other. Ezra Mendelsohn observes that from the start American Zionism was "similar to other varieties of ethnic nationalism in America." It did not encourage American Jews to speak Hebrew or to return to the homeland, and, like other mobilized diasporas in the United States, it always stressed that support for Jewish nationalism was "in no way conflicting with [the Zionists'] intense Americanism at home, just as Americans of Irish origin who fought to oust England from Ireland were perfectly good Americans."[54]

To be sure, the divisions among American Jews over the legitimacy and necessity of the Zionist experiment in Palestine largely ended after the Holocaust and especially with the establishment of the state of Israel.[55] Even after the state was established, the Diaspora focused mainly on integrating itself and European Jewish newcomers into American society and on eradicating post-Holocaust American anti-Semitism. The three major Jewish defense groups—the Anti-Defamation League, the American Jewish Committee, and the American Jewish Congress—struggled against racial and ethnic stereotypes, in ways that helped establish universalistic liberalism as Jewish Americans' postwar ethnic identity. This emphasis on integration also did not leave much room to cope with the trauma of the Holocaust.

Even with the very real emotional attachment they felt for Israel, Jewish Americans feared that political expressions of support for the new state would bring charges of dual loyalty that could not be allowed. Indeed, Diaspora leaders forced Israel to recognize that for American Jews America is the promised land. A document negotiated between Israel's first Prime Minister, David Ben-Gurion, and Jacob Blaustein, then president of the American Jewish Committee, declared in 1950 that "the Jews in the United States, as a community and as individuals, have only one political attachment and that is to the United States. . . . They owe no political allegiance to Israel."[56]

Ben-Gurion's brand of Zionism largely ignored Jewish American contributions to Israel's War of Independence and relegated diasporic Zionist efforts, "no matter how . . . helpful they might be to the Jewish State, . . . [to] lower status in the hierarchy of Jewish values."[57] In turn, Jewish Americans believed that, unlike other Jewish centers in the world, their experience was not going to recede into insignificance, but would continue to develop alongside the newly established state. Nevertheless the definitions of this duality varied according to ideological camps. Regarding religious identity, from the beginning of the century until the 1950s, Jewish Americans were generally removed from regular religious observance and synagogue life. Only with the postwar move to suburbia did synagogues begin to grow and proliferate and Jewish community institutions to thrive. As religion took a more central place in American public life, Jews in suburban America began to enter mainstream American society. The social radicalism of the second generation of descendants of Jewish immigrants did not find favor among the third generation that came of age at this time. This new generation, following the pattern of their non-Jewish neighbors, expressed a greater interest in the religious element of their identity, but in a distinctly American way. Synagogue services and organizational structures borrowed heavily from Protestant practices, with the creation of Sunday schools, sisterhoods, and so on. Altogether, the return to religious worship, based in large part on a search for roots and authenticity that could in other circumstances have denoted a retreat into cultural isolationism, became a clear signal of Jewish acculturation and integration into the broader society, which adopted religious practices informed by American values. American Judaism at this juncture had little to do with Israel, a stance that was reinforced by the often hostile policy of the Eisenhower administration toward the homeland.[58] Even further, organized Jewish lobbying for Israel did not come into its own until the early 1960s. The growing legitimacy of ethnicity in American public life in the 1960s led to the growing politicization of U.S. Jews and brought to the fore the diasporic component of their identity. The openness of American society and the assertion of identity that came with it had several important influences on the community, leading to changes among American Jews that would soon have significant political repercussions. On the one hand, Jewish intermarriage rates, which had held steady at 4%–6% for half a century, rose dramatically from 1965, reaching 30% in 1974 and more than 50% by the mid-1980s.[59] On the other hand, differences of many kinds became more acceptable in American society, in ways that enabled younger Jews to claim their distinctiveness in a bolder manner than their parents' generation had done. This was also the period when Jewish day schools throughout the United States began to proliferate, including the Conservative and Reform movements, whose leaders gradually subscribed to the Orthodox view "that only through day school education can Judaism survive [in the United States]."[60] The effects of general social change were also reflected in the push for gender desegregation, leading Jewish women to challenge traditional practices and claim roles as cantors and rabbis. At the same time Jewish Orthodoxy also gained confidence, "in sharp contrast to the timidity that often characterized the movement in the first two thirds of this century."[61] Its younger representatives were no longer hesitant to express opposition to liberal Judaism, including the separation of synagogue and state, "the hallmark of American Jewry."[62]

This activism found a new outlet in the energy and emotions that the Eichmann trial and the 1967 war released among Jewish Americans, which were channeled into the establishment of pro-Israeli organizations and the reorganization of traditional Jewish American institutions with greater emphasis on the Israeli dimension. Israel's victory also helped American Jews to finally begin the process of reckoning with the Holocaust. "Their psychologically empowering discovery . . . [that there would be] no annihilation of the Jews at this time, not in the face of superior Jewish armed forces" was so cathartic that they were finally able to confront this existential trauma. The Diaspora's ability to embrace both the Holocaust and Israel was augmented by America's domestic developments as "Jews ceased to be a (sort of) race (somewhat) apart, and became (white) Americans—not as mere assimilationist but with vehement reference to Israel and to the Holocaust."[63] Israel grew more dependent on American support, and assumption of a strategic alliance with the United States made Jewish Americans more important to the maintenance of Jewish existence in the homeland and gave them a strong and clear purpose around which to lobby and organize. They underwent "a kind of a mass conversion to Zionism, and the UJA, through Israel, evolved into 'America's Jewish religion.'"[64] The new role of Israel provided Conservative and Reform Jewish Americans more secular alternatives to Orthodox categories of Judaism. For Reform Jews in particular, this was a significant departure from their earlier opposition to Zionism and part of their recognition that their fate as Diaspora Jews was intimately—and legitimately—intertwined with that of the state of Israel. These developments also raised questions as to the political implications of their faith.

The 1967 war was also significant for ethnic relations within the United States. The war and its aftermath were major causes of a fundamental political and social realignment among groups that had previously fought as a united front in favor of civil rights and the general advancement of minorities. Many Jewish Americans distanced themselves from their previous partners in the desegregation movement and the American left. Israel-bashing, especially among radical black activists and the "new left," was generally perceived by Jewish Americans as a barely disguised form of anti-Semitism. The shock of the 1973 Yom Kippur War heightened Jewish sensitivity to the continued insecurity of Jews. A significant and highly visible minority of Jewish Americans and Jewish organizations began to move rightward politically, a phenomenon which had been virtually unimaginable ten or twenty years before. One indication of the move rightward was the Jewish approach to the Jackson-Vanik Amendment, which linked the issue of trade with the Soviet Union to Soviet willingness to permit Jewish emigration and which ran counter to the spirit of detente. The effort to free Soviet Jews gave American anti-communism "a new moral argument" and increased Jewish American clout in U.S. foreign policy. This higher profile was enhanced by Jewish American campaigns against the Arab economic boycott of Israel and against the anti-Zionist propaganda prevalent among third world and communist countries, which culminated in the 1975 U.N. vote equating Zionism with racism.[65]

The new Diaspora-Israeli alliance pushed aside the Israeli demands from Jewish Americans to immigrate. The dilemma of Israel's democratic character and its contentious treatment of the Palestinian issue was minimized when safeguarding Israel's existence was at stake. From the late 1970s, however, with the rise to power of the Likud Party and the growing divisions within Israel regarding peace, diasporic political positions became more diverse. These divisions were encouraged by Israeli efforts to establish Jewish American counterparts in the United States that as "Friends of ——" raised funds and lobbied to support their political agenda in Israel, in effect expanding their constituencies to include nonvoters in the Diaspora. It was at this juncture that liberal Jewish Americans established the New Israel Fund to promote a liberal agenda for Israeli politics and society. This organization represented an early departure from the traditional patterns of Jewish American giving to the United Jewish Appeal toward nonstate institutional frameworks.

Although the internal diasporic rift was largely kept quiet, it surfaced whenever the American government collided with Israel's Likud-led government. This was the case with the 1982 Reagan plan; more dramatically with the issue of loan guarantees under the George H. W. Bush administration in 1991 and 1992; and throughout this period with the controversial subject of settlements in the occupied territories. Yet, when criticism of Israel came from sources traditionally, or even categorically, seen as hostile to Israel or to Jews in general, American Jews were generally reluctant to accede. In an environment of broadly based and harsh criticism by the United States, other governments, the media, and other institutions, most American Jewish spokespeople declined to give what they saw as aid and comfort to enemies of Jews and of Israel.[66] By the late 1980s, as the question of Israel's moral standing became increasingly disputed, many Jewish Americans felt that Israeli affairs might jeopardize their own standing in America. The 1985 Pollard Affair, in which an American Jewish intelligence analyst was convicted of spying for Israel, was deeply disturbing to Jewish Americans. They were shocked to discover how Israel's actions could quickly expose them to the old charge of double loyalty.

Israel's controversial relationship with South Africa's apartheid regime also increased the tensions between Israel and the Diaspora by exacerbating tensions between Jews and African Americans in the United States. With the first Palestinian *intifada*, the diversification and erosion of Jewish American support for Israel became evident.[67]

By 1990 the deep penetration of Israel into Jewish American life and organizational structures raised concerns about Israeli meddling and manipulating of Jewish American affairs.[68] Looking from an Israeli foreign policy perspective, in 1990 it seemed that an "Israel-centric perspective" in mobilizing the Diaspora reached a dangerous level when American Israel Public Affairs Committee and other Jewish organizations felt so empowered that they began to adopt an independent foreign policy agenda in the Middle East.[69] Remarking on the Israeli government's pressure on American Jewry to stand behind the homeland, even against the U.S. government official position, David Vital writes that "Israel and its affairs tend to continuously rob [Jewish Americans] of their long sought for and so very recently acquired peace of mind."[70]

By 2000 many Orthodox Jewish American articulated disappointment with the pronounced secularist shift in Israeli society, which for them was reinforced by the widespread willingness to give up the West Bank and parts of East Jerusalem. Even modern Orthodox—who uphold halachic theology but also allow for Western democratic norms and values in their daily life and espouse the Zionist vision without its messianic elements—became disillusioned with what they saw as liberal post-Zionist reluctance to preserve the Jewishness of Israel. Norman Lamm, president of Yeshiva University and an important voice of modern Orthodoxy in the United States, draws a direct parallel between the "demographic and cultural catastrophe" brought on American Jewry by the lax practices of the Reform and (less so) Conservative Judaism and the deleterious impact of Israel's post-Zionists on Israel's loss of its Jewish character.[71]

Ironically, just at the time when it seemed that in Israel moderate Orthodox forces were on the verge of losing the Israeli *Kulturkampf* to both secularists and post-Zionists on the left and extreme religious nationalists and the ultra-Orthodox on the right, America embraced a modern Orthodox candidate for the vice presidency. These developments prompted some Orthodox leaders inside the United States to contemplate how to better build the future of their vibrant community by developing an "improved" brand of a modern Jew on American soil, rather than directing their energies toward the biblical homeland. Even more ironically, such rethinking came at a time when non-Orthodox Jewish Americans work harder than ever before to expand their message into Israeli society.

Throughout the Oslo peace process, leaders of the American Jewish community acted as unofficial emissaries in the efforts to open new diplomatic channels to countries that had no diplomatic relations with Israel, to lift the Arab boycott, to reward Arab and Islamic states which normalized relations with the Jewish state, and to encourage others to do the same.[72] Many Reform and Conservative Jews promoted a Palestinian-Israeli rapprochement because they viewed the Israeli occupation of the West Bank and Gaza as belying the liberal political principles they championed in the United States and which, they argued, were the foundation of Israel's natural and close alliance with the United States. These movements saw the era of peace as an opportunity to disseminate their American views of a multifaceted Jewish identity inside Israel and to bring their vision of Jewish pluralism to the Israeli public, which is already more eager for greater openness. Yet the fact that Reform Judaism in the United States, and its extension in Israel, allied itself with the Israeli peace camp (i.e., the Israeli left) and ascribed much importance to its positions on peace with the Palestinians as part of its religious creed alienated some of its potential constituents among the Russian immigrants. Dimitri Slivniak, an astute observer of Russian immigrants' life in Israel, argues that this liberal tradition represents "a different cultural and social environment, not ours"— and expresses American-inspired "politically correct" positions. This American liberalism on the Arab-Israeli conflict was inconsistent with the views of many Russian immigrations. These attitudes are unattractive to post-Soviet Jews who are staunchly liberal in their religious orientations and in their belief in the market economy, but have a more conservative, right-wing outlook on security and cultural matters more in tune with American neoconservatives.[73]

All in all, by 2000 the diverse American Orthodox camp was divided between two poles: the moderates who considered religious imposition inside Israel as "ideologically dubious and pragmatically unwise" and the more ardent group that declared the old alliance with secular Zionism defunct.[74] Some in the latter camp even began to question the centrality of Israel to their Jewish theology to the point of embracing the prenationalist *haredi* approach. This spectrum of views is visible in the Orthodox Union, the leading Orthodox organization in the United States. In 1996 the organization attempted to strengthen its own vision of Jewish identity in Israel by creating a branch of the American National Conference of Synagogue Youth, aimed at "combating the trends of Americanization, secularization, and alienation." This organization also targeted "semireligious" youth and Russian immigrants in secular Israeli cities.

When Security Overshadows Identity

By 2000 the Jewish *Kulturkampf*, both within and outside Israel, reshaped the relationship between Israel and the Diaspora in several ways. First, the peace process and the widespread notion of increasing normality widened the gulf between Jewish universalists and Jewish particularists. As identities were pushed to the fore, the splits within Israel regarding the direction of peace negotiations further divided American Jews over their vision for U.S. Middle East policy.[75] When in summer 2000 Prime Minister Barak negotiated with Palestinian leader Yasser Arafat at Camp David, Jewish American leaders issued conflicting messages both supporting and opposing the Israeli government's position. The issues that divided Israel became resonant within the Diaspora, and a new symbiosis between diasporic organizations and domestic Israeli social and political formations solidified, which served the Jewish identity interests of groups both inside and outside Israel. Conversely, many Israeli groups actively recruited Jewish allies in the Diaspora to buttress their domestic political and social agendas and, consequently, pushed Diaspora voices to the center of the Israeli *Kulturkampf*, with particular emphasis on the question of religious pluralism. A third development was a growing assessment within the Diaspora that Israel remained a very important factor for their own identity in the United States and that they have a vested interest in the evolution of the Israeli polity—a development that reflected their own worldview on religious pluralism, security issues, and sociopolitical affairs.

With the notion that "Israel is no longer waging an existential battle for its survival ... against an external enemy," a 2000 Jewish Agency for Israel study chronicled the vast proliferation of largely Diaspora-supported voluntary enterprises which had become so visible in the struggle to shape Israeli-Jewish identity.[76] In sum, the core of support for Israel remained, and there had not been a reduction of interest in Israeli affairs. On the contrary, a desire for reinvigoration and intensification of the Jewish American-Israeli relationship surfaced on both sides, albeit marked by a comprehensive transformation of kinship affinity.

The crushing failure of the Oslo peace process and the waves of violence that ensued dramatically shifted the focus from identity back to existential security. To some extent reminiscent of the shock of the 1967 war, almost overnight both the internal and international Jewish *Kulturkampf* ceased as the community reunified and recreated solidarity to face the new threat. When the Barak government appeared to be willing to compromise Jewish sovereignty in Jerusalem, some observers expressed their concern "that a hand-over of the Temple Mount and parts of Jerusalem threatens to undermine the Jewish identity of American Jews and tear away the already delicate fabric of their relationship with Israel."[77] Indeed, many in the Diaspora were adamant that the Temple Mount was the inheritance of all Jews and must be discussed within the wider Jewish community rather than solely by the Israeli government. Their position was reinforced when Arafat made Jerusalem into a Muslim-Jewish battle. Malcolm Hoenlein, the executive vice chairman of the Conference of Presidents, stated, "Israel has a right to make decisions that affect its security. All Jews have a right to discuss it, but it's up to the government of Israel. The Temple Mount is a different issue. It belongs to all Jews, it is the inheritance of all Jews, and all Jews have vested interests in it."[78] Even within the Conservative movement, there was vocal disagreement over the issue of Jerusalem, with American members refusing to accept the idea of their left-leaning counterparts in Israel that a compromise over the Temple Mount was only a political matter rather than a core religious identity one.[79]

The events of 9/11 and the emergence of violent terrorist threats on U.S. soil brought the security dilemma home to American Jews and made the American-Israeli nexus of Jewish security closer than ever before. Widespread

Arab/Muslim defamation of Jews as perpetrators behind the attacks further amplified this new sense of threat and solidarity.[80] Even younger, highly assimilated American Jews were awakened to the reemergence of the Jewish security dilemma and to the subtle interconnections between anti-Americanism and anti-Semitism. One young Jewish American writer, who was suddenly reminded of his own father's flight from Nazism, wrote in the *New York Times Magazine*, "Arab governments have transformed Israel into an outpost of malevolent world Jewry, viewing Israelis and Jews as interchangeable emblems of cosmic evil."[81] In this time of peril, the debates over identity were once again trumped by Jewish existential questions.

Conclusion

The Jewish condition today is fundamentally different than a century ago. It is no longer characterized by deep divisions between and within proponents and opponents of Jewish sovereignty. Ezra Mendelsohn is correct when he writes that the simplicity of Jewish politics today derives from the fact that nationalism has triumphed over all other diasporic solutions. The antimodern ultra-Orthodox, the Jewish left and the cultural Bundists, the liberal assimilationists and the Jewish cosmopolitans, the local nationalists and anti-Zionist Reform integrationists—all believed (until World War II) that the "Jewish question" must find its solution in the lands of the dispersion. Yet in the post–1948 era all aspects of Jewish life, above all, Jewish politics, are tied to "the growing hegemony of Israel":

> In Jewish politics, as in the politics of so many groups in the twentieth century, the nation-state has enjoyed great triumph, even if it is not entirely victorious. The cosmopolitan, culturally and religiously divided Jewish people is united today in support of the Hebrew-speaking Jewish nation-state where an ever-growing number of Jews actually lives, and where many more visit in order to gain inspiration.[82]

Despite the growing hegemony of Israel for Jewish identity and consciousness worldwide, this influence is far from being total. At the beginning of the twenty-first century the Jewish world remains bifurcated between Israel and the United States, with Jewish populations of approximately five and a half million in each center. Given this reality, all other Diaspora centers are secondary or marginal in negotiating Jewish identity. However, the situation of American Jews is somewhat anomalous. Their external environment is rarely hostile—and never overtly so. The comfortable and influential status they have achieved in their country is arguably as consequential for world Jewry as the resumption of Jewish sovereignty in Israel. To begin with, the prosperity of Jewish Americans has enabled them to assume a world leadership role by providing smaller Jewish communities elsewhere with everything from educational funding and leadership training to political intercession on behalf of

Jewish human rights. Yet, the same prosperity that enables them to assist external Jewish communities is not without its own considerable inconveniences. Or more precisely, the perception abroad of that prosperity and its attendant benefits lead to considerable inconveniences for the Jewish communities that enjoy its largesse. The perceptions of excessive Jewish power in America have been especially acute in recent years when characteristically shrill and hysterical voices attribute to American Jews authorship of U.S. foreign policy in many domains. Though the impact of Israel and American Jewry on the two million to three million Jews residing in other countries is often direct and powerful, there is no formal mechanism for consultation among these communities. As a result, communication and cooperation is often ad hoc and haphazard. The question of Jewish identity—religious, ethnic, or national—remains entangled with the question of Jewish power and security in Israel and the United States. Other Jews may continue to face peril and other challenges related to identity and security in their countries of domicile, but the two large centers dominate their voices or even speak on their behalf.

For diasporas which are part of the rich and accommodating tapestry of American society, the difficulty of maintaining the content of their respective ethnocultural and religious identities in America has led to an increasing dependence on ties to the homeland for identity sustenance. This interaction is particularly powerful and durable when diasporic and homeland (ethnonational) identities are strongly linked with religious affiliation, as in the case of the Hindus, Punjabi Sikhs, Catholic Poles, Irish, Armenians, and Jews vis-à-vis Israel. The saliency of the religious component in the identity of these groups is strengthened by its ties to their ethnonational origin and the strong resonance of a homeland, which is deeply intertwined in the religion. In the American context, the religious component of these diasporic identities is also embellished because other ideational components and forces of communal cohesion—ethnicity, language, geography, and nationalism, which form the core of identity inside the homeland—are constantly eroded in the face of a strong assimilationist culture. In addition, in the current U.S. context, religion is appreciated and culturally valued much more than ethnicity.

We may be seeing a new kinship vision emerging out of a transnational struggle for Jewish pluralism. This vision seems to affirm the old American Zionist formula in which the Jewish American community is not to be subsumed into or subordinated to the Israeli homeland. Rather, the two communities are to live side by side in a symbiotic relationship of mutual influences. As early as 1914, when future Supreme Court Justice Louis Brandeis assumed leadership of the American Zionist organization, he said: "To be good Americans, we must be better Jews, and to be better Jews we must become Zionists."[83] Whereas previously Israeli Zionism demanded a privileged Israeli voice in defining Jewish interests and identity, now not only does the Diaspora largely determine its own way of life in America, but it has also demanded and gradually gained access to a voice in Israeli Jewish affairs. This new Zionist vision of reciprocity strengthens both pillars of world Jewry today in America and Israel, while simultaneously encouraging their kinship solidarity. Thus, against the thesis regarding the growing separation between Israel and the Diaspora, on the contrary, one sees a new affirmation, intensification, and redefinition of Jewish kinship.

NOTES

1. Naftali Rothenberg, "Jews in Israel and the United States: Diverging Identities," in *Jewish Survival: The Identity Problem at the Close of the Twentieth Century*, ed. Ernest Krausz and Gitta Tulea (New Brunswick, NJ: Transaction, 1999), 166–67. See also Steven T. Rosenthal, *Irreconcilable Differences? The Waning of the American Jewish Love Affairs with Israel* (Hanover, NH: Brandeis University Press, 2001).

2. Jerome A. Chanes, "Who Does What? Jewish Advocacy and Jewish 'Interest,'" in *Jews in American Politics*, ed. L. Sandy Maisel and Ira N. Forman (Lanham, MD: Rowman & Littlefield, 2001), 101.

3. See, for example, Ephraim Yuchtman-Yaar and Yochanan Peres, *Between Consent and Dissent: Democracy and Peace in the Israeli Mind* (Lanham, MD: Rowman & Littlefield, 2000), 162–63; and Arian Asher, *The Second Republic: Politics in Israel* (Chatham, NJ: Chatham, 1998), 10.

4. For an excellent analysis of the dynamics of the ultra-Orthodox economy, see Eli Berman, "Sect, Subsidy, and Sacrifice: An Economist's View of Ultra-Orthodox Jews" (unpublished paper, 1999).

5. Ari Shavit, "A Jewish Soul," *Ha'aretz Magazine*, Feb. 2004.

6. Arian, *Second Republic*, 3.

7. Rabin was assassinated in November 1995 by Yigal Amir, a young Israeli religious nationalist student who was influenced by rabbinic authorities of his camp (in Israel and the United States) that articulated the view that by agreeing to relinquish segments of the Holy Land to Gentiles Rabin was deemed *rodef* and *moser*—two obscure halachic precepts that made the prime minister liable to be killed. See Milton Viorst, *What Shall I Do with This People? Jews and the Fractious Politics of Judaism* (New York: Free Press, 2002), 239–42; and Martin Kramer, "The Middle East, Old and New," *Daedalus* 126.2 (Spring 1997): 94.

8. *Ha'aretz*, June 26, 2000.

9. *Ha'aretz*, Oct. 5, 2000.

10. For a discussion of these early efforts, see Zalman Abramov, *Perpetual Dilemma: Jewish Religion in the Jewish State* (Cranbury, NJ: Associated University Press, 1976), 375–76.

11. Ibid., 206.

12. Alan M. Dershowitz puts forward the "Jewish question" for the twenty-first century as "Can we survive our success?" He writes: "The good news is the American Jews—as *individuals*—have never been more secure, more affluent, and less victimized by discrimination or anti-Semitism. The bad news is that American Jews—as a *people*—have never been in greater danger of disappearing through assimilation, intermarriage, and low birth rates"; *The Vanishing American Jew: In Search of Jewish Identity for the Next Century* (Boston: Little, Brown, 1997), 1.

13. For the debate over the study of Jewish American demography and the different interpretations of population surveys, see Bernard Wasserstein, "Post-Diaspora Jewry and Post-Zionist Israel" (paper presented at the international conference entitled "Diasporas: Transnational Identities and the Politics of the Homeland," University of California, Berkeley, Nov. 12–13, 1999).

14. Egon Mayer, Barry Kosmin, and Ariela Keysar, *American Jewish Identity Survey, 2001* (New York: Graduate Center of the City University of New York, 2001).

15. Sidney Goldstein, "Profile of American Jewry: Insights from the 1990 National Jewish Population Survey," in *American Jewish Year Book*, vol. 92: *1992*, ed. David Singer and Ruth R. Seldin (New York: American Jewish Committee, 1992), 12–132.

16. Interview with Rabbi Ammiel Hirsh, Dec. 29, 1999.

17. David Abel, "Jews Find New Meaning in Ritual," *Boston Globe*, Dec. 5, 2001, B1.

18. Cited in Jonathan D. Sarna, *American Judaism: A History* (New Haven: Yale University Press, 2004), 326.

19. See Ori Z. Soltes, "Memory, Tradition, and Revival: Mapping and Identifying the Political Structure of the Jewish Community Worldwide," in *Occasional Papers on Jewish Civilization, Israel, and the Diaspora* (Washington, DC: Program for Jewish Civilization, Georgetown University, 2005), 14.

20. Daniel Levy and Natan Sznaider, *The Holocaust and Memory in the Global Age* (Philadelphia: Temple University, 2006).

21. The term is borrowed from Robert Wuthnow.

22. See Avi Beker, "A Different Model of a Jew," *Ha'aretz* (Hebrew edition), Aug. 14, 2000, B2.

23. Conor Cruise O'Brien, *God Land: Reflections on Religion and Nationalism* (Cambridge: Harvard University Press, 1987), 3.

24. Joseph Dan, "Jewish Sovereignty as a Theological Problem," *Azure* 16 (Winter 2004): 123–24.

25. Bernard Wasserstein, "The Politics of Holiness in Jerusalem," *Chronicle Review*, Sept. 21, 2001 (= section 2 of *Chronicle of Higher Education*).

26. Joseph B. Soloveitchik, *Fate and Destiny: From the Holocaust to the State of Israel* (Hoboken, NJ: Ktav, 2000).

27. While fewer than 10% of American Jews are Orthodox, they comprise over 80% of American immigrants; Yair Sheleg, "The North American Impact on Israel Orthodoxy" (New York: American Jewish Committee, 1999), foreword.

28. See "American Jewish Attitudes towards Israel and the Peace Process" (public opinion survey conducted for the American Jewish Committee by Markets Facts, Aug. 7–15, 1995), 63.

29. See statement by the Central Conference of American Rabbis, May 1999, http://ccarnet.org/index.cfm?. For the opinions of the two leading shapers of the political ideology of the Reform movement on this issue, see Albert Vorspan and David Saperstein, *Jewish Dimensions of Social Justice: Tough Moral Choices of Our Time* (New York: Union of American Hebrew Congregations Press, 1998), 137.

30. Electronic Newsletter of the World Union for Progressive Judaism, *WUPJ News* 9 (March 11, 1999).

31. See Harvey Meirovich, "The Shaping of the Masorti Movement in Israel" (New York: American Jewish Committee, 1999), 6.

32. Asher Arian, *Politics in Israel: The Second Generation* (Chatham, NJ: Chatham, 1985), 5.

33. For the best book on the subject, see Charles S. Liebman and Eliezer Don-Yehiya, *Civil Religion in Israel* (Berkeley: University of California Press, 1983). For an analysis of how the civil religion helped in creating Israel's perceived sense of "exceptionalism" and the implications of this collective identity for the foundation of Israel's national security, see Gil Merom, "Israel's National Security and the Myth of Exceptionalism," *Political Science Quarterly* 114.3 (Fall 1999): 409–93.

34. Baruch Kimmerling, "Between Hegemony and Dormant *Kulturkampf* in Israel," in *In Search of Identity: Jewish Aspects of Israeli Culture*, ed. Dan Urian and Efraim Karsh (London: Cass, 1999), 49–72.

35. Peter Berkowitz, "A Dramatic Struggle over Self-Definition," *Wall Street Journal*, June 1, 2000, A20.

36. See Yoav Peled, "Towards a Redefinition of Jewish Nationalism in Israel? The Enigma of Shas," *Ethnic and Racial Studies* 21.4 (July 1998): 703.

37. Bernard Susser and Charles S. Liebman, *Choosing Survival: Strategies for a Jewish Future* (Oxford: Oxford University Press, 1999), 94.

38. See Elan Ezrachi, "Jewish Renaissance and Renewal in Israel: A Report of the Dorot and Nathan Cummings Foundation" (Jan. 2001), 18.

39. See the statement by Samuel H. Sislen, executive director of the Masorti Foundation for Conservative Judaism in Israel, in "Strengthening Israel, Strengthening Conservative Judaism," *Women's League Outlook* (Fall 1999).

40. See Ellen Schnitser, "The Impact of American Liberal Jewish Identity in Israel: The Case Study of Russian Speaking Immigrants" (unpublished paper, Tel Aviv University, April 2003).

41. In November 1999, activists of the General Assembly of America's Jewry held in Atlanta, moved to establish a single umbrella organization, the United Jewish Communities. In what was described by one Israeli journalist as "more than a bureaucratic upheaval," the new body took aim at redirecting funds to bolster Jewish identity in a process that empowers U.S.-based local federations and gives them greater say over spending in Israel. The new body unified all Jewish communities across America—through a merger of the United Jewish Appeal, the United Israel Appeal, and the Council of Jewish Federations. See Nitzan Horowitz, "Historic Assembly to Be a Melting Pot, as U.S. Jewish Organizations Merge," *Ha'aretz*, Nov. 17, 1999; and Marilyn Henry, "GA Ends with United Body, Divisive Issues," *Jerusalem Post*, Nov. 21, 1999.

42. See Nir Boms, "Redefining Israel: The Changing American-Jewish Community of Israel as Indicated by Changes in Jewish-American Philanthropy" (MA thesis, University of Maryland/Baltimore Hebrew University, 2000), 98.

43. Yossi Shalom and Shahar Ilan, "Chief Rabbi: Holocaust Pales Next to Reform," *Ha'aretz*, Jan. 26, 1999, 1.

44. Jack Wertheimer, "Judaism without Limits," *Commentary* 104.1 (July 1997): 24.

45. With the rise of intermarriages among Jews in the United States, American Reform rabbis have eased the difficult process of Jewish conversion in order to enable tens of thousands of American Gentiles to become Jewish. The Orthodox do not recognize these conversions and regard Reform and Conservative converts as non-Jews; J. J. Goldberg, *Jewish Power: Inside the American Jewish Establishment* (Reading, MA: Addison-Wesley, 1996), 338.

46. According to Goldberg (ibid., 338), the Lubavitcher Rebbe "had built a powerful trans-Atlantic political machine to press his view on a reluctant Israeli Orthodox political establishment. They in turn, had pressured [Prime Minister] Shamir."

47. David Landau, "Who Is a Jew? A Case Study of American Jewish Influence on Israeli Policy" (New York: American Jewish Committee, 1996), 10–11.

48. While the vast majority of Israeli Orthodox and ultra-Orthodox (about 80%) reject the idea of a Palestinian state in the occupied territories, a large majority of "nonobservant" (75%) or "somewhat-observant" (62%) Israeli Jews support such an outcome as part of a permanent agreement. These divisions resemble those within the

Diaspora. See Asher Arian, "Israeli Public Opinion on National Security" (Tel Aviv: Jaffe Center for Strategic Studies, Aug. 1999), 46.

49. Abraham Ben Zvi, "Partnership under Stress: The American Jewish Community and Israel" (Tel Aviv: Jaffe Center for Strategic Studies, Aug. 1998), 35.

50. For the statement, see Shahar Ilan, "Progressive Jews: 'What Synagogue Are We Not Going To?'" Ha'aretz (English edition), Feb. 21, 1999, 6.

51. Cited in Rabbi G. Hirsch's keynote address, published in the Electronic Newsletter of the World Union for Progressive Judaism, Special Convention Issue (March 11, 1999), 5. The writers were attacked vehemently by secular Israelis who argue that by endorsing Reform and Conservative Judaism and by calling on Israelis to join these movements, they were undermining the vision of a secular/humanistic Jewish-Israeli movement. For A. B. Yehoshua's response to these charges, see Free Judaism 14 (April 1999): 38 (Hebrew).

52. Cited in the periodical report of the Minister of Diaspora and Social Affairs, Jerusalem (Feb. 20, 2000).

53. Cited in "Making Meaning: Participants' Experience of Birthright Israel" (Maurice and Marilyn Cohen Center for Modern Jewish Studies, Brandeis University, Nov. 2000), 1.

54. Ezra Mendelsohn, On Modern Jewish Politics (New York: Oxford University Press, 1993), 79, 133.

55. Jewish Americans organized large rallies on behalf of the new state, pleaded with the Truman government to recognize and stand behind it, and raised tens of million of dollars for arms procurement in support of its 1948 war efforts. See David Schoenbaum, The United States and the State of Israel (Oxford: Oxford University Press, 1993), 58–62. For a discussion of the Jewish American role in President Truman's decision to accord recognition to the state of Israel, see Alexander DeConde, Ethnicity, Race, and American Foreign Policy: A History (Boston: Northeastern University Press, 1992), 131–36.

56. Schoenbaum, United States and the State of Israel, 64.

57. Arthur Hertzberg, "Israel and the Diaspora: A Relationship Reexamined," Israel Affairs 2.3–4 (Spring/Summer 1996): 172.

58. Abraham Ben Zvi, Decade of Transition: Eisenhower, Kennedy, and the Origins of the American-Israeli Alliance (New York: Columbia University Press, 1998), 56–57, 96.

59. See "Jewish-Americans beyond the Pale," Economist, Nov. 2, 1991, 29.

60. Jonathan D. Sarna and David G. Dalin, Religion and State in the American Jewish Experience (Notre Dame: University of Notre Dame Press, 1997), 246.

61. Samuel C. Heilman, Portrait of American Jews: The Last Half of the 20th Century (Seattle: University of Washington Press, 1995), 146.

62. Sarna and Dalin, Religion and State, 262.

63. Paul Breines, "Deliver Us from Evil," Washington Post Book World, Feb. 4, 2001, 13. For a critical treatment of such Holocaust-related dynamics, see Peter Novick, The Holocaust in American Life (New York: Houghton Mifflin, 1999).

64. Menahem Kaufman, "Envisaging Israel: The Case of the United Jewish Appeal," in Envisioning Israel: The Changing Ideals and Images of North American Jews, ed. Allon Gal (Jerusalem: Magnes, 1996), 222.

65. Reform leader Albert Vorspan writes that the U.N. decision "made all Jews consider themselves Zionists"; see Great Jewish Debates and Dilemmas: Jewish Perspectives on Moral Issues in Conflict in the Eighties (New York: Union of American Hebrew Congregations, 1980), 19.

66. Charles S. Liebman, "Israel in the Mind of American Jews," in *Israel and Diaspora Jewry: Ideological and Political Perspectives*, ed. Eliezer Don-Yehiya (Jerusalem: Bar-Ilan University Press, 1991), 34.

67. For an extensive treatment of the widening gulf between Israeli and American Jews since the 1980s, see Rosenthal, *Irreconcilable Differences?*

68. By that time a web of over seventy pro-Israel political action committees had been established which channeled $4.7 million to pro-Israel candidates during the 1987–88 election cycle. See Stuart E. Eisenstat, "Loving Israel—Warts and All," *Foreign Policy* 81 (Winter 1990–91): 93.

69. Aaron S. Klieman, *Israel and the World after 40 Years* (Washington, DC: Pergamon-Brassey, 1990), 178.

70. David Vital, *The Future of the Jews: A People at the Crossroads* (Cambridge: Harvard University Press, 1990), 136.

71. David Landau, "The Voice of Post-Tolerance," *Ha'aretz* (Hebrew edition), Oct. 17, 1996.

72. Janine Zacharia, "The Unofficial Ambassadors of the Jewish State," *Jerusalem Post*, April 2, 2000, 1.

73. Dimitri Slivanik, "Emigration according to Herzel," *Eretz Acheret* 19 (Nov.–Dec. 2003): 18–21 (Hebrew).

74. The more ardent group advocates a balance between civil and religious life in Israel based on the idea that the "ways of the Torah are ways of pleasantness and all its pathways are peace." See David Berger, "Reflections on the State of Religious Zionism," *Jewish Action* 60.1 (Fall 1999): 12–15.

75. For a detailed discussion of this phenomenon, see Jonathan Broder, "Netanyahu and American Jews," *World Policy Journal* 15.1 (Spring 1998): 89–98.

76. "The Many Faces of Judaism in Israel: Mapping Jewish Unity Organizations" (Jewish Agency for Israel, 2000), 3.

77. Tamar Hausman, "Sacrifice of Temple Mt. 'Risks Ties to U.S. Jews,'" *Ha'aretz*, Jan. 5, 2001.

78. Cited in *Jerusalem Report*, Aug. 28, 2000, 56.

79. See Gail Lichtman, "Mounting Temple Controversy," *Jerusalem Post Magazine*, Jan. 26, 2001, 10–13.

80. A survey conducted by the *Forward* found that 75% of American Jews felt more threatened than they did prior to 9/11, and half of these Jews cited their Jewishness as the reason for their increased fear; see Eliahu Salpeter, "World Jewry and the War against Global Terrorism," *Ha'aretz*, Nov. 7, 2001.

81. Jonathan Rosen, "The Uncomfortable Question of Anti-Semitism," *New York Times Magazine*, Nov. 4, 2001, 48.

82. Mendelsohn, *On Modern Jewish Politics*, 144–45.

83. Cited in Robert A. Burt, "On the Bench: The Jewish Justices," in *Jews in American Politics*, ed. L. Sandy Maisel and Ira N. Forman (Lanham, MD: Rowman & Littlefield, 2001), 69.

BIBLIOGRAPHY

Abramov, Zalman. *Perpetual Dilemma: Jewish Religion in the Jewish State*. Cranbury, NJ: Associated University Press, 1976.
"American Jewish Attitudes towards Israel and the Peace Process." Public opinion survey conducted for the American Jewish Committee by Markets Facts, Aug. 7–15, 1995.

Arian, Asher. "Israeli Public Opinion on National Security." Tel Aviv: Jaffe Center for
    Strategic Studies, Aug. 1999.
———. *Politics in Israel: The Second Generation*. Chatham, NJ: Chatham, 1985.
———. *The Second Republic: Politics in Israel*. Chatham, NJ: Chatham, 1998.
Ben Zvi, Abraham. *Decade of Transition: Eisenhower, Kennedy, and the Origins of the
    American-Israeli Alliance*. New York: Columbia University Press, 1998.
———. "Partnership under Stress: The American Jewish Community and Israel." Tel
    Aviv: Jaffe Center for Strategic Studies, Aug. 1998.
Berger, David. "Reflections on the State of Religious Zionism." *Jewish Action* 60.1 (Fall
    1999): 12–15.
Berman, Eli. "Sect, Subsidy, and Sacrifice: An Economist's View of Ultra-Orthodox
    Jews." Unpublished paper, Boston University, National Bureau of Economic
    Research, 1999.
Boms, Nir. "Redefining Israel: The Changing American-Jewish Community of Israel
    as Indicated by Changes in Jewish-American Philanthropy." MA thesis, Univer-
    sity of Maryland/Baltimore Hebrew University, 2000.
Broder, Jonathan. "Netanyahu and American Jews." *World Policy Journal* 15.1 (Spring
    1998): 89–98.
Burt, Robert A. "On the Bench: The Jewish Justices." In *Jews in American Politics*.
    Edited by L. Sandy Maisel and Ira N. Forman. Lanham, MD: Rowman &
    Littlefield, 2001.
Chanes, Jerome A. "Who Does What? Jewish Advocacy and Jewish Interest." In *Jews in
    American Politics*. Edited by L. Sandy Maisel and Ira N. Forman. Lanham, MD:
    Rowman & Littlefield, 2001.
DeConde, Alexander. *Ethnicity, Race, and American Foreign Policy: A History*. Boston:
    Northeastern University Press, 1992.
Dershowitz, Alan M. *The Vanishing American Jew: In Search of Jewish Identity for the
    Next Century*. Boston: Little, Brown, 1997.
Eisenstat, Stuart E. "Loving Israel—Warts and All." *Foreign Policy* 81 (Winter 1990–91).
Ezrachi, Elan. "Jewish Renaissance and Renewal in Israel: A Report of the Dorot and
    Nathan Cummings Foundation." Jan. 2001.
Goldberg, J. J. *Jewish Power: Inside the American Jewish Establishment*. Reading, MA:
    Addison-Wesley, 1996.
Goldstein, Sidney. "Profile of American Jewry: Insights from the 1990 National
    Jewish Population Survey." In *American Jewish Year Book, 1992*, vol. 92. Edited
    by David Singer and Ruth R. Seldin. New York: American Jewish Committee,
    1992.
Heilman, Samuel C. *Portrait of American Jews: The Last Half of the 20th Century*. Seattle:
    University of Washington Press, 1995.
Hertzberg, Arthur. "Israel and the Diaspora: A Relationship Reexamined." *Israel
    Affairs* 2.3–4 (Spring/Summer 1996).
Kaufman, Menahem. "Envisaging Israel: The Case of the United Jewish Appeal." In
    Envisioning Israel: The Changing Ideals and Images of North American Jews. Edited by
    Allon Gal. Jerusalem: Magnes, 1996.
Kimmerling, Baruch. "Between Hegemony and Dormant *Kulturkampf* in Israel." In *In
    Search of Identity: Jewish Aspects of Israeli Culture*. Edited by Dan Urian and Efraim
    Karsh. London: Cass, 1999.
Klieman, Aaron S. *Israel and the World after 40 Years*. Washington, DC: Pergamon-
    Brassey, 1990.
Kramer, Martin. "The Middle East, Old and New." *Daedalus* 126.2 (Spring 1997).

Landau, David. "Who Is a Jew? A Case Study of American Jewish Influence on Israeli Policy." New York: American Jewish Committee, 1996.

Levy, Daniel and Sznaider, Natan. *The Holocaust and Memory in the Global Age.* Philadelphia: Temple University, 2006.

Liebman, Charles S. "Israel in the Mind of American Jews." In *Israel and Diaspora Jewry: Ideological and Political Perspectives.* Edited by Eliezer Don-Yehiya. Jerusalem: Bar-Ilan University Press, 1991.

Liebman, Charles S., and Eliezer Don-Yehiya. *Civil Religion in Israel.* Berkeley: University of California Press, 1983.

'Making Meaning: Participants' Experience of Birthright Israel." Maurice and Marilyn Cohen Center for Modern Jewish Studies, Brandeis University, 2000.

"The Many Faces of Judaism in Israel: Mapping Jewish Unity Organizations." Jewish Agency for Israel, 2000.

Mayer, Egon, Barry Kosmin, and Ariela Keysar. *American Jewish Identity Survey, 2001.* New York: Graduate Center of the City University of New York, 2001.

Meirovich, Harvey. "The Shaping of the Masorti Movement in Israel." New York: American Jewish Committee, 1999.

Mendelsohn, Ezra. *On Modern Jewish Politics.* New York: Oxford University Press, 1993.

Merom, Gil. "Israel's National Security and the Myth of Exceptionalism." *Political Science Quarterly* 114.3 (Fall 1999): 409–93.

Novick, Peter. *The Holocaust in American Life.* New York: Houghton Mifflin, 1999.

O'Brien, Conor Cruise. *God Land: Reflections on Religion and Nationalism.* Cambridge: Harvard University Press, 1987.

Peled, Yoav. "Towards a Redefinition of Jewish Nationalism in Israel? The Enigma of Shas." *Ethnic and Racial Studies* 21.4 (July 1998).

Rosenthal, Steven T. *Irreconcilable Differences? The Waning of the American Jewish Love Affair with Israel.* Hanover, NH: Brandeis University Press, 2001.

Rothenberg, Naftali. "Jews in Israel and the United States: Diverging Identities." In *Jewish Survival: The Identity Problem at the Close of the Twentieth Century.* Edited by Ernest Krausz and Gitta Tulea. New Brunswick, NJ: Transaction, 1999.

Sarna, Jonathan D. *American Judaism: A History.* New Haven: Yale University Press, 2004.

Sarna, Jonathan D., and David G. Dalin. *Religion and State in the American Jewish Experience.* Notre Dame: University of Notre Dame Press, 1997.

Schnitser, Ellen. "The Impact of American Liberal Jewish Identity in Israel: The Case Study of Russian Speaking Immigrants." Unpublished paper, Tel Aviv University, April 2003.

Schoenbaum, David. *The United States and the State of Israel.* Oxford: Oxford University Press, 1993.

Sheleg, Yair. "The North American Impact on Israel Orthodoxy." New York: American Jewish Committee, Oct. 1999.

Soloveitchik, Joseph B. *Fate and Destiny: From the Holocaust to the State of Israel.* Hoboken, NJ: Ktav, 2000.

Soltes, Ori Z. "Memory, Tradition, and Revival: Mapping and Identifying the Political Structure of the Jewish Community Worldwide." In *Occasional Papers on Jewish Civilization, Israel, and the Diaspora.* Washington, DC: Program for Jewish Civilization, Georgetown University, Summer 2005.

Susser, Bernard, and Charles S. Liebman. *Choosing Survival: Strategies for a Jewish Future.* Oxford: Oxford University Press, 1999.

Viorst, Milton. *What Shall I Do with This People? Jews and the Fractious Politics of Judaism.* New York: Free Press, 2002.

Vital, David. *The Future of the Jews: A People at the Crossroads.* Cambridge: Harvard University Press, 1990.

Vorspan, Albert. *Great Jewish Debates and Dilemmas: Jewish Perspectives on Moral Issues in Conflict in the Eighties.* New York: Union of American Hebrew Congregations Press, 1980.

Vorspan, Albert, and David Saperstein. *Jewish Dimensions of Social Justice: Tough Moral Choices of Our Time.* New York: Union of American Hebrew Congregations Press, 1998.

Wasserstein, Bernard. "The Politics of Holiness in Jerusalem." *Chronicle Review*, Sept. 21, 2001 (= section 2 of *Chronicle of Higher Education*).

———. "Post-Diaspora Jewry and Post-Zionist Israel." Paper presented at the international conference entitled "Diasporas: Transnational Identities and the Politics of the Homeland," University of California, Berkeley, Nov. 12–13, 1999.

Wertheimer, Jack. "Judaism without Limits." *Commentary* 104.1 (July 1997).

Yuchtman-Yaar, Ephraim, and Yochanan Peres. *Between Consent and Dissent: Democracy and Peace in the Israeli Mind.* Lanham, MD: Rowman & Littlefield, 2000.

6

Politicians' Perceptions of the "Muslim Problem": The Dutch Example in European Context

Sam Cherribi

Religious pluralism poses a particular challenge for both E.U. governance and politics within E.U. member states. The Netherlands, a
country with one of the longest traditions of religious pluralism—
known since the seventeenth century as a place of refuge for minorities facing religious persecution—has recently had to grapple with
events that challenge its historical reputation. In the mid-1980s,
when migrants were given the right to vote in local elections in the
Netherlands through a pioneering act of national legislation, leaders
of political parties, including then Prime Minister Ruud Lubbers,
went to mosques in the country and actually spoke some Turkish and
Moroccan Arabic to encourage immigrant citizens to exercise their
right to vote. By the late 1990s, however, as Muslim populations
came to be more visible in metropolitan areas, the political elite
and public opinion in the Netherlands were beginning to seriously
question the wisdom of having allowed a constant stream of Muslim
guest workers and their families over two to three decades. As the
experience of Belgium, France, Germany, and Scandinavia over
the past decade demonstrates, this shift in political context is not
unique to the Dutch case.

Policy responses to ethnic and religious pluralism have differed
from country to country, as have integration policies. But despite
these different approaches, the general assessment among publics,
politicians, and the press is that none of the attempts to integrate
Muslim religious minorities into European countries has been successful. These widespread perceptions have contributed to recent
failures to deepen governance at the European level. In May and June
2005, voters in French and Dutch referendums rejected the proposed
European constitution by a significant margin. The "no" camp's

success in evoking serious concern about Muslim migration in Europe and the prospect of Turkish E.U. membership contributed to the outcome.

What do European elites think about Europe's "Muslim problem"? This essay explores the question by drawing on a series of interviews conducted with members of national parliaments in June 2001 and June 2002. The interviews revealed some striking convergence across the political spectrum concerning the transnational dimension of the Middle East problem; approaches to illegal immigration; and appropriate Muslim attitudes towards existing laws and institutions. Some left-right differences were in evidence concerning proposed solutions to the illegal immigration problem and the perceived impact of the September 11, 2001, attacks on how European publics think about the Muslims in their midst.

This essay proceeds in three steps. It first examines the social science literature on migration and citizenship and its relevance to the issue of Muslims in Europe. Scholars are increasingly acknowledging the importance of a transnational lens that incorporates attention to religion, but our knowledge of how European elites are framing the Muslim problem remains remarkably thin. A second section sets out the results of two sets of interviews conducted with European parliamentarians and underscores striking convergences across the political spectrum in how the issue of Muslim migration is constructed. A third section examines the Dutch case in more detail in the wake of the 2004 murder of filmmaker Theo van Gogh. The Netherlands represents a dramatic example of the political discovery of a Muslim problem with far-reaching implications for the future of religious pluralism and democracy.

Islam and the Study of Immigration in Europe

Islam is now the fastest growing religion in Europe, and Muslims in some countries constitute the second largest religious group.[1] As of 2005, it is estimated that more than 20 million Muslims lived in the enlarged European Union. The largest number resided in France (4 million to 5 million), Germany (over 3 million), the United Kingdom (more than 1.5 million), Spain (about 1 million), and Italy and the Netherlands (close to 1 million each). The number of Muslims was lower in Belgium (400,000–500,000), Greece (up to 400,000), Austria and Sweden (more than 300,000 each), and Denmark (up to 180,000), with Muslims constituting 3%–4% of all residents in these countries in the aggregate.[2] Growing numbers have gone hand in hand with greater visibility, particularly in capitals and larger cities where most Muslims reside, in what are often described as "enclaves." Levels of political membership have varied. Half or more of the Muslims in France, the United Kingdom, the Netherlands, and Belgium are citizens of those countries, a fact often lost on those Europeans who fail to make distinctions between legal and illegal immigrants or between citizens and foreign nationals.

The study of migration, an emergent and interdisciplinary area that encompasses a wide range of substantive topics and analytical paradigms, has been slow to take up the issue of Muslim migration in Europe.[3] Saskia Sassen notes that social scientists are becoming aware of the "massive domestic and international transformations that are increasingly reconfiguring states and the interstate system."[4] In this vein, work on E.U. governance has drawn attention to transnational dynamics, including how local voting rights for migrants, dual nationality, and E.U. citizenship undermine the principle of a singular nationality underlying the nation-state model. Nevertheless, state-centric approaches continue to dominate the literature. An influential comparative study of the postwar politics of immigration in Britain, Germany, and the United States, for example, argues that the nation-state and its policy instruments have proven to be quite resilient in the face of immigration.[5]

Within this state-centric literature, familiar typologies map onto issues of Muslim migration and integration only imperfectly. Ruud Koopmans and Paul Statham set out and criticize a familiar distinction among three types of citizenship "regimes."[6] One is labeled "ethnic" or "exclusive"; it makes access to the political community very difficult or impossible. Germany was the ideal type here, until recently when the country changed its requirements for German citizenship. This type still characterizes Austria and Switzerland. A second type is "republican" in the French sense of the term, or otherwise described as "assimilationist," which provides comparatively easy access to citizenship via, for example, automatic citizenship if one is born in the country. France and the traditional U.S. melting pot conception are examples here, but this regime, Koopmans and Statham note, "requires from migrants a high degree of assimilation in the public sphere and gives little or no recognition to their cultural difference."[7] A third regime is described as "multicultural" or "pluralist" and offers easy formal acquisition of citizenship, as well as the rights of citizens to maintain their cultural difference. Examples of this type of pluralist citizenship regime include the contemporary United States, Canada, Australia, and in Europe—Britain and the Netherlands.

As Koopmans and Statham point out, this typology oversimplifies the variety of citizenship regimes in Europe. In particular, their category of pluralist regimes suggests too rosy a picture of the opportunities and constraints facing immigrants. They outline some of the problems associated with the "multicultural approaches" applied in Britain and the United Kingdom, where "the problem has not been a lack of policy instruments to tackle disadvantage based on ethnic, cultural or racial differences, but rather that these instruments have sometimes reinforced and solidified the very disadvantages they were supposed to combat." In the Netherlands in particular, a vicious circle has emerged "in which state policies have reinforced the image of migrants as a problematic, disadvantaged category in need of constant state assistance—not only in the eyes of the majority population, but also in those of many migrants and their representative organizations."[8] Migrants in the Netherlands, while they enjoy greater legal protections and prospects for citizenship than in Germany, continue to face a high level of informal discrimination, evident in the far-reaching segregation of public schools and in uneven access to the labor market.

Gary Freeman introduces some other useful categories for getting beyond the familiar tripartite division among migration regimes.[9] He makes a very useful distinction between four areas of migration policy: "managing legal immigration, controlling illegal migration, administering temporary worker programs, and processing asylum seekers and refugees."[10] Muslim immigrants fall into each of Freeman's four categories, but the vast majority is legal, having come to Europe as guest workers in the 1960s and later bringing their families. Freeman's work focuses primarily on how political elites control decisions about immigration policies and how these are for the most part kept from public scrutiny. He discusses the processes by which immigration policies emerge, with pro-immigration lobbying from antiracist movements, lawyers, intellectuals, and the media.[11] These "client politics" help to explain historical differences and similarities across countries in terms of immigration and integration policies. But they appear to have less analytical utility since the late 1990s, when Muslim migration began to emerge as an object of public and electoral scrutiny. Client politics has increasingly given way to heated controversy, marked by negative stereotypes and alarmist demographic predictions.

The politicization of Muslim migration should not be understood as a post-9/11 phenomenon. By the late 1990s, despite the diversity in ethnic backgrounds and in the immigration trajectories of the millions of Muslims then living in Europe, Aristide Zolberg and Long Litt Woon note a widespread tendency among European publics to think about "these disparate groups" as sharing "an essentialized negative identity as dangerous strangers."[12] Controversy surrounding Islam had already begun, taking different forms in the various European contexts. In the Netherlands, for example, "homosexuality versus Islam" became the defining issue in the public arena, whereas in France it was and continues to be the veil.[13] Even the security dimension of the issue can be traced back to the 1990s. Writing in 1999, both authors already described the "European malaise" as "exacerbated by the rise of international terrorism, some of which has originated in Muslim countries and is sustained by organizations that speak in the name of Islam."[14]

More recent analyses examine the depth of stereotypes in play. In a comparative study focused on perceptions of North African immigrants, Mustapha Nasraoui discerns clear patterns of negative representation in the media, public opinion, and political discourse. In the popular mind, he argues, such immigrants are defined by "three stereotypes: bestial sexuality, disease and a capacity to contaminate, as well as a predisposition to criminality."[15] Work by Tore Bjorgo, centered on the Scandinavian experience, shows how such stereotypes have been combined with apocalyptic demographic forecasts. Anti-immigrationists claim to see a "Muslim invasion." Immigration "is in reality part of a conspiracy to conquer Europe for Islam, they claim. In a few decades from now, they will have taken control of territory and the political system by means of a 'demographic time bomb,' the argument goes."[16]

There is also connection between the perceptions and status of immigrants, the economic situation of the country, the problem of crime and criminality, and support for the far right.[17] The fortunes of the far right do not ebb and flow in isolation. Although past research suggested that the far-right vote is a protest vote, more recently research showed that supporters of extreme right parties in Europe are actually often voting in support of the party's policies.[18] Research also suggested that the news media, by focusing on crime, play into the far right's issue agenda, at least in the Belgian case.[19] Marcel Lubbers and Peer Scheepers show that in France the presence of immigrants is a powerful predictor of far-right success. "Between regions," they argue, "large variance exists in Front National support, which is explained partly by the number of immigrants present, but only indirectly by the unemployment level."[20]

There is little evidence that European publics differentiate among different kinds of Muslims in their midst. Recent research shows just how diverse the Muslim presence is. Chantal Saint-Blancat conducted research on Islamic populations within European host societies—a comparative analysis of the religious behaviors and social strategies of Maghrebin, Turkish, and Pakistani communities—and discerns three main currents: a fundamentalist "re-Islamization," a revival of more "traditional Islam," and a "secularized Islam," where the "religious dimension is progressively abandoned in favor of an essentially cultural identification."[21] European publics tend not to be educated about such distinctions. For that matter, research on the sources of attitudes toward immigrants reveals that hostile attitudes are not specifically tied to the religion, race, or language of the immigrants, but rather the perception that they are "outsiders" or foreigners, and those who are hostile to one out-group are likely to be hostile to another out-group, though the level of hostility may be more intense against one or another out-group.[22] Some recent research in the Netherlands reveals that for Dutch people social distance is highest toward people from Muslim countries (Morocco and Turkey) and lower for people from Central Europe (Bulgaria) and nonimmigrant minority groups.[23] Looking at Europe as a whole with Eurobarometer data, based on fieldwork conducted during October and November 2005, immigration and terrorism appear to be on the rise as main concerns of European citizens, and support for further E.U. enlargement reveals that most people favor enlargement with countries such as Norway or Switzerland, but are more hesitant when it comes to Croatia, Bulgaria, Romania, and Ukraine, and a majority is opposed to enlargement with Turkey, the only Muslim country on the list.[24] Given the high levels of concern among publics, insight into the perceptions of political elites takes on greater political and analytical importance.

Politicians' Perceptions of Europe's Muslim Problem

The social science literature on migration, citizenship, and comparative immigration policy tells us very little about what leading politicians actually think about European Muslims and their place within European society.[25] In order to address this gap, I conducted two sets of interviews with leading European parliamentarians. The first set took place in June 2001, three months before the attacks on the World Trade Center and the Pentagon. The second, more extensive set of interviews, took place in June 2002, nine months after the attacks, and involved twenty members of national parliaments (MNPs) who attended the weeklong session of the Assembly of the Council of Europe in Strasbourg. The juxtaposition of both sets of discussions sheds light on the impact of 9/11 on changing perceptions of Europe's Muslim problem.

The June 2001 group included eight non-Muslim MNPs from a variety of different parties in a number of E.U. countries. Our discussion made clear that already, at that time, there was a major concern among political elites in Europe about what they called the Muslim problem. The main concerns articulated included the following:

- the impact of population growth among second- and third-generation Muslim immigrants on the demographics of Europe's major cities
- the distinctive clothing worn by Muslims increasingly visible in the public sphere
- the growth of Islamic schools and European Muslim media outlets
- the influence of Islamic countries on European Muslim populations, including the fear of possible terrorism and espionage
- the violence and crime associated with Muslim young men and teenage boys
- the treatment of Muslim women by Muslim men
- illegal immigrants from sub-Saharan Africa, who regularly come ashore from Morocco, Algeria, and Tunisia onto the coasts of Europe, as well as Albanians crossing into Italy and Kurds from Turkey and Iraq, who had been among the most visible of the regular influx of political refugees with Muslim backgrounds

This first discussion led me to conclude that before the "war on terror" began, the Muslim problem in Europe was largely perceived as one of immigration and Islamization, or of numbers and culture. This overriding perception appeared to hold across the political spectrum.

The more formal interviews I conducted one year later, in the aftermath of 9/11, following the Seville Summit, also showed that MNPs from the left and right shared similar perspectives. A week before the interviews in Strasbourg, the summit brought E.U. heads of state together to negotiate and agree upon how to deal with the issue of illegal immigration. (Other issues on the agenda included the E.U. enlargement process and overall E.U. governance.) The summit made some movement toward adopting common policies, an avowed E.U. priority since the Finland Summit in 1999. But progress was slow. In trying to find an appropriate balance between keeping out illegals and improving the integration of legal immigrants, the leaders agreed to increase external border security at ports and airports, to pass new rules that encourage heavier penalties for smuggling people, to review visa requirements for countries outside the E.U. zone, to adopt a policy by the end of 2002 to hurry to repatriate those who do not qualify to remain (especially from Afghanistan), and to speed up the adoption of common rules for asylum seekers.

A main area of concern was how to respond to countries that do not co-operate with the European Union in restricting illegal immigration. Ultimately a compromise was reached between those countries that wanted tough warnings (led by Britain and Spain) and others more worried about how this would be interpreted by poor countries (led by France and Sweden). The official compromise solution reached was that the European Union "may unanimously find that a third country has shown an unjustified lack of cooperation in joint management of migration flows." It warned that "inadequate cooperation could hamper the establishment of closer relations," while at the same time insisting that any measures would be taken "without jeopardising the objectives of development cooperation." One BBC correspondent concluded: "This is all rather vague and allows for a decision either way, which is why both sides will claim success. That is the nature of E.U. summits."[26] Seville was an effort, however preliminary, to "develop multilateral approaches and factor in the changed character of unilateral sovereign authority."[27]

In the wake of the summit, I selected a representative sample of MNPs to address three questions:

- "What is your opinion about the outcome of the Seville Summit?"
- "Do you think about Muslims as different from other immigrants and do you have any concerns about Muslim migrants in Europe and specifically in your country?"
- "Did 9/11 change anything?"

Because the left-right dimension is an important one for distinguishing political opinions in the E.U. context, I selected the MNPs with attention both to party and national affiliations.[28] I also targeted a relatively equal number of MNPs from northern and southern European countries. The sample of twenty included MNPs from parties on the left and right in Spain, Portugal, Italy, Greece, France, Belgium, Germany, the Netherlands, Finland, and the United Kingdom.

The interviews revealed some remarkable geographical and partisan convergence around (1) the transnational nature of the problem in the Middle East, (2) the importance of immigration as a problem confronting Europe, and (3) the perceived need for Muslim immigrants to be respectful and accepting of the laws of the land in which they live.

The Transnational Nature of Middle East Problems

The transnational nature of the problems in the Middle East, and the Israeli-Palestinian conflict in particular, was mentioned by MNPs from all parties as a crucial source of tensions within Europe. The following examples illustrate the general perception that problems in the Middle East translated into tensions in European cities between Jewish and Muslim communities and more generally between Muslims and non-Muslims. Among the key statements were the following:

> We have to consider both sides and be critical of both sides. The Middle East is the main issue and the source of the tensions in Europe. (right MNP)

> I think this issue is tearing at the heart of the Muslims in Europe, who want to see peace in that area. (left MNP)

> Look at the recent demonstrations by the young Arabs, especially Moroccans, in the old Jewish city of Amsterdam, waving anti-Israel banners. I was horrified to see Nazi swastikas compared to Sharon and the Star of David. This is a major source of tension in our country. (right MNP)

> Jerusalem is the problem. The Israelites say tomorrow Jerusalem, it is their *espoir de vivre*. They want to die in Jerusalem. The Muslims want to do the same thing. . . . I'm afraid that I don't think there is a solution. And in Europe the Jews identify with Israel and the Muslims identify with Palestinians, resulting in a problem outside of the location of the problem. (right MNP)

> I think that the Arab states want this conflict because it is a catalyst of hate and it helps them to focus attention on problems elsewhere and not in their own country. . . . As long as the conflict is not solved, we will have frictions in France and these kinds of problems. . . . All extremists will use the Palestinian question to gain votes, extremists on the right and left. (left MNP)

> We will always have a tension in Europe if we do not solve this problem. (right MNP)

> There is a Muslim identity. The conflict is exportable and this is what people don't want to understand. Because the migrants in France and maybe even in Holland feel as if they are in the same position as the Palestinians. (left MNP)

> We have a lot of Turks and Muslims and Middle Eastern Palestinians in Greece but they do not really practice Islam in a fundamentalist way. The problem now in the Middle East is making [these] people think in a more radical way. (right MNP)

These comments reflected, in part, the context of early 2002 and concerns about a lack of progress in the Middle East peace process. In April of that year, for example, there were several peace demonstrations in major European cities. At the same time, the interviews pointed to strong links between the issue of Muslim immigration, on the one hand, and the international context, on the other.

Europe's Illegal Immigration Problem

There was also agreement between left and right on the importance of the problem of illegal immigration, the centrality of E.U.-level attempts to address the issue, and the need to follow through on the progress made in Seville. As one MNP on the right put it: "The biggest problem is illegal migration. We have one and a half million illegal migrants, still coming in from Eastern Europe as well." Another on the left cast the problem in broadly similar terms: "Illegal immigration is a major problem. You can never solve the problems of immigration in Europe without solving the problems of the countries exporting illegal migrants. As long as that is not solved, we will only fight against a sea of trouble."

Many of the MNPs expressed disappointment with the decisions taken at the Seville Summit. The left-right dimension is useful for identifying the reasons why they believed the decisions taken in Seville on immigration were not sufficient. Politicians on the left tended to see the problem as stemming from poverty in poor countries, while those on the right were more likely to see it stemming from weak laws and poor enforcement. Proposed solutions differed accordingly. One MNP on the left argued: "I don't think we need to stop migration, we need to work with the countries of origin to prevent illegal migration. We have to work on poverty reduction so people will not feel the need to migrate." A Spanish MNP from the conservative camp, by contrast, drew attention to Madrid, with its "barrios that are terrible, violent, and where the children of migrants are thieves." The Moroccan government was encouraging illegal immigration to Spain, he argued, a situation "we cannot tolerate."

Nineteen of twenty MNPs interviewed were disappointed with the outcome of Seville, the sole exception being one of the then Spanish Prime Minister's party colleagues. MNPs on both sides of the political spectrum saw too little too late. The comment of a right MNP was typical: "We've been opening the door too long and without any rules, and that is why the problem cannot be solved instantly because it was ages or years of negligence."

Respect for European Laws

There is also agreement between left and right on the importance of immigrants having respect for and being willing to live by the laws of the country. This was offered directly, without prompting, by a number of MNPs irrespective of political leaning. All agree on the need for Muslim immigrants to respect democracy and the laws of the country in which they live. Two left MNPs made the point with reference to their respective countries:

> I am concerned about respect for the constitution. The Dutch politicians missed all opportunities to tame Islam. We were idealistic and supporting Islamic schools and we left people to be free to build their mosques without any conditions, especially people who do not think like us when it comes to the same values. There is a big difference

between Christian fundamentalists radicals and Muslim extremists, the latter do not respect the law [and] the constitution but the former do. Even the SGP [a fundamentalist Christian party] totally respect the law. This is the danger of Muslim fundamentalism. (left MNP)

As long as they want to integrate in Finnish society and respect the Finnish laws, then I have no problem. (left MNP)

Similar thoughts were expressed on the other side of the political spectrum:

The Spanish migrants [in the 1950s] were respecting totally, were fully accepting and deferential towards the laws of the host country be-cause they knew that if they did not do so they would be ejected. It's not like the migrants today. (right MNP)

Believe me, I have nothing against Islam. I am a secular man. All I ask Muslims to do is to respect and obey our laws. I cannot tolerate that women are circumcised, and I cannot tolerate polygamy and radicalism and fundamentalism. (right MNP)

The degree of consensus around the importance of Muslim immigrants hav-ing respect for democracy and the laws of the European countries in which they live is striking. It was much more pronounced in 2002 than in 2001, a possible reflection of concerns about Muslim fundamentalism and extremism in the wake of 9/11.

Left-Right Differences

In the interview sample, left and the right tended to agree about the impor-tance of the problem of illegal immigration for Europe. But there were some important differences of emphasis. One concerned different understandings of the source of the problem and its eventual solution. In general, those on the left believed that nothing has been done to counter the problem of poverty in the sending countries, which is, in their view, the main reason why immi-gration occurs. Those on the right believe that Europe does not have tough enough border controls, backed up by the money and the vision for security necessary to prevent illegals from entering. Those on the left were more op-timistic about the possibilities for time to solve the problems of European integration in the future. Those on the right did not see it as a question of time or of having the right amount of money paid to poor countries. They believed that the problem could be handled only through law enforcement and low or no tolerance of illegals.

Left and right were also more likely to disagree about the impact of 9/11. The Muslim problem in Europe, as perceived by those on the right, became more visible after the attacks and therefore more important. It was a problem that already existed, but 9/11 shaped the perception of the urgency and prox-imity and possible consequences for Europe. One right MNP put it this way:

I don't think that the malaise in Europe now is because of 11 September. The 11th of September only made everything more urgent and more visible than before. Micro-criminality [petty theft] and rape were crimes that were often committed by illegal migrants and these people are ruining the lives of the good immigrants. The Italians now have the impression that they invited people into their homes and now they themselves are becoming prisoners in their own homes and in their own streets. (right MNP)

Another right MNP saw more serious problems:

I think that 9/11 has aggravated everything because it gave the young Arabs who are revolutionary the idea that they don't need an army or any big means to destroy the enemy. They can use terrorism. This is very grave. (right MNP)

Those on the left, on the other hand, were more likely to argue that 9/11 changed things mainly in that it led to anti-Muslim feeling among native Europeans:

I think that 11 September aggravated this psychological dimension of insecurity. It is unbelievable that in many villages where there are no minorities or people of color, that people voted Le Pen. (left MNP)

9/11 was one of the factors making Pim Fortuyn more visible and preparing the Dutch to be an obedient audience. (left MNP)

9/11 only furthered the environment of hate. . . . I am Jewish and this is very bad also for the future of minorities in Europe in general, also Jewish minorities. I was on the train from Brussels to Paris and there was a woman talking with me in the same way that Le Pen had been talking about the Holocaust, she denied the gas chambers and she denied the Holocaust, and she said that she was glad that the Socialist government left in France because they were all Jews and that all terrorists are Jews. An environment of hate is bad for everyone. She was sitting in first class and she didn't know that I am a Jew. The Muslims have to know that if they feel bad about what happens to them now, look what happens to people who have been integrated for years and who are integrated in this country. Any environment of hate can generate more hate and it can become uncontrollable. (left MNP)

In the conversations with a group of MNPs in June 2001, there was already some consensus about what was described as the Muslim problem in Europe. At that time, the issue had a number of different aspects, but fundamentalism and extremism were not mentioned by the parliamentarians, and the problems in the Middle East were also not mentioned as having transnational implications for Muslims and non-Muslims living in Europe. A year later, a major concern had become the transnational nature of the Middle East problem, perceived threats of Muslim extremism within Europe, and the implications of this for social relations between immigrants and natives in European countries. As noted above, established research shows that prejudice and anti-immigrant rhetoric is already particularly focused on Muslim immigrants and Islam in Europe.[29] My interviews with MNPs show that European political elites are especially concerned about conflicts and tensions between peoples in their own countries and see increasing links to developments outside the Continent. This international dimension is likely to grow only more salient in years to come.

Ultimately, the major concern of these parliamentarians was the future of politics within their own national societies. The interviews took place against the backdrop of a series of controversies. Far-right parties in Belgium, the Netherlands, and France had made electoral gains with the immigration issue. Jean-Marie Le Pen's success in the first round of the French presidential elections in March 2002 was an especially important marker. Other notable events included the publication of an anti-Muslim book by well-known Italian journalist Oriana Fallaci in 2002; the riots and burning of North African businesses in southern Spain in 2000; the attacks on mosques and Muslims in the Netherlands, Germany, and the United Kingdom in the weeks after 9/11; the continued public support for the far-right nationalist party Vlaams Blok in Belgium; and the support for the Danish and Dutch anti-immigration parties and recent restrictions on marrying foreigners and bringing in foreign spouses in those countries. The common thread among these examples in recent years was public concern about the growing Muslim populations in European countries.

Add to this the impact of international events in the Middle East and elsewhere, and you have the potential for anti-Muslim politics in years to come. The events since June 2002 have unfortunately made this potential very clear. With the terrorist bombings in Madrid in March 2004, now known as Europe's 9/11 or 11-M, these concerns have become even more pressing. 11-M magnifies and augments all of the concerns about Europe's Muslim problem that European political elites expressed in the interviews I conducted in June 2002. It was also apparently (according to those who took credit for the bombs) a product of the war in Iraq, a war that most European publics were strongly against and a war over which most European political elites felt they had little control. The London bombings of July 2005 marked a further critical juncture, as did the riots that rocked France in the fall of that year.

The problem after Spain's 11-M and the London bombings is not only the potential terrorist coming into the country, but also potential terrorist already within. The reactions of Western European politicians in the European media coverage following the 11-M attacks on Spain, for example, show that there are now even more serious concerns about the possibility of the Muslim populations in Western European democracies becoming radical and turning against the countries in which they are (often second-generation) citizens. "Recruiting for Jihad" was the headline in the Dutch *NRC*, the country's leading elite newspaper. *Le Figaro* in France carried a similar story. In the aftermath of 11-M, European political elites on the left and the right agreed on the potential threat from within Europe's borders.

Extremism and Intolerance in the Netherlands

In the Dutch context, the nightmare became a reality on November 2, 2004, the day George W. Bush was reelected president of the United States. The U.S. presidential election usually is top billing in European news media, but this time a more troublesome story competed for the headlines: the cold-blooded murder of Theo van Gogh, controversial columnist and filmmaker, on one of Amsterdam's main streets, as he was bicycling to his office late that morning. Van Gogh, who produced the controversial film *Submission: Part I*, pleaded for his life, imploring his assailant, "let's talk about this"—a typical consensus-oriented Dutch expression ("laten wij even overlegen"). The killer instead took a knife, slit van Gogh's throat, and then with the same knife pinned a six page letter to his chest. The letter was addressed to Ms. Ayaan Hirsi Ali, a Somalian-born asylum seeker who became a Dutch member of Parliament in 2003, whom the killer wrote would be the next one to die for her role as author and narrator of *Submission* and her statements against the Prophet.

The murder of van Gogh took place less than two months after the eleven-minute film was aired in late August 2004 and after Hirsi Ali had appeared on an intellectual cultural talk show called "Zomergasten" (summer guests), in which guests select and discuss bits and pieces that have a special meaning for them. She chose to debut her short film. Although this late-night program does not have large audience, within twenty-four hours the entire country concentrated on *Submission*, which was picked up by the mainstream press and broadcasting outlets. In the weeks after it was first aired on Dutch public television, the film's main message about Muslim men abusing veiled women was repeated over and over again in news and current affairs programs that reminded audiences of the possible "enemy within" the country.

While the anti-Islam drumbeat in the Dutch media had been relatively constant since the 2002 election campaign, in which the new party of Pim Fortuyn came to power, the media frenzy about the film took it to the next level. Prominent ethnic minority intellectuals in the country, such as Dutch member of Parliament Ali Lazrak, who was born in Morocco and came to the country as a guest worker in the 1970s, claimed that the Dutch media was more "racist and anti-Muslim" than any other European country.[30] According to Geert Mak, a prominent Dutch journalist, novelist, and essayist, the Dutch media failed to interview any Moroccan intellectuals who could say something meaningful and instead gave the floor to those who further stoked the flames, such as a Dutch imam (a Dutch convert to Islam) who said he would prefer that one of the country's newly prominent far-right members of Parliament, Geert Wilders, "would die of cancer."[31] Mak was frustrated with the Dutch media for choosing to interview those who supported a milder form of jihad, rather than the many Muslim intellectuals who are not religious but are very concerned about the atmosphere of mistrust and discrimination against Muslims in the country. The Dutch media have been one sided in giving voice to anti-Muslim perspectives, while largely ignoring the critical culture within the Muslim communities and eschewing interviews with many highly educated and professionally successful Muslims.

The news of Theo van Gogh's murder spread quickly throughout Europe and the world. Prime Minister Jan Peter Balkanende was quoted on Radio 1 the next day as saying that the country was at war, and Belgian Prime Minister Guy Verhofstadt said "our neighboring country is on the brink of civil war." The Danish newspaper *Politiken* warned that this could be like "*Kristallnacht* in 1938," and reporter Craig S. Smith of the *New York Times* had trouble finding the appropriate words to translate the obscenities used by Dutch demonstrators.[32]

The film and its coverage in the Dutch press may indeed have contributed to the anti-Muslim violence in the following weeks of 2004, with Muslims being the predominant but not the only target. A report published by the Research and Documentation Centre of the Anne Frank Foundation and the University of Leiden noted 174 violent incidents between November 2 and November 30, including cases of verbal abuse, intimidation, graffiti, physical violence, vandalism, bomb attacks, and arson. Of these incidents, 106 were targeted at Muslims or Muslim institutions or property. Jewish and Christian targets made up the rest. The mainstream Dutch media did not seem overly concerned by this outbreak of hostility toward Muslims. By December 2004 *Elsevier*, Holland's version of *Time* magazine, put Ayaan Hirsi Ali on the cover and named her "Dutchman of the Year." Dozens of Muslim women, citizens of the Netherlands, challenged Hirsi Ali in the courts to prevent her from making *Submission: Part II* because they claimed it would be counterproductive, but they lost on freedom-of-speech grounds. Hirsi Ali herself said in an interview on CBS's *60 Minutes* in March 2005 that she was determined to make another film and "will not be silenced by terrorists."

An *Elsevier*-like profile of Hirsi Ali appeared in the *New York Times Magazine* in April 2005, just weeks after *60 Minutes* aired its sympathetic interview with her and broadcast parts of her controversial film. Christopher Caldwell began the six-page article: "Daughter of the Enlightenment: Ayaan Hirsi Ali is a Somali-born feminist and a Dutch legislator who has rejected her Muslim faith to become an outspoken advocate for 'European values.' It's a cause that some of her opponents want her to die for."[33] Both of these stories failed to provide important information about past and present examples of the critical culture existing within Muslim communities and societies. It appears from these stories that Hirsi Ali is novel and heroic for standing up for Muslim women all over the world, yet the news stories fail to mention that not a single prominent Muslim woman from the largest Muslim populations (Turks and Moroccans) in the Netherlands has publicly supported her.

The coverage also failed to point out that Hirsi Ali's critique of Islam is one that that was made by prominent women in countries such as Morocco, Algeria, Tunisia, Egypt, and Lebanon more than two decades ago and is a critique that continues to be made today. In both the Dutch and the U.S. coverage of her story, it is as if her criticisms of gender bias, wife beating, honor killings, and sexual abuse had never before been echoed in Europe or Muslim societies. Yet in France, two to three years before *Submission* was made, French Muslim women started a movement called "Ni put ni soumise," criticizing the two views that they found themselves in between—the fundamentalists' view that unveiled women are like prostitutes and the mainstream French perspective that all veiled women have "submitted."

Hirsi Ali appears to defy the left-right continuum. Until recently she was an active member of the VVD, a market-oriented liberal party. At the same time, she sometimes sat with Geert Wilders in the Parliament, a former VVD member of Parliament who broke away from his party in early 2004, because he felt it was too soft on migration and the question of Turkish membership in the European Union. The two of them coauthored a widely cited article in the *NRC Handlesblatt* under the title "Liberal Jihad." Certain of Hirsi Ali's stances also appeal to the left. The feminist magazine *Op Zij* supported Hirsi Ali's stands on women's issues, and *Vrij-Nederland*, a prominent left-wing magazine, published an article in which well-known Labor politicians urged her to join their party.

As the case of Hirsi Ali illustrates, criticism of Islam is increasingly prominent across the political spectrum in the Netherlands. The murder of Theo van Gogh and its aftermath further fueled concerns and prejudices among the Dutch. Destructive stereotypes and generalizations about one Muslim community are magnified by attention from the media,[34] and there has been little effort to engage the different Muslim communities in Holland in a constructive conversation about the future of Dutch society. While the worst fears about civil strife have faded since November 2004, Holland's reputation as a country of tolerance and pluralism has suffered serious harm.

Events of the last decade have sorely tested European democracies. Muslim immigration, which had proceeded largely outside the spotlight of electoral politics, moved to the center of political controversy. Even before 9/11 leaders across the political spectrum identified a Muslim problem, defined less in terms of the negative stereotypes associating Islam with extremism than in terms of the alleged inability of the newcomers to adapt to the European way of life. The Netherlands, long considered a bastion of tolerance, was not immune to this trend. On the contrary, as the public uproar following the murder of van Gogh demonstrated, deep-seated anti-Muslim prejudices coexist in that country, alongside a generous welfare state and progressive policies designed to promote pluralism and multiculturalism. How the Netherlands—and Europe as a whole—masters the political, social, and cultural tensions that have emerged over the past decade will have a decisive impact on the future and health of democracy on the Continent.

NOTES

1. Jørgen Nielsen, *Towards a European Islam* (London: Macmillan, 1999); Gilles Kepel, *The War for Muslim Minds: Islam and the West* (Cambridge: Harvard University Press, 2004); Oussama Cherribi, "The Growing Islamization of Europe," in *Modernizing Islam: Religion in the Public Sphere in Europe and the Middle East*, ed. John L. Esposito and Francois Burgat (Newark: Rutgers University Press, 2003), 193–214; Yvonne Haddad, ed., *Muslims in the West: From Sojourners to Citizens* (Oxford: Oxford University Press, 2002); and Jytte Klausen, *The Islamic Challenge: Politics and Religion in Western Europe* (Oxford: Oxford University Press, 2006).

2. See http://eisnet.eis.be/own/graph/2005/en03/eure;2943;414.pdf.

3. Caroline Brettell and James Frank Hollifield, eds., *Migration Theory: Talking across the Disciplines* (London: Routledge, 2000); Patrick Ireland, *The Policy Challenge of Ethnic Diversity: Immigrant Politics in France and Switzerland* (Cambridge: Harvard University Press, 1994); and Will Kymlicka, *Multicultural Citizenship: A Liberal Theory of Minority Rights* (Oxford: Clarendon, 1995).

4. Saskia Sassen, "Regulating Immigration in a Global Age: A New Policy Land-scape," *Annals of the American Academy of Political and Social Sciences* 570 (2000): 65–77 at 65.

5. Christian Joppke, *Immigration and the Nation-State: The United States, Germany, and Great Britain* (Oxford: Oxford University Press, 2000).

6. Ruud Koopmans and Paul Statham, "Migration and Ethnic Relations as Field of Political Contention: An Opportunity Structure Approach," in *Challenging Immigration and Ethnic Relations Politics: Comparative European Perspectives*, ed. Ruud Koopmans and Paul Statham (Oxford: Oxford University Press, 2000), 19.

7. Ibid.

8. Ibid., 27.

9. Gary P. Freeman, "The Consequence of Immigration Policies for Immigrant Status: A British and French Comparison," in *Ethnic and Racial Minorities in Advanced Industrial Democracies*, ed. Anthony Messina, Luis Fraga, Laurie Rhodebeck, and Frederick Wright (New York: Greenwood, 1992).

10. Freeman, ibid.; idem, "Modes of Immigration Politics in Liberal Democratic States," *International Migration Review* 29.4 (1995): 881–902; idem, "The Decline of Sovereignty? Politics and Imimgration Restriction in Liberal States," in *Challenge to the Nation-State: Immigration in Western Europe and the United States*, ed. Christian Joppke (Oxford: Oxford University Press, 1998); and idem, "Can Liberal States Control Unwanted Migration?" *Annals of the American Academy of Politics and Social Sciences* 534 (1994): 17–30 at 17.

11. Freeman "Decline of Sovereignty?" 103.

12. Aristide R. Zolberg and Long Litt Woon, "Why Islam Is Like Spanish: Cultural Incorporation in Europe and the United States," *Politics and Society* 27.1 (March 1999): 5–38 at 6.

13. Oussama Cherribi, "Olanda (s)velata: Intolleranza, populismo e media" [Outing the Dutch: intolerance, populism, and the media], *Comunicazione politica* 4.2 (2003): 141–65. See also idem, "Outing the Dutch: Intolerance, Populism, and the Media" (paper presented at the annual meeting of the International Communication Association, San Diego, May 2003).

14. Cherribi, "Olanda (s)velata," 6.

15. Mustapha Nasraoui, "The Image of Muslim Arabic Culture and the Integration of the North African Immigrant in Europe," *Journal of Mediterranean Studies* 11 (2001): 215–23.

16. Tore Bjorgo, "Xenophobic Violence and Ethnic Conflict at the Local Level," in *Challenging Immigration and Ethnic Relations Politics: Comparative European Perspectives*, ed. Ruud Koopmans and Paul Statham (Oxford: Oxford University Press, 2000), 379. See also Teun A. van Dijk, *Elite Discourse and Racism* (Newbury Park, CA: Sage, 1993).

17. Stefaan Walgrave and Knut De Swert, "The Making of the (Issues of the) Vlaams Blok: On the Contribution of the News Media in the Electoral Success of the Belgian Extreme-Right Party" (paper presented at the annual meeting of the American Political Science Association, Boston, 2002).

18. Wouter van der Brug and Meindert Fennema, "Protest or Mainstream? How the European Anti-Immigrant Parties Have Developed into Two Separate Groups by 1999," *European Journal of Political Research* (forthcoming); and Wouter van der Brug, Meindert Fennema, and Jean Tillie, "Anti-Immigrant Parties in Europe: Ideological or Protest Vote?" *European Journal of Political Research* 37 (2000): 77–102.

19. Walgrave and De Swert, "Making of the (Issues of the) Vlaams Blok."

20. Marcel Lubbers and Peer Scheepers, "French Front National Voting: A Micro and Macro Perspective," *Ethnic and Racial Studies* 25.1 (2002): 120–49 at 120.

21. Chantal Saint-Blancat, "Hypotheses concerning Islam as Religion Transplanted into Europe," *Social Compass* 40.2 (1993): 323–41.

22. Paul M. Sniderman, Pierangelo Peri, Rui J. P. de Figueiredo Jr., and Thomas Piazza, *The Outsider: Prejudice and Politics in Italy* (Princeton: Princeton University Press, 2002).

23. Hajo Boomgaarden, "News and Ethnic Prejudice: Threat Framing of Immigrants and Its Impact on Anti-immigration Sentiments" (paper presented at the annual meeting of the International Communication Association, Dresden, Germany, June 2006).

24. "Eurobarometer 64: First Results" (Dec. 2005), 8–9, 30–32.

25. Veit Bader, "The Cultural Conditions of Transnational Citizenship: On the Interpretation of Political and Ethnic Cultures," *Political Theory* 25 (Dec. 1997): 771–813; Rogers Brubaker, *Citizenship and Nationhood in France and Germany* (Cambridge: Harvard University Press, 1992); Mark J. Miller, *Foreign Workers in Western Europe: An Emerging Political Force?* (New York: Praeger, 1981); idem, "The Political Impact of Foreign Labour," *International Migration Review* 16.1 (1982): 27–60; Randall Hansen and Patrick Weil, *Dual Nationality, Social Rights, and Federal Citizenship in the U.S. and Europe: The Reinvention of Citizenship* (London: Berghahn, 2002); Ruud Koopmans, "Explaining the Rise of Racist and Extreme Right Violence in Western Europe: Grievances or Opportunities?" *European Journal of Political Research* 30 (1996): 185–216; idem, "Germany and Its Immigrants: An Ambivalent Relationship," *Journal of Ethnic and Migration Studies* 24.4 (July/Aug. 1999): 627–47; Rey Koslowski, *Migrants and Citizens: Demographic Change in the European State System* (Ithaca: Cornell University Press, 2002); David Kyle and Rey Koslowski, eds., *Global Human Smuggling: Comparative Perspectives* (Baltimore: Johns Hopkins University Press, 2001); Aristide R. Zolberg and Peter Benda, eds., *Global Migrants, Global Refugees: Problems and Solutions* (London: Berghahn; 2001); Michael Dummett, *On Immigration and Refugees* (Thinking in Action; London: Routledge, 2001); and Saskia Sassen, *Guests and Aliens* (New York: New Press, 1999).

26. For an excellent summary of the agreements reached at the Seville Summit, see the text of the speech by British Prime Minister Tony Blair on June 24, 2002, available at http://www.number-10.gov.uk/output/Page1719.asp.

27. Sassen, "Regulating Immigration in a Global Age," 65.

28. Hermann Schmitt and Jacques Thomassen, "Distinctiveness and Cohesion of Political Parties," in *Political Representation and Legitimacy in the European Union*, ed. Hermann Schmitt and Jacques Thomassen (Oxford: Oxford University Press, 1999), 119.

29. Koopmans, "Explaining the Rise of Racist and Extreme Right Violence"; Ruud Koopmans and Paul Stratham, "Ethnic and Civic Conceptions of Nationhood and the Differential Success of the Extreme Right in Germany and Italy," in *How Social Movements Matter*, ed. Marco Guigni, Doug McAdam, and Charles Tilly (Minneapolis: University of Minnesota Press, 1999), 225–51.

30. Author's discussions with Ali Lazrak, Dec. 2004.

31. Geert Mak, *Gedoemd tot Kwetsbaarheid* [Damned to vulnerability] (Amsterdam: Atlas, 2005), 41.

32. Ibid., 12.

33. Christopher Caldwell, "Daughter of the Enlightenment," *New York Times Magazine*, April 3, 2005, 26–31.

34. Abram de Swaan, "Nederland Schomelt van Balorig naar Kwaadsappig," *De Volkskrant*, Feb. 25, 2006, 1 het Betoog; and Aranka Klomp and John Kroon, *The Netherlands 2006: The Mood after the Hysteria* (Amsterdam: Prometheus, 2005).

BIBLIOGRAPHY

Bader, Veit. "The Cultural Conditions of Transnational Citizenship: On the Interpretation of Political and Ethnic Cultures." *Political Theory* 25 (Dec. 1997): 771–813.

Bjorgo, Tore. "Xenophobic Violence and Ethnic Conflict at the Local Level." In *Challenging Immigration and Ethnic Relations Politics: Comparative European Perspectives*. Edited by Ruud Koopmans and Paul Statham. Oxford: Oxford University Press, 2000.

Boomgaarden, Hajo. "News and Ethnic Prejudice: Threat Framing of Immigrants and Its Impact on Anti-immigration Sentiments." Paper presented at the annual meeting of the International Communication Association, Dresden, Germany, June 2006.

Brettell, Caroline, and James Frank Hollifield, eds. *Migration Theory: Talking across the Disciplines*. London: Routledge, 2000.

Brubaker, Rogers. *Citizenship and Nationhood in France and Germany*. Cambridge: Harvard University Press, 1992.

Caldwell, Christopher. "Daughter of the Enlightenment." *New York Times Magazine*, April 3, 2005, 26–31.

Cherribi, Oussama. "The Growing Islamization of Europe." In *Modernizing Islam: Religion in the Public Sphere in Europe and the Middle East*, 193–214. Edited by John L. Esposito and Francois Burgat. Newark: Rutgers University Press, 2003.

———. "Olanda (s)velata: Intolleranza, populismo e media" [Outing the Dutch: intolerance, populism, and the media]. *Comunicazione politica* 4.2 (2003): 141–65.

———. "Outing the Dutch: Intolerance, Populism, and the Media." Paper presented at the annual meeting of the International Communication Association, San Diego, May 2003.

Dummett, Michael. *On Immigration and Refugees*. Thinking in Action. London: Routledge, 2001.

Freeman, Gary. "Can Liberal States Control Unwanted Migration?" *Annals of the American Academy of Politics and Social Sciences* 534 (1994): 17–30.

———. "The Consequence of Immigration Policies for Immigrant Status: A British and French Comparison." In *Ethnic and Racial Minorities in Advanced Industrial Democracies*, 17–32. Edited by Anthony Messina, Luis Fraga, Laurie Rhodebeck, and Frederick Wright. New York: Greenwood, 1992.

———. "The Decline of Sovereignty? Politics and Immigration Restriction in Liberal States." In *Challenge to the Nation-State: Immigration in Western Europe and the United States*. Edited by Christian Joppke. Oxford: Oxford University Press, 1998.

———. "Modes of Immigration Politics in Liberal Democratic States." *International Migration Review* 29.4 (1995): 881–902.

Haddad, Yvonne, ed. *Muslims in the West: From Sojourners to Citizens*. Oxford: Oxford University Press, 2002.

Hansen, Randall, and Patrick Weil. *Dual Nationality, Social Rights, and Federal Citizenship in the U.S. and Europe: The Reinvention of Citizenship*. London: Berghahn, 2002.

Ireland, Patrick. *The Policy Challenge of Ethnic Diversity: Immigrant Politics in France and Switzerland*. Cambridge: Harvard University Press, 1994.

Joppke, Christian. *Immigration and the Nation-State: The United States, Germany, and Great Britain*. Oxford: Oxford University Press, 2000.

Kepel, Gilles. *The War for Muslim Minds: Islam and the West*. Cambridge: Harvard University Press, 2004.

Klausen, Jytte. *The Islamic Challenge: Politics and Religion in Western Europe*. Oxford: Oxford University Press, 2006.

Klomp, Aranka, and John Kroon. *The Netherlands 2006: The Mood after the Hysteria*. Amsterdam: Prometheus, 2005.

Koopmans, Ruud. "Explaining the Rise of Racist and Extreme Right Violence in Western Europe: Grievances or Opportunities?" *European Journal of Political Research* 30 (1996): 185–216.

———. "Germany and Its Immigrants: An Ambivalent Relationship." *Journal of Ethnic and Migration Studies* 24.4 (July/Aug. 1999): 627–47.

Koopmans, Ruud, and Paul Stratham. "Ethnic and Civic Conceptions of Nationhood and the Differential Success of the Extreme Right in Germany and Italy." In *How Social Movements Matter*. Edited by Marco Guigni, Doug McAdam, and Charles Tilly. Minneapolis: University of Minnesota Press, 1999.

———. "Migration and Ethnic Relations as Field of Political Contention: An Opportunity Structure Approach." In *Challenging Immigration and Ethnic Relations Politics: Comparative European Perspectives*. Edited by Ruud Koopmans and Paul Statham. Oxford: Oxford University Press, 2000.

Koslowski, Rey. *Migrants and Citizens: Demographic Change in the European State System*. Ithaca: Cornell University Press, 2002.

Kyle, David, and Rey Koslowski, eds. *Global Human Smuggling: Comparative Perspectives*. Baltimore: Johns Hopkins University Press, 2001.

Kymlicka, Will. *Multicultural Citizenship: A Liberal Theory of Minority Rights*. Oxford: Clarendon, 1995.

Lubbers, Marcel, and Scheepers, Peer. "French Front National Voting: A Micro and Macro Perspective." *Ethnic and Racial Studies* 25.1 (2002): 120–49.

Mak, Geert. *Gedoemd tot Kwetsbaarheid* [Damned to vulnerability]. Amsterdam: Atlas, 2005.

Miller, Mark. *Foreign Workers in Western Europe: An Emerging Political Force?* New York: Praeger, 1981.

———. "The Political Impact of Foreign Labour." *International Migration Review* 16.1 (1982): 27–60.

Nasraoui, Mustapha. "The Image of Muslim Arabic Culture and the Integration of the North African Immigrant in Europe." *Journal of Mediterranean Studies* 11 (2001): 215–23.

Nielsen, Jørgen. *Towards a European Islam*. London: Macmillan, 1999.

Saint-Blancat, Chantal. "Hypotheses concerning Islam as Religion Transplanted into Europe." *Social Compass* 40.2 (1993): 323–41.

Sassen, Saskia. *Guests and Aliens*. New York: New Press, 1999.

———. "Regulating Immigration in a Global Age: A New Policy Landscape." *Annals of the American Academy of Political and Social Sciences* 570 (2000): 65–77.

Schmitt, Hermann, and Jacques Thomassen. "Distinctiveness and Cohesion of Political Parties." In *Political Representation and Legitimacy in the European Union*. Edited by Hermann Schmitt and Jacques Thomassen. Oxford: Oxford University Press, 1999.

Sniderman, Paul, Pierangelo Peri, Rui J. P. de Figueiredo Jr., and Thomas Piazza. *The Outsider: Prejudice and Politics in Italy*. Princeton. Princeton University Press, 2002.

van der Brug, Wouter, and Meindert Fennema. "Protest or Mainstream? How the European Anti-immigrant Parties Have Developed into Two Separate Groups by 1999." *European Journal of Political Research* (forthcoming).

van der Brug, Wouter, Meindert Fennema, and Jean Tillie. "Anti-Immigrant Parties in Europe: Ideological or Protest Vote?" *European Journal of Political Research* 37 (2000): 77–102.

van Dijk, Teun. *Elite Discourse and Racism*. Newbury Park, CA: Sage, 1993.

Walgrave, Stefaan, and Knut De Swert. "The Making of the (Issues of the) Vlaams Blok: On the Contribution of the News Media in the Electoral Success of the Belgian Extreme-Right Party." Paper presented at the annual meeting of the American Political Science Association, Boston, 2002.

Zolberg, Aristide, and Peter Benda, eds. *Global Migrants, Global Refugees: Problems and Solutions*. London: Berghahn, 2001.

Zolberg, Aristide, and Long Litt Woon. "Why Islam Is Like Spanish: Cultural Incorporation in Europe and the United States." *Politics and Society* 27.1 (March 1999): 5–38.

7

America's Muslims: Issues of Identity, Religious Diversity, and Pluralism

John L. Esposito

America's religious landscape, its religious pluralism, has been transformed dramatically since the last decades of the twentieth century. The American melting pot, however diverse in its origins, has become far more religiously and ethnically pluralistic. A Judeo-Christian and secular country has now expanded its "religious boundaries/borders" to include large populations of Muslims, Hindus, Buddhists, Sikhs, and others. Nowhere is this seen more pointedly than in the contrast of America's landscape in the first half of the twentieth century, dominated by churches and synagogues, and today when mosques, Islamic centers, and Hindu and Buddhist temples dot the American landscape.

Perhaps the most dramatic change has been the growth of Islam and Muslims in America and Europe. In contrast to only several decades ago when they were almost invisible in America and Europe, today Islam and Muslims are the second largest religion and community in the West. The Muslims have become participants in neighborhoods, schools and universities, and the workplace. It is no longer correct to simply speak of Islam versus the West, for Islam is very much within, an integral part, of the West. The capitals or major cities of Islam are not only "over there" in overseas exotic-sounding places like Cairo, Damascus, Baghdad, Mecca, Islamabad, and Kuala Lumpur, but also "here" in New York, Detroit, Washington, Boston, Des Moines, Los Angeles, London, Bradford, Paris, Marseilles, Stockholm, Rotterdam, and Brussels.

Muslims were present in America prior to the nineteenth century principally as a result of the slave trade. However, most slaves were forced to convert to Christianity. In the late nineteenth century, Muslims came to America with waves of immigrant laborers from the Arab world. A major and significant increase in the Muslim population occurred in the mid-to-late twentieth century as many came from the Middle East, South and Southeast Asia, and Africa. In contrast to Europe, where large numbers of Muslims were immigrant laborers needed by the booming economies of the 1960s and 1970s, many who came to America were well-educated professionals, intellectuals, and students. They came for political and economic reasons, leaving behind the constraints of life under authoritarian regimes and failed economies to seek a better life.

The Muslim Mosaic

The Muslim population of America today is far from monolithic in composition and in attitudes and practices. Islam in America is a mosaic of many ethnic, racial, and national groups, immigrants, or their descendents from various parts of the world, as well as indigenous African Americans. The majority of American Muslims are Sunni, but there is a strong minority of Shii. Racial, ethnic, and sectarian differences are often reflected in the composition and politics of some mosques. While many mosques incorporate the diversity of Muslims in America, the membership of others remains drawn along ethnic or racial lines. Their issues, like those of other religious minorities, are those of faith and identity: assimilation versus integration, the preservation and practice of religious faith in an American society informed by Judeo-Christian or secular values, the relationship of religious tradition to the demands of current realities, empowerment in American politics and culture. This situation is further complicated by the problematic historical relationship between Islam and Christianity, in particular between the West and Muslim societies, experiences that range from memories of the Crusades and European colonialism to charges of American neocolonialism, a distorted image of Islam, and Islamophobia. The situation has been compounded by September 11, 2001, and its impact on the status of American Muslims, as seen by issues ranging from racial profiling and hate crimes to the erosion of civil liberties, the Bush administration's foreign policies, and attacks from right-wing ideologues and the militant Christian right.

Integration, Assimilation, or Isolationism?

Living as a minority in a dominant non-Muslim culture as well as experiencing the negative fallout from the acts of violence and terror committed by Muslim extremists and from the effects of Islamophobia, many Muslims have experienced a sense of marginalization, alienation, and powerlessness.

Ingrid Mattson, a professor of Islamic studies at Hartford Seminary and vice president of the Islamic Society of North America, identifies three paradigms adopted by Muslims in America. First, "paradigms of resistance" view the United States as a *jahili* society—pagan, hedonistic, irreconcilably opposed to a society based on obedience to God's commands (an Islamic society). This results in a strong sense of isolationism and resistance to participation in American politics and society, which are viewed as void of morality. Second, "paradigms of embrace" view the United States as their new home/adopted country. Advocates cite the Qur'an in justifying Muslim participation in the ruling apparatus of a non-Muslim country. Many try to show that the constitutional democratic structure of America is almost equivalent to the political structure of an ideal Islamic state—that the American Constitution is concordant with Islamic principles. Third, "paradigms of selective engagement," the category within which the majority fall, strive to define their place as religious minorities in a country that allows great religious freedom. If some have advocated isolationism and others have been disillusioned or skeptical about their ability to bring about anything but superficial change in the American system, many others have increasingly proposed and worked to build an American Muslim identity as well as Muslim communities and institutions.[1]

Religion and Culture

Integral to the experience of Muslims in America, like other religious or ethnic minorities before them, are questions of faith, identity, and culture: Are they Muslims in America or American Muslims? Can Muslims become part and parcel of a secular, predominantly Judeo-Christian, pluralistic American society without sacrificing or losing their identity? Can Muslims be fully Muslims in a non-Muslim state that is not governed by Islamic law? Are American society and the American legal system capable of allowing for particular Muslim religious and cultural differences within the Constitution's broader universal claims?

Like other religious and ethnic groups before them, Muslims on the Americanization path have faced issues of integration and assimilation. Many have been influenced by a "myth of return," the belief, no matter how long they have lived here, that they were/are going to return to their native lands at some point in the future. Thus, they did not try to learn English or integrate and participate in American society. Others have felt torn between the "American dream" and the belief that its pursuit would require abandoning their faith and culture. However, as second- and third-generation Muslims increasingly find their identity as Americans, ties to home countries weaken. Many Muslim youth increasingly reject their parents' and grandparents' efforts to define Islam in culture-specific terms and work to create an American Islam that meets the challenges of its own egalitarian ideology. Many have in fact assimilated and been acculturated to a significant degree, educated in America and for the most part accepting or integrating American values with their Islamic heritage. An American Muslim identity is rapidly emerging. The interplay between American values and Islamic values and the mutual reconstitution of each is leading to an understanding of Islam more in tune with dominant American values such as religious tolerance, pluralism, multiculturalism, and multireligious coexistence.

Post-9/11

The impact of 9/11 and the threat of al-Qaeda and global terrorism, post-9/11 American foreign and domestic policy, and growing Islamophobia have made the situation for American Muslims more precarious. The experience of America as liberal, democratic, tolerant, and multicultural has been counterbalanced by the Muslim perception of America as a unipolar global force, using its power to, in the words of one Muslim observer, "redraw the map of the Middle East and broader Muslim world." Charges of racial profiling, the use of secret evidence and the Patriot Act, and the arrest and detention of thousands for planning or engaging in acts of terrorism with very few convictions have fed concerns about indiscriminate arrests and the erosion of Muslim civil liberties.

At the same time, if engagement in the American political system has in the past been hesitant or considered undesirable by many, recent years have witnessed a significant shift. Muslims have become more rooted and conversant with American politics, participated in national and local elections, sought to pursue and defend their domestic and international interests, and developed political action groups and nongovernmental organizations such as the Muslim Political Action Committee, Islamic Society of North America, Islamic Circle of North America, International Institute of Islamic Thought, Council on American-Islamic Relations, Muslim American Society, Muslim Alliance of North America, Institute for Social Policy and Understanding, and Center for the Study of Islam and Democracy. They have increasingly responded to the negative impact of 9/11 on the image of Islam, its identification with violence and terrorism, growing Islamophobia, and threats to or violations of civil liberties.

Central both to the American Muslim experience and to the image of Islam have been issues of pluralism and democracy. Ironically, not only many conservative Muslims but also many fundamentalists and militants as well as non-Muslim experts and critics have questioned whether Islam is compatible with modern notions of pluralism and democracy. This question, which has in fact been addressed for more than a century, has taken on new urgency in recent years. While the limits of this study preclude looking at the political and religious debates of the past, a brief review of contemporary Islamic discourse and several prominent Muslim voices of change will reveal the ways in which Islamic reformers have been grappling with issues of pluralism, tolerance, and democratization. Like reformers in other religious traditions, and most recently in Roman Catholicism (where the reform process led to Vatican II), reformers are often a vanguard that in the face of significant obstacles lay the groundwork for a constructive religious engagement and response to the challenges of contemporary life. Although a global phenomenon, among the more influential voices have been Muslims in the West. They have been influenced by their experiences of America and through their writings and roles as religious leaders or public intellectuals made significant contributions to Islamic reform in the West and in the Muslim world. Among the key areas of their contributions are those that have validated and informed notions of identity, citizenship, and especially pluralism and democracy.

Changing Perceptions of Pluralism

Islam from its origins developed in and responded to a pluralistic world: multireligious, tribal, racial, and ethnic. Both Islamic faith and history (the Qur'an, the example [*sunnah*] of the prophet Muhammad, Islamic law, and Muslim institutions) reflect a pluralism that, although deficient by modern standards, was relatively advanced when compared to Christianity (the far more exclusivist approach of Western Christendom was intolerant of other faiths). Muslims regarded Jews and Christians as people of the book, whose major prophets and original revelations were seen as coming from the one, true God. As "protected" (*dhimmi*) people, in exchange for payment of a head tax (*jizya*), Jews and Christians under Muslim rule could live and practice their faith, guided by their religious leaders. Non-Muslims could and did hold positions of responsibility in society. While conservative Muslim voices continue to celebrate and defend this historic practice, which by modern standards of pluralism and equality of citizenship amount to second-class status, Muslim reformers from Egypt to Indonesia have advocated full and equal citizenship for non-Muslims, to enable a more egalitarian and pluralist society of Muslims and non-Muslims.

Questions of citizenship and the exercise of political rights became increasingly significant for Muslim minorities in the latter half of the twentieth century. At no time had Muslim minority communities been so numerous, widespread, and permanent. Both the swelling numbers of Muslim refugees and the migration of many Muslims to Europe and America made the issue of minority rights and duties within the majority community an ever greater concern for Islamic jurisprudence. What is the relationship of culture to religion? Are Muslims who live in the United States American Muslims, Muslim Americans, or simply Muslims in America? Similar questions existed and exist in Europe and have been addressed, for example, by European Muslims like Tariq Ramadan in his *To Be a European Muslim*. However, if in the past, Muslims found their answers by looking to the *ulama* and muftis in Muslim countries, today contemporary issues of the relationship of faith to culture, the status and rights of minorities, pluralism and tolerance, and the compatibility of Islam and democracy are also addressed by Muslim intellectuals and religious scholars in America and Europe.

The Transatlantic Muslim Diaspora and the Islamic World

The remarkable demographic and religious emergence of Islam as a major faith in the West has not only underscored the importance of Islam in Europe and America but also transformed relations between Muslims in the West and those in predominantly Muslim countries.[2] For centuries the development and flow of Islamic faith and knowledge came from the Muslim world, from the writings and interpretations of a range of intellectuals and activists (Islamic modernists in the Arab world and South Asia like Jamal al-Din al-Afghani,

Muhammad Abduh, Rashid Rida, Ahmad Khan, and Muhammad Iqbal) to the early trailblazers of contemporary Islamic revivalism (like Hasan al-Banna, Sayyid Qutb, Mawlana Mawdudi among others).[3] This transfer of information and communication was one way. Today the information sources and flow of ideas have broadened just as the Islamic community or *umma* itself has expanded and become more global geographically. Today information, ideas, financial resources, and influence flow in both directions on a multilane superhighway.[4] It is a movement encompassing diverse people, ideologies, institutions, and mass communications. Two-way communication and exchange occur through scholars' and activists' travel, speaking engagements, publications, video and audio tapes, and increasingly in cyberspace. The process is also multileveled, involving individuals (scholars, preachers, and activists), movements, and countries.

America: A Climate for Ijtihad

The diaspora or periphery, in particular the Muslims of America as well as Europe, has become *a* center, and in time may become *the* center in fact if not in religious sentiment, for the actual development of Islamic thinking on many important areas of reinterpretation (*ijtihad*) and reform in theology, law, and history. While much of the Islamic world (Muslim countries) remains under authoritarian regimes with limited freedoms of assembly, thought, speech, and expression as well as shrinking financial and institutional resources, the opportunities afforded in the West have presented conditions for significant growth and development.

In recent decades, the more open religious, political, and intellectual climate in the West has produced a broad range of American- and European-educated scholars, activists, and political leaders whose writings and training of a new generation have increasingly had a significant impact on Islamic thought and activism. Many have pursued and debated reformist methodologies in Qur'an and *hadith* criticism as well as legal reform. Intellectually, Muslim experiences of the West have produced serious thinking about simply following past traditions versus employing a more thoroughgoing process of reinterpretation and reform (*taqlid* and *ijtihad*). Among the more visible and influential scholars and public intellectuals from America have been Seyyed Hossein Nasr, Ismail al-Faruqi, Fazlur Rahman, Abdul Aziz Sachedina, Fathi Osman, Sulayman Nyang, Sherman Jackson, Mahmoud Ayoub, Khaled Abou El Fadl, Muqtedar Khan, and others who have addressed issues of faith and practice, religious leadership and authority, religious and political pluralism, tolerance, minority rights (Muslim and non-Muslim), and gender.

Islam and Pluralism: Past and Present

Islam recognizes both Jews and Christians as "people of the book," those who have special status because God revealed his will through his prophets, including Abraham, Moses, and Jesus, which both communities respectively follow.

Indeed, the Qur'an 2.62 states: "Those who believe—the Jews, the Christians, and the Sabeans—whosoever believe in God and the Last Day and do good works, they shall have their reward from their Lord and shall have nothing to fear, nor shall they come to grief." Muslims accept Jesus's teachings of love and compassion for humankind and obedience to God but reject what they regard as later Christian interpolations or distortions of the gospel message due to foreign influences, such as the Trinity, Jesus's transformation from prophet to the Son of God, and Jesus's vicarious atonement or self-sacrifice for the salvation of humankind (Muslims believe that salvation is an individual matter and cannot be achieved for one person by the deeds of another).

Some Muslims have been suspicious of interfaith dialogue because it was initiated by Christians who remain associated with memories of European colonialism, the crown and cross/Christian missionaries, and the continued political and economic dominance of the Western world. Could pluralism be just another form of a hidden imperialism in religious garb, Muslims wondered? Nevertheless, in a matter of decades, Muslims have become partners in dialogue, religious and civilizational, locally and globally, in international and domestic dialogues with the Vatican, World Council of Churches, National Council of Churches, United States Conference of Catholic Bishops, and local interreligious dialogues in cities and towns in many parts of the world. Dialogue and issues of pluralism, religious and political, have become an important part of contemporary Islamic discourse.

Mainstream Muslim religious scholars and activists today reexamine and redefine their faith based upon the premise that pluralism is a foundational principle of nature and one confirmed by the Qur'an. They emphasize the equality of all humanity, citing the Qur'anic teaching that God created a world of different nations, ethnicities, tribes, and languages (30.22; 48.13) and that pluralism in systems, civilizations, and laws is to be permanent (5.48, 69). They believe that the purpose of these differences was not the promotion of war and discord, but, rather, a sign from God that all people should strive to better understand each other. Thus, they argue, Islam favors mutual acceptance and appreciation since, according to the Qur'an, difference is intended to encourage competition in virtue among nations and guarantee progress (2.251). Several major Muslim intellectuals, whose writings, ideas, and students have had an impact on Muslims in the West as well as in Muslim majority countries, exemplify this broad-based phenomenon and contemporary Islamic discourse on pluralism and democratization.

Voices of Pluralism and Democracy

As noted previously, Muslims continue to struggle with basic issues of identity and participation in American society. Are they American Muslims or Muslims in America? Some describe the prevailing orientations as Muslim democrats or Muslim isolationists, others use terms like progressive or liberal Muslims versus conservative or fundamentalist Muslims.

The unity of the Muslim community can seem stronger than the reality. On issues such as the defense of Islam and Muslims, they are often in agreement and will mobilize and act together. However, the dividing line is political participation, representing very different conceptions of the role of Islam and Muslims in America.[5] Isolationists view America from a conservative theological viewpoint and through its foreign policies toward the Muslim world. They see America as a land of unbelief (*kufr*), neither governed by nor geared toward *sharia*. America's democracy, pluralism, and freedom are seen as producing an immoral, sexually promiscuous, and permissive society. Their critics, reformers or Muslim democrats, often point out that isolationists are formalists who fail to appreciate the fact that "both the American constitution and the Islamic state seek justice, protection and the moral and material well-being of their citizens."[6] Isolationists view America as an evil empire whose foreign policies are regarded as anti-Muslim; its promotion of democracy and human rights in Muslim countries is perceived as based upon a double standard. Rejecting America's political system does not preclude participation and prospering in America's economy. Muslim democrats accuse Muslim isolationists of creating intellectual and political ghettos but believe that they have become more marginalized as greater numbers of Muslims have become more organized and mobilized to fight for their rights and interests nationally and internationally. Muslim democrats are not blind to America's shortcomings and double standards but appreciate and value the principles of America, the freedoms and opportunities it offers, which often stand in sharp contrast to existing conditions in many Muslim countries.

Muqtedar Khan of the University of Delaware, born and raised in India, with a PhD in government and international relations from Georgetown University, describes the accomplishments of Muslim democrats as first and foremost their liberal interpretation of Islam, formulated in America and implemented through Muslim organizations and institutions. The result is that during the past three decades

> Muslim democrats have shifted the Muslim community's focus from battling the West to building bridges with it. They have rejuvenated the tradition of *ijtihad*, or independent thinking among Muslims, and now speak openly of *fiqh al-aqliat* (Islamic law, or interpretation of the *sharia*, in places where Muslims are a minority). They have emphasized Islamic principles of justice, religious tolerance, and cultural pluralism. They have Islamized Western values of freedom, human rights and respect for tolerance by finding Islamic sources and precedents that justify them.[7]

Over the years, Muslim reformist thought has slowly taken shape in America. A review of several Muslim intellectuals highlights several core theological and legal questions and the reinterpretations of sacred texts and history employed to articulate a rationale for modern and postmodern reform. Their ideas are not only important in and for themselves but also because they reflect similar positions held by many other reform-minded Muslims.

Religious exclusivism is part of the theological heritage and religious worldview of many Muslims and has been a major factor affecting the formation of American Muslim identity, their integration, assimilation, or isolationism, and attitudes toward religious pluralism. Many Muslims, like many Christians, have believed that the truth of their faith necessarily precludes salvation for the other. Islam and American society are seen in terms of belief versus unbelief, truth versus falsity, with little middle ground. A variation on this outlook is one which, though not formally exclusivist, so privileges Islam and a sense of supercessionism that other faiths are very much seen as the other.

Mahmoud Ayoub of Temple University, born and raised in Lebanon and educated at the University of Pennsylvania and Harvard University, maintains that religious exclusivism is not in accord with Islam's worldview and teachings. The Qur'an declares, "To everyone we have appointed a way and a course to follow" (5.48), and "For each there is a direction toward which he turns; vie therefore with one another in the performance of good works. Wherever you may be, God shall bring you all together [on the day of judgment]. Surely God has power over all things" (2.148).

Similarly, Abdul Aziz Sachedina of the University of Virginia, a prolific scholar and religious leader, maintains that religious exclusivism is not simply part of Islamic history but has been a common phenomenon in all world religions. All have had a tendency to act as if they had a patent on divine revelation, espousing supremacy rather than accommodation when faced with another religious viewpoint. This lack of religious pluralism, the assertion by each religion that it alone is the one true religion, which renders competing traditions false and valueless, is the biggest problem facing interreligious dialogue. The result has too often been a clash between cultures and dehumanization of the other.[8]

Ayoub points out that "religious diversity is a normal human situation ... the consequence of the diversity of human cultures, languages, races, and different environments."[9] Ayoub sees a synthesis in Islam of the Qur'anic dialectic between unity and diversity, revealed in the Qur'an's affirmation (2.213) of the existence of "the Book which is the heavenly archetype of all divine revelations and of which all true scriptures are but earthly exemplars."[10] He seeks to bridge the gap between affirmation of the truth of one's faith and acceptance of others by also identifying two basic understandings of Islamic identity in the Qur'an—formal membership in an institutionalized religion and a deeper, personal identity based upon a believer's individual faith, or *iman*. Since the truth or falsity of an individual's faith can be determined only by God, Ayoub maintains, faith is the "primary, universal and overarching principle" that leads to the recognition of a genuine religious identity open to the acceptance of religious pluralism.[11]

For Sachedina, the unique characteristic of Islam—belief in the oneness of God (*tawhid*)—unites the Muslim community with all humanity because God is the creator of all humans, irrespective of their religious traditions. Furthermore, the Qur'an teaches that on the day of judgment all will be judged, irrespective of sectarian affiliation, on their moral performance as members of the world community. He concludes: "The idea that 'the People are one community' is the foundation of a theological pluralism that presupposes the divinely ordained equivalence and equal rights of all human beings."[12] Thus, for Sachedina, salvation ultimately depends not simply on belonging to a specific faith but on ethical or moral conduct.

In Islam issues of identity, pluralism, and participation within society are more often than not defined and understood within the context of Islamic law and institutions. More conservative or traditional Muslims in America and Europe have often placed, or believed they have to place, their self-definition and relationship to non-Muslim societies within the classical division of the world into the house/land of Islam (*dar al-Islam*), with the requirement that *sharia* be the law of the land, and the house/land of war (*dar al-harb*). As a result, some immigrants and religious leaders have believed that since *sharia* is not applied in the West, it is a house/land of unbelief (*dar al-kufr*) to be avoided or lived in on a temporary basis and in relative isolation from the broader non-Islamic society. In recent years, many reform-minded Muslims have either said that these classical divisions or understandings contradict the Qur'an or that they reflect past conditions and interpretations that are no longer useful or relevant in modern times:

> That universal narrative [of the Qur'an] that emphasized the common destiny of humanity was severed from its universal roots by the restrictive Islamic conception of a political order based on the membership of only those who accepted the divine revelation to Muhammad. As this exclusivist community gained control of its public order and directed its political and military might in order to secure its dominance beyond the sphere of faith [*dar al-iman*] to create the sphere of submission [*dar al-islam*], territories administered by the Muslim state, the jurists formulated the rulings legitimizing Muslim dominance, if not necessarily the ascendancy of the Islamic faith, over the world.[13]

Others have turned to alternative traditional concepts to legitimate their identity and residence in America such as house/land of treaty (*dar al-sulh*) or house/place of security (*dar al-amm*), which enabled Muslims in the past to live in non-Muslim territories. They argue that America is more Islamic and offers more security and protection than many current Muslim states. Still others, believing that all the preceding categories from the past are no longer relevant to current global conditions, prefer to speak of the West (and indeed residence and citizenship in any non-Muslim territory) as a house/land of invitation to Islam (*dar al-dawa*).[14]

The Muslims of America have been challenged to define their Islamic identity while accommodating multiple levels of diversity and pluralism. For many immigrant Muslims, forging a new national identity while retaining their identity as a Muslim minority in a secular society, with a predominant Judeo-Christian legacy, has raised many issues. Fathi Osman, an Egyptian

American scholar, trained at Al-Azhar University and among the first generation of Muslims to earn a PhD from Princeton University, has been an influential guide. Having lived in Britain and now for many years in America, Osman has written extensively on issues of Muslim identity in the West and on pluralism, tolerance, and democracy in Islam.

Writing in the context of a global Muslim diaspora that now comprises more Muslims than at any time in history and in which many in America and Europe are permanent communities, Osman counters the concern that Islam requires Muslims to live in a state guided by Islamic law and thus compels those who live abroad (outside *dar al-Islam*) to return when feasible to an Islamic community-state. He affirms the legitimacy of permanent Muslim minority communities, maintaining that Muslim unity does not mean that all Muslims must live in single state.

If the tendency of conservatives and fundamentalists has been to emphasize a more monolithic and exclusivist vision, reformers emphasize the Islamic roots for a more global, diverse, and pluralistic worldview. Differences and divisions, ethnic and racial pluralism, are acknowledged as grounded and legitimated in Qur'anic passages such as 30.22 and 49.13. Thus, they conclude that the Qur'an mandates that Muslims cohabit the earth and share together with others of diverse backgrounds and faiths and cooperate in developing humankind. In Islamic history, the experiences of the early Islamic caliphates and later of Andalusia are cited as examples of coexistence and cooperation when peoples of different beliefs and ethnicities held positions in government and society and were able to practice their faith.[15]

The classic starting point for moving beyond the confines of exclusivism and pluralism has been the Qur'anic doctrine of the people of the book. The Qur'an acknowledges the shared spiritual space among the monotheistic faiths, the common vision of the three Abrahamic faiths—Judaism, Christianity and Islam. Thus, the major task for early Muslims was to secure their identity within the God-centered worldview which they shared with other faiths. A primary text to support this understanding is Qur'an 2.213, which affirms three aspects that are fundamental to the Qur'anic conception of religious pluralism: the unity of humankind under one God, the particularity of religions brought by the prophets, and the role of revelation in resolving differences among these faith communities. All prophets represented the same revelation, although different aspects were emphasized at different times. While the specificity of religions is not denied, the need to look beyond their differences in belief and practice is also stressed.[16] Sachedina concludes: "Islam recognizes and even confirms its salvific efficacy within the wider boundaries of monotheism."[17] However, as he acknowledges, despite Qur'an 2.213's message of pluralism, during the early centuries of imperial expansion the *ulama* often legitimated the acts of their ruler-patrons by claiming that this verse was abrogated by other verses requiring Muslims to fight unbelievers.

Islam, like other faiths, has had to balance its sense of uniqueness or special dispensation with recognition of others faiths. The Qur'an's recognition of Christians and Jews as valid faith communities is counterbalanced by the fact that the Muslim community is still considered the "ideal" or the "best" community. Thus, the ultimate question or "acid test of pluralism is whether a religion is willing to recognize members of other religions as potential citizens in the world to come. Is such citizenship conferred *in spite* of or *because* of the person's membership in another religion?"[18]

Pluralism and Minorities in Islam (Dhimmi) Revisited

Muslim attitudes and relations with non-Muslims have been guided in the past by the concept/doctrine of the *dhimmi* (protected peoples). Reformers in recent years, from Egypt to Indonesia and North America to Europe, have reexamined and reinterpreted the prevailing understanding of this concept. Some maintain that rather than implying second-class status, the word *dhimma* (found only in the *hadith* and not in the Qur'an) was intended to designate a special covenant of protection between Muslims, on the one hand, and Jews and Christians, on the other. Similarly, the notion of people of the book is revisited by those who call for a new translation of the Arabic phrase *ahl al-kitab*. Since Arabic *ahl* always signifies a family relationship, its usual translation into English as "people of the book" should more correctly be "family of the book." The result is a more pluralistic understanding of the Qur'anic message. Just as the Qur'an enjoins Muslims and all people of faith to love and be kind to their families, so too this injunction applies to the familial relationship which exists between Islam/Muslims and Jewish and Christian communities.

A somewhat similar conclusion is derived from the Qur'anic principle of coexistence and the willingness of the dominant Muslim community to recognize the people of the book as self-governing communities that are free to determine own internal affairs. Yet, historically Islamic law never accepted the equality of believers and nonbelievers but institutionalized inferiority of non-Muslims—contrary to the pluralistic spirit of the Qur'an—as "necessary" for the well-being of Muslim public order. Because non-Muslims had deliberately spurned the offer of Islam, their inferior status was not imposed, but freely chosen in the opinion of the legal scholars.[19] Heresy and apostasy, although ill defined, remained punishable crimes.

The globalization of religion and with it the new religious context of Muslims in America has led some, in particular Osman, to situate religious pluralism beyond the children of Abraham (Jews, Christians, and Muslims) within the broader and more inclusive Qur'anic category (17.70) of the children of Adam. Thus, Muslim interreligious dialogue must be extended to Hindus, Buddhists, Taoists, and other faiths on the basis of Qur'an 7.172–73, which "teaches that every human being has his or her spiritual compass, and has been granted dignity by God (17.70). Moreover, Muslims are not simply to respect others but have a Qur'anic obligation to guarantee freedom of faith and opinion (2.256) and freedom of expression for all people (2.282)."[20] Recognition and acceptance of the Islamic roots for this notion of the children of Abraham provide the basis for development of universal relations and global pluralism. Ayoub adds: "We Muslims must look at the great religious figures—

prophets, philosophers and the great teachers of human history—and discover how they fit into this broad Islamic framework."[21]

Islam and Democracy

For more than a century, Muslims have grappled with the issue of Islamic reform and Islam's relationship to modernization and to democracy. In recent decades, especially with the rise of militant Islam and global terrorism, a persistent question has been whether Islam is compatible or incompatible with democracy. Employing an approach similar to that initiated by a generation of Islamic modernists in the first half of the twentieth century, such as Egypt's Muhammad Abduh and Pakistan's Muhammad Iqbal, Muslim scholars today reinterpret concepts and institutions such as consultation (*shura*) and consensus (*ijma*) and legal principles such as equity (*istihsan*) and the general welfare (*maslaha*) to provide the bases for the development of modern Muslim notions or authentic versions of democracy, from the acceptance of parliamentary government and civil society to the rule of law and the equality of women and minorities. While some reinterpret traditional beliefs to essentially legitimate Western-generated forms of democracy, others develop their own forms of political participation and democracy appropriate to Islamic values and realities. Most are carefully crafted to demonstrate or claim continuity between the Islamic tradition and heritage and modern reforms.

The traditional and fundamental concept is consultation (*shura*), the process by which the elders of the early community selected or elected Muhammad's successors, the first caliphs, and a practice incumbent upon rulers in making important decisions. The meaning and function of consultation are reinterpreted and extended beyond its identification with the institution of the caliphate. The religious authority behind *shura*, its derivation from prophetic practice and not merely as a formal or ceremonial exercise conducted by the caliphs, is underscored. More importantly, some reformers argue that Qur'an 4.59 and 4.83 refer in the plural to those entrusted with authority, thus indicating that authority belongs to organizational bodies rather than to individual rulers.[22] This rationale lays the groundwork for the acceptance of parliamentary or other elected representative bodies.

Early Islamic history, in particular the selection of the Four Rightly Guided Caliphs, is also used to argue that elections are Islamically acceptable. Though each caliph was chosen, all went to the public in the mosque to receive an oath of approval or allegiance (*baya*). Osman defines *baya* as the "mutual pledge from the ruler to follow *sharia* and earn the public's approval and support through his services, and from the people to support the ruler and advise him."[23] Thus, public approval (*baya*) serves as confirmation of the election process.

Osman's interpretation emphasizes the importance of the majority of the people or consent of the governed. His *ijtihad* is based upon the claim that the Qur'an does not teach that relying on a few people necessarily leads to perfect decisions and that prophetic tradition urges the individual to yield to the majority when a serious split occurs. Precedents in the lives of both the Prophet and the early caliphs attest to the fact that decisions were made according to majority opinion even when they differed from the leader's opinion.[24] Just as voting has become an accepted method for choosing governing boards of unions, professional organizations, and student associations, so too voting should be considered legitimate for choosing a government.[25]

Khaled Abou El Fadl of UCLA Law School, educated at Princeton University, covers similar ground with a somewhat different interpretation and conclusion. The caliphate was based on a contract (*aqd*) between the caliph and *ahl al-hall wa al-aqd* (the people who have the power of contract) who give their *baya* (allegiance or consent) to the caliph; *sharia* defines the terms of the contract. However, when it came to determining who had the power to choose and remove the ruler, Muslim jurists differed significantly. Some argued that the public at large had the power; the vast majority of jurists argued, more pragmatically, restricting it to the *ahl al-aqd*, those with the necessary power to insure the obedience or, in the alternative, the consent of the public. Consent in premodern Muslim discourses was the equivalent of acquiescence. Thus, although Islamic political theory generated concepts that suggest an idea of representative government, they were never fully endorsed. "In the dominant paradigm both ruler and ruled are God's agents in implementing the divine law."[26]

The Role of Sharia

As constitutional debates in Afghanistan and Iraq have most recently underscored, central to the question of the compatibility of Islam and democracy is the role of *sharia*, Islamic law. To what extent is government subject to and limited by *sharia* law? Although *sharia* is often simply described as Islamic law, a critical distinction between *sharia* and *fiqh* is necessary. Strictly speaking *sharia* refers to normative revealed principles, values, and legal rules of *sharia*, and *fiqh* to its human interpretation, production, and application (the corpus of Islamic law), which were historically and socially conditioned. This distinction underscores the relative, fallible, human dimension of Islamic law as well as its dynamic nature, which enables it to be reinterpreted and reformed to respond to multiple and diverse situations.

Many reformers, in particular those identified with the Islamic modernist movement in the late nineteenth and early twentieth centuries and those who continued to follow their legacy, express the divine-human, immutable-mutable dimensions of Islamic law by distinguishing duties to God (*ibadat*, worship, unchanging religious observances such as prayer five times a day, the fast of Ramadan, pilgrimage to Mecca) from duties to others (*muamalat*, social transactions or relations). The distinction between *sharia* and *fiqh* and between Islamic law's duties to God and duties to others underscores the extent to which much of Islamic law—from forms of government and notions of governance to individual and collective rights and gender relations—may be seen as reflecting time-bound, human interpretations that are open to adaptation and change.

As previously noted, an essential characteristic of a legitimate Islamic government is that it is a subject to and limited by *sharia* law. Some reformers argue that there is a distinction between the supremacy of law and the supremacy of a specific set of legal rules, which can provide the basis for an accommodation with democratic principles.

The supremacy of *sharia* has often been understood as the requirement that governments operate within the limits or parameters of *sharia*, in particular the limits (*hudud*) or laws and punishments set by God for adultery, theft, and drinking of alcohol. Reformers argue that the rule of law need not be taken to mean that government is bound by a codebook of specific rules but rather they must make or interpret laws in light of Islamic criteria such as justice, public welfare, and human dignity.[27] Thus, rather than insist that the legal system must be based upon or reimplement past Islamic legal systems, a rationale advocated by some reformers and employed by some governments has been to require that no law be contrary to Islam or basic Islamic principles.

Reformists' methodologies that emphasize the need to read and interpret texts within contexts and to distinguish between *sharia* and *fiqh* conditioned by sociohistorical contexts were seen quite sharply in March 2005. On March 18, Amina Wadud, a professor at Virginia Commonwealth University, led a community of men and women in Friday congregational prayer in New York City. On March 30, Tariq Ramadan, a prominent European Muslim intellectual and activist, called for an international moratorium on the *hudud*. Wadud's pioneering study, *The Quran and Woman: Rereading the Sacred Text from a Woman's Perspective*, a rereading and reinterpretation of the Qur'an, argues that the Qur'an properly read and understood reveals a message of equality and is gender inclusive. Thus, patriarchal interpretation and implementation, not the Qur'an, are responsible for those beliefs, practices, and values which have often been used to marginalize or limit women's rights and roles in society. While there is a tradition of female leaders in Islam and some recognition that women can lead an all-women congregation in prayer, public/mixed-gender prayers challenged traditions developed and maintained by most religious scholars and leaders. Amid worldwide controversy, Wadud's action and promise of similar prayer gatherings in other cities in North America, some sponsored by the Progressive Muslim Union of North America, reflect the growing empowerment of Muslim women and the use of new methodologies and interpretations of sacred texts and law.

Ramadan, whose most recent book is *Western Muslims and the Future of Islam*, issued an equally revolutionary reformist challenge to traditional interpretations of *sharia*, specifically the *hudud*, with a call for an immediate international moratorium on corporal punishment, stoning, and the death penalty in all Muslim countries.

As previously discussed, a fundamental question of contemporary Islamic identity that Muslim majority societies and Muslims around the world confront is the role of *sharia*, in particular how or whether to implement the penalties (*hudud*) prescribed in the Islamic penal code. Ramadan notes that today there are a spectrum of positions regarding implementation of the *hudud*, from those who insist on its immediate and strict application to those who see the *hudud* punishments as obsolete and out of place in contemporary Muslim societies. He calls upon Muslims to reject "formalist legitimization," which has had a devastating impact on women, especially the poor, and to reconcile themselves with the message of Islam, which "demands education, justice and the respect of pluralism. Societies will never reform themselves by repressive measures and punishment but more so by the engagement of each in civil society and the respect of the popular will as well as just legislation guaranteeing the equality of women and men, poor and rich before the law."[28] Like Wadud and other reformers, Ramadan challenges the blind acceptance of past regulations, calls upon all Muslims (the laity as well as the *ulama*) to reexamine and address this issue, emphasizes the importance of reading texts within contexts, and affirms the right and need for fresh interpretations or reinterpretations (*ijtihad*) of Islamic law where needed.

Conclusion

The American Muslim experience, like that of Christians and Jews before them, reflects struggles of faith and identity (integration versus assimilation), political participation, institution building, and acculturation. They have faced the challenge of constructing an American identity that incorporates faith and values within America's melting pot or, more recently, its multicultural society. The twenty-first century will prove a dynamic and challenging one for Muslims worldwide. The Islamic community or *umma* itself reflects the impact of globalization both in its changing demographics and intellectual and political developments. The struggle of diaspora communities in America as in Europe to define or, more accurately, redefine, identity, and empower themselves to forge American and European Muslim identities has produced a dynamic period of transformation. A broad range of interpreters and interpretations has emerged. In various ways, Muslim scholars, students, and ideas have emerged as new voices and actors for change, impacting and influencing the development of Islam both in the West and in the Muslim world.

NOTES

1. Ingrid Mattson, "How Muslims Use Islamic Paradigms to Define America," in *Religion and Immigration: Christian, Jewish, and Muslim Experiences in the United States*, ed. Yvonne Yazbeck Haddad, Jane I. Smith, and John L. Esposito (Walnut Creek, CA: AltaMira, 2003), chap. 11.

2. See, for example, Steven Vertovec and Ceri Peach, eds., *Islam in Europe: The Politics of Religion and Community* (New York: St. Martin's, 1997); Philip Lewis, *Islamic Britain: Religion, Politics, and Identity among British Muslims* (London: Taurus, 1994); Jørgen Nielsen, *Towards a European Islam* (New York: St. Martin's, 1999); Yvonne Haddad and Jane Smith, eds., *Muslim Communities in North America* (Albany: State University of New York Press, 1994); Jane I. Smith, *Islam in*

America (New York: Columbia University Press, 1999); and Sulayman Nyang, *Islam in the United States of America* (Chicago: Kazi, 1999).

3. For information on their thought, see John O. Voll, *Islam: Continuity and Change in the Modern World*, 2nd ed. (Syracuse: Syracuse University Press, 1994); and John L. Esposito, *Islam and Politics*, 3rd ed. (Syracuse: Syracuse University Press, 1998).

4. John L. Esposito, "The Muslim Diaspora and the Islamic World," in *Islam in Europe: The New Social, Cultural, and Political Landscape*, ed. Shireen T. Hunter (Westport, CT: Greenwood, 2002).

5. Muqtedar Khan, *American Muslims: Bridging Faith and Freedom* (Beltsville, MD: Amana, 2002), 27.

6. Ibid., 28.

7. Ibid., 30–31.

8. Abdul Aziz Sachedina, *The Islamic Roots of Democratic Pluralism* (Oxford: Oxford University Press, 2001), 22.

9. Mahmoud Ayoub, "Islam and the Challenge of Religious Pluralism," *Global Dialogue* 2.1 (Winter 2000): 55.

10. Ibid., 56.

11. Mahmoud Ayoub, "Islam and Christianity: Between Tolerance and Acceptance," in *Religions of the Book: The Annual Publication of the College Theology Society*, vol. 38, ed. Gerard S. Sloyan (Lanham, MD: College Theology Society, 1992), 28.

12. Sachedina, *Islamic Roots of Democratic Pluralism*, 28.

13. Ibid., 50.

14. Tariq Ramadan, *Western Muslims and the Future of Islam* (New York: Oxford University Press, 2004), 72.

15. Mohamed Fathi Osman, "The Children of Adam: An Islamic Perspective on Pluralism" (occasional paper, Center for Muslim-Christian Understanding, 1997), 21.

16. Sachedina, *Islamic Roots of Democratic Pluralism*, 23.

17. Ibid., 27.

18. Ibid., 38.

19. Ibid., 97.

20. Osman, "Children of Adam," 18.

21. Ayoub, "Islam and the Challenge of Religious Pluralism," 57.

22. Ibid., 46.

23. Osman, "Children of Adam," 47.

24. Ibid., 48.

25. Ibid., 49.

26. Khaled Abou El Fadl, *Islam and the Challenge of Democracy* (Princeton: Princeton University Press, 2004), 11.

27. Ibid., 30–31.

28. Available at http://www.tariqramadan.com/.

BIBLIOGRAPHY

Ayoub, Mahmoud. "Islam and Christianity: Between Tolerance and Acceptance." In *Religions of the Book: The Annual Publication of the College Theology Society*, vol. 38. Edited by Gerard S. Sloyan. Lanham, MD: College Theology Society, 1992.
———. "Islam and the Challenge of Religious Pluralism." *Global Dialogue* 2.1 (Winter 2000).

El Fadl, Khaled Abou. *Islam and the Challenge of Democracy*. Princeton: Princeton University Press, 2004.

Esposito, John L. *Islam and Politics*, 3rd ed. Syracuse: Syracuse University Press, 1998.

———. "The Muslim Diaspora and the Islamic World." In *Islam in Europe: The New Social, Cultural, and Political Landscape*. Edited by Shireen T. Hunter. Westport, CT: Greenwood, 2002.

Haddad, Yvonne, and Jane Smith, eds. *Muslim Communities in North America*. Albany: State University of New York Press, 1994.

Khan, Muqtedar. *American Muslims: Bridging Faith and Freedom*. Beltsville, MD: Amana, 2002.

Lewis, Philip. *Islamic Britain: Religion, Politics, and Identity among British Muslims*. London: Taurus, 1994.

Mattson, Ingrid. "How Muslims Use Islamic Paradigms to Define America." In *Religion and Immigration: Christian, Jewish, and Muslim Experiences in the United States*. Edited by Yvonne Yazbeck Haddad, Jane I. Smith, and John L. Esposito. Walnut Creek, CA: AltaMira, 2003.

Nielsen, Jørgen. *Towards a European Islam*. New York: St. Martin's, 1999.

Nyang, Sulayman. *Islam in the United States of America*. Chicago: Kazi, 1999.

Osman, Mohamed Fathi. "The Children of Adam: An Islamic Perspective on Pluralism." Occasional paper, Center for Muslim-Christian Understanding, 1997.

Ramadan, Tariq. *Western Muslims and the Future of Islam*. New York: Oxford University Press, 2004.

Sachedina, Abdul Aziz. *The Islamic Roots of Democratic Pluralism*. Oxford: Oxford University Press, 2001.

Smith, Jane I. *Islam in America*. New York: Columbia University Press, 1999.

Vertovec, Steven, and Ceri Peach, eds. *Islam in Europe: The Politics of Religion and Community*. New York: St. Martin's, 1997.

Voll, John O. *Islam: Continuity and Change in the Modern World*, 2nd ed. Syracuse: Syracuse University Press, 1994.

8

Religious Diversity in a "Christian Nation": American Identity and American Democracy

Robert Wuthnow

For all the talk about diversity, over 80 percent
of Americans are Christian and over 90 percent
believe in God. And that is why attempts to secularize our society in the name of diversity are intellectually and morally indefensible. To be blunt,
were it not for our Judeo-Christian heritage, freedom would not exist. Not here, not anywhere.
    —William A. Donohue, "Censoring Religious
            Speech," paid advertisement in
        New York Times, September 20, 2004

Scholars generally agree that the United States has become more
diverse in recent decades as a result of immigration. The largest
number of immigrants has come from Mexico and from other
Spanish-speaking countries. Large numbers have also come from
China, Korea, Vietnam, and other countries in east Asia.[1] To the extent that these immigrants were religious in their countries of origin or have become religiously involved in the United States, the
majority are assumed to be Christian and thus have mainly added
to the ethnic diversity of the Christian population and, according
to some observers, revitalized American Christianity in the way
previous waves of European immigration did.[2] The recent immigration is distinctive, though, in also adding significantly to the range
of religious traditions represented in the United States. While there
have been a few Muslims, Hindus, Buddhists, and adherents of
other non-Western religious traditions in the United States for more

than a century, the numbers associated with these traditions have become significantly larger. In considering religious diversity, it is also important to recognize that Americans' awareness of major religious traditions other than Christianity and Judaism has undoubtedly increased, as a result of travel, mass communications, education, and the nation's integration into world markets.

The growing reality and awareness of religious diversity has raised normative questions about the implications of this diversity for the functioning of American democracy. These include such important considerations as whether norms of tolerance are sufficiently robust to protect the rights of new religious communities and produce amicable relationships among them and their neighbors; whether this diversity will require clearer distinctions between church and state or will perhaps erode those distinctions; whether current laws and regulations are capable of dealing with the new complexities, raised by larger numbers of religious holidays and dress and dietary customs; and especially in a climate of concern about terrorism whether democratic ideals involving the free expression of religion can be sustained.

Important as it is to ponder these normative questions, basic empirical questions also need to be addressed. In a democracy, public opinion is presumed to matter, both for its own sake and because it influences how the public votes and how it responds to movements engaged in political advocacy. Insofar as religious organizations make up an influential share of American civil society, it is also important to know what their members think and do. Among the important empirical questions that must be considered, therefore, are questions about the public's awareness of minority religious communities, the public's attitudes toward these groups, how the public thinks about the religious aspects of America's historic identity, and how religious organizations may be encouraging their members to respond to the new diversity.

From 1999 through 2005, I served as director of the Responses to Religious Diversity Project at Princeton University. The project, funded by the Lilly Endowment, sought to understand how the majority Christian population of the United States is responding to the growing presence of other religions, particularly Muslims, Hindus, and Buddhists. Unlike previous sociological studies that have focused on new immigrant congregations and other non-Western religious groups, this project was concerned with the cultural impact of these groups and the implications of this impact for American identity and American democracy.[3] The project was initiated on the premise that diversity involving interaction between adherents of Christianity and adherents of other religions poses different challenges than the more usual varieties of diversity considered in discussions of religious pluralism (such as Protestants and Catholics or white and black Baptists).[4]

The project was a multimethod study that included historical, qualitative, and quantitative research. The historical component involved examining the writings of key religious and political leaders from the time of initial European exploration of the North American continent to the present in order to understand and, indeed, emphasize the extent to which responses to non-Christian religions have *always* been an important feature of American culture, rather than a consideration that emerged only at the end of the twentieth century. The qualitative component involved more than three hundred in-depth interviews. Some of these were conducted with informants at strategic organizations, such as interfaith ministries, antidefamation and civil rights organizations, seminaries, and campus ministries. The majority were conducted among clergy and laity in fourteen cities selected to provide geographic diversity. In each city, interviews were conducted at one mosque, one synagogue, one Hindu temple, and one Buddhist temple or meditation center. Interviews were then conducted at the church closest to each of these mosques, synagogues, temples, or meditation centers. The quantitative component was a nationally representative survey of the adult population of the United States. This survey, the Religion and Diversity Survey, was conducted between September 18, 2002, and February 25, 2003. Thus, it began approximately one year after the September 11, 2001, attacks and ended prior to the start of the U.S. war in Iraq. Up to nineteen calls were made to selected households, and respondents were offered a $10 incentive for participating. A total of 2,910 individuals age eighteen and over, living in the continental United States, were interviewed. Several other surveys have asked a few questions about U.S. attitudes toward Muslims, Hindus, and Buddhists, but the Religion and Diversity Survey is unique in the following respects: it asks questions about the extent, nature, and venues of contact between the general public and each of these religious groups; it asks how many people in the general public have attended worship services at mosques or at Hindu or Buddhist temples; it asks detailed questions about stereotypes of each group (such as whether the group is violent or peace loving); it includes questions about whether the U.S. government should restrict the rights of these religious groups in various ways; and it includes extensive questions about respondents' religious beliefs, practices, and congregational activities, such as whether the respondent thinks all or only some religions are true, whether the respondent has attempted to make converts among adherents of other religions, and whether the respondent's congregation has sponsored interfaith services or other interreligious activities.

The full results of the Responses to Religious Diversity Project are reported in my book *America and the Challenges of Religious Diversity*.[5] In that volume, I examine the changing history of debate about non-Western religions; describe the current beliefs and practices of American Muslims, Hindus, and Buddhists; delineate the various levels (cultural, political, religious) at which these new forms of religious diversity pose challenges; examine how the response to other religions varies and is integrated into the beliefs and practices of spiritual shoppers, inclusive Christians, and exclusive Christians; discuss the particular accommodations that occur in interreligious marriages; show what congregations are (or, in most cases, are not) doing to promote interreligious understanding; and examine the successes and failures of organizations that have tried specifically to facilitate interreligious interaction. Here, I summarize the most important descriptive results of the Religion and Diversity Survey and offer some conclusions about the distinctive ways in which religious diversity is being received in the United States, compared with other countries in which Christianity has historically been dominant, notably Western Europe. The discussion proceeds as follows: a description of the scope of influence of Muslims, Hindus, and Buddhists in the United States; an overview of attitudes toward these groups among the adult population of the United States; an assessment of the extent to which Americans still perceive themselves to be living in a "Christian nation" and the impact of this perception on their attitudes toward non-Christian religions and other minority groups; and a discussion of the tensions within American culture surrounding religious diversity and the implications of these tensions for American democracy.

Two caveats are in order. The first is that my concern is specifically with *religious* diversity. I do not deny that racial diversity, particularly the continuing inequality between African Americans and white European Americans, remains an important issue, nor that other forms of diversity rooted in gender, sexual orientation, social class, and ethnicity are important. For instance, the large number of Latino and Asian immigrants in the United States has added considerably to the diversity of the Christian population, and in my larger study, I examined the implications of these other varieties of diversity. The fact that the United States has been culturally diverse and the fact that racial divisions have been especially acute have often served as a template on which considerations of the new religious diversity are overlaid. I nevertheless emphasize *religious* diversity here, because for many Americans—indeed, nearly all Americans—religion is taken seriously enough that how they think about other religions runs to the core of how they understand their own. Second, I regard religion as sufficiently important that it affects not only how people think and behave in their personal lives (the *privatized* aspect of religion, as it is sometimes called), but also how they think and behave in public. My evidence persuades me that Americans are more deeply theological, if often in ways that theologians would regard as naïve, than most Americans themselves realize. Thus, it is far too easy to regard the current religious diversity simply through the lens of such rubrics as cultural pluralism or religious markets. Religious assumptions profoundly affect our culture and our political behavior.

The Scope of Influence

Studies of religious diversity that focus on the presence of non-Western religions in the United States have generally tried to assess this presence through estimates of numbers of adherents. These estimates vary widely, depending on whether they are drawn from surveys (in which immigrants are often underrepresented), extrapolated from estimates based on mosque or temple attendance, or reported by advocacy groups.[6] Even the most generous of these estimates suggests that Muslims, Hindus, and Buddhists make up a very small percentage of the U.S. population—so small, in fact, that some observers argue that the nation is no more diverse than it ever was or, at least, that the present diversity is not very important.[7] But it is no more accurate to assess the presence of non-Western religions simply in terms of adherents than it would be to understand the place of African Americans only in terms of their proportion in the population, or Jews through theirs.

A better way to assess influence is to ask about integration into the wider society. This approach is commonly used in studies of race and ethnicity and, of course, in discussions of immigrants' assimilation. From census figures, it is reasonable to assume that most immigrants from predominantly Muslim, Hindu, and Buddhist countries are immigrants who are part of the middle or upper-middle class, in terms of education levels, employment in business and the professions, and income. In a paper with Conrad Hackett that examined Muslims, Hindus, and Buddhists in a large survey of the U.S. population and selected cities, I was able to demonstrate that these religious groups are well integrated in terms of these standard measures of social status.[8] However, there are discrepancies, for instance, between the incomes earned by the adherents of these groups and those of Christians and Jews with comparable levels of education. We also found the adherents of these non-Western religious groups to be less integrated in terms of political knowledge and participation than the majority religious population. Again, there were variations from group to group. Among all these groups, though, the likelihood of having friends and acquaintances outside their own group appeared to be quite high.

Interpersonal contact across religious lines points to another instructive way to assess the scope of influence of minority religions in the United States. For instance, Jews make up only about 2% of the U.S. population, yet a large proportion of non-Jews in the United States report having friends or acquaintances who are Jews.[9] Whether such friendships actually exist or are only *presumed* to exist is arguable. However, the perceptions themselves are important. In the Religion and Diversity Survey, I was able to examine further the extent to which the U.S. population claims to have contact with Muslims, Hindus, and Buddhists. Because the meaning of terms such as "friends" and "close friends" in surveys has been shown to be quite variable, I asked people about *contact* and then, for those who indicated having had any contact with each group, asked about the frequency, venues, and outcomes of such contact. The results are summarized in table 8.1. Relatively few Americans claim to have had a "great deal" of contact with Muslims, Hindus, or Buddhists. The rates are 6%, 3%, and 3%, respectively. However, if those who have had either a "great deal" or "fair amount" of contact are combined, the figures rise to 24%, 14%, and 14%, respectively. These figures are one indication that the perceived presence of Muslims, Hindus, and Buddhists is substantially greater than the tiny fraction of Americans who are actually adherents of these religions might suggest. Moreover, if everyone who claims to have had at least "a little" contact is considered, then almost half of the public (48%) has had some exposure to Muslims, and about a third (35% and 34%, respectively) has had some exposure to Hindus and Buddhists.

Table 8.1 also shows the venues in which Americans who have had contact with Muslims, Hindus, or Buddhists believe this contact has occurred. According to these responses, most of the contact occurs in the workplace or

TABLE 8.1. Personal Contact with Religious Groups (percent)

	Muslims	Hindus	Buddhists
How much?			
a great deal	6	3	3
a fair amount	18	11	11
only a little	24	21	20
almost none	19	23	21
none	32	41	44
Among those with any contact, context is . . .			
work	41	35	29
neighborhood	15	12	18
shopping, personal business	37	45	42
other	6	6	8
Outcome is mostly . . .			
pleasant	64	67	76
mixed	27	24	19
unpleasant	6	5	3
How often discuss religion?			
never	47	52	38
almost never	19	22	24
occasionally	26	20	29
often	8	5	9
Contacts mostly with . . .			
black Muslims	22		
other Muslims	58		
immigrant Buddhists			41
convert Buddhists			42

Source: Religion and Diversity Survey.

through shopping and other personal business dealings. Upward of three-quarters in each case locate their contact in these contexts. Fewer than a fifth say their contacts have occurred in their neighborhood. And fewer than one in ten indicate some other venue, suggesting that relatively few religious lines are being crossed in actual worship settings or within families.[10]

When asked to assess the outcome of these contacts, most Americans say their contacts with Muslims, Hindus, and Buddhists have been pleasant. The figures range between two-thirds and three-quarters of those who have had any contact. However, the fact that a third say their contacts with Muslims have been mixed or unpleasant may be an indication of incipient religious tension, especially in view of some other responses to which we will turn momentarily.

In asking about interreligious contact, I thought it important to ask whether this contact actually involved discussions of religion. If it did, this might be an indication of efforts to forge greater understanding of religious differences. It might also suggest religious arguments or attempts at proselytization. The results are ambiguous, but are probably best interpreted to suggest that religious discussions are seldom part of interreligious contact. Whereas fewer than one person in ten claims to have had such discussions "often," approximately two in three claims to have "never" or "almost never" discussed religion. The unlikelihood of having discussed religion is also consistent with the fact that most interreligious contact of this kind is infrequent and occurs in workplace and business settings, rather than in more intimate contexts.

The data about contacts point to one other important distinction. While it is often assumed that Muslims, Hindus, and Buddhists are immigrants, estimates suggest that between a quarter and a third of American Muslims are African Americans who have converted to Islam and that as many as half of American Buddhists are probably converts.[11] The figures for contact would support these estimates. Twenty-two percent of those who had contacts with Muslims said their contact was with black Muslims, and 58% said it had been with other Muslims (the remainder were unsure). The percentages who had contact with immigrant Buddhists and with convert Buddhists were almost equal (41% and 42%, respectively).

Yet another way of assessing the influence of non-Western religions is to ask about perceived familiarity with the *teachings* of these religions. The results are shown in table 8.2. The distributions of responses are similar to those we have just considered for contact. A relatively small proportion of the American public claims to be "very familiar" with the teachings of Islam, Hinduism, or Buddhism (5%, 3%, and 5%, respectively). If those who claim to be at least "somewhat familiar" with these teachings are included, then the proportions point to fairly sizable minorities of the public: 33% say they are somewhat familiar with the teachings of Islam, 22% with the teachings of Hinduism, and 30% with the teachings of Buddhism. How we think about these figures depends, of course, on what standard of comparison is used. Had one assumed that non-Western religions make up such a small proportion of the American population that these religions hardly matter, then the fact that a quarter to a third of the population claims some familiarity with Islam, Hinduism, or Buddhism suggests that religious diversity is a larger issue than one might have supposed. For those who believe knowledge of other religions besides one's own should be the norm, these figures are, of course, disappointing. Indeed, they are disappointing even in comparison with what most Americans *think* the norm should be. When asked, "Do you think people should learn more about religions other than their own, or is it better to avoid learning too much

TABLE 8.2. Perceived Familiarity with Religious Teachings (percent)

Question: How familiar are you with the basic teachings of each religion?	Islam	Hinduism	Buddhism
very familiar	5	3	5
somewhat familiar	28	19	25
somewhat unfamiliar	20	22	20
very unfamiliar	46	56	49
don't know	1	1	1

Source: Religion and Diversity Survey.

about other religions," 83% of the public responded "should learn more," while only 13% said "better to avoid."

Whenever conclusions are drawn about familiarity with religious teachings, qualifications must, of course, be stated. Most Americans claim to be quite familiar with the teachings of Christianity, yet surprisingly few can name the four gospels or the city in which Jesus was born. The same would undoubtedly be true were Americans asked factual questions about Muslim or Buddhist teachings. In the qualitative interviews we conducted, this lack of familiarity was often painfully evident. Even people who regarded themselves as spiritual syncretists often had little knowledge of the world's major religious traditions.

For present purposes, though, the conclusion I draw from the research is that religious diversity—meaning diversity that includes religions outside of Christianity and not just the traditional denominational and confessional varieties within Christianity—is a significant cultural fact in the United States. It is more significant than the occasional presence of a mosque or temple would suggest. It is significant for a large minority of the public, because they have had personal contact with Muslims, Hindus, or Buddhists or because they have somehow gained a modicum of familiarity with the teachings of these religions. Religious diversity is also significant, as we shall see next, because most Americans have opinions about Muslims, Hindus, and Buddhists.

Attitudes toward Muslims, Hindus, and Buddhists

Research on racial prejudice and anti-Semitism has always emphasized its cognitive component, especially the role that negative stereotypes play in prejudicial feelings and discrimination. Positive stereotypes often accompany negative ones, but usually do not counteract the potentially harmful effects of such views. In the case of Muslims, opinion in the American public is mixed, but many Americans emphasize negative traits. On the much-considered question of whether the Muslim religion is violent or peace loving, 40% of the public says that "violent" is a word that applies and 40% says "peace loving" applies

TABLE 8.3. Perceived Traits of Religious Groups (percent who say word applies)

Question: Please tell me if you think each of these words applies to (religion).	Islam	Hinduism	Buddhism
fanatical	47	25	23
violent	40	16	12
peace loving	40	53	63
backward	34	29	27
closed minded	57	35	30
tolerant	32	45	56
strange	44	43	42
appealing	16	19	26

Source: Religion and Diversity Survey.

(table 8.3). Even larger proportions, though, think the Muslim religion is "closed minded" (57%) or "fanatical" (47%). While 32% think Islam is "tolerant," 44% think it is "strange," and 34% regard it as "backward." Only 16% find it "appealing."

Americans' attitudes toward Hindus and Buddhists are more positive than they are toward Muslims, but a sizable minority of the public holds negative views of these religions as well. Americans are more likely to regard Hinduism and Buddhism as peace loving (53% and 63%, respectively) than they are to say these religions are violent (16% and 12%). They are also more likely to consider them tolerant (45% and 56%) than closed minded (35% and 30%). However, about four in ten Americans think Hinduism and Buddhism are strange (43% and 42%). A quarter think these religions are backward. And a quarter think they are fanatical.

One could argue that such attitudes reflect the private opinions of individual Americans and thus have little bearing on public policy. However, the public also has opinions about public policies toward minority religions. On these issues, a majority of Americans generally respond in ways that reflect the nation's official culture of religious freedom, protection of civil liberties, and restraint on government intrusion in religious affairs. Nevertheless, the number of Americans who are willing to abridge these norms is chilling. For instance, 60% of the public favors the government collecting information about Muslim religious groups in the United States (table 8.4). Almost four in ten favors making it harder for Muslims to settle in the United States. A quarter of the public actually favors making it illegal for Muslim groups to meet in the United States. Willingness to monitor or restrict the activities of minority religious groups is not limited to Muslims. Half the public favors the government collecting information about Hindu and Buddhist groups in the United States. A fifth would make it illegal for Hindu or Buddhist groups to meet. Two-thirds of the public favors keeping a close watch on all foreigners in the United States. Two-thirds also favor passing a law to reduce the number of immigrants

TABLE 8.4. Surveillance of Religious Groups (percent who favor or oppose)

Question: Please tell me if you favor or oppose the U.S. government doing each of the following.	Favor	Oppose
collecting information about Muslim religious groups in the United States	60	34
making it harder for Muslims to settle in the United States	38	55
keeping a close watch on all foreigners in the United States	66	30
passing a law to reduce the number of immigrants coming into the country	64	32
collecting information about Hindu religious groups in the United States	51	41
collecting information about Buddhist religious groups in the United States	48	44
making it illegal for Muslim groups to meet in the United States	23	72
making it illegal for Hindu groups to meet in the United States	20	74
making it illegal for Buddhist groups to meet in the United States	20	74
collecting information about some Christian groups in the United States	51	44

Source: Religion and Diversity Survey.

coming into the country. These attitudes are not limited only to foreigners and members of non-Western religions. Half the public also favors the government collecting information about some Christian groups in the United States.

Willingness to curb the rights of Muslims, foreigners, and other groups has undoubtedly been reinforced by the concerns about terrorism, prompted by the 9/11 attacks on New York and Washington. Many civil liberties groups, for instance, believe the Patriot Act that extended government surveillance activities would not have been passed under other circumstances. In the Religion and Diversity Survey, 31% of respondents said they were "extremely worried" or "very worried" about the threat of another terrorist attack against the United States. Yet, it is not accurate to say that negative attitudes toward Muslims and other non-Western religious groups can be *explained* by concerns about terrorism. Indeed, those surveyed who were most worried about terrorism were only slightly more likely to hold negative views of Muslims than those who were less worried. Other surveys that have compared U.S. attitudes toward Muslims before and after 9/11 also disconfirm the notion that negative attitudes are simply a function of fears about terrorism.[12]

America as a Christian Nation

Whatever people may think about individual coworkers or neighbors who happen to be Muslim or Hindu or Buddhist, there is a significant tension in American culture between a long-standing and still deeply held view among sizable numbers of Americans that America is a Christian nation, on the one hand, and norms of civic liberty that recognize the reality and the rights of non-Christian groups, on the other. The extent to which Americans continue to associate their nation with Christianity is evident in table 8.5. Nearly four

TABLE 8.5. Christian America (percent who agree or disagree)

Question: Please tell me whether you agree strongly, agree somewhat, disagree somewhat, or disagree strongly.	Agree	Disagree
the United States was founded on Christian principles	78	18
America has been strong because of its faith in God	79	19
our democratic form of government is based on Christianity	55	40
in the twenty-first century, the United States is still basically a Christian society	74	24
religious diversity has been good for America	86	12
the public schools should teach children the Ten Commandments	64	35
America owes a great deal to the immigrants who came here	76	22
foreigners who come to live in America should give up their foreign ways and learn to be like other Americans	46	52
nothing in other countries can beat the American way of life	70	27

Source: Religion and Diversity Survey.

Americans in five agree that the United States was founded on Christian principles. An equally large proportion believes America has been strong because of its faith in God. Three-quarters agree that in the twenty-first century the United States is still basically a Christian society. More than half believe our democratic form of government is based on Christianity.

These attitudes may be abstract or theoretical, but they are accompanied by other attitudes that have had more practical implications. For instance, two-thirds of Americans believe the public schools should teach children the Ten Commandments—an issue that has inspired rallies, voter petitions, and judicial action in numerous states. As they do on other issues, Americans also register assent on questions that suggest appreciation of diversity. Thus, 86% say religious diversity has been good for America (although, chances are, the diversity in mind has more to do with Baptists and Methodists than Hindus and Muslims), and three-quarters grant that America owes a great deal to the immigrants who came here. At the same time, there are nationalistic sentiments that range from the simple pride in the American way of life that most Americans feel to the view—held by almost half the public—that foreigners should give up their foreign ways and learn to be like other Americans.

It is worth mentioning that views about America being a Christian nation are not only widespread but also strongly associated with political divisions in the United States. For instance, there is an almost perfect correlation between states in which respondents in the Religion and Diversity Survey scored high on an index of attitudes about America being a Christian nation and the so-called red states that voted for George Bush during the 2000 presidential election.[13]

Christian Exclusivism?

I suggested earlier that attitudes toward the new religious diversity in the United States must be understood in terms of *religion*. We should not assume, as some observers do, that religious diversity can be understood simply as marketplace behavior, in which interchangeable organizations hawk religious goods the same way fast food chains do. That has been an easy view for scholars to accept, who care only about numbers and incipient signs of religious vitality, instead of taking claims about religious truth as seriously as many believers do. The culture of pluralism and civility *does* influence how Americans respond to religious diversity, but it does not mean that all Americans are eager to embrace this diversity.

The tension that Americans experience in confronting religious diversity can be illustrated by two remarks of George W. Bush. Shortly after 9/11, President Bush made several speeches in which he pointedly said to Muslims that he respected their faith. Yet, he had earlier said that according to his Bible only Christians have a place in heaven. Like Bush, American culture is influenced by norms of respect, tolerance, and a kind of live-and-let-live approach to religious and philosophical differences, on the one hand, and a historic commitment to the doctrine that only Christianity is ultimately true, on the other.

We have already seen some of this tension in the responses to questions about whether religious diversity is good and non-Western religions should be accepted. A similar tension is evident when Americans are asked directly about the truth of various religions (table 8.6). On the one hand, three-quarters believe that all major religions, such as Christianity, Hinduism, Buddhism, and Islam, contain *some* truth about God, while only a sixth of the public disagrees. A slight majority of the public thinks that these major religions are *equally good* ways of knowing about God, and four people in ten take the view that all religions basically teach the same thing. These responses all suggest that many Americans may come close to thinking that religions are as interchangeable as Coke and Pepsi. However, a majority of Americans also think that Christianity is the *best* way to understand God, and more than four in ten believe Christianity is the *only* way to have a true personal relationship with God. In short, Christianity goes well beyond brand loyalty for many Americans. It remains a truth system in which a person must believe in order to know God.

For those who believe that Christianity is uniquely or especially true, the obvious implication is that followers of other religions are pursuing falsehood and are thus in need of proselytization. In the public at large, 79% of Americans say it is very important or fairly important "for Christians to share their faith with non-Christians." As other scholars have observed, this may mean little more than observing the Golden Rule. Still, half of all Americans (49%) say it is very important or fairly important "for Christians to encourage people from other faiths—such as Muslims, Hindus, or Buddhists—to become Christians," regardless of whether Christians actually do anything to make converts is the question. In the Religion and Diversity Survey, I asked those who claimed they were Christians "how many times have you talked specifically with anyone who was not a Christian to persuade them to become a Christian?" Almost half (48%) said they had done this at least once in the past year. About a third (31%) said they had done so several or many times.

These responses suggest that there may be as much proselytizing of non-Christians by Christians, as some media reports of campaigns to convert

TABLE 8.6. Attitudes about Christianity and Other Religions (percent who agree or disagree)

Question: Please tell me whether you agree strongly, agree somewhat, disagree somewhat, or disagree strongly.	Agree	Disagree
all major religions, such as Christianity, Hinduism, Buddhism, and Islam, contain some truth about God	74	17
all major religions, such as Christianity, Hinduism, Buddhism, and Islam, are equally good ways of knowing about God	54	39
all religions basically teach the same thing	42	55
Christianity is the only way to have a true personal relationship with God	44	53
Christianity is the best way to understand God	58	39

Source: Religion and Diversity Survey

Hindus or Muslims have described. However, this is where norms of civility—and, indeed, of avoidance—prevail. When those who said they had talked with a non-Christian to persuade them to become a Christian were asked *who* they had tried to persuade, only 5% mentioned a Hindu, 7% mentioned a Buddhist, and 10% mentioned a Muslim. In comparison, 45% said the person was an atheist. But, by far, the largest number (88%) had simply talked with "someone who didn't go to church."

What Churches Are Doing

Norms of avoidance are also prominent when church members are asked about the programs in which they have participated at their churches. Only a third have participated in a class or study group that discussed how to share their faith with others (table 8.7). From the previous responses, these programs probably did prompt church members to share their faith, but probably not with Muslims or Hindus. Indeed, only 10% had been involved with a program to tell people of other faiths about Jesus. More of that activity appears to be directed overseas, at least judging from the fact that 43% of church members say they have attended a meeting at which a missionary or religious leader spoke about efforts to bring Christianity to people in other countries. Where norms of avoidance are most evident, though, is in positive efforts to promote greater understanding of other religions. Only one church member in ten had participated in a class or study group that focused on the beliefs and practices of some other religion besides Christianity or Judaism, such as Islam, Hinduism, or Buddhism. Only one church member in six had participated in a worship service that included a non-Christian leader, and an equally small proportion

TABLE 8.7. Interreligious Programs of Churches (percent)

Question (asked of church members only): During the past year, have you personally participated in any of the following at your congregation?	
a class or study group that focused on the beliefs and practices of some other religion besides Christianity or Judaism, such as Islam, Hinduism, or Buddhism	10
a worship service or other event at your congregation in which a non-Christian religious leader spoke, such as a Jewish, Muslim, Hindu, or Buddhist leader	15
any program or activity that was specifically concerned with improving relations between Christians and Jews	13
any organized program to tell people of other faiths—such as Muslims, Hindus, or Buddhists—about Jesus	10
a service program or volunteer activity sponsored by your congregation that also included people who belong to other religions, such as Muslims, Hindus, or Buddhists	16
a meeting at which a missionary or religious leader spoke about efforts to bring Christianity to people in other countries	43
a class or study group that discussed how to share your faith with others	36

Source: Religion and Diversity Survey.

had been involved with an interreligious service or volunteer program. The qualitative interviews we conducted confirmed that few churches are making more than token efforts to promote interreligious contact or understanding.[14]

American Identity and American Democracy

The foregoing provides a basis for considering questions about the larger significance of religious diversity for American identity and American democracy. Four implications are particularly worth emphasizing.

First, responses to adherents of non-Western religions in the United States are likely to differ from those in Western Europe and elsewhere, because of the distinctly *religious* character of U.S. culture. As is often documented in news coverage and polls, participation at worship services and belief in God continues to be more widespread in the United States than in most Western European countries. Two less easily documented differences are also important: the fact that American civil religion, as Robert Bellah calls it,[15] differentiated itself from the beginning by associating the emerging nation with revivalist religion, and the fact that the most politically activist part of American religion in recent decades has been evangelical Protestantism. From the former, Americans derive their continuing sense of the United States as a Christian nation, and the latter produces most of the arguments at present about Christianity being exclusively true. In my larger research, I have shown that Christian exclusivism is one of the strongest predictors of negative sentiments toward Muslims, Hindus, Buddhists, so-called foreigners, and immigrants more generally (including Asian and Hispanic immigrants). These negative sentiments are more closely associated with Christian exclusivism than with any of the standard factors that social scientists typically emphasize, such as level of education, race, gender, or lack of exposure to travel or other culturally broadening opportunities. This does not mean that negative sentiments toward religious minorities are necessarily more acute in the United States than in Europe. Numerous other factors, including the composition of those minority communities, their place in the labor force, and whether they are granted or denied citizenship, are also important.[16] However, it does mean that efforts to mobilize restrictions against non-Western religious minorities are more likely in the United States than in Europe to draw on religious sentiments and to enlist the efforts of religious organizations.

A second conclusion follows closely from the first, namely, that political rhetoric in the United States is particularly colored with religious language. In general terms, this observation will come as no surprise to anyone having witnessed recent presidential elections, though the prominence of religious language in U.S. political discourse continues to be a topic of comment by European observers. What is less often noted is the interplay between arguments rooted in distinctly Christian rhetoric and the realities of religious diversity. To return to my example of George W. Bush's mixed messages about Muslims, it is rare (perhaps unthinkable) for any public official in the United

States to make overt remarks about the superiority of Christianity over other religions. Yet in practice, officials continue to offer prayers to a God that would be unrecognizable in Hinduism or Buddhism, to champion the inclusion of "under God" in the Pledge of Allegiance, and to encourage the display and teaching of the Ten Commandments. The point is not that these efforts are necessarily out of order. It is rather that they are often associated with a sense that American traditions are being lost, with concerns about moral decay, uncertainty, and change. The more likely targets of these concerns are homosexuals, the elite media, academics, and federal judges. However, we must also consider that America ceasing in so many ways even symbolically to be a Christian nation is at the heart of these concerns. In personal interviews, people report that greater religious diversity will surely strengthen, not threaten, their own faith and that of their particular congregation. Yet they also worry that their children will marry someone of a different faith, that Muslims or Hindus will build a mosque or temple in their community, and that it will be much harder in the future to know what to believe.

Third, it follows from what I have described as a tension between norms of civil liberty and ideas about Christianity that this tension exists not only between different parts of the population but also within individuals and groups. In short, it influences the reasoning and rhetoric that now characterize the public sphere. For instance, arguments about separation of church and state are increasingly recast in language about the *rights* of religious groups to be heard and to exercise power. These arguments are voiced by religious leaders who believe churches should be places from which to mobilize political advocacy. They have become common in arguments about government funding of faith-based service agencies. Rights language is often used by religious groups for other purposes as well, such as protecting the rights of the unborn. The positive aspect of these developments for American democracy is that there is an apparent commitment to play by the rules and to speak in the same terms. However, it is less clear if those who believe in the absolute truth of Christianity, or in other absolute values, can find appropriate means of expressing their views or will feel increasingly alienated from the political process.

Finally, and more speculatively, I want to suggest the possibility that increasing religious diversity has inadvertently contributed to the emergence of a de facto religious establishment. I have in mind the possibility that evangelical Protestants (accompanied by some traditionalist Catholics) have become a de facto religious establishment and have become more self-aware and active as a political bloc over the perceived threat of religious diversity to their way of life. This is at first blush an odd suggestion, especially in view of the fact that some studies find only about 7% of the U.S. population to be active churchgoing evangelical Protestants.[17] It is also odd, because it flies against so much current thinking about the disestablishment of religion and the consequent rise of religious markets, which, to some observers, appear as nothing more than happy testimony to the positive effects of competition. Still, it is difficult to find any group in American religion as well represented in the White House and in other high positions of power as evangelical Protestants have been during the past two decades. It is equally difficult to find any other group more vocal, or more actively courted during major national elections, or any other group as willing to argue against historic understandings of separation of church and state. It is also difficult to find any other religious group identified, however superficially, as making up 40% of the population and considering themselves, however diverse, as a single political constituency. In the years since the collapse of the Soviet Union, territories in Eastern Europe, Central Asia, and the Middle East have witnessed a resurgence of religious, ethnic, and tribal identities. That resurgence has also prompted some within the United States to argue that religiously grounded first principles must be the basis for a new U.S. foreign policy. As some suggest, there is a natural affinity between conservative religious rhetoric and a policy language of strictness, resolve, and indeed waging war.[18] If there is a de facto religious establishment now reasserting itself in the United States, then the more secularized public discourse that has flourished in Europe since the end of the religious wars in the seventeenth century may well be worth careful consideration.

NOTES

1. Richard Alba and Victor Nee, *Remaking the American Mainstream: Assimilation and Contemporary Immigration* (Cambridge: Harvard University Press, 2003).

2. R. S. Warner, "Work in Progress toward a New Paradigm for the Sociological-Study of Religion in the United States," *American Journal of Sociology* 98.5 (1993): 1044–93.

3. Ethnographic studies of new immigrant and non-Western religious communities in the United States include Diana L. Eck, *A New Religious America: How a "Christian Country" Has Now Become the Most Religiously Diverse Nation on Earth* (San Francisco: Harper, 2001); Helen Rose Ebaugh and Janet Saltzman Chafetz, eds., *Religion and the New Immigrants: Continuities and Adaptations in Immigrant Congregations* (Walnut Creek, CA: AltaMira, 2000); and R. Stephen Warner and Judith G. Wittner, eds., *Gatherings in Diaspora: Religious Communities and the New Immigration* (Philadelphia: Temple University Press, 1998).

4. In this respect, my approach differs from that of William R. Hutchison in his valuable book *Religious Pluralism in America: The Contentious History of a Founding Ideal* (New Haven: Yale University Press, 2003). The history of religious pluralism has, of course, profoundly influenced the legal framework in which current court cases involving new religious diversity are considered, as shown in Nancy L. Rosenblum, ed., *Obligations of Citizenship and Demands of Faith: Religious Accommodation in Pluralist Democracies* (Princeton: Princeton University Press, 2000); and Stephen Macedo, *Diversity and Distrust: Civic Education in a Multicultural Democracy* (Cambridge: Harvard University Press, 2000).

5. Robert Wuthnow, *America and the Challenges of Religious Diversity* (Princeton: Princeton University Press, 2005); see also idem, "Presidential Address 2003: The Challenge of Diversity," *Journal for the Scientific Study of Religion* 43.2 (June 2004): 159–70.

6. These estimates are discussed in Wuthnow, "Presidential Address 2003."

7. Michael Hout and Claude S. Fischer, "Religious Diversity in America, 1940–2000" (paper presented at the annual meeting of the American Sociological Association, Chicago, Aug. 2001).

8. Robert Wuthnow and Conrad Hackett, "The Social Integration of Practitioners of Non-Western Religions in the United States," *Journal for the Scientific Study of Religion* 42.4 (Dec. 2003): 651–67.

9. Ibid.

10. More extensive analysis of the questions about Buddhists in this section has been published in Robert Wuthnow and Wendy Cadge, "Buddhists and Buddhism in the United States: The Scope of Influence," *Journal for the Scientific Study of Religion* 43.3 (Sept. 2004): 361–78.

11. Wendy Cadge, *Heartwood: The First Generation Practices Theravada Buddhism in America* (Chicago: University of Chicago Press, 2004); and Wendy Cadge and Courtney Bender, "Yoga and Rebirth in America: Asian Religions Are Here to Stay," *Contexts* 3.1 (2004): 45–51.

12. Ismail Royer, "U.S. Public Opinion toward Islam and Muslims after the Sept. 11 Attacks," *Islam Today* (April 2, 2002), www.islamonline.net; and Andrew Kohut, "Views of Islam Remain Sharply Divided" (Pew Research Center Commentary, Sept. 9, 2004), people-press.org.

13. Wuthnow, *America and the Challenges of Religious Diversity*, chap. 7.

14. Gustav Niebuhr, in research on interreligious programs, has come to a more optimistic conclusion (personal communication); however, his study deliberately looked for such instances, whereas mine examined what the typical congregation in close proximity to a non-Christian congregation was doing.

15. Robert N. Bellah, *The Broken Covenant: American Civil Religion in a Time of Trial* (Boston: Beacon, 1975).

16. These factors are examined in Lauren M. McLaren, "Anti-Immigrant Prejudice in Europe: Contact, Threat Perception, and Preferences for the Exclusion of Migrants," *Social Forces* 81 (March 2003): 909–36; see also Yasemin Soysal, *Limits of Citizenship: Migrants and Postnational Membership in Europe* (Chicago: University of Chicago Press, 1994); and Peter van der Veer, "Transnational Religion" (working paper 01-06h, Center for Migration and Development, Princeton University, 2003).

17. Christian Smith, *American Evangelicalism: Embattled and Thriving* (Chicago: University of Chicago Press, 1993).

18. George Lakoff, *Moral Politics: How Liberals and Conservatives Think* (Chicago: University of Chicago Press, 2002).

BIBLIOGRAPHY

Alba, Richard, and Victor Nee. *Remaking the American Mainstream: Assimilation and Contemporary Immigration.* Cambridge: Harvard University Press, 2003.

Bellah, Robert N. *The Broken Covenant: American Civil Religion in a Time of Trial.* Boston: Beacon, 1975.

Cadge, Wendy. *Heartwood: The First Generation Practices Theravada Buddhism in America.* Chicago: University of Chicago Press, 2004.

Cadge, Wendy, and Courtney Bender. "Yoga and Rebirth in America: Asian Religions Are Here to Stay." *Contexts* 3.1 (2004): 45–51.

Ebaugh, Helen Rose, and Janet Saltzman Chafetz, eds. *Religion and the New Immigrants: Continuities and Adaptations in Immigrant Congregations.* Walnut Creek, CA: AltaMira, 2000.

Eck, Diana L. *A New Religious America: How a "Christian Country" Has Now Become the Most Religiously Diverse Nation on Earth.* San Francisco: Harper, 2001.

Hout, Michael, and Claude S. Fischer. "Religious Diversity in America, 1940–2000." Paper presented at the annual meeting of the American Sociological Association, Chicago, Aug. 2001.

Hutchison, William R. *Religious Pluralism in America: The Contentious History of a Founding Ideal.* New Haven: Yale University Press, 2003.

Kohut, Andrew. "Views of Islam Remain Sharply Divided." Pew Research Center Commentary, Sept. 9, 2004. people-press.org.

Lakoff, George. *Moral Politics: How Liberals and Conservatives Think.* Chicago: University of Chicago Press, 2002.

Macedo, Stephen. *Diversity and Distrust: Civic Education in a Multicultural Democracy.* Cambridge: Harvard University Press, 2000.

McLaren, Lauren M. "Anti-Immigrant Prejudice in Europe: Contact, Threat Perception, and Preferences for the Exclusion of Migrants" *Social Forces* 81 (March 2003): 909–36.

Rosenblum, Nancy L., ed. *Obligations of Citizenship and Demands of Faith: Religious Accommodation in Pluralist Democracies.* Princeton: Princeton University Press, 2000.

Royer, Ismail. "U.S. Public Opinion toward Islam and Muslims after the Sept. 11 Attacks." *Islam Today,* April 2, 2002. www.islamonline.net.

Smith, Christian. *American Evangelicalism: Embattled and Thriving.* Chicago: University of Chicago Press, 1993.

Soysal, Yasemin. *Limits of Citizenship: Migrants and Postnational Membership in Europe.* Chicago: University of Chicago Press, 1994.

van der Veer, Peter. "Transnational Religion." Working paper 01-06h, Center for Migration and Development, Princeton University, 2003.

Warner, Stephen R. "Work in Progress toward a New Paradigm for the Sociological-Study of Religion in the United States." *American Journal of Sociology* 98.5 (1993): 1044–93.

Warner, Stephen R., and Judith G. Wittner, eds. *Gatherings in Diaspora: Religious Communities and the New Immigration.* Philadelphia: Temple University Press, 1998.

Wuthnow, Robert. *America and the Challenges of Religious Diversity.* Princeton: Princeton University Press, 2005.

———. "Presidential Address 2003: The Challenge of Diversity." *Journal for the Scientific Study of Religion* 43.2 (June 2004): 159–70.

Wuthnow, Robert, and Wendy Cadge. "Buddhists and Buddhism in the United States: The Scope of Influence." *Journal for the Scientific Study of Religion* 43.3 (Sept. 2004): 361–78.

Wuthnow, Robert, and Conrad Hackett. "The Social Integration of Practitioners of Non-Western Religions in the United States." *Journal for the Scientific Study of Religion* 42.4 (Dec. 2003): 651–67.

PART II

Democratic Responses to the New Religious Pluralism

9

Radical Evil in Liberal Democracies: The Neglect of the Political Emotions

Martha C. Nussbaum

The Fragility of Toleration

Toleration is an urgent preoccupation in all modern, liberal democracies.[1] All such democracies are based on an idea of equal respect for citizens. But all contain a plurality of religious and secular "comprehensive doctrines" (to use John Rawls's phrase),[2] doctrines in terms of which people make sense of life to themselves and search for its moral basis and its ultimate meaning. It would seem that equal respect for citizens, in such circumstances, requires respect for their freedom and equality, as they pursue matters of such fundamental importance. All such democracies therefore have strong reasons to support an idea of toleration, understood as involving respect, not only grudging acceptance, and to extend toleration to all religious and secular doctrines, limiting only conduct that violates the rights of other citizens. This norm is widely shared.

There is no modern democracy, however, in which toleration of this sort is a stable achievement. Toleration is always under siege from the forces of intolerance, and constant vigilance is required lest a powerful group impose its ways on an unwilling and relatively powerless minority, particularly in an era in which all nations are experiencing greater religious diversity and pluralism. In the United States, Christian language and sentiments are often casually introduced in public policy statements, in ways that suggest the unequal dignity of non-Christians.[3] In France, intolerance has become official state policy in the ban on conspicuous religious articles of dress in public schools. Although this law purports to be even-handed, it in fact discriminates against Muslims and Jews, since Christians do not regard the wearing of large crosses as a religious obligation, whereas the Muslim headscarf and (for some Jews) the yarmulke are regarded as obligatory. In India, the particular subject of much of my current writing, a democracy that once prided itself on respect for pluralism and indeed on a real love of religious and ethnic diversity has been under siege from political groups who would like to convert it into a Hindu state. During the political hegemony of the Hindu right (ended for the time being by the election of May 2004), textbooks used by young children expressed a Hindu-fundamentalist conception of the nation and its history and even denigrated minorities (readers said things like "Kabir is a nice boy even though he is a Muslim"). In the state of Gujarat, state government continues to defend text-books that portray Adolf Hitler as an admirable leader.[4] The Muslim minority's right to the equal protection of the laws is no longer secure; the highest levels of state and even national government support gross violations of the rights of this minority.[5] And although the 2004 election has brought many good changes and a ringing affirmation of the ideas of toleration and equal respect, the future is by no means assured.[6]

Why is toleration, attractive in principle, so difficult to achieve? The nor-mative case for toleration was well articulated by John Locke in his influential *A Letter concerning Toleration*, a work that has profoundly influenced all sub-sequent proposals in the Western tradition. But Locke made no attempt to diagnose the forces in human beings that militate against toleration, despite the fact that he acknowledged that his own ban on force and fraud was in-sufficient to solve the problem; his attractive proposal thus rests on a fragile foundation. Kant, I shall argue, did much more, combining a Lockean account of the state with a profound diagnosis of "radical evil," the tendencies in all human beings that militate against stable toleration and respect. But Kant did little to connect these two parts of his thought about religion. Nor did he propose any mechanism through which the state might mitigate the harmful influence of radical evil, thus rendering toleration stable. As he was well aware, this left the tolerant state in a precarious situation.

One solution to the problem of radical evil was proposed by Rousseau, the source for most aspects of Kant's doctrine of radical evil. Rousseau famously argued that the tolerant state, in order to be stable, needs to inculcate senti-ments that support toleration, in the form of a "civil religion." His proposal shows profound human insight. But its coercive features would surely be unac-ceptable to Locke and Kant, and they should be unacceptable to us.

How, then, should modern pluralistic societies solve the problem of rad-ical evil? How can a respectful pluralistic society shore up the fragile human basis of toleration, especially in a world in which we need to cultivate toleration not only within each state, in an era of increasing diversity, but also *among* peoples and states, in this interlocking world? I shall argue that part of the solution is indeed Kant's: the protection of a vigorous critical culture, together with the freedoms of speech, press, and assembly that such a culture requires. More, however, is required: the problem cannot be resolved without careful thought about how a liberal state, without becoming an illiberal Rousseauian state, can nonetheless cultivate emotions that support equal respect and a toleration that is more than grudging obedience to law.

Toleration and Equal Respect: The Lockean State

John Locke's understanding of toleration is complex, making it impossible to understand the argument of his *Letter* fully without connecting it to the rest of his political thought. Let me attempt, however, a summary. Locke insists that in matters of religious belief and religious conduct (so long as it does not violate the rights of others) the state must strive to protect "absolute liberty, just and true liberty, equal and impartial liberty" (12).[7] Not only must the state refuse the use of coercion to compel religious homogeneity, it must strenuously protect all its citizens from coercion on the part of others. Moreover, no person is to be "prejudice[d]...in his civil enjoyments" (27) because of religion. Magistrates must go beyond nonpersecution to zealous protection of all citizens in their rights, so that "the goods and health of subjects be not injured by the fraud or violence of others" (35). The state must leave religion strictly alone, except insofar as it ventures into areas that the state rightly regulates, such as property.

For both citizens and state actors, the norm of toleration requires not only the grudging preservation of rights, but also a spirit of "charity, bounty, and liberality" (27). Church officials ought to advise their members of "the duties of peace and good-will towards all men; as well towards the erroneous as the orthodox" (32). They should "industriously exhort" their members and especially civic magistrates to "charity, meekness, and toleration" (32).

Locke advances several different arguments for this norm. Some rely on Christian texts and doctrines. Some rely on a skeptical attitude toward religious beliefs. One influential strand of argument relies on the Protestant idea of "free faith": genuine religious belief cannot be coerced. What concerns me here, however, is a line of argument that I take to be both central to the work and more pertinent to our modern debates than any other. Modern readers of Locke may justly feel that some of his arguments are too "internal," requiring a framework of Protestant ideas for their success. But this criticism cannot be made against the line of argument that concerns me—that all citizens have rights, that is, rightful claims over liberty, property, and other prerequisites of well-being. Moreover, these rights are equal. It is simply wrong for these equal rights to be undermined on grounds of religious difference. Summarizing his argument, Locke emphasizes the centrality of this strand in his argument: "The sum of all we drive at is, that every man enjoy the same rights that are granted to others" (69).

This argument is based on Locke's general political theory and, in particular, on his idea of the social contract and its relation to rights. I shall not pursue those connections further here. However we understand the origin of Locke's doctrine of rights, it is a powerful idea for modern pluralistic democracies, one that most of them already accept, however much they differ concerning the metaphysical grounding of rights-claims and the precise nature of the rights in question. I take the key idea in this Lockean argument to be an idea of respect for persons. To say that persons have rights and should not be interfered with is a way of saying that persons deserve respect from one another. With regard to the fundamentals of well-being, they are all equally placed and equally entitled, and their equal entitlements must not be interfered with, either by the state or, through the inaction of the state, by one another.

Locke recognizes that people are not always generous and peaccable. Indeed, his insistence on the duty of churches to exhort their members to toleration, generosity, and peace acknowledges the presence of a problem: people are inclined to go against the Lockean ideal. Locke's political surroundings did much to illustrate such violations. But nothing is said about how a Lockean state can grapple with this problem, beyond asking people to be nice to one another. Perhaps Locke believes that the problem is only temporary, the artifact of recent religious strife and bad clerical behavior. Moral psychology cannot be said to be Locke's strongest point as a philosopher. He simply lacks interest in the psychological underpinnings of intolerance, tending to blame it, instead, on bad individuals who can be replaced by good individuals.

Locke thus leaves his own project in a position that is at best uncertain, at worst highly unstable. Without trying to figure out why intolerance is so ubiquitous, however speculative all such accounts are bound to be, it is difficult to justify a conception of the state, for surely part of justifying a political conception is showing that over time it can be stable, and stable, as Rawls puts it, "for the right reasons," that is, stable not just as a grudging *modus vivendi*, but as something people can really endorse as good for their lives. Locke leaves us uncertain whether this condition has been fulfilled.

Radical Evil

Kant is deeply influenced by the social contract doctrines of both Locke and Rousseau. His state is basically Lockean in structure, uses a roughly Lockean understanding of rights, and understands the limits of state action in roughly Locke's way. Kant does, however, feel the need to fill the gap in Locke's account, by supplying a moral psychology of evil and intolerance that will explain why intolerance and other forms of evil are likely to remain a permanent problem in human societies. In *Religion within the Boundaries of Mere Reason*, Kant articulates his famous doctrine of "radical evil," a doctrine that is closely related to Rousseau's moral psychology, but one that Kant develops in a powerful and original way.[8]

Evil is radical, according to Kant, that is to say, it goes to the root of our humanity, because human beings, prior to any experience, have a propensity to both good and evil, in the form of tendencies that are deeply rooted in our natures.[9] We are such that we can follow the moral law, but there is also something about us that makes it virtually inevitable that under certain circumstances we will disregard it and behave badly.

What are those conditions? Animality itself is not the problem; animality is basically neutral (6.32, 57–58). Here is where Kant locates the error in Stoicism, which he portrays (wrongly)[10] as involving the doctrine that our moral struggle is against animal inclination alone (6.57–58). The tempter, the invisible enemy inside, is something peculiarly human, a propensity to competitive self-love, which manifests itself whenever human beings are in a group. The appetites all by themselves are easily satisfied, and animal need is limited (6.93). The human being considers himself poor only "to the extent that he is anxious that other human beings will consider him poor and will despise him for it." But a sufficient condition of such anxiety is the mere presence of others:

> Envy, addiction to power, avarice, and the malignant inclinations
> associated with these, assail his nature, which on its own is un-
> demanding, *as soon as he is among human beings*. Nor is it necessary
> to assume that these are sunk into evil and are examples that lead
> him astray; it suffices that they are there, that they surround him, and
> that they are human beings, and they will mutually corrupt each
> other's moral disposition and make one another evil. (6.94, emphasis
> original)

Kant's account is powerful. Although he surely is too sanguine about the opportunity of many of the world's people to satisfy bodily need,[11] he is also surely right in holding that mere satisfaction is not the biggest cause of bad behavior. Even when people are well fed and housed, and even when they are reasonably secure with respect to other prerequisites of well-being, they still behave badly to one another and violate one another's rights. And even though an innate propensity is a difficult thing to demonstrate, Kant is surely right when he suggests that people require no special social teaching in order to behave badly, and indeed regularly do so despite the best social teaching.

Kant is offering a general explanation for the origins of bad behavior, not a particular explanation of intolerance. But it has an obvious relevance to Locke's problem. Wherever people are together, they form themselves into religious (and ethnic) groups and vie for superiority among themselves. This process, difficult to explain with reference to the internal ideologies of the religions, which may be strongly in favor of peace and compassion—as Locke pointed out for the case of Christianity—is well explained by Kant's positing of a propensity to competition that is activated by the mere presence of a plurality.

Kant's account of radical evil, while attractive in many respects, seems incomplete. It is all very well to say that there are propensities in human beings such that the presence of others will elicit competition and aggressive behavior; but Kant says little about their nature. Perhaps he thinks that there is nothing more to be said: radical evil is just the disposition to manifest competitive and morality-defying behavior in the presence of others. It seems to me that we can say more. In two books on the emotions,[12] I argue that understanding the roots of bad behavior requires thinking about human beings' problematic relationship to their own mortality and finitude, their desire to transcend conditions that are painful for any intelligent being to accept. The earliest experiences of a human infant contain a jolting alternation between blissful completeness, in which the whole world seems to revolve around its needs, and an agonizing awareness of helplessness, when good things do not arrive at the desired moment and the infant can do nothing to ensure their arrival. The expectation of being attended to constantly—the "infantile omnipotence" so well captured in Freud's phrase "His Majesty the baby"—is joined to the anxiety, and the shame, of knowing that one is not in fact omnipotent, but utterly powerless. Out of this anxiety and shame emerges an urgent desire for completeness and fullness that never completely departs, however much the child learns that it is but one part of a world of finite needy beings. And this desire to transcend the shame of incompleteness leads to much instability and moral danger. In writing about the role of shame and disgust in the process of group formation and social intolerance, I have argued that the type of social bad behavior with which I am most concerned in this essay can be traced to child's early pain at the fact that it is imperfect, unable to achieve the blissful completeness that in certain moments it is encouraged to expect. This pain leads to shame and revulsion at the signs of one's own imperfection. And then, what most concerns me here, shame and revulsion, in turn, are all too often projected outward onto subordinate groups who can conveniently symbolize the problematic aspects of bodily humanity, those from which people would like to distance themselves.

Thus my account of prejudice and hatred, whether religious or ethnic or sex based, is more complicated than Kant's, invoking not only mere plurality but also the hatred of weakness, helplessness, and (ultimately) death that is omnipresent in our relationship to our humanity.[13] And I argue that a primary reason why people form groups of the sort that engage in bad behavior toward others is a (futile) attempt to recover completeness and safety. By defining their own group as the good "normal" one, lacking in nothing, and by surrounding themselves on all sides with such people, people gain the illusion of safety and control, projecting onto subordinate others the weaknesses that they wish not to accept in themselves. By stigmatizing and persecuting others, they conceal from themselves their own weakness and vulnerability.

Thus, unlike Kant, I think that radical evil is not a bare disposition to behave badly in certain circumstances. It has an underlying content and a narrative history. Radical evil concerns the pursuit of transcendence and the hatred of finitude: it is about narcissism, we might say, and the fear of death that is such a powerful prop to human narcissism. Thus the remedy for radical evil will have to address the problem of narcissism—not curing it, for life is too painful for human beings ever to accept it as it is, but mitigating its role in human life.

To say this is not to say that all desires for transcendence are politically problematic. First of all, without casting aspersion on human weakness one may certainly strive to make human life as good as it can possibly be, fighting to overcome disease, injustice, and sloth—what I have elsewhere called "internal transcendence."[14] Many philosophers who do not connect morality to any otherworldly source, and many who do, recommend that sort of transcendence. But there are also specifically religious types of transcendence that seem to have no conceptual link to narcissism. The longing for a life after death, in which one will be reunited with one's loved ones, is certainly a longing to transcend the painful conditions of human life, but it is perfectly compatible with, and even entails, a recognition that human beings are, as Rousseau puts it, "naked and poor," insufficient to control the most important goods in life. It thus has no tendency on its own to lead to the denigration of the disabilities of the body or of birth and death. So my analysis in no way suggests that it would be better for religious believers to give up belief in transcendent sources of value; indeed the narcissism I repudiate, which denies human weakness and vulnerability, is usually repudiated, as well, by the major religions, much though people may often hijack religion in the service of narcissistic projects. This is important, since I want to recommend my antinarcissistic principles as part of a liberal "overlapping consensus" that may be affirmed by people with many different reasonable comprehensive doctrines (to use Rawls's terms).[15]

The narrative history of radical evil that I have sketched here has implications for the social treatment of evil that Kant's far more abstract account does not. For now, however, let me return to Kant's generic account, which is compatible with mine, although it does not entail it.

Whenever human beings are together, then, according to Kant, bad behavior is a likely outcome, and intolerance is one prominent form that such bad behavior typically takes, as one prominent form of competitive self-love. Intolerance, then, is not an easily eradicated social condition. People will in general seek to violate the rights of others and in particular will seek to establish the superiority of their own religious doctrines. Although Kant himself does not explicitly connect his doctrine of evil to the specific problem of intolerance, the connection is strongly suggested by his argument.

To individual human beings, Kant gives extensive advice. In particular, to counteract the bad tendencies in their nature they have the duty to surround themselves with a group of people who are all working for the victory of the good tendencies over the bad. People are unlikely to achieve such a victory stably on their own, but in a group of like-minded strivers they have a better chance, forming a countersociety that will strengthen the moral disposition and protect it from the temptations that worldly society offers. That is the role Kant sees for religion: it is a social force that supplies a support structure for morality. Given that we are all morally weak and liable to error, we have an ethical duty to join such a society, leaving our ethical state of nature to join an ethical community. Kant then argues that not just any ethical community will do: it has to be a religious community, meaning one that is united by the idea of a higher moral being.

Much of the text is then devoted to distinguishing good religious communities from bad, asking what sort of religious community could actually do the job Kant has laid out. Most existing churches, Kant argues, are actually a bad moral influence, since they teach people to placate God in extraneous ways and in other ways undermine the purity of the moral incentive. But more or less any of the major faiths can become an acceptable church, if reconstructed in the right (moral, rational) way.

What, however, of the Lockean state? Given the ubiquity of the propensity to evil, what can such a state do to protect itself against the forces of bad behavior generally and intolerance in particular? Well, it can certainly use coercion to protect people's property rights and other rights that they have under the social contract. Here Locke and Kant are in agreement. But I have suggested that this leaves equal respect in a fragile position. So it would be nice to think that the state could find some further ways of supporting good behavior in general, toleration in particular.

For Kant, the choice to enter a church must always remain a choice. He is just as averse as Locke is to the Hobbesian idea of state-based religious coercion. He argues against it on both moral and prudential grounds. "Woe to the legislator who would want to bring about through coercion a polity directed to ethical ends," he writes, "for he would thereby not only achieve the very opposite of ethical ends, but also undermine his political ends and render them insecure" (6.96). Moreover, even when people make a bad choice and join a bad church, or even declare themselves atheists, Kant is convinced that respect for autonomy requires respecting their liberty. Like Locke, he insists that no person's civil liberties may be infringed on grounds of religious membership or practice; but he goes even further than Locke, protecting atheists as well as believers. The most the state can demand is that churches include nothing in their constitutions that contradicts the duties of members as citizens of the state. (Here Kant remains close to Locke.)

So there is a problem: respect for autonomy requires us to tolerate bad churches, which is what Kant thinks most actual churches are. Such churches actually strengthen evil and thus undermine toleration. What, then, can the Lockean state do to protect itself?

Kant's answer, and the only answer he believes he *can* give, consistently with his defense of autonomy, is that the state can and should foster a vigorous critical culture, including strong protections for the freedom of speech and debate. This, of course, is a lifelong preoccupation of Kant's and one that his political problems made a constant focus of his attention. Moreover, this state support should extend to generous funding for education and support for scholarship. Kant frequently emphasizes in the strongest possible terms that a focus on public education is a crucial linchpin of public enlightenment. In *Idea for a Universal History* he writes:

> As long as states apply all their resources to their vain and
> violent schemes of expansion, thus incessantly obstructing the
> slow and laborious efforts of their citizens to cultivate their minds,
> and even deprive them of all support in these efforts, no progress
> in this direction can be expected. For a long internal process of care-
> ful work on the part of each commonwealth is necessary for the
> education of its citizens. But all good enterprises which are not grafted

on to a morally good attitude of mind are nothing but illusion
and outwardly glittering misery.[16]

In "The Contest of Faculties" he emphasizes, again, that reliance on private
educational efforts is likely to prove insufficient:

> To expect that the education of young people in intellectual and moral
> culture, reinforced by the doctrines of religion, firstly through
> domestic instruction and then through a series of schools from the
> lowest to the highest grade, will eventually not only make them good
> citizens, but will also bring them up to practise a kind of goodness
> which can continually progress and maintain itself, is a plan which is
> scarcely likely to achieve the desired success.[17]

The argument is apparently that private efforts will be sporadic and un-
coordinated. The educational system should not be permitted to develop in a
haphazard way, while the state spends all its money on war. Education will
produce an enlightened public culture, thus mitigating violence, only if "it
is designed on the considered plan and intention of the highest authority
in the state, then set in motion and constantly maintained in uniform opera-
tion thereafter."[18] Kant clearly thinks that maintaining an enlightened public culture has multiple aspects: support for schools and universities; strong
protection for civil liberties; and, especially important, a strong emphasis
on publicity in all political matters and on institutions that facilitate and protect
public debate.[19]

In the *Religion*, Kant focuses particularly on the role that critical religious
scholarship plays in bringing good churches into existence and publicizing the
possibilities of rational and moral religion. He gives numerous examples of the
ways in which biblical scholarship can bring a recalcitrant text into line with
the moral law. It is to be hoped that such scholarship will gradually lead to
greater public support for rational religion and to diminished support for bad
churches. Critical biblical scholars must have good political conditions for their
work to be effective: "It is self-evident that they must not on any account be
hindered by the secular arm in the public use of their insights and discoveries
in this field, or be bound to certain dogmas" (6.113; cf. 6.133). In addition to
maintaining academic freedom and freedom to speak and publish, the state
apparently has the affirmative task of underwriting the employment of such
scholars (6.113).

All this is fine, as far as it goes. But the same principle that protects the
scholarship Kant likes also protects the scholarship that he detests. (Certainly
other scholars would have to have the same free speech protections; nor is it
easy to imagine a meaningful policy of academic freedom that would fund
scholars on the basis of their moral/political viewpoint.) The same public
openness that creates the conditions for rational religion to come into existence
also gives wide scope for the mobilization of prejudice and intolerance. This
being the case, the state that Kant envisages remains in a fragile condition. He

has to rely on the sophistication and rationality of a general public who are, as he himself knows, very much inclined to the emotional and rhetorical appeals of the bad churches. In his suspiciousness about the passions and sentiments, he seems unwilling to propose any emotional dimension to the public rhetoric in favor of rational religion and the good churches. To the extent that they do prevail, it must be because of good scholarship and enlightened argument.

Kant advances beyond Locke in his profound understanding of human psychology, and thus of the threats to a liberal society of the type he defends. But his liberalism, combined with his mistrust of the passions, prevents him from doing much about those threats.

The dilemma with which Kant's thought leaves us becomes more acute still when we consider the global society to which Kant's thought so powerfully pointed the way. As Kant knew and stressed, one of the worst expressions of radical evil lies in the conduct of nations toward other nations. Wars of conquest, colonial domination, all these are outgrowths of the competitive tendencies that Kant so well identified, and it is not surprising that intolerance of the different beliefs and ways of life of others is so often a part of these projects.[20] But if the state seems to be impotent to stop threats to the stability of its own tolerant policies internally, it has a harder time still once we articulate the human goal in world terms, as that of respecting humanity wherever it is and of protecting the religious freedom, and in general the freedom to pursue one's own comprehensive doctrine, for all world citizens. Many people who can be led to behave with toleration to their own fellow nationals forget about this principle completely when they are abroad. Thus a tolerant world order will be far harder to produce than a stably tolerant Lockean state.

A Civil Religion?

Because Kant's moral psychology is not altogether new, the problem that it raises for the liberal society is also not new. Rousseau, whose psychology is in essence the source of Kant's, understood that the state that is going to protect toleration needs to think about the moral emotions and needs to adopt some program for their cultivation. In the important section of *On the Social Contract* about the civil religion,[21] Rousseau argues that complete toleration in spiritual matters is of great importance, but that it needs to be undergirded by the promulgation of a civil religion consisting of "sentiments of sociability, without which it is impossible to be a good citizen or a faithful subject" (226). This religion, a kind of moralized deism fortified with patriotic beliefs and sentiments, will hold the state together and create moral unanimity among citizens. Its dogmas include the existence of a powerful beneficent deity and a life after death, the happiness of the just, the punishment of the wicked, the sanctity of the social contract and the laws, *and* the unacceptability of intolerance (226).

Around all of these dogmas the sovereign will create ceremonies and rituals, engendering strong bonds of sentiment connected to morality and patriotic duty. The civil religion functions as the common moral core of all the acceptable forms of religion; people may add to this core various metaphysical and spiritual beliefs: "Each man can have in addition such opinions as he pleases, without it being any of the sovereign's business to know what they are" (226). But all must adhere to the core, both with respect to conduct and with respect to belief.

Rousseau believes that this device will solve the problem of stability in the tolerant state, giving people sources of motivation to behave well to one another, much in the way that, for Kant, a church of the right kind will strengthen the good dispositions and undermine the bad. For Kant, however, respect for autonomy requires that the choice to enter a church be left entirely free. Rousseau, by contrast, permits the sovereign to enforce the civil religion by coercive means, including banishment and even capital punishment. State coercion applies not only to conduct harmful to others, but also to nonharmful conduct expressing lack of adherence to the civil religion; and it applies, as well, to nonconforming belief and speech. In particular, Rousseau insists on a belief not only in civil, but also in theological toleration. Thus state coercion extends to a great deal in the way of religious opinion, since Rousseau believes that "it is impossible to live in peace with those one believes to be damned" (226). If we think about the relationship of Rousseau's ideas to the actual doctrines of the major religions in his own time, we can see quickly that in Rousseau's state Roman Catholics will not be tolerated (a fact he applauds), and many if not most forms of Protestantism will not be either.

Rousseau has taken the problem of evil seriously and made a proposal that may be sufficient to cope with it. Obviously, however, his solution would be unacceptable to Locke, Kant, and anyone who finds the idea of a Lockean state attractive. Such a state is built on the idea that respect for persons entails respect for their comprehensive doctrines. This starting point requires broad toleration of religious opinion, including theological opinions about the salvation of others, so long as these opinions do not issue in conduct that violates the civil rights of others. Rousseau has purchased stability at much too high a price. We may see Kant's emphatic insistence on freedom of speech, scholarship, and association as an implicit repudiation of Rousseau, as well as a reflection on his own situation under a series of different Prussian leaders.

Another grave problem with Rousseau's civil religion, as with all attempts at a civil religion based on patriotic sentiment and the idea of willingness to die for one's country, is that this religion provides a very bad basis for international relations. The very sentiments that cement the homogeneity of Rousseau's society make it suspicious and intolerant of foreigners and conduce to warlike behavior against foreigners. Rousseau likes this consequence. Indeed, one reason why he feels the need for a civil religion to supplement Christianity is that he finds Christianity too passive, meek, and mild.[22] But anyone who finds Kant's idea of a peaceful and tolerant world community attractive will find here yet further reasons to take exception to Rousseau.

Rousseau's psychological insight, however, does not disappear once one rejects his solution. He seems right to insist that the state needs to take the problem of evil seriously and to devise some sort of public psychology to address it, a civil religion if you will. And yet Kant seems right in his insistence that the problem of radical evil cannot be addressed by state coercion of free political and religious debate; this cure is worse than the disease. At the margins we may legitimately debate the legal regulation of some forms of hate speech, asking how immediate the threat to safety and stability must be in order for such speech to be legally regulable. But in general we should agree with Kant: the very value of respect for persons that leads us to want a Lockean state also prevents us from protecting it with a coercive civil religion of Rousseau's sort.

What is the solution to this dilemma? How can a respectful pluralistic society shore up the fragile bases of toleration, especially in a time of increasing domestic religious pluralism and in a world in which we need to cultivate toleration not only internally, but also between peoples and states?

Kant was surely right in thinking that one very important part of the solution is the vigilant protection of freedoms of speech, press, and scholarship. Intolerance thrives in a situation in which opinion is curtailed, and we may observe that intolerant groups usually if not always seek the curtailment of these freedoms as a road to domination. Consider the situation of the Hindu right in India today. These groups want, in essence, to turn a pluralistic respectful Lockean state into a nonrespectful Hindu-first society in which norms of ethnic purity are used to establish who is a first-class and who is a second-class citizen. Central to their operations are attacks on academic freedom, the freedom of scholars to publish dissident views (of history, of religion, of politics), and the freedom of opinion generally.[23] It seems just right in this case for the proponents of pluralism and toleration to focus on shoring up the Kantian freedoms, as an essential bulwark of the other political liberties. But this case shows, as well, that a possibly fatal threat to the very existence of a Lockean democracy can arise and become strong even though the Kantian freedoms have been, until now anyway, pretty well protected. So what more might be done, along Rousseauian lines but without his illiberal strategies?

One thing that a society may certainly do, and that most societies do already, is to attach rituals and ceremonies to the basic freedoms protected by the society, inspiring citizens to love those values by linking the values to music, art, and ritual. This stratagem is dangerous, given the propensity of all forms of patriotism to lead to demonization of foreigners and local "subversives." We see in the case of the Hindu right in India how such patriotic values can be hijacked and turned to the services of radical evil. Nonetheless, it seems to me that there are reasonable ways to institutionalize such ceremonies that do not buy into these dangers. Where toleration is concerned, a reasonable civil religion would include, for example, a celebration of the diversity of traditions and comprehensive doctrines that are contained within a nation, as a source of its strength and richness. In general, there is much that the tolerant state may do by way of persuasion and rhetorical undergirding, without infringing on the freedoms of speech, assembly, and publication of those who think differently.

An attractive further proposal was made by John Stuart Mill in his essay entitled "The Utility of Religion."[24] Here Mill, recognizing the importance of religious sentiments in giving force to moral motivation, suggests what (following Auguste Comte and others) he calls "the religion of humanity," a moral ideal that could be promulgated through public education.[25] According to this moral ideal, a good person is one who cares deeply about humanity generally. Her thoughts and feelings learn the habit of being carried away from her own parochial concerns; they are habitually fixed on this "unselfish object, loved and pursued as an end for its own sake." She learns to view helping others as a part of her own good: she identifies her good with that of humanity as a whole, and thinks of her afterlife as the life of those who follow her. She learns, in these ways and others, that helping others is not a sacrifice, but an intrinsic good. Thus she learns a "morality grounded on large and wise views of the good of the whole, neither sacrificing the individual to the aggregate nor the aggregate to the individual, but giving to duty on the one hand and to freedom and spontaneity on the other their proper province" (108).

To the imagined objection that human beings cannot really learn to be motivated by universal concerns, Mill responds with some very insightful remarks about patriotism and its force: "When we consider how ardent a sentiment in favourable circumstances of education, the love of country has become, we cannot judge it impossible that the love of that larger country, the world, may be nursed into similar strength, both as a source of elevated emotion and as a principle of duty" (107).[26]

These ideas are closely linked to some that I develop in *Upheavals of Thought* concerning compassion as a moral sentiment that can be cultivated by public institutions and public education. I argue that a liberal society, without offending against respect for pluralism, can still employ a moral ideal of this sort and promote a moral education aimed at underwriting it. This ideal would serve as a basis for public political culture, in connection with public norms of equality and respect. In effect, such a moral education would be the psychological underpinning to public norms that can command a Rawlsian "overlapping consensus," and thus, as I argue, it need not be seen as divisive or illiberal when made part of a public education.[27]

How, more precisely, would this moral education be institutionalized? A good part of it, I argue, would in fact take the form of developing institutions that express the views of equal respect and due attention to the needs of all: a just tax system, a just health care system, a just welfare system. But institutions remain stable only when human beings have the will to sustain them, a fact that the collapse of social democracy in the United States, since the Reagan era, has made an all too vivid reality. Therefore, I argue, public education at all levels (and private education too) should focus on putting forward something like Mill's religion of humanity, conveying the sense that all human lives are of equal worth and that all are worthy of being lived with dignity and a decent minimum level of well-being.

More concretely, public education can cultivate awareness of the problems human beings face on the way to their well-being, in different parts of one's own nation and in different parts of the world, and can impart a sense of urgency concerning the importance of giving all world citizens decent life chances. Children can learn with increasing sophistication the economic and political obstacles that human beings face on the way to their well-being and can learn to see ways in which a just society might overcome these problems. At the same time, education can try to minimize the role of greed and competitive accumulation in society, by portraying greedy accumulation in a negative light and showing how it subverts the legitimate strivings of others—a teaching to which the major religious and secular comprehensive doctrines certainly give lip service, even if they do not always insist on it in practice.

Where toleration is concerned, the "religion of humanity" takes, in the first instance, an institutional form, in the form of strong protections for religious liberty and a support for the idea of equal respect for comprehensive doctrines. (A doctrine of nonestablishment is one very usual and valuable means of promoting equal respect.)[28] Enhanced penalties for crimes involving ethnic, racial, and religious hatred would also be prominent parts of the institutional side of such a program, expressing society's very strong disapproval of intolerance and the actions to which it can give rise.[29]

Although my proposal is Kantian in the sense that no civil penalties attach to people who speak in favor of greed, inequality, and even intolerance, so long as they do no harm to others, it seems appropriate for public education and the media culture of a democratic society to focus on imparting norms that do support the values of a liberal society and a decent world culture. Thus, where toleration is concerned, I would support education at all levels aimed at conveying understanding of and respect for different religious and secular comprehensive doctrines and different ethnic and national traditions. Although knowledge does not guarantee good behavior, ignorance is a virtual guarantee of bad behavior: stigmatization of the other is much easier when people know nothing, or nothing complicated, about a different religious or cultural tradition, whether local or foreign. But education can surely go further, fostering a sense of respect for persons and of their equal worth, their equal entitlement to lives with human dignity, of which religious freedom is one big part.

Because my own understanding of radical evil is more complex than Kant's, I also argue, in my recent *Hiding from Humanity: Disgust, Shame, and the Law*, that public culture needs to devote special emphasis to minimizing the negative effects of narcissism and of the aggression that is so closely connected with people's unwillingness to tolerate their own neediness, finitude, and embodiment. Many aspects of the inhibition of narcissism will, once again, be institutional: I insist, for example, that disgust is never a sufficient reason to render a practice illegal, when it causes no harm to others with respect to their established rights; and that shame is never a good device to use in criminal punishment. And I consider many ways in which the law can protect citizens from shaming and minimize the harmful effects of stigma. But much of the program must be, once again, informal and educational, devising ways to bring children up in a climate that fosters equal respect and minimizes the baneful social influences of disgust and stigmatization and instills a positive attitude toward aspects of our embodied life, such as sexuality, aging, and physical and mental disability, that are usually difficult to confront.

Here we see the limitations in Mill's proposal, for, Victorian that he is, he thinks of compassion as something that can be fostered directly, without attending to the body or sexuality, or the ways in which other people's bodily disabilities remind us unpleasantly of our own frailty—and the ways in which anxieties in these areas become sources of trouble.

There is no reason why a more psychologically complex version of Mill's "religion of humanity" cannot be widely taught and promulgated by liberal, democratic societies—in public (and private) education at all levels, in the rhetoric of leaders and other political actors, in the normative thinking of the judiciary. I believe (and have argued more fully in *Hiding from Humanity*)[30] that such norms can become the object of an "overlapping consensus" of the type that Rawls envisages in *Political Liberalism*.[31] That is to say, people who have different religious and secular comprehensive doctrines can agree that for political purposes it is important to inhibit narcissism and to foster equal respect. People will, of course, differ about the deeper underlying rationale for supporting these goals. Some, for example, will have a religious rationale. In *Hiding from Humanity* I combined an analysis of emotions based on cognitive psychology and psychoanalysis with ethical arguments; this psychological material is part of my own "comprehensive doctrine" and is not a necessary underpinning for the political norms, which may be defended in various different ways, religious, ethical, and economic. In other words, my project is isomorphic to Rawls's idea of political principles that can be supported from a number of different epistemological, metaphysical, and ethical vantage points.

Religious and other views of the good that do not support toleration and equal respect will not be suppressed or denied the right to speak and argue, as Rawls again emphasizes.[32] But insofar as the people who hold them also hold, with more than grudging lip service, the political principles of a tolerant pluralism, they will very likely come to feel a strain between these public views and their religious commitments. Sometimes this will lead to modifications in the (interpretation of) the religious view itself, as has happened with Roman Catholicism after Vatican II. The deliberate expression of respect for other religions that is now an orthodox part of Catholic doctrine (as in Pope John Paul II's 1998 speech to the U.N. General Assembly, stating that all religions are avenues to the truth) is surely in part a way of reconciling church doctrine with political principles that most major world democracies and their citizens officially accept. Similarly, Gandhi's radical reinterpretation of Hinduism as not resting on caste distinctions, though in part inspired by his own spiritual investigations, was surely also inspired by political thought about the norms of the future pluralistic democracy and how Hinduism might support rather than undercut them. Religions may stick to their intolerant guns, but if they do, and if citizens affirm the political principles as both valuable and important, such religions are likely to gain fewer adherents over time, since people dislike living with such emotional and cognitive tensions. As Rawls emphasizes, to show

that a proposal is respectful of religion we are not obliged to show that all religions fare equally well under it.[33]

The norms (and supportive emotions) of the political culture should always be fostered together with support for a robust critical culture of the sort
that Kant favors. In this way we reassure those who disagree with us, showing
them that our proposal is not a Rousseauian civil religion. In this way, too, we
express a commitment to equal respect for persons, even when their views are
not the ones enshrined in the dominant public culture. And, as Mill emphasized in *On Liberty*, we protect the ideas of the public culture from becoming
mere empty shells, with no passion sustaining them, if we do debate them
vigorously and constantly.

But because my program is more psychologically complex, more unsettling, than Mill's, it is going to need real artists to carry it out, not just well-
intentioned public servants. Such artists can play a role in at least three
different ways. First, they may participate in constructing emotions supportive
of the political norms, for people who do not yet support them or do not fully
support them (especially children and young people). Second, they may give
people a sense of how important the political norms are, again by attaching
them to emotions that support them and embody a sense of urgency. As Rawls
remarks, it is not enough that people support norms of toleration and equal
respect: they must also think that these political goals are quite important,
worth really trying hard to secure and maintain, because these political goals
may sometimes require sacrifices of their own self-interest.[34] Emotions constructed by art and rhetoric frequently play a valuable role in such a process.
Third, a "public poetry" of the type I envisage can also support the efforts of
those who already believe in the political norms, giving them hope (as they
participate in the public celebration of their own values) that these good norms
may eventually prevail and are not merely a foolish utopianism.

Public Poetry

Now we must leave the realm of abstraction and turn to political history, for
there are indeed examples of the good kind of civil religion or public poetry in
our recent history, and if we keep them before us as paradigms, we will understand a little more about our task.

If I were publishing this essay in India, I would turn at this point to
Rabindranath Tagore, who was the archentrepreneur of a public poetry of
diversity and inclusion. In his songs, dance-dramas, and poems, he celebrated
the richness of a nation that derives from its diversity; at the same time, he
celebrated the body, with all its complexity, its sexuality, its aging, as a source of
joy.[35] By casting middle-class Hindu women (students in his school) in leading
roles in his sexy dances, he made a powerful statement against the stigmatization of female sexuality. Amartya Sen's mother, who was one of his leading
student dancers, movingly described to me the scandal of her debut on the
Calcutta stage, dancing the role of Spring in Tagore's dance-drama about the

seasons of the year. Before her death in 2005 she often demonstrated for me how Tagore himself seductively danced the role of the human being who waits for the spring, beckoning to her, until she leapt in with joyful abandon.

I note that India had, and still has, a big fight about which poem to choose for its national anthem. One candidate, still favored by the Hindu right, which constantly seeks to reverse the decision, was the poem "Bande Mataram" ("Hail to the Motherland") by nineteenth-century Bengali novelist Bankimchandra Chatterjee, an aggressive warlike ode to a type of national unity based upon blood, homogeneity, and the land—the very idea of unity that the leaders of the Hindu right love, because it fits with their racial ideas of genuine citizenship.[36] The speaker expresses slavish devotion to the Motherland, depicted as a goddess; he kisses her feet, and he identifies morality and law, explicitly, with this death-seeking mother-goddess. The poem is suffused with anxiety about military weakness and the humiliation of colonial domination, which it seeks to purge in an orgy of violence. Writing in 1915, in his novel *The Home and the World*, Tagore depicted the song as closely connected to a narrow type of patriotism that repudiated the claim of Muslims to be equal citizens of India and that put slavish devotion to the Motherland ahead of principles of justice.[37]

The other candidate, which won, was a poem by Tagore: "Jana Gana Mana."[38] The poem celebrates the diversity of India's people, mentioning their ethnic and regional variety. It depicts all citizens as loving their country and revering the universal principles of right and justice on which it is founded; even the river Ganges and the waves of the Indian ocean sing this name.[39] The poem has no warlike message; although it mentions victory, the victory in question consists in protecting all of India's people and achieving well-being and justice for them. Its idea of unity is one of mutual love among people who are different. It is not surprising that the Hindu right fights so aggressively to change this anthem and even circulate false stories about it, such as the story that it was originally written to celebrate a visit by King George V (when it was really written after Tagore decided that he could not celebrate that visit, in place of the desired celebratory anthem).

I believe that this anthem really does some work in reaffirming and strengthening commitment to the political values it embodies. I cannot doubt, when I see activists singing it with conviction and enthusiasm, after spending weeks taking down testimony of women who were raped and tortured in the religious massacre in Gujarat, that the poem and the emotions it inspired renew hope in people whose experience might lead them to the brink of hopelessness. It also helps to teach values of pluralism and respect to children who have not yet made a choice in the struggle between pluralism and Hindu fundamentalism. And, by being sung on solemn public occasions, especially occasions celebrating India's independence and its founding as a nation, it gives a sense of emphasis and importance to the values on which the nation was in fact founded, values that are under siege in today's India. Of course, a national anthem cannot do much work in isolation from other aspects of the political culture. If Tagore's proposals for education had been more widely institutionalized, there would have been a stronger support structure for these values in public education. But at any rate the anthem leads in the right direction, especially when people are aware, as everyone is, that it was deliberately chosen, and is still being deliberately chosen, over against another anthem that embodies a different vision of India. (Hindu right websites insist that although "Jana Gana Mana" is in fact the national anthem, "Bande Mataram" is equally important and is India's "national song.")

But since I am a citizen of the United States and know its struggles and foibles better than those of any other nation, let me now choose U.S. examples of a civil religion addressed to the formation of political emotions.

Walt Whitman's Poetry

Although I have written so much about this topic before, Walt Whitman's effort to construct a public poetry supportive of democracy cannot be overlooked, since, unofficial though it is, it is a paradigm of what I have in mind, and it has deeply influenced most subsequent examples. I will simply ask you to excuse the poverty of detail in this account on the ground that chapter 15 of *Upheavals of Thought*, which treats Whitman's poetry as an example of the idea of the reform or "ascent" of love, contains the details that I think most important.

Whitman understood, and repeatedly asserted, that the civic fabric of a democracy cannot be held together by laws and institutions alone: "To hold men together by paper and seal or by compulsion is no account" ("Blue Ontario's Shore," 130). What is needed is something "which aggregates all in a living principle" (131)—and that, he insists, can be supplied only by poets. Writing during the Civil War, he says that the United States needs poets more than any other country does: "Their Presidents shall not be their common referee so much as their poets shall" (133).

Why are poets needed? This is a large topic, but the connection of poetry with the emotions is a central part of it. An insistent theme in Whitman's poetry is the relationship we have to minorities in our society: African Americans, women, and homosexuals. Whitman understood that laws can *say* that all citizens are equal, but only poetry can construct sentiments that lead all citizens to acknowledge that equality, because only poetry can characterize the suffering of exclusion in a way that moves us to put an end to it, and only poetry can characterize what we stigmatize and hate in ways that make us see it differently. Crucial to this project is forging a new idea of the body. My own very Whitmanesque view about the nature of radical evil is that a certain shame and disgust at our very humanity leads, under many social circumstances, to the stigmatization of others. Whitman saw his task, therefore, as creating a new relationship to the body, one of love and delight rather than shame and disgust. Like Tagore, Whitman understood that emotions supportive of respect for all the different citizens of a great nation, whatever their race, gender, or religion, required working vigilantly against the tendency to stigmatize the different by portraying people or groups as disgusting, as bearers of some type of bodily contamination or dirtiness. This human tendency, which I call projective disgust, is a flight from something in ourselves; it therefore can be countered only by a reconstructed relation to ourselves and our bodily fluids, which Whitman again and again tries to forge—above all in "I Sing the Body Electric," but throughout "Song of Myself" and many shorter poems as well.

Whitman's poetry, like Mill's religion of humanity, contains ideas of transcendence. First of all, it contains ideas and images of what I have called "internal transcendence": the transcendence of racism and other forms of oppression in justice, the transcendence of the Civil War in the form of a restored nation aspiring to justice, the transcendence of the hatred of difference in the form of an image of New York, which represents for Whitman the idea that people different and unsettling to one another might live in peace and chaotic, turbulent amity. Second, it also contains a Millean idea of the continuity of all lives, the way in which the lives of soldiers dead in the war survive in the blades of grass upon their tomb, the way in which all of us survive in our fellow world citizens and the progress of humanity. It repudiates as harmful not the bare desire for transcendence, but rather a disgust at one's human body, which is seen by Whitman to be strongly linked with the repudiation of particular groups and people. (To his list, we should add the repudiation of people with bodily and mental disabilities, who are all too often shunned because of an anxiety they evoke in the people who would like to think their bodies free from flaw.)[40]

Public poetry is likely to be unsettling, as Whitman's poems have always been found unsettling. And yet the sheer richness of language and image in them leads the reader in, until the difficult and challenging images prove acceptable—even images of the relationship between self and soul as one of homoerotic intercourse, images of women being freed to bathe and dance with naked men, images of black men eating with white men and even exchanging clothing with them. When one considers the extraordinary fact that a poet who frankly challenged all the sources of disgust and stigma in American society is beloved and is taught to every schoolchild in the country, and even holds a central place in conservative politician William Bennett's A Book of Virtues, one can see the magnitude of the task that Whitman has accomplished.

King's "I Have a Dream" Speech

Martin Luther King Jr.'s famous "I Have a Dream" speech is read by all schoolchildren. They cut their public-emotional teeth on it, so to speak, and in the process form emotions relating to race and the relationship between race and American ideals. The speech had, and has, two quite different goals: to portray as beautiful and attainable a world of racial equality and to convince African Americans that this goal must be attained through nonviolence. The two goals are connected, since the portrayal of the goal as wonderful and attainable is a large part of what might convince someone to persist with King's Gandhian program: violence feeds on despair. But the first goal reaches more broadly: King addresses the white majority, as well as his supporters and, within that minority, people not yet convinced that the goal is worth pursuing, as well as people who already grant that it is worth pursuing. So King has a very difficult rhetorical task. King's brilliant success in these tasks owes a great deal to his ability to draw on the rhetorical traditions of American history and, at the same time, on the Bible.

The first words of the speech are "Five score years ago," words that immediately establish it as a commentary on Lincoln's Gettysburg address; its first reference is to Lincoln's signing of the Emancipation Proclamation. This proclamation's "great beacon light of hope" is now contrasted to the prior situation of Negro slaves, "seared in the flames of withering injustice." So already biblical images of heaven and hell make their appearance, and life in the antebellum South is compared to being consigned to hell unjustly— something that only flawed human beings could have done. The next paragraph, however, makes it clear that one hundred years later, the life of Negroes in America is still hell rather than heaven: they are "crippled by the manacles of segregation and the chains of discrimination," and are "exile[s]" in their own land. With the image of exile, King cleverly positions African Americans within the exodus narrative of slavery and freedom, evoking in his audience the emotions connected with that narrative, with which small Jewish and Christian children are taught to identify at a very early age.

But then King sharply changes course, to evoke yet another American tradition: fiscal responsibility. We have come, he says, to "cash a check." The Constitution and the Declaration of Independence were a "promissory note" on which America has "defaulted . . . insofar as her citizens of color are concerned." Instead, America "has given the Negro people a bad check which has come back marked 'insufficient funds.' But we refuse to believe that the bank of justice is bankrupt. We refuse to believe that there are insufficient funds in the great vaults of opportunity in this nation." This part of the speech is little quoted, but for me it is especially shrewd. Most of the speech relies on prophetic biblical imagery, which most Americans will find resonant, but perhaps not all. Here King reaches out to the rather unpoetic and unreligious American who just has a sense of fiscal rectitude. He says that national ideals are like a promissory note and that justice is like a bank that surely has sufficient funds to pay that note. Instead of the common racist trope that black Americans are shiftless and lazy, we have an opposing image: white racists are like people who pass a bad check. (At the same time, he reassures his black audience, saying that there is enough money in the bank for all, there is no need of violence to get it out.)

Suffusing the images of servitude and freedom that follow are insistent references to tactile bodily sensations: the "sweltering summer of the Negro's legitimate discontent" (a phrase that alludes to the actual heat of the August day in Washington, but whose Shakespearean reference also implicitly contrasts the Negro's legitimate strivings with Richard III's crafty manipulations); the "warm threshold which leads into the palace of justice," as if its comforting touch can even now be felt by the weary feet of the marchers; the bodies of Negro men and women which, "heavy with the fatigue of travel, cannot gain lodging in the motels of the highways and the hotels of the cities." In this way, in a very Whitmanesque manner, he conjures up a physical empathy with Negro bodies, transcending the disgust and stigmatization that usually makes it impossible for whites to empathize with the way a Negro body feels.[41]

Now we arrive at the most famous parts of the speech, at King's remarkable mingling of American ideals with biblical prophetic rhetoric. It seems unnecessary to mention the parts that every one of us knows, and has heard, with the marvelous cadences of King's extraordinary voice; but I have particular admiration for the exodus-style characterization of Mississippi as "a desert state, sweltering with the heat of injustice and oppression," but scheduled to become "an oasis of freedom and justice." It is so odd to think of Mississippi as a desert land that the metaphor forces thought: what is really desert, and what is fertile oasis, in this country of ours? I also have particular admiration for the way in which the governor of Alabama is first characterized as a fairy tale witch, his "lips ... presently dripping with the words of interposition and nullification," but then the future of Alabama rises up out of the end of that same sentence, as a future where all children, black and white, "walk together as sisters and brothers." Although I am not sure, I believe that this sentence makes reference to "Hansel and Gretel" where we first have the witch who has imprisoned the little children, and then, after she is gotten out of the way, the children rise up and, at the end of the opera anyway, join hands together—an image linked to the history of German racism, now turned around to stand for a future of racial equality.[42]

The famous ending of the speech, in which King evokes "America the Beautiful" and urges freedom to ring from each state, is Whitmanesque for the way in which the states are personified, in quite sexy ways: the "heightening Alleghenies of Pittsburgh," the "curvaceous peaks of California." And then, his sly humor comes back, as he says, let freedom ring "from every hill and every molehill of Mississippi." I am inclined to think that the sly humor in the speech is one of its great points, for it says to the audience, "We are nobody's fools, we are no sentimentalists. We know a molehill when we see it. We also know a Richard III, we know a witch, when we see them. But we overlook that, to pursue the cause of freedom." The path of nonviolence looks, then, like something smart people can embrace without feeling stupid. (Gandhi was also a master at this sort of thing, combining extremely sophisticated wit with theatricality that moved large masses.)[43]

The closing of King's speech broadens the message of freedom, making it not just about the freeing of black people, but about the freeing of all people: racism enshackles us all, so it is all who need to be freed, "black men and white men, Jews and Gentiles, Protestants and Catholics," all will be able to sing together. But all, this time, will not just sing "America the Beautiful" together, they will sing "in the words of the old Negro spiritual, 'Free at last! Free at last! Thank God Almighty, we are free at last!'"

How, more precisely, does King construct emotions in his audience? Let us focus on the primary two: anger and hope. To make an audience angry, as Aristotle long ago observed, you need to make them feel that they—or someone they care about—have been wronged, in a way that is significant and not trivial, and that the wrong was not merely inadvertent or negligent, but willfully inflicted. Obviously enough, King's references to hell, to the bad check, to the weary bodies of people who cannot stay in a hotel, and to the dripping mouth of the governor of Alabama engender such beliefs. Could such beliefs have been summoned up without King's use of imagery and his references to the biblical and literary traditions? Probably, in people who had them already, as most of the audience did. For them, the key aspect of King's manipulation of anger lies in the way in which, by connecting anger to hope, he defuses the urge to violence. But what about uncommitted members of the audience? And, since the speech was written for posterity and not only for a single occasion, what about schoolchildren who read it now to learn about the civil rights struggle? For those children, the vivid bodily depiction of fatigue and insult is crucial in getting the propositions involved in anger to be really believed, really taken in beneath the surface of the mind.

So too, I believe, with hope. To have hope, one must believe that an important future good is possible. One might have had a speech that said, "There is an important goal we are pursuing, and we can achieve it if we work hard." But who would really listen to that or believe in it, while standing with weary feet in Washington on a hot August day? King's depiction of the contrast between the "dark and desolate valley of segregation" and the "sunlit path of racial justice," his resonant use of the prophetic "every valley shall be exalted"—whose familiarity is one part of what makes it easy to take in beneath the mind's surface—the repetition of the phrase "I have a dream" and the vivid depiction of a possible future time corresponding to that dream, the references to the familiar text of "America the Beautiful," which surely must be possible and attainable, because we already sing it as if it *is* reality—all this positions the hope-for goal as both glorious, deeply significant, and as available, no idle dream, but a dream that will become reality.

It is hardly necessary to mention the fact that high-minded philosophical sentiments compatible with this hope, if written as you or I would write them or even as John Stuart Mill would have written them, could not on their own have moved large masses of people to support its cause. King's poetic and rhetorical genius played a key role in getting people to support the nonviolent movement and in getting still other people to understand what it was all about. In this way, rhetoric and emotion changed history. If King had not been this sort of poet, we can hardly say what would have happened next.

King, to my mind, advances a civil religion in the best sense. In its Gandhian vision of nonviolence and its reliance on the tradition of constitutional rights, it is a civil religion in a way that is compatible with the vision of Locke and Kant; it does not rely on Rousseauian coercion. Moreover, although the speech relies for some of its effects on familiarity with Judeo-Christian prophetic texts, it uses those texts in a nonsectarian way, as it also uses Shakespeare and "America the Beautiful." Its sentiments, and its images too, can be endorsed by people who do not belong to that religious tradition, and also by people who do not have any religion.

Roosevelt and Public Photography

During the Depression, Franklin Roosevelt faced a large rhetorical challenge: how to mobilize public support for the policies of the New Deal, in an America that had never before supported such social welfare measures. The task was complex, for Americans traditionally had not wanted to extend economic relief to people except in the case of a natural disaster. Nor had they been inclined to have compassion for people whose problem was poverty: for they thought of these people as slothful and irresponsible. Here I draw on brilliant work by legal sociologist Michele Landis Dauber,[44] who argues that Roosevelt, understanding these attitudes, deliberately set out to convince Americans that an economic disaster has all the features of a natural disaster that are most relevant, where the emotion of compassion is concerned. Using an analysis of compassion similar to the Aristotelian one I propose in *Upheavals of Thought*,[45] Dauber shows that winning compassion for the victims of economic disaster required convincing the American public that the calamity they suffered was serious, that they were not to blame for it (any more than one would be to blame for being the victim of an earthquake or a flood), and that it was the sort of thing that any human being might suffer.

Dauber analyzes many pieces of public rhetoric and many works of art connected to the New Deal, including John Steinbeck's great novel *The Grapes of Wrath*. My focus here, however, will be on her analysis of the photographs commissioned by various New Deal agencies, in particular the Resettlement Administration. Hiring a staff of talented photographers, including Dorothea Lange, Walker Evans, Ben Shahn, Lee Russell, and Arthur Rothstein, the administration gave them specific instructions about how and what to photograph; it also chose, later, which photographs to print and which to "kill." Those selected were shipped to newspapers and magazines around the country, included in reports given to the Congress, and displayed at conventions of social workers, so that the images rapidly came to stand for the Depression itself.

How did these images construct compassion for a skeptical American public? The seriousness of the plight of the poor was the easiest thing to depict. Images showing lines of people applying for various types of relief—unemployment checks, bread, soup—made vivid the lack of basic necessities in lives hit hard by the Depression. Other images showed the dwellings of the poor and the even worse conditions in which migrant laborers were forced to live. Much more difficult were the other elements of compassion. Lack of blame and the idea of similar possibilities actually go together closely: for a spectator will think, "I myself might suffer that," only if it is clear that the cause of misery is not badness or laziness on the part of the suffering person. Roosevelt's agents thought about this problem very hard. First, they forbade photographers to show images of strikes (a favorite subject of Dorothea Lange before this), since that would scare viewers and make them think of the poor as bad troublemakers who brought their misery on themselves. Instead, people quietly queuing up for bread were preferred, in which, Dauber argues, the "blameless character of the needy" was shown in their orderliness and patience.

Second, the images selected were shorn of biography, in order to prevent thoughts about individual moral character and possible blame from cluttering the mind of the spectator. The only cause of misery that we are permitted to focus on is the Depression itself. In the queue photographs that were selected (as contrasted with those that were killed), "the viewer is prevented from identifying the men as individuals by the hats, shadows, and hazy focus that obscure details of physiognomy. These are people made equal in their loss." Other photographs of intimate suffering have a surface clarity and appeal, but at the same time discourage any interest in the biography of the individual represented. "Thus we have," Dauber concludes, "in some of the most enduring visual images of the Depression, vivid pictures of babies being nursed by migrant women who are otherwise wholly anonymous, without clues as to family status, location, or historical circumstances."[46]

This appeal to emotion through a carefully crafted use of the arts was, I believe, a key feature in the success of Roosevelt's New Deal programs. The fact that nobody is thinking much about these matters today goes some way to explaining the slide back to the view that the poor cause their own misery[47] and, in turn, to the decline of the American welfare state. Both Roosevelt and King exemplify my argument: progressive movements for equal respect ignore rhetoric and the construction of emotion at their peril.

We seem to have moved rather far from our original focus on religious and ethnic relations. But poverty is among the greatest sources of stigma in all societies, and this case, which shows how stigma can be overcome by an intelligent public deployment of emotion, contains obvious lessons for the cases with which my argument has been most concerned. It is also an instance of a "religion of humanity" in Mill's sense.

Chicago's Millennium Park

The poetry of great cities is a particularly powerful source of public emotion-construction in the American tradition. New York and Chicago, in particular, have given rise to a type of civic poetry and art that expresses a love of differences and celebrates the great energy that comes from difference when difference is respected and not feared. Here we must return to Whitman, whose public poetry of inclusiveness for all America, during and in the wake of the horror of the Civil War, was modeled on his love of New York and his sense of what New York stood for. "Walt Whitman, a cosmos, of Manhattan the son," he announces himself early in "Song of Myself," and immediately he juxtaposes to the idea of New York the key values of his ideal America: "Whoever degrades another degrades me. / And whatever is done or said returns at least to me. . . . / By God! I will accept nothing which all cannot have their counterpart of on the same terms."

What is the connection between these values and the idea of New York? Whitman shortly makes it explicit:

Through me many long dumb voices,
Voices of the interminable generations of prisoners and slaves,
Voices of the diseas'd and despairing and of thieves and dwarfs,
... And of the rights of them the others are down upon,
Of the deform'd trivial, flat, foolish, despised, ...
Through me forbidden voices,
Voices of sexes and lusts, voices veil'd and I remove the veil.

New York is a metaphor for the turbulent diversity that is Whitman's America—and for the daring and energy of that diversity, all the forbidden people and things that dare to speak their names there. One can see that Whitman is addressing the roots of shame and disgust in a way that goes to the heart of intolerance as I understand it. He says that if we learn to love and celebrate what is noisy, messy, tumultuous—including, prominently, our own messy sexuality—then we will be less likely to hate and oppress others. It is not surprising that New York figures centrally in the climactic lines of Whitman's elegy to Abraham Lincoln, as the only place the poet calls his "own": "Lo, body and soul—this land, / My own Manhattan with spires, and the sparkling and hurrying tides, and the ships."[48]

I am reminded of the painter Red Grooms, who said this, in an interview, about his great painting "Ruckus Manhattan": "What I wanted to do was a novelistic portrait of Manhattan from Battery Park to Grant's Tomb. I also felt it had to include the dark sides of life as well as the lighter ones: prostitutes, thieves and gamblers, tourists, shoppers, babies, moms and dads. I wanted to get it all in, it got quite busy."

In both Whitman and Grooms, this poetry of diversity is not free from difficulty. The dark side of life is dark. But there is a kind of love the whole enterprise, and the suggestion is that this love, which is at bottom a love of the messier parts of ourselves, can carry us forward. When we do not like our fellow citizens or approve of what they do, we can still love them as parts of the great city that we celebrate and are. The poetry of inclusion beckons to us, offering pleasure as we investigate corners of life we usually view with suspicion. These include, as Whitman knew so well, aspects of human sexuality that we usually cordon off as forbidden territory, telling ourselves that what makes us uncomfortable is outside and other. Thus Whitman's invitation to love the body provides a solvent for turbulent hatreds that grow out of our inability to tolerate ourselves.

But enough of New York. At this point, Chicago patriot that I am, I want to describe Chicago's new Millennium Park, opened by the city in summer 2004, which creates a public space that is its own poem of diversity. As you approach the park from Michigan Avenue, you encounter, first, the Crown Fountain, designed by Spanish artist Jaume Plensa. On two huge screens, fifty-feet high and about twenty-five yards apart, one sees projected photographic images of the faces of Chicagoans of all ages and races and types. At any given time two faces are displayed, changing expression in slow motion, with wonderfully comic effect. Every five minutes or so, the faces spit jets of water, as if from out of their mouths, onto the waiting bodies of delighted children, who frolic in the shallow pool below and between the screens—often joined, at first shyly and gingerly, by parents and even grandparents. (My daughter, a cultural historian, calls this an "ejaculatory esthetic." Well, yes. That is its charm. As Whitman said of the young men bathing, so of these faces: "They do not think whom they souse with their spray.")

If you watch all this from a certain angle, you will also see the sprouting plumes of the Frank Gehry band shell curling upward, a silver helmet, lying on its side, a relic of war that has decided to abandon aggression and turn into a bird. From yet another angle, you see the buildings of Michigan Avenue, and the clouds above, reflected as crazy curves in Anish Kapoor's sculpture "Cloud Gate," a huge inverted stainless steel kidney bean. The buildings look nice straight, and they look even more delicious curved or, I am tempted to say, queered. People of all sorts lie on the ground underneath the sculpture to get a view, or walk around it looking, with laughter, at their own distorted reflections. Meanwhile, on Gehry's improbably curving bridge over the highway—a bridge that seems to go nowhere in particular—people meander, pause, talk to strangers. The interactive public space celebrates diversity together with astonishing beauty, and both together with the pleasures of the body, as young and old paddle contentedly or stare at the reflected clouds.

What attitudes and emotions are constructed by this magical place? Well, certainly a love of diversity in one's fellow citizens and a sense that diversity is a source of pleasure, not of anxiety. Then too, a delight in getting wet—for one of the features of the park least anticipated by its designers has been the extent to which not just children, but people of all ages, want to stand in front of those spewing fountains, enjoying an odd kind of sensuous, if not exactly sexual, intercourse with Chicagoans of many races and genders and ages. Also, not insignificantly, a sense of the ridiculous in oneself and others, a sense that when the body looks odd and funny, or when fluids suddenly shoot out from some part of the body, that is good rather than bad. Also, again not insignificantly, a kind of calmness, a willingness to lie around, to walk slowly, to pause and greet people.

Radical evil is not a piecemeal affair. What Kant, Mill, and Whitman rightly want is a wholly new view of human relations, not simply progress on this or that issue. And it is clear that radical evil is alive and flourishing in the United States. Suspicion and mistrust of other peoples and groups appear to be growing, the underside of the new diversity. Rather than being encouraged to see the world as an international society in which we must all support the aspirations of people everywhere to decent and dignified lives, we are all too often encouraged to think in terms of U.S. preeminence and to see other nations as looming threats to U.S. power and safety—what I would call a narcissistic view of politics. Domestically, the dominant religion increasingly asserts its hegemony over minority religions and nonreligion, and public rhetoric too often gives sanction to this aim. In the proposed constitutional amendment to ban gay marriage, we see deep-rooted anxieties about sexuality taking a hateful and repressive form.

To counteract the influence of all this division, we need not only good liberal doctrines and arguments and not *only* (though it is crucial) the vigilant protection of free speech. We need a poetry of the love of free citizens *and* of their noisy chaotic sometimes shockingly diverse lives, constructing emotions that provide essential undergirding for good laws and institutions. Without this, good liberal principles, as Whitman said, are just dead words on paper. Whitman, Roosevelt, Tagore, and King understood, and Mayor Daley (with the help of Frank Gehry, Anish Kapoor, and Jaume Plensa) understands this point well. If we are to survive as a pluralistic nation, we had better hope there are more out there like them.

NOTES

I am grateful to Thomas Banchoff and other participants in the Georgetown conference for their helpful comments. This essay was also presented at a conference on Moral Psychology at the University of Texas at Austin, as a Parthemos Lecture at the University of Georgia, as an Andreas Papandreou Memorial Lecture in Athens, at Jawaharlal Nehru University in New Delhi, India, and at several other colleges and universities. For helpful comments on earlier versions, I am very grateful to Julia Annas, Richard Bernstein, Daniel Brudney, Stephen Darwall, John Deigh, George Papandreou, Zoya Hasan, Rachel Nussbaum, Eric Posner, Tanika Sarkar, Walter Sinnott-Armstrong, and Cass Sunstein. A related paper about India has appeared as Martha Nussbaum, "Education and Democratic Citizenship: Beyond the Textbook Controversy," *Islam and the Modern Age* (New Delhi) 35 (2005): 69–89; a slightly different version as idem, "Freedom from Dead Habit," *The Little Magazine* (New Delhi) 6 (2005): 18–32. For comments on issues pertaining to India, I am grateful to Barnita Bagchi, Jasodhara Bagchi, Zoya Hasan, Mushirul Hasan, Sumit Sarkar, and Krishna Kumar.

1. I use the term *toleration* because the European philosophical tradition uses it, although I insist from the start that I am talking about an attitude that includes respect, not merely grudging acceptance. The American founders found the word *toleration* too weak; George Washington, for example, wrote to the Jewish congregation at Newport: "It is now no more that toleration is spoken of, as if it was by the indulgence of one class of people, that another enjoyed the exercise of their inherent natural rights." Locke, however, did not think the word incompatible with a justification that focused on natural rights.

2. John Rawls, *Political Liberalism*, expanded ed. (New York: Columbia University Press, 1996).

3. See my book about the U.S. situation: *Liberty of Conscience: Defending Our Tradition of Religious Equality* (New York: Basic Books, forthcoming).

4. For all of this, see my *Democracy in the Balance: Violence, Hope, and India's Future* (Cambridge: Harvard University Press, forthcoming). Hitler's policy toward the Jews was openly admired by M. S. Golwalkar, a key founder of the Hindu right in the 1930s.

5. See my "Genocide in Gujarat," *Dissent* (Summer 2003): 15–23; and idem, "Body of the Nation: Why Women Were Mutilated in Gujarat," *Boston Review* 29.3–4 (2004): 33–38.

6. In his first speech as Prime Minister, Manmohan Singh, the first minority member ever to serve as India's Prime Minister, said this: "Divisive forces were allowed

a free play, which I believe is extremely injurious to orderly development. . . . We as a
nation must have a firm determination that these things should never happen."

7. Page references are to Locke's *A Letter concerning Toleration* (1689) (repr. New
York: Prometheus, 1990). Locke's argument are probably not very original: most of
them, for example, can be found in Roger Williams's *The Bloudy Tenent of Persecution*
(1644); see my discussion in *Liberty of Conscience*, chap. 2.

8. Quotations are from Kant's *Religion within the Boundaries of Mere Reason*, trans.
and ed. Allen Wood and George Di Giovanni, Cambridge Texts in the History of
Philosophy Series (Cambridge: Cambridge University Press, 1998). Page numbers are
from the Akademie edition, which are given in the margins of this translation.

9. Kant actually uses two different terms for the good and evil tendencies. The
"propensity" to evil, for which Kant uses German *Hang* and Latin *propensio*, is defined
as "the subjective ground of the possibility of an inclination"; it is distinguished from a
"predisposition" (*Anlage*), the term Kant uses for the tendency to good, in that a
propensity can be innate while yet being represented as not being such (see 6.29). This
distinction and the use Kant makes of it are obscure, but what he clearly wants to
achieve is to suggest that we naturally incline to evil and yet have a genuinely free will.
I am grateful to Daniel Brudney for discussion on this point.

10. See my "Equity and Mercy," in *Sex and Social Justice* (Oxford: Oxford University Press, 1999); and also idem, *The Therapy of Desire: Theory and Practice in
Hellenistic Ethics* (Princeton: Princeton University Press, 1994), chap. 11. I suggest
that Seneca locates the origins of evil in the "circumstances of life," that is, the competitive striving for goods that human life as it is brings forth. His account is not exactly
Kant's, because he does not hold that bodily appetite is easily satisfied; nor does he
posit an innate tendency to competition. But the similarity of the two accounts is
considerable.

11. Thus Seneca's account is in some ways stronger than Kant's.

12. Martha C. Nussbaum, *Upheavals of Thought: The Intelligence of Emotions*
(Cambridge: Cambridge University Press, 2001); and idem, *Hiding from Humanity:
Disgust, Shame, and the Law* (Princeton: Princeton University Press, 2004).

13. See Nussbaum, *Hiding from Humanity*.

14. See "Transcending Humanity" in my *Love's Knowledge* (New York: Oxford
University Press, 1990). Here I am responding to a challenge by Charles Taylor. Later
Robert Adams replied to my reply to Taylor in his excellent book *Finite and Infinite
Goods* (New York: Oxford University Press, 1999), and he and I then had an exchange
on the topic in the symposium on his book in *Philosophy and Phenomenological Research*
64 (March 2002). My article is entitled "Transcendence and Human Values" (445–52).

15. In chapter 7 of *Hiding from Humanity* I develop my own conception of political
liberalism and argue that my political psychology is compatible with a respect for a
reasonable pluralism of comprehensive doctrines.

16. Hans Reiss, *Kant: Political Writings*, 2nd ed. (Cambridge: Cambridge University Press, 1991), 49.

17. Ibid., 188–89.

18. Ibid., 189.

19. See "Perpetual Peace" in ibid., 126–27.

20. Ibid., 106, where Kant discusses the way in which immoral schemes of colonial domination are facilitated by the pretext of pious intentions: "And all this is the
work of powers who make endless ado about their piety, and who wish to be considered as chosen believers while they live on the fruits of iniquity" (107).

21. I cite from Jean-Jacques Rousseau, *Basic Political Writings*, trans. and ed. Donald A. Cress (Indianapolis: Hackett, 1987). "On Civil Religion" is §4.8, pp. 220–27.

22. See ibid., 225: "Christianity preaches only servitude and dependence. Its spirit is too favorable to tyranny for tyranny not to take advantage of it at all times. True Christians are made to be slaves."

23. See Nussbaum *Democracy in the Balance*, especially chap. 7.

24. "Utility of Religion" in J. S. Mill's *Three Essays on Religion* (New York: Prometheus, 1998), 70–122.

25. For a discussion of the essay and the influence of Comtean ideas in nineteenth-century English philosophy generally, I am indebted to a fine unpublished paper by Daniel Brudney.

26. Mill goes on to discuss Cicero's *De officiis*, noting that the standard of conduct it proposes is not unduly high and that most educated Romans at least tried to follow it. Cicero and many others did unhesitatingly sacrifice their lives to the common good, as they conceived it; we need only broaden this conception (Mill argues) to include not just one's own country, but humanity as a whole.

27. See Nussbaum, *Upheavals of Thought*, chap. 8.

28. See Nussbaum, *Liberty of Conscience*, chap. 3.

29. For an argument that these penalties do not involve an illegitimate penalizing of political speech, see Nussbaum, *Hiding from Humanity*, chap. 5.

30. Ibid., chap. 6.

31. On overlapping consensus, see Rawls, *Political Liberalism*, 133–72.

32. See the important sections entitled "Free Political Speech" (ibid., 340–47) and "The Clear and Present Danger Rule" (348–56). Rawls argues that the standard defended in *Brandenburg v. Ohio* is too restrictive. His own view is that political speech may be abridged only in a constitutional crisis in which there is imminent danger to the survival of the basic structure of the state itself. I do not intend to defend this view, which seems to me extreme.

33. Ibid., 197–200.

34. Ibid., 154–58.

35. On Tagore, see Nussbaum, "Education and Democratic Citizenship"; and also idem, *Democracy in the Balance*, chap. 1.

36. Here is Sri Aurobindo's English translation of the lyrics of "Bande Mataram":

> Mother, I bow to thee!
> Rich with thy hurrying streams,
> Bright with thy orchard gleams,
> Cool with thy winds of delight,
> Dark fields waving, Mother of might,
> Mother free.
> Glory of moonlight dreams
> Over thy branches and lordly streams,
> Clad in thy blossoming trees,
> Mother, giver of ease.
> Laughing low and sweet!
> Mother, I kiss thy feet,
> Speaker sweet and low!
> Mother, to thee I bow.

Who hath said thou art weak in thy lands,
When the swords flash out in twice seventy million hands
And seventy millions voices roar
Thy dreadful name from shore to shore?
With many strengths who art mighty and stored,
To thee I call, Mother and Lord!
Thou who savest, arise and save!
To her I cry who ever her foemen drave
Back from plain and sea
And shook herself free.
Thou art wisdom, thou art law,
Thou our heart, our soul, our breath,
Thou the love divine, the awe
In our hearts that conquers death.
Thine the strength that nerves the arm
Thine the beauty, thine the charm.
Every image made divine
In our temples is but thine.

Thou art Durga, Lady and Queen,
With her hands that strike and her swords of sheen,
Thou art Lakshmi Lotus-throned,
Pure and perfect without peer,
Mother, lend thine ear.
Rich with thy hurrying streams,
Bright with thy orchard gleams,
Dark of hue, O candid-fair
In thy soul, with jeweled hair
And thy glorious smile divine,
Loveliest of all earthly lands,
Showering wealth from well-stored hand!
Mother, mother mine!
Mother sweet, I bow to thee,
Mother great and free.

37. See Rabindranath Tagore, *The Home and the World*, trans. Surendranath Tagore (London: Penguin, 1985), esp. 29, where the wife observes: "And yet it was not that my husband refused to support *Swadeshi*, or was in any way against the Cause. Only he had not been able whole-heartedly to accept the spirit of *Bande Mataram*. 'I am willing,' he said, 'to serve my country; but my worship I reserve for Right which is far greater than my country. To worship my country as a god is to bring a curse upon it.'"

38. For an English translation of "Jana Gana Mana" and to hear the melody, also written by Tagore, which is itself very far from warlike and suggestive of dance rhythms, go to www.tourindia.com/insignia/anthem.htm. People typically sway to the rhythms of the tune as they sing. The addressee of the song is God, conceived of, as I say, in Tagore's deist/Comtean sense, as a universal principle of right and justice. It is for the victory of this principle that the song asks at the end:

Thou art the ruler of the minds of all people,
Dispenser of India's destiny.

Thy name rouses the hearts of the Punjab, Sindhu, Gujarat, and Maratha.
Of the Dravid and Orissa and Bengal.
It echoes in the hills of Vindhyas and Himalayas,
Mingles in the music of the Jamuna and Ganga
And is chanted by the waves of the Indian sea.
They pray for thy blessings and sing thy praise,
The saving of all people waits in thy hand,
Thou dispenser of India's destiny.
Victory, victory, victory to thee.

39. These ideas are expressed in terms of Tagore's conception of the religion of humanity, which is very similar to Mill's and has a similar Comtean source. See Rabindranath Tagore, *The Religion of Man* (London: Unwin, 1931). On Comte's influence on Tagore, see Jasodhara Bagchi, "Anandamath and the Home and the World: Positivism Reconfigured," in *Rabindranath Tagore's the Home and the World: A Critical Companion*, ed. P. K. Dutta (Delhi: Permanent Black, 2003), 174–86.

40. See Martha C. Nussbaum, *Frontiers of Justice: Disability, Nationality, Species Membership* (Cambridge: Harvard University Press, 2006).

41. Lest readers forget how physical the stigmatizing of African Americans was in our country, I recall that my father (born in Macon, Georgia) forbade our African American cleaning women to use the same toilet as any of us and even forbade me to offer a local black child (daughter of live-in help in the neighborhood) to drink from a glass of water in our kitchen.

42. King's sophistication and his wide knowledge of world literatures surely makes this reading a strong possibility. As with most great popular literature, from ancient Athenian tragedy to the present day, some allusions will be recognized by all, some by relatively few.

43. Told that Lord Curzon prayed to God every day, Gandhi replied, "What a pity that God gives him such bad advice." Asked by a journalist what he thought of Western civilization, he said, "I think it would be a very good idea." This sort of thing was typical and helped his followers to feel that to follow him in nonviolence was not to be a chump.

44. Michele Landis Dauber, "Fate, Responsibility, and 'Natural' Disaster Relief: Narrating the American Welfare State," *Law and Society Review* 33 (1999): 257–318; and idem, "Helping Ourselves: Disaster Relief and the Origins of the American Welfare State" (PhD diss., Northwestern University, 2003).

45. This is no coincidence, since Dauber was a student of mine, but the causal relationship does not make the view false. Something like it has been endorsed by most of the Western philosophical tradition.

46. These quotations are from Dauber, "Helping Ourselves," chap. 4, although there is a similar discussion in her "Fate, Responsibility."

47. See the sociological study of compassion in America by Candace Clark, *Misery and Company* (Chicago: University of Chicago Press, 1997), which concludes that many if not most Americans hold this belief; see also my *Upheavals of Thought*, chap. 6.

48. "When Lilacs Last in the Dooryard Bloom'd," 12, 89–90. Another great New York poem is Whitman's "A Broadway Pageant," which depicts a parade celebrating a treaty between the United States and Japan, and, as the poet imagines himself blending into the dense and diverse crowd to watch the Japanese visitors, New York becomes a symbol of the whole nation: "Superb-faced Manhattan! / Comrade Americanos! To us, then at last the Orient came."

BIBLIOGRAPHY

Adams, Robert. *Finite and Infinite Goods*. New York: Oxford University Press, 1999.

Bagchi, Jasodhara. "Anandamath and the Home and the World: Positivism Reconfigured." In *Rabindranath Tagore's the Home and the World: A Critical Companion*, 174–86. Edited by P. K. Dutta. Delhi: Permanent Black, 2003.

Clark, Candace. *Misery and Company*. Chicago: University of Chicago Press, 1997.

Dauber, Michele Landis. "Fate, Responsibility, and 'Natural' Disaster Relief: Narrating the American Welfare State." *Law and Society Review* 33 (1999): 257–318.

———. "Helping Ourselves: Disaster Relief and the Origins of the American Welfare State." PhD diss., Northwestern University, 2003.

Locke, John. *A Letter concerning Toleration* (1689). New York: Prometheus, 1990.

Mill, J. Stuart. *Three Essays on Religion*. New York: Prometheus, 1998.

Nussbaum, Martha. "Body of the Nation: Why Women Were Mutilated in Gujarat." *Boston Review* 29.3–4 (2004): 33–38.

———. *Democracy in the Balance: Violence, Hope, and India's Future*. Harvard University Press (forthcoming).

———. "Education and Democratic Citizenship: Beyond the Textbook Controversy." *Islam and the Modern Age* (New Delhi) 35 (2005): 69–89.

———. "Freedom from Dead Habit." *The Little Magazine* (New Delhi) 6 (2005): 18–32.

———. *Frontiers of Justice: Disability, Nationality, Species Membership*. Cambridge: Harvard University Press, 2006.

———. "Genocide in Gujarat." *Dissent* (Summer 2003): 15–23.

———. *Hiding from Humanity: Disgust, Shame, and the Law*. Princeton: Princeton University Press, 2004.

———. *Liberty of Conscience: Defending Our Tradition of Religious Equality*. New York: Basic Books (forthcoming).

———. *Love's Knowledge*. New York: Oxford University Press, 1990.

———. *Sex and Social Justice*. Oxford: Oxford University Press, 1999.

———. *The Therapy of Desire: Theory and Practice in Hellenistic Ethics*. Princeton: Princeton University Press, 1994.

———. "Transcendence and Human Values." *Philosophy and Phenomenological Research* 64 (March 2002): 445–52.

———. *Upheavals of Thought: The Intelligence of Emotions*. New York: Cambridge University Press, 2001.

Rawls, John. *Political Liberalism*. New York: Columbia University Press, 1996.

Reiss, Hans. *Kant: Political Writings*. 2nd ed. Cambridge: Cambridge University Press, 1991.

Rousseau, Jean-Jacques. *Basic Political Writings*. Translated and edited by Donald A. Cress. Indianapolis: Hackett, 1987.

Tagore, Rabindranath. *The Home and the World*. Translated by Surendranath Tagore. London: Penguin, 1985.

———. *The Religion of Man*. London: Unwin, 1931.

IO

Islam and the Republic: The French Case

Danièle Hervieu-Léger

All European societies are now faced with Islamic diasporas that disturb established ways of dealing with religion in the public space.[1] The diversity of responses to those diasporas reflects multiple political traditions in these societies and the mixed character of the Muslim populations involved in the process. The Pakistanis of Great Britain, the Turks who have mainly settled in Germany, and the North Africans who make up the largest part of the Muslim community in France do not conceive Islam in the same way. Neither do they have the same manner of approaching the conflicts that arise from their confrontation with the norms and values of modern, democratic societies. In the emergent and the imperative public debate about how to approach these diasporas, the plurality of Islam, both historic and present, is rarely taken into account. Its capacity to adapt to the democratic rules of the game is called into question, as if it were self-evident that an authoritative Islamic approach is discernible in the corpus of doctrinal and legal texts that supposedly bind all believers. In point of fact, the Muslim tradition has progressively restrained the active practice of interpreting its sacred texts and adapting them to new conditions. From a historical and sociological point of view, however, the presence or absence of particular texts and their interpretation is not decisive. Social reality consists of various "experienced Islams"—different ways of living against the backdrop of the norms embedded within texts and traditions.[2] To wonder whether Islam per se is compatible with the values and principles of secular, democratic societies will be in vain, as long as we do not raise the question of how the Muslims who seek recognition in these societies experience their various Islams.

The presence of Islam in France is far from a new phenomenon. There is no need to recall the importance of the Muslim presence in colonial France or the long-standing settlement of immigrant populations from Muslim countries on the French metropolitan territory. It suffices to say that the Paris Mosque was inaugurated in 1926 as a mark of France's gratitude to the many Muslims who died defending the nation during the First World War. Until 1981, it was the official symbol and the most visible institution of Islam in France. Yet the popular perception is that the French have only recently discovered the existence of Islam in their midst. Of course, this anxious awareness is linked to the psychological shock of the rise of Islamist movements in all Muslim countries and especially in Algeria, by far a most sensitive area for the French. But the essential part of the phenomenon lies in the transformation, over the last thirty years, of the social conditions of immigrants who came from the Maghreb to work in France, with the permanent settlement of families in the host country and the coming of age of new generations born in France of Muslim extraction.[3] For this population who has never lived elsewhere, the idea of a "return to the original land"—which, in principle, is what Islam entices all its believers to do when they live in the land of the unfaithful—has not only lost all concrete plausibility but is no longer a dream that mobilizes them. It is in a situation where they have settled in France for good that these Muslims demand to live their religious life if they have one. The multiplication of prayer rooms since the early eighties (approximately three thousand today), followed by the construction of architectural mosques wherever numerous Muslim populations live, has concretized this stabilization, while giving Islam local and often conflictual visibility.

The presence of Islam in the public space has gradually grown. The presence of Muslim chaplains in the army and, above all, in prisons—where Islam is, de facto, the leading religion—is drawing considerable attention.[4] The growing demand that special spaces oriented toward Mecca be reserved for Muslims in cemeteries has been met with favorable reception by certain mayors in large cities, including Paris. This claim indeed has had a considerable symbolic impact: it shows that being buried in France is now the fate of a large majority of the Muslims living in the country. Furthermore, it means that they have given up the idea of a late repatriation to their Muslim countries of origin. All aspects of religious faithfulness must now be implemented in a country that is no longer a "host" or "temporary residence" country, but a native land for Muslims with French passports—now a majority—to exercise citizenship. This claim for recognition has asserted itself all the more strongly where economic, social, and cultural integration is difficult. For the young, the most vulnerable to threats of exclusion, religion can become a place for the conquest of dignity and the construction of identity.[5] Many young Muslims claim to live, publicly and collectively, according to an Islam which they have appropriated as a fundamental dimension of their cultural and social identity. For many, this is the only cultural and symbolic possession they can specifically claim vis-à-vis the French of French extraction. It allows them to transform enduring exclusion into difference willingly embraced.

Such constructions of identity take different shape according to actual living conditions, social and cultural dispositions, and life experience. In the case of France, the recurring question in the public debate about the compatibility of Islam with Republican principles also hides another, more directly practical question: whether these diverse experienced Islams are likely to fit into the system regulating the exercise of religion within "the limits of the Republic." The problem of the assimilability of Islam, artificially represented as an immutable, monolithic whole, in the very abstract environment of laïcité (secularism), hides the fact that the legal and administrative framework within which these values are supposedly inscribed is itself the result of a historical compromise. This compromise took place over a long period of time and with many confrontations and will likely continue to evolve.

The challenge posed by Islam, which has now become France's second religion, is not primarily that of its possible absorption within the existing secular framework. It is that of the dynamics of transformation in which laïcité is now engaged, whether willingly or not, due to its confrontation with the inescapable presence of a plural, French Islam on French soil. To say this does not mean that we radically relativize the principles on which the French conception of citizenship is founded. Neither does it imply that we consider unnecessary a fundamental reflection on, say, whether the Muslim problematic of humanity's dependence on God may or may not be compatible with the modern conception of individual autonomy, the basis of all democratic constructions. From the point of view of laïcité, however, this is not an issue for the state. According to one of its major principles, the state should not intervene in the field of dogma, even if the latter's claims are in contradiction with the law. The state should act neither as the promoter of any religious ethic nor as the arbiter of any "religiously correct" order. It is strictly in charge of the maintenance of public order—the guarantee of individual liberties and the defense of the rights of the young. It is important to remember here that laïcité is not a philosophy or a system of thought. It is fundamentally a legal construction embedded in various legal and interpretative frameworks over time.

Against this backdrop, an understanding of the challenge posed by the Islamic diaspora necessitates an analysis of the historical logic that has governed the elaboration of the French model of laïcité. By grasping the fluidity of the model one can better address the question of its adaptation to a new landscape in which contemporary Islam both exemplifies and induces its further evolution.

Citizenship and Religion: The Weight of History

It should first be remembered that on the eve of 1789 the Roman Catholic Church was undoubtedly the pivotal institution of French society. It legitimized political institutions and, through the king's coronation, gave its religious foundation to the principle of dynasty. It governed the calendar and the time and space of both collective and individual life. It held the registry office and ruled teaching, medicine, and social institutions. If it did not control mentalities quite as much as is sometimes assumed, it nevertheless exercised considerable influence through social structures. Its economic power was considerable, and its capacity to impose norms remained vast, despite the contestation of the emergent critical intellectual milieus of the Enlightenment.

In the space of a few months, between May and September 1789, this formidable machinery of control collapsed. The constitutional monarchy that followed the *ancien régime* immediately moved to secularize the political order. The legitimacy of monarchy, therefore, lost its religious foundation and henceforth rested on a contract between the king and the nation. This new understanding of sovereignty was set down in Article 3 of the Declaration of the Rights of Man: "No corporate body, no individual may exercise any authority that does not expressly emanate from it."

This new configuration of the connections between power and individuals made politics the founding principle of social cohesion. At its center was the essential figure of the citizen, solely defined by legal status and thus torn from the determinations and dependencies imposed through family, community, and social groups. In the new world thus launched, the citizen was defined solely by belonging to the national community. In principle this belonging abolished all specific identities conferred by being part of an ethnic, regional, linguistic, religious, or other group. The unity of the "community of citizens" was built with individuals made legally independent from any attachments set by birth and its related social destiny.[6]

It followed that no one could be prevented from participating in political life on the grounds of their religious affiliation. The proclamation of the principle of religious freedom in Article 10 of the Declaration of the Rights of Man in 1789 was a decisive step in this political revolution. It effectively supplanted the religious monopoly of the Roman Catholic Church, both in society and in the religious sphere. Religious minorities were progressively granted all the rights related to citizenship. Protestants were soon given back the right to vote and be elected, as well as to be admitted to all professions. The emancipation of Jews took place in September 1791. The constitution adopted on September 3, 1791, guaranteed as a "natural and civil right" the freedom for each citizen "to practice the faith he is related to." But the price for this emancipation was that all communities—and notably religious communities—had to renounce efforts to assert themselves as such, with their own specific rights, in the public space.

The assertion of religious freedom raised the question of the status of Catholicism within the nation. This question concretely crystallized the split between the new regime and the Catholic Church. Indeed, the Assembly refused to recognize Catholicism as a state religion three times. The modern construction of *laïcité* that culminated with the principle of the separation of church and state established in 1905 already existed in embryo in this first establishment of the relationships between state and religion. It corresponded to a "political conception implicating the separation between the civil and religious societies, the state exercising no religious power and the churches no political power."[7]

This process of dissociating politics and religion was itself inscribed in a movement of "differentiating institutions," which had started a long time before the Revolution and extended beyond it. Through this long-term movement, spheres of social activity progressively attained their own autonomy. Politics, religion, morals, law, art, culture, economics, and community and family life came to be considered largely separate domains. Each was organized following its own rules relatively independent from others. In this movement, religion was progressively removed from the overarching position it claimed in traditional society. It gradually lost its capacity to rule, as the guardian of revealed truth, over all domains of social life and all aspects of individual and collective behavior. Yet if the disjunction of politics and religion—the nodal point of this trajectory which is part of modernity—has taken place in most Western countries at various rhythms and with various modalities, nowhere but in France has it assumed such a dramatically conflictual character.[8]

The war of the two Frances—the juxtaposition of a conservative, Catholic France and a progressive, Republican France—was extremely violent. Following the passage of the 1905 law, the confrontation slowly ebbed, in part through the reconciliation of French society in the trenches during World War I. One century after the institution of the 1905 law this model of separation of church and state is the object of a very large national consensus, with active and even enthusiastic support from French bishops (despite major wrangles over education policy in the 1980s and 1990s).[9] Today the relationship between Roman Catholicism and the Republic is not the issue, but instead how to protect a durable historical compromise in the face the growth of Islam.

At the heart of the compromise and the consensus it embodies is a particular understanding of an acceptable religion within the framework of the Republic. This understanding might be termed denominational (*confessionnelle*). It conceives of the relationship of religion to the state exclusively through representative religious institutions. This definition rests on two premises. One is the private character of the individual religious choice; the other is the modality, mainly of worship and rituals, in which these choices are normally supposed to be expressed in a collective way. This double postulate governs the framework inside which religious activity, in the French context, requires protection from the public power. Another condition is required: that the religious institution be able to ensure social and disciplinary supervision among its followers, so that the state need not intervene at any time in the specific life of these communities.

The specifically French model of consistorial Judaism, established by Napoleon in 1808, is the perfect illustration of an implementation of this denominational model. It was the renunciation of the national component of the Jewish identity—a renunciation inseparable from the plenary integration of Jews into the French nation—that made possible the acknowledgement of Judaism as "one of the official religions of France." In order for Judaism to count among the religions accredited by the state, it had to form itself as a denomination endowed with a central authority and defining a specific faith. In other words, it had to conform to an organizational framework that was, for the most part, copied from that of the Catholic Church. In the terms of the

1905 law, the Republic no longer formally recognized any faith. Yet, it had de facto perpetuated a typically Roman Catholic denominational conception of religion, which defines the religious community by ultimately reducing it to a congregation, gathering for worship under the responsibility of an authority recognized as legitimate by its members.

As it happened, this denominational definition of a religious community, compatible with the assimilationist model of national identity inherited from the Enlightenment and the French Revolution, also fit the institution of the Catholic Church with its hierarchical structure. In fact it is directly derived from it. Here, beyond their historical competition, we can measure the affinity between the Catholic apparatus—organized into a religious power both hierarchic and territorial, inseparable from a strict division of religious work between priests and laypeople—and the universalist and administrative model that the Republic has implemented in all possible domains. It is not only because of its historic domination within the national space that the Roman Catholic model has been set up as the organizational reference for all religions within the framework of French laïcité. It is also because the institutional construction of the church represents the implicit point of reference for the institutional construction of the Republic itself. Laïcité managed to contain the social and symbolic power of the Catholic institution by opposing its own, symmetric, social, and symbolic apparatus: the territorial network of state schools versus the parish network; the authority figure of the schoolmaster countering the priest; the representation of a community of citizens against the representation of the communion of saints; and so on. As Pierre Nora underscores, the Republic could fight and defeat the power of the Catholic Church only by opposing a countermodel of a "true civil religion," including its own pantheon, martyrs, liturgy, myths, rites, altars, and temples.[10] The denominational definition of "religion within the limits of the Republic," which has been imposed on the Catholic Church and all other religious institutions, also stems from this game of mirrors. This paradoxical affinity can be considered as one of the keys to the "secular conciliation" which has taken place between yesterday's opponents with the help of time.

Can Islam Become Denominational?

For this system to function beyond Catholicism, it is necessary that religious institutions fit into the denominational mould. To interact with the public powers, they must be able to bring forth qualified representatives likely to be acknowledged as authoritative by believers. This requires, in turn, an organization that can ensure the internal regulation of community life. For this double condition to be satisfied, religious institutions must be able to impose among themselves a regime of validation of belief through which institutional authority is the last guarantor of the truth shared by the believers.

The question arises as to whether Islam in France, with all its contemporary diversity, is likely to fit into this denominational model. After desperately trying to identify and even promote "representative interlocutors" with whom to negotiate and normalize the place of Islam within French society, state authorities themselves have confirmed that at this point the answer is negative. Islam has no clergy or institution—at least in France—that can take responsibility for the ideological and institutional regulation of its communities. Furthermore, French Islam is eminently polycentric, with strong competition between various groups intending to define authentic Islam and control its concrete presence: mosques, schools, radios, newspapers, associations, local communities, and so on. Bruno Etienne, who stresses this point, distinguishes three levels of rival structures in French Islam. The first level is that of "very small communities, locally organized, that have almost no connections with one another, that simply try to organize the life of Muslims from the point of view of worshipping." The second level encompasses "associations set up by foreign states aiming to control their nationals." The third level is "the Muslim leagues supporting the problematic of Muslim minorities as defined by Orthodox Islam."[11] "Each of these structures produces clerks, preachers and imams, all more or less autonomous," Etienne writes. They compete in particular for the control of mosques and prayer rooms.

The French state is confronted with a mosaic of groups of different ideologies and ethnic or national origins, partly under the control of competing organizations.[12] It is therefore powerless to put into use regulatory mechanisms which postulate the existence of a unique, visible institutional authority entitled to speak in the name of the whole "Muslim denomination" (*confession musulmane*). Over the last fifteen years, France's various governments of both the left and the right have taken initiatives designed to create such an authority.

The Conseil de réflexion sur l'islam en France (Council for Reflection on Islam in France) was created in 1988 by Pierre Joxe, then Minister of the Interior. Organized around "significant" figures of Islam, it had authority not only to organize the Muslim cult, but also to help the dialogue between its various movements. It notably helped reach an agreement on the beginning date for Ramadan. The right-wing government that came to power in 1993 put an end to this experiment and instead tried to make the Paris Mosque the federative authority for French Islam. This attempt did not go far. The Conseil consultatif des musulmans de France (Consultative Council of French Muslims), created under this egis, produced the Charte du culte musulman français (Charter of the French Muslim Faith), officially certified by French Minister of Interior Charles Pasqua, on January 10, 1995. However, this approach implied the acknowledgement of the primacy of Algerian Islam. This led a group opposed to the monopoly of the Paris Mosque to create, during that same year, a Haut conseil de la communauté musulmane (High Council of the Muslim Community), which linked back to a wide array of associations. This high council subsequently proved the object of the government's largely unsuccessful efforts to help bring about an official representative authority for French Islam.[13]

This fragmentation of French Islam has far-reaching consequences for the question of training religious specialists with the capacity to lead worship services and local communities effectively. One of the major problems con-fronting French Islam is the poor preparation of many imams. Their role formally comes down to presiding over collective prayer, yet their responsibil-ities extend as community life expands. There have been various initiatives to create training schools for imams, but the results have been disappointing. Foreign recruitment of imams remains widespread.[14]

Despite these difficulties, the state, in the person of Jean-Pierre Chevène-ment, the Minister of the Interior, tried to relaunch the process of institution-alizing French Islam in the late 1990s. In May 1998 he released a communiqué stating that, "far from giving up the idea of a legitimate interlocutor, the state will approve the one proposed as long as it can be considered as such by the largest number." Even though it might take time, he continued, the state had not renounced intervention, "within the framework of Republican laïcité, to provide Muslim compatriots with a recognition of their culture and the means to put an end to discrimination."[15]

The Construction of the Conseil français du culte musulman (French Council of the Muslim Faith)

The plan took shape in November 1999 with the announcement of the Is-tichara consultation. A proposal was sent to an ensemble of "qualified per-sonalities" and representatives of the main currents of French Islam in charge of associations and the larger mosques. With very few exceptions, the con-cerned parties agreed to participate in this project. At the request of the min-ister and as a preamble to this undertaking, a majority of the representatives signed a "declaration of intention concerning the rights and obligations of the Muslim faith in France." The process was not without controversy. Disputes centered on the possibly discriminatory character of addressing such a call for allegiance only to Muslims and on particular language put forward regarding apostasy.[16]

The minister's view was that this text should help the emergence of a col-legial authority representing the various trends of French Islam, on the model of the Fédération protestante. Some voices began to rise among the Union des organizations islamiques en France (Union of Islamic Organizations in France) to express particular concern about the exclusive privilege this project gave to the dimension of worship in religious activity—in keeping with the denominational problematic defined by laïcité.[17] However, a master agreement was finally signed in May 2001, under the egis of the new Minister of the In-terior, Daniel Vaillant. It made provisions for the creation of a Conseil français du culte musulman (French Council of the Muslim Faith) with the status of association Loi 1901 (nonprofit association). Election to this authority was to take place in two stages, on a territorial basis:[18]

> Each edifice of the Muslim faith run by an officially registered asso-ciation shall designate delegates, whose number shall be in proportion

of its size. . . . Gathered in regional assemblies, these base delegates shall then elect delegates to meet at a national level and form a general assembly. This general assembly shall play the role of a constituent assembly and establish the representative authority of the Muslim faith in France.

Two major events perturbed the predicted course of the consultation process. September 11, 2001, was the first and most dramatic. Among French Muslims, except for some sporadic demonstrations of limited range in the suburbs, there was an immediate and unanimous reaction of condemning the terrorist attacks, sharing in the sorrow of the American people, and refuting in advance any confusion that might arise. Around the same time, there arose a new movement to contest the consultation led by the very charismatic Great Mufti of Marseille, Soheib Bencheikh. The claim was that the new council might "trivialize Islamism" and, under the guise of recognition, actually promote fundamentalist activism. If anything, this sharp reactivation of the internal tensions in the French Muslim community led Vaillant to accelerate the approval procedure for the new body. The date for the vote was set for May 26, 2002, between the presidential and legislative elections.

Electoral politics then muddied the waters. The extreme-right leader Jean-Marie Le Pen emerged as the challenger to Jacques Chirac in the second round of the presidential election. Concerned about political uncertainties and anxious that the council vote might turn out unfavorably Algerian Islam, its representatives petitioned for a postponement. The strong debate that ensued centered on the possible risks of legitimizing the most fundamentalist movements and laid bare the balance of power among organizations laying claim to represent French Islam: the Paris Mosque, the Fédération nationale des musulmans de France (National Federation of French Muslims), linked with the Moroccan state, and the more radical Union des organizations islamiques en France, close to the Muslim Brotherhood.

In the end, however, Muslim leaders united in a determination that the council should succeed. This was probably reinforced by the increase of xenophobia and racism shown in support for Le Pen. Nicolas Sarkozy, Minister of the Interior in the new right-wing government, announced his refusal "to see fundamentalism sit at the table of the Republic." At the same time, however, he pressed ahead on the path trodden by his predecessors.

The consultation finally took place in April 2003: four thousand *grands électeurs* representing some one thousand places of worship elected the general assembly of the Conseil français du culte musulman. The Paris Great Mosque had fewer elected representatives than the Fédération nationale des musulmans de France and especially the Union des organizations islamiques en France. Nevertheless, the council ratified the state's nomination of Dalil Boubakeur as its president. This tension between base and leadership weakened the council from the outset and was particularly visible in debates about headscarves in French schools that had gained momentum since the early 1990s.

The *Loi sur les signes religieux ostensibles* (Law Concerning Ostensible Religious Signs)

The polemics started in 1989 around the case of a Paris suburban secondary school where three young girls refused to take off their headscarves. The event received considerable media coverage and soon became one of national importance. It was not just a matter of opposition between the religious and the *laïc*. It deeply divided the *laïcs* themselves, between supporters of an open and tolerant *laïcité* and defenders of strict neutrality within the public space. It also revealed internal conflicts within the Muslim population, torn between the goal of assimilation at an individual level and the assertion of a collective identity.

Fueled by political parties, teachers' trade unions, and diverging intellectual voices, these ideological passions appeared to decline by the late nineties. The reasonable rulings returned by the Conseil d'état embodied a more pragmatic approach to the issue. These rulings concerned student exclusion on the one hand and, on the other, the implementation of ministerial circulars (in 1993 and 1994) mentioning the principles of *laïcité*, yet leaving school principals in charge of handling the problem—preferably through negotiation—at the local level.

The very small number of students concerned (a little over one hundred per year on average), as well as the good results of the local mediation authorities implemented by the minister, gave an impression of relative calm. Yet early in the new decade, voices rose requesting a global and final settlement of the litigation. In this movement, which once again mobilized the *laïc* camp, principals of secondary and high schools were among the most prominent proponents of regulations to be imposed universally. The main impetus behind the reopening of the debate was not a multiplication of Islamic headscarf affairs in schools. These remained a marginal phenomenon. Mobilization around the issue was probably more a reflection of an identity crisis plaguing state school teachers, whose traditional mission of training citizens and promoting social unity was in disarray. The request for a law banning all ostensible religious signs in school was an attempt—perhaps the last—to reassert the specificity of a national political culture based on a strictly individual conception of equality.

From this point of view, the "question of Islam" reveals a much wider issue—that of the survival of the French universalist model of citizenship in the face of calls for the recognition of the special rights of minorities.[19] It is impossible to develop here everything at stake in this major mutation of democratic cultures and the specific implications for the French construction of *laïcité*. We will explore only a few questions that relate to how law has been received inside the French Muslim community.

On the initiative of the president of the Republic, a commission was formed in July 2003 under chairmanship of the *deputé* Bernard Stasi. It gave its approval to the passage of a law prohibiting all ostensible religious signs within the school space. The law itself was adopted by the Parliament in

ISLAM AND THE REPUBLIC 213

December 2004 and generated a new wave of passionate discussions about the acceptable interpretation of forbidden "ostensible signs." Following a Chirac speech in December 2003 that endorsed the recommendations, Conseil français du culte musulman President Dalil Boubakeur, who at first had been opposed to the very principle of a law, announced that he would summon the Muslims to respect it if passed. At the same time, the Conseil français du culte musulman vice president, close to the Union des organizations islamiques en France, invited the Muslim community to mobilize against the law.

Such distortions reveal the depth of the tensions within the representative authority of French Muslims and, beyond that, the uncertainties that remain as to the definition of a cultural compromise through which French Islam can progressively adapt itself within the public space. At the same time, the debate about the law also engaged other religious communities in France. They were just as divided over the thrust of the law and the particular religious signs it actually prohibited. The question of Islam and its interconnections with *laïcité* thus paradoxically became less "singular." The discussion about the law and its implications for religious freedom actually focused as much on the turbans of Sikh students as on Muslim girls' headscarves. The negative reaction of the great churches, both Catholic and Protestant, as well as the Jewish community, with respect to efforts to confine religion to the private sphere broadened the discussion far beyond the specific problem of Islam.

The entry of Islam into the common debate about the place of religion in the public space is one aspect of a more diffuse process of cultural adaptation. Here the remarkable upsurge of interreligious initiatives and associations has played an important role.[20] This process is far from being completed, and new developments are likely. Nevertheless, one can already point to changes in mentalities on both sides of the controversy. It is notable that representatives of all the currents in the Conseil français du culte musulman unanimously condemned, in the name of Islam, the kidnapping of French journalists in Iraq and helped to organize large demonstrations for their release. Public opinion viewed this reaction favorably. Positive media coverage has accompanied Conseil français du culte musulman initiatives and cast them as significant evidence that French Muslims *do*—as they claim—belong to the French national community. The Conseil français du culte musulman is often portrayed as positive evidence of a "humanist Islam" strongly opposed to the attraction of radicalism or terrorism.[21]

Chosen Islam: The Construction of a Religious Identity Anchored in Modernity

There is no doubt that the long path toward the assimilation of the Islamic faith into a Republican organization of religious practice may contribute to the reinforcement of radical movements that are unsatisfied with this new definition of Islam and therefore turn toward communitarian isolationism and militant activism. The risk exists, yet acknowledging the situation does not mean viewing it as an irreducible manifestation of the singularity of Islam, whose very nature would destine it to remain a foreign body in a democratic, secular nation.

If we endeavor to explore the various forms of Islam as experienced by its followers, we will discover a diversified, evolving reality with little or no connection with the idea of an Islam frozen in its singularity amid an environment of religious modernity. Evidence so far explored reveals that French Islam in many ways partakes of the typical tendencies of this modernity. Researchers who have delved into these questions most deeply reject the blanket question whether Islam per se is likely to modernize. They convincingly demonstrate that young French Muslims do partake of this modernity culturally, even as they denounce its failings and deadlocks, in the name of a self-given definition of religious faithfulness. Through this assertion of their Muslim identity, the Islam of the diaspora emerges as a modern Islam.

The basic element in this concrete dynamics of inventing an Islam anchored in modernity is that, in general, the religious identity of these young Muslims is chosen rather than inherited. To choose Islam postulates that one can make another choice. This is particularly apparent in the interviews by Leïla Babès of young boys and girls from northern France. Whether they were exposed to Islam by their parents or grandparents in their childhood or whether they were given some kind of religious education within the family framework—all describe their present religious identity in terms of an individual, voluntary appropriation. This requires some personal research and implies that they have acquired the necessary knowledge to practice religion. Such an approach can be expressed as integration or reintegration into the family tradition. "Islam was the religion of my parents, but over the last two or three years it has become mine," said one young girl interviewed. This suggests a break with or distancing from the traditional, ethnic Islam, whose customs were a way for the preceding generation to retain its cultural and symbolic heritage and to maintain a connection with the country of origin. This distance is especially visible (notably among young girls) when traditional Islam is identified as a religion of constraints and prohibitions. Generally speaking, Islam as it is experienced by these new believers excludes the ritualistic submission to rules of observance.

What these young Muslims seek is an experience often separate from any personal understanding of the theological and spiritual foundations of practice. According to Babès, this double movement—valorizing their choice, while rationalizing their relationship with observance—shows a process of individualizing belief that marks the gradual insertion of Islam into the space of religious modernity. Religious membership may have (as is often the case) a strong dimension of questioning modernity, and all the more so when the parties concerned are further excluded from the benefits and promises of modern values. Nevertheless, religion becomes a path of self-construction which places those who follow it into the modern culture of the individual. The young who state that they "have chosen Islam," beyond some cultural heritage more or less passed on or taken on are thus part of a general movement which progressively imposes the figure of the "convert"—along with that of the "pilgrim" traveling the nonpredetermined stages of his or her path of identification—as one of the central figures in the modern religious landscape.[22] They manifest a funda- mental postulate of religious modernity: that "authentic" religious identity can only be chosen. The focus of this conversion act—be it to "enter," "return to," or "renew" one's religious faith—is that it acknowledges the personal commit- ment of the individual, autonomous believer. At the same time, it involves a global reorganization of life along new normative lines and incorporation into a community. Religious conversion is thus a remarkably effective modality of self-construction in a world of plural identities, where there is no longer a central principle to organize individual and social experiences.

The study by Farhad Khosrokhavar underscores that this religious path of self-construction particularly concerns the young who are economically and socially excluded and usually feel hated by a society that makes no room for them. Islamization to them primarily reorganizes the meaning of their own lives. To become a Muslim means both to access self-esteem and to acquire a socially recognizable identity. This religious integration of one's own individ- uality takes place in different ways, depending on the social situation of the concerned parties. Khosrokhavar distinguishes the "Islam of integration"— which allows young Arabs of the lower-middle class to put forward, socially, a visible denominational identity—from the "Islam of exclusion" of the young in the most precarious situations. The latter turn their marginality into a radical religious requirement to separate themselves from an evil world. Excluded by society, they choose, in the name of their new faith, to cut themselves off from it. Social necessity thus turns into religious virtue.

What remains in all cases is that entering into Islam implies a global change of course. Not only does the new coherence, stemming from a religious reading of the world, help to hold rage at a distance, but it also involves a practical reorganization of the relation to time and space for those concerned.[23] It redefines their relationship with the public space and regulates ordinary behaviors.[24] The concrete living conditions of the young converts to Islam specify the social and symbolic implications of their religious identification. Yet the logic of self-construction behind this identification—which makes them sort out and piece together practices and beliefs and which results in plural modes of relation to the believers lineage—does not differentiate young Muslims from the young believers of other religions, presumably adapted or adaptable to modernity. This has been shown in the interviews led by Khos- rokhavar among young Muslim girls demanding to wear the Islamic head- scarf, the utmost symbol of the nonassimilability of Islam into modern Eu- ropean society. This analysis points out the remarkable polysemy of a sign marked by opacity, carefully maintained by the young girls concerned, that allows them to play with their Muslim identity. They can settle their ambig- uous relationship with both family and social environment, conquer their identity as women by giving their fathers and brothers a fictive proof of submission, while they are actually escaping from it or even reinventing the cultural memory they lack in order to have access to self-esteem.[25] Like any of the great religions present in societies "that have moved out of religion," Islam is a toolbox, a supply of symbolic references.[26] In the absence of a code of meanings imposed on them and on the whole society, individuals can draw elements from it. With these, they can construct a small narrative of belief, inside of which the social relations and experiences they go through are likely to find their meaning.

Islam as a Mirror of Religion in Modernity

In all the great religions, religious symbols lend themselves easily to being reused and pieced together in myriad individual ways, a kind of institutional deregulation. This dynamic can be traced to the inevitable disqualification of the authorities in charge of defining, in each tradition, the "true belief" that compels recognition from the faithful. The autonomy of the believing subject, which has asserted itself as the norm in a society of individual entities, weakens the traditional system regulating beliefs and practices. In each tradition, in the name of the acknowledged "authenticity" of each believer's individual course, the devices formerly institutionalizing conformity of belief are gradually invalidated. This causes an atomization of faith, as has been shown in many inquiries.[27] Yet this atomization makes other real concerns crop up for the be-lievers, such as how to validate their own, self-constructed identities. For these free-floating believers to capitalize on the benefits of their identity, they must find, in one way or another, the means to confirm with other believers that they validly belong to the faith lineage they claim to be a part of. For a sociology of religious modernity, this brings up another question. What are the modalities capable of structuring both the quasiunlimited itineraries of belief identifica-tion and the continuity of a tradition that is no longer—or less and less—expressed in the discourse of a religious authority or acknowledged as the sole guardian of this continuity? This does not make Islam in the diaspora appear as totally singular. On the contrary, the question invites one to ask more broadly what takes place in a religion torn from a culture, where collective significances were naturally validated through the family transmission of values and norms, when it is directly confronted with the absence of an institutional system val-idating the belief. Islam, as we have said, has neither church nor clergy, and this lack of institutionalization is the key to its incapacity to adapt to the modern religious scene.[28]

Now let us put the question backward. Islam in the diaspora is structurally deregulated and—as are other religions—caught in a logic of the individu-alization of belief. It therefore pushes to the limits the tendencies observed in the less-and-less regulated spaces of Christianity and Judaism: namely, a joint emergent evolution, apparently contradictory, of two systems that take over the institutional validation of beliefs and practices. On the one hand, it is a flexible, tolerant, and fluid system of mutual faith validation, in which individuals authenticate for one another their common belonging to a belief lineage. On the other hand, it is a crystallization of small community systems of faith validation that offer to the religiously regenerated an absolute certainty: a body of truths ensured by perfect coherence in the behavior of the group.

What has indeed been described in the inquiries on which this reflection is based? Babès evokes a "positive Islam," tolerant and open, in which individuals, together, proclaim that they belong to the family of Islam, while they want to be fully integrated into society as a whole. They mutually acknowledge one another as Muslims in that they share a common memory, the same conviviality (which the practice of Ramadan particularly affords them), and an ensemble of ethical references. This Islam is involved in a process of internal secularization, miles away from the "neocommunitarianism" described by other researchers, including Khosrokhavar. The latter emphasizes that, by tearing themselves away as completely as possible from the contamination of the impure world around them, the new believers commit themselves to a global reorganization of their rules of life. Even though the debate should take place between the researchers concerned, the question is not which vision best matches the present evolution of Islam among the young.[29] It is rather how best to chart the outline of the twofold movement that characterizes the entire religious landscape of secularized societies today. Indeed, established religious organizations must accommodate the invasion in their midst of a system marked by individualization and the mutual validation of belief. By gradually imposing a "weak standard" of the true faith, this new system tends to slowly dissolve the traditional routine of institutional validation.

At the same time, religious institutions are faced, both internally and externally, with a multiplicity of small communitarian systems of validation, which counter the trend toward individualization with "strong standards" of shared truth. Those attracted by such standards are generally convinced that the weakness of these institutions—their laxity or their fear of conflicts—facilitates the irrepressible rise of an individualization and subjectivization of faith. To counteract these trends, they erect around their group a wall of a self-defined orthodoxy. The rise of neotraditionalism and neocommunautarianism in Catholicism, Protestantism, and Judaism falls precisely within this trend. As Olivier Roy puts it very clearly in his excellent essay published in 2005, the contemporary forms of Muslim "integralism" are part of this general movement. Unlike traditional forms of fundamentalism, the contemporary integralisms (or neofundamentalisms) put forward first and foremost the sacralization of believers' life rather than the resacralization of society as such.[30] They claim a personal regeneration which is shared and confirmed within strong communities confronting the compromises of dominant culture and politics.[31]

To describe this situation more precisely, one can say that, in France or anywhere in Europe, two typical, contrary movements are working their way through the modern-day religious landscape. The first movement, directly connected to the dominant culture of the individual, tends to relativize the norms of belief and religious practice. In stressing the value of personal research and individual appropriation of meaning, it almost dilutes and sometimes explicitly contests the notion of obligation connected to these beliefs and practices. If there is a community in this context, its vocation is not to attest to the prepostulated homogeneity of beliefs, but to demonstrate a mutually acknowledged convergence of its members' personal approaches. Within this perspective, the accepted recognition of differences is as important as the assertion of beliefs shared by the group. The community link is supposed to take form again and again, from a "spiritual credit" granted to one another by individuals involved in the search for a common expression. The identification of the limits within which this common expression remains possible is thus established as the basic principle of an endlessly reworked definition of community identity. One can note that this conception of community is often associated with the idea of "ethical convergence" found in the great religious traditions—a convergence which looks toward the utopian horizon of a possible unification of individual "quests for meaning." A large number of interviews led by Babès among young people connected in various degrees to the Islamic-Christian dialogue give interesting indications to that effect.

To this dynamic conception of the community, another, radically different movement opposes the solidity of the small worlds of collective certainties which efficiently ensure the ordering of individual experiences. The community concretizes the unicity of truth proclaimed by the group. To belong implies that one accepts this communitarian mode which encompasses beliefs and practices and sets clear boundaries with respect to outsiders. The idea of community as a process here corresponds to the system of mutual validation of belief. Still, the substantive definition of the community matches the communitarian system of validation of belief. Not only do these directly oppose each other, but they both defy the institutional vision that places the established, preexisting community before the individual members who make it up and update their beliefs in various ways. In a system of institutional validation, it is all the past, present, and future believers together that make up the authentic community. Small communities are historical condensations of the lineage of belief. They do not exhaust the reality of the "great community" (the Chosen People, the *umma*, or the church) which is their point of reference. The institutional religious authority has the acknowledged right to speak in the name of the community. As its guardian and ultimate arbiter it controls the centrifugal or separatist dynamics that may arise among the various smaller communities within it.

When this institutional regulation falls apart or when, in the case of Islam in the diaspora, it does not exist in the first place, the twin movements of individualization and communitarization develop their contradictory effects. In France, the future of *laïcité* directly depends on its capacity to develop—beyond the institutional issue of religion that was its historical reference—a robust public sphere in which new forms of individual and collective religious identity and practice can unfold within a democratic context. From this point of view, Islam is not an absurd case requiring a specific solution. It is the foremost test of the ability of our institutions and political culture to face the challenges of religious modernity. The suggestion that the presence of Islam lays bare these challenges in all European societies makes us wonder whether the treatment of Islam in each of them might not be, in many ways, the best mirror in which to compare the dynamics of religion throughout contemporary Europe.

NOTES

1. Chantal Saint-Blancat, *L'islam de la diaspora* (Paris: Bayard, 1997).

2. Among the works which come more closely to the scope of this perspective are Nancy Venel, *Musulmans et citoyens* (Paris: PUF, 2004); and, in the case of Germany, Valérie Amiraux, *Acteurs de l'islam entre allemagne et turquie: parcours militants et expériences religieuses* (Paris: L'harmattan, 2001).

3. About the settling process, see Gilles Kepel, *L'islam des banlieues: naissance d'une religion en France* (Paris: Seuil, 1987).

4. Farhad Khosrokhavar, *L'islam dans les prisons* (Paris: Balland, 2004).

5. See Leïla Babès, *L'islam positif: la religion des jeunes musulmans en France* (Paris: L'Atelier, 1997); Farhad Khosrokhavar, *L'islam des jeunes* (Paris: Flammarion, 1997); Jocelyne Cesari, *Musulmans et républicains: les jeunes, l'islam et la France* (Paris: Complexe, 1997); and Nancy Venel, *Musulmanes françaises: des pratiquantes voilées à l'université* (Paris: L'harmattan, 1999).

6. Dominique Schnapper, *La communauté des citoyens: sur l'idée moderne de nation* (Paris: Gallimard, 1994).

7. Henri Capitant, ed., *Vocabulaire juridique* (Paris: PUF, 1936).

8. For in-depth analysis regarding the historical construction of the French problematic about the relationships between religion and politics, see Danièle Hervieu-Léger, *Catholicisme: la fin d'un monde* (Paris: Bayard, 2003).

9. This support was particularly clearly expressed during the commemoration of the centennial anniversary of the 1905 law, the bishops insisting that the edifice then implemented remain untouched.

10. Pierre Nora, ed., *Lieux de mémoire*, vol. 1: *La république*, and vols. 2–4: *La nation* (Paris: Gallimard, 1984–87).

11. Bruno Etienne, *L'islamisme radical*, Le livre de poche (Paris: Hachette, 1987), 308–9.

12. Such as la Grande Mosquée de Paris, la Fédération nationale des musulmans de France, l'Union des organisations islamiques de France, and l'Association foi et pratique (Jamah-al-Tabligh).

13. For a clear presentation of the complex issues at stake in the institutionalization of Islam in France since the early eighties, see Jocelyne Cesari, *Etre musulman en France aujourd'hui* (Paris: Hachette, 1997), 163–202.

14. Institut européen des sciences humaines, founded in 1993 in Château-Chinon, by the Union des organizations islamiques en France; l'Institut d'études islamiques, created from an idea by Didier Ali-Bourg in 1993; Institut de formation d'imams de la Mosquée de Paris, inaugurated on October 4, 1993, in the presence of the Minister of the Interior and the Minister of Culture. See Cesari, ibid., 191–95.

15. *Le monde*, May 21, 1998.

16. "The right of every person to change religion," formally mentioned in the first version of the text, has disappeared in the second one, as it is supposed to be included de facto in the acceptance of total freedom of faith guaranteed by *laïcité*. About this controversy and the whole consulting process, see Xavier Ternisien, *La France des mosquées* (Paris: Albin Michel, 2002), chap. 12.

17. The Union des organisations islamiques en France was created in 1983 by the Tunisian Abdallah Ben Mansour and the Iraqi Mahmoud Zouheir. Recruiting mainly among Muslim students of Arab origin in France, it draws its inspiration from the doctrine of the Muslim Brotherhood. Refraining from fundamentalism, it advocates living a totally Muslim life in the context of French society.

18. Differing from, say, the Belgian consultation, which organized the designation of representatives on an ethnic basis.

19. See, for example, Dominique Schnapper, *La démocratie providentielle: essai sur l'égalité contemporaine* (Paris: Gallimard, 2002).

20. Anne Sophie Lamine, *La cohabitation des dieux: pluralisme religieux et laïcité* (Paris: PUF, 2004).

21. On the major mutation encompassing all the various forms of Islam in the diaspora, see Jocelyne Cesari, *L'islam à l'épreuve de l'occident* (Paris: la Découverte, 2004).

22. Danièle Hervieu-Léger, *Le pèlerin et le converti: la religion en mouvement* (Paris: Flammarion, 1999).

23. François Dubet, *La galère: jeunes en survie* (Paris: Fayard, 1987).

24. Khosrokhavar, *L'islam des jeunes*, 67–77.

25. François Gaspard and Farhard Khosrokhavar, *Le foulard et la république* (Paris: la Découverte, 1995), part 1: "Du côté des jeunes filles voilées."

26. Marcel Gauchet, *La religion dans la démocratie: parcours de la laïcité* (Paris: Gallimard, 1998).

27. A general table of these researches is presented in Grace Davie and Danièle Hervieu-Léger, eds., *Identités religieuses en Europe* (Paris: la Découverte, 1996).

28. Jean Paul Charnay, *Sociologie religieuse de l'islam* (Paris: Hachette, 1994), 451. For this author, who pleads for a "specific" sociology of Islam, the absence of a clearly institutionalized division of religious work, the discarding of mystery (436), and the absence of a stable and significant connection between faith and observance (437) are the main traits which underscore the singularity of Islam vis-à-vis the classical conceptualization of religious sociology. In fact, these remarks aim more at the "christianocentrism" of religious sociology questioned by the author than an irreducible singularity of Islam as such.

29. Cf. Babès, *L'islam positif*, 151–52.

30. Olivier Roy, *La laïcité face à l'islam* (Paris: Stock, 2005), 135–42.

31. See, for example, Gabriel A. Almond, R. Scott Appleby, and Emmanuel Sivan, *Strong Religion: The Rise of Fundamentalisms around the World* (Chicago: Chicago University Press, 2003).

BIBLIOGRAPHY

Almond, Gabriel A., R. Scott Appleby, and Emmanuel Sivan. *Strong Religion: The Rise of Fundamentalisms around the World*. Chicago: Chicago University Press, 2003.

Amiraux, Valérie. *Acteurs de l'islam entre allemagne et turquie: parcours militants et expériences religieuses*. Paris: L'harmattan, 2001.

Babès, Leïla. *L'islam positif: la religion des jeunes musulmans en France*. Paris: l'Atelier, 1997.

Capitant, Henri, ed. *Vocabulaire juridique*. Paris: PUF, 1936.

Cesari, Jocelyne. *Etre musulman en France aujourd'hui*. Paris: Hachette, 1997.

———. *L'islam à l'épreuve de l'occident*. Paris: La Découverte, 2004.

———. *Musulmans et républicains: les jeunes, l'islam et la France*. Paris: Complexe, 1997.

Charnay, Jean Paul. *Sociologie religieuse de l'islam*. Paris: Hachette, 1994.

Davie, Grace, and Danièle Hervieu-Léger, eds. *Identités religieuses en Europe*. Paris: La Découverte, 1996.

Dubet, François. *La galère: jeunes en survie*. Paris: Fayard, 1987.

Etienne, Bruno. *L'islamisme radical*. Le livre de poche. Paris: Hachette, 1987.

Gaspard, François, and Farhad Khosrokhavar, *Le foulard et la république*, part 1: "Du côté des jeunes filles voilées." Paris: La Découverte, 1995.

Gauchet, Marcel. *La religion dans la démocratie: parcours de la laïcité*. Paris: Gallimard, 1998.

Hervieu-Léger, Danièle. *Catholicisme: la fin d'un monde*. Paris: Bayard, 2003.

———. *Le pèlerin et le converti: la religion en mouvement*. Paris: Flammarion, 1999.

Kepel, Gilles. *L'islam des banlieues: naissance d'une religion en France*. Paris: Seuil, 1987.

Khosrokhavar, Farhad. *L'islam dans les prisons*. Paris: Balland, 2004.

———. *L'islam des jeunes*. Paris: Flammarion, 1997.

Lamine, Anne Sophie. *La cohabitation des dieux: pluralisme religieux et laïcité*. Paris: PUF, 2004.

Nora, Pierre., ed. *Lieux de mémoire*, vol. 1: *La république*; vols. 2–4: *La nation*. Paris: Gallimard, 1984–87.

Roy, Olivier. *La laïcité face à l'islam*. Paris: Stock, 2005.

Saint-Blancat, Chantal. *L'islam de la diaspora*. Paris: Bayard, 1997.

Schnapper, Dominique. *La communauté des citoyens: sur l'idée moderne de nation*. Paris: Gallimard, 1994.

———. *La démocratie providentielle: essai sur l'égalité contemporaine*. Paris: Gallimard, 2002.

Ternisien, Xavier. *La France des mosquées*. Paris: Michel, 2002.

Venel, Nancy. *Musulmanes françaises: des pratiquantes voilées à l'université*. Paris: L'harmattan, 1999.

———. *Musulmans et citoyens*. Paris: PUF, 2004.

II

Pluralism, Tolerance, and Democracy: Theory and Practice in Europe

Grace Davie

This essay has three sections—two short and one more extended. The first indicates the conceptual difficulties that arise in the study of religious pluralism and democracy and draws in particular on the work of James Beckford—more precisely on his discussion of religious pluralism as a social construct.[1] The second offers a brief excursus into the field in which religious pluralism was first explored in sociological debate—the study of new religious movements and the questions that such movements raise for democracy. Interestingly, in the last decade or so, the discussion of new religious movements has substantially "relocated"; more precisely it has shifted south and east, away from the Anglo-Saxon world, in which it began, and into continental Europe and the post-communist world, provoking a new set of questions for those interested in the democratic process.

The third section forms the core of the essay, in that it opens the discussion to a numerically far more significant section of Western populations, that is, the growing other faith communities now present in Europe and the gradual process of accommodation, or otherwise, as these communities become part of their chosen societies. It is the *relationship* between newcomer and host society that constitutes the pivot of the argument. The British case is developed in some detail, with the French and Dutch cases offering interesting points of comparison. In a short conclusion, the conceptual ideas are revisited in light of both empirical data and public controversy.

Conceptual Clarity

James Beckford has written extensively in the sociology of religion. A major thread lies in his constant efforts to relate the debates within the sociology of religion subfield to those of the parent discipline. It is imperative that we overcome "religion's insulation against, and isolation from, the principal currents of social scientific thinking"[2]—hence the arguments presented in *Religion and Advanced Industrial Society*.[3] *Social Theory and Religion* continues the story, this time paying careful attention not only to religion itself, but to how those things which "count as religion" are conceptualized and regulated in everyday life. In short, Beckford presents a constructivist account, primarily concerned with the ways that religion as a category is "intuited, asserted, doubted, challenged, rejected, substituted, re-cast, and so on."[4] Unsurprisingly, the outcomes are different in different situations.

How then does this apply to religious pluralism? Beckford goes straight to the heart of the matter: in much sociological discourse, several ideas have been conflated in one term. At one level, the word *pluralism* describes the extent of religious diversity—clearly societies differ in this respect. Similarly, religious groups vary in the degree to which they enjoy acceptance or recognition in the public sphere, differences that can be determined empirically. The third meaning of the term is qualitatively different—it evokes the moral or political values associated with increasingly varied forms of religion and whether these changes should, or should not, be encouraged. The inference is clear enough: there is a persistent confusion between what is and what ought to be, and until we get this straight, there are bound to be misunderstandings in public, as well as sociological, debate.

Take, for example, the ways in which different societies accommodate religious differences. Legal or constitutional arrangements provide the starting point—analyses that call on a range of different disciplines, not least a knowledge of law. Rather more penetrating, however, are Beckford's remarks concerning the "normal" or "taken for granted" in any given society's acceptance or regulation of religion. The examples from France outlined in the following section will exemplify the point admirably; they also reveal the need to observe with care the chain of events through which the default positions have been—consciously or unconsciously—put in place. An inevitable question follows from this: can they be changed and if so, by whom? Who, in other words, has the right to recognize or to reject the parameters of religious life in any given society? Definitional issues are central to these discussions.

The notion of tolerance opens another Pandora's box. Once again it means different things to different people—along a continuum which runs from a tacit acceptance of a restricted list of religious activities to a positive affirmation of forms of religion very different from the norm. Tolerance, moreover, operates at different levels: individuals who are tolerant of religious differences may exist in societies that have difficulty with the idea, and vice versa. Nor is there any direct correlation between pluralism (in its various forms) and toleration, though it is at least likely that those who affirm that religious diversity is beneficial rather than harmful are more likely to be tolerant of forms of religion that are able to coexist. They will be less happy with forms of religion that aspire to monopoly status. The converse is equally true.

Enough has been said to alert the reader to the pitfalls. A more detailed elaboration, including interesting examples from the literature, can be found in Beckford's own work. How then do these ideas work out in practice?

New Religious Movements: A Challenge to Democracy?

Sociologists of religion were among the first to pay attention to new religious movements—that is, to acknowledge their presence, to explain what was happening, and to endorse their right to exist—so much so that the work on new religious movements began to assert a disproportionate presence in the sociological literature devoted to religion. Case studies proliferated, often in the form of doctoral theses, alongside handbooks, encyclopedias, and thematic analyses.

This, moreover, was an Anglo-Saxon industry—one that fitted well with American denominationalism and reasonably well with the more moderate pluralism (in both a descriptive and normative sense) of Britain. In Latin Europe, sociological work in the 1960s had a rather different emphasis; it, too, was concerned with nonstandard beliefs and practices, but in the form of popular religion—more precisely of popular Catholicism.[5] Interesting regional studies were central to this endeavor. Some thirty years on, the situation has changed dramatically. New religious movements remain a crucial aspect of the sociological agenda, but in different parts of the world—notably in France and in the post-communist countries of Europe.[6] The reasons are clear enough and reveal an entirely positive feature of sociological attention to this field: an awareness of the issues that such movements raise, not so much for themselves, but for the societies of which they are part. The questions, moreover, go to the core of the sociological debate, in which the careful conceptualizations of Beckford resonate at every stage.

Clearly the presence of new religious movements indicates an increase in religious diversity (in terms of the number and range of religious organizations in any one society and of the choices open to the believer). But even a cursory glance at the data reveals not only that new religious movements take root more easily in some places than in others, but that they are treated in very different ways. By and large, societies which have been religiously plural from the start or which have learned over time to accommodate diversity simply extend this to new forms of religious life (albeit more easily to some than to others). Conversely, societies which once enjoyed a religious monopoly or quasimonopoly react rather differently; here the resistance to new religious movements raises important issues of religious freedom. Normative questions can no longer be avoided—indeed in many parts of Europe, they dominate debate. The French case is not the only European society where this occurs, but it has become something of a cause célèbre. It offers an interesting worked example of the themes set out above.

A first step in understanding the specificity of the French situation was taken by Beckford himself in 1985, an account which draws directly on David Martin's analysis of secularization.[7] The connections are crucial: just as the historic churches form different patterns across Europe in terms of their modes of secularization, so too do the minority groups, including new religious movements. The patterns, moreover, are far from random—particular features can be identified which are likely to have predictable effects both for the process of secularization and for the management of new forms of religious life. One such is the role of the state. In France the state assumes a moral quality, becoming itself an actor in the religious field; no other European society exhibits this tendency to quite the same degree. The particular difficulties facing new religious movements in France derive very largely from this situation. In effect they are hemmed in on two sides, by a monopoly church (historically speaking) and a monopoly state; they are victims of a classic double whammy. The reasons, as ever, can be found in the past.[8]

A full account of the French situation would go back to the *ancien régime* and the alliance between throne and altar that dominated this period, to the French Revolution and the articulation of ideals that have become central to French self-understanding, to the vicissitudes of the nineteenth century as one regime gave way to another, and to the early years of the Third Republic in which religious issues dominated political debate—culminating in the formal and notably acrimonious separation of church and state.[9] The 1905 law effecting this separation has symbolic importance in France: it is the moment when church finally gives way to state as the dominant institution in French society. Two parallel organizations emerge, one Catholic and one secular, each with its own set of beliefs, institutions, and personnel. Even more important, however, are the default positions set in place in the course of this process: what did and what did not count as religion in the French context? The system that was worked out at the beginning of the twentieth century was predicated on a particular understanding of religion, one which could encompass the Catholic Church and the historic forms of Protestantism and Judaism, but not much else.

The situation at the beginning of the twenty-first century, examined in some detail by Danièle Hervieu-Léger,[10] is markedly different. Innovative forms of religious belief, including new religious movements,[11] have exploded in France just as they have everywhere else, causing immense strain on the system. More precisely, the checks and balances so carefully worked out in 1905 are thrown into disarray. A model that has served France well for the best part of a century cannot cope, either conceptually or institutionally, with the forms of religion that are presenting themselves at the turn of the new millennium. Hervieu-Léger puts this as follows:

> The system topples when the mesh of the confessional net is strained
> by the multiplication of groups and movements claiming religious

status and demanding the benefits of a freedom taken for granted in democratic societies. In reaction to the anarchic proliferation of self-proclaimed and extradenominational religious groups, *laïcité's* deep-rooted suspicion that religious alienation poses a constant threat to freedom is tending to resurface.[12]

A whole range of factors come together in these sentences: the frameworks (both legal and conceptual) set in place in 1905, the quintessentially French notion of *laïcité* (itself related to French understandings of the Enlightenment), the transformation of the religious scene in the late twentieth century, and the clearly normative reactions of French officialdom and the French public to these changes. These reactions reveal the fundamental points: first, the definitional issue (what can and cannot count as religion and who should decide); and, second, a persistent and at times worrying reflex (a widespread and very French belief that religion as such might be a threat to freedom). The size of the questions is, it seems, inversely related to the size of the movements in question; equally striking are the contrasts with the United States.

Very similar debates are now happening in other parts of Europe, not least those that were under communist domination in the postwar decades. Here the historic forms of religion had been pushed to the margins, never mind the minorities. Post-1989, the structures and ideologies of communism imploded, releasing spaces for religion that had not existed for several generations. In most places the mainstream churches have reemerged to fill the gaps, some more successfully than others, but new forms of religion have also flooded in through open borders. The questions that follow are by now familiar: which forms of religion are to be welcomed and which are not, and who is to make these very difficult decisions? The debate has repeated itself in one country after another in the search not only for democratic institutions, but for the philosophies that underpin these. Just as in France, it is the rapid deregulation of the religious field that has prompted the discussion; the catalyst is the same in each case.

The place of the mainstream churches within these debates is interesting. Paradoxically, or perhaps not, in those parts of Europe where the mainstream churches themselves were victims of pressure or worse, there is in many places a marked resistance to new forms of religious life. The historic churches, having reclaimed the center, are reluctant to share their hard-won freedoms with a multitude of competing denominations. Instead these essentially territorial institutions conspire to protect both the physical spaces of which they are part and the populations who live therein. Looked at from a different point of view, there is an evident clash between European understandings of religion and American congregationalism. In the minds of European church leaders, especially those emerging from decades of resistance under communism, there is little to choose between the more enthusiastic Protestant missionaries (many of which come from the United States) and new religious movements as such. Both challenge the territorial rights of indigenous forms of religion.

Attempts to manage these encounters are fraught with difficulty. They involve, among other things, the writing of constitutions and the administration of finance and property, the details of which impinge on many vested interests, calling into question assumptions about local as well as national power. A detailed discussion of these issues goes well beyond the limits of this essay, except to remark that Beckford's conceptual clarity is not always as present in these discussions as it ought to have been.[13] Given the tumultuous circumstances in which such arrangements were worked out, this is hardly surprising; at times, however, the attempts to find solutions to these very difficult issues create almost as many problems as they solve—these are debates that will continue for some time.

Other Faith Communities

New religious movements raise important issues for the democratic process; the numbers involved are, however, relatively small. Very much larger are the religious minorities that have arrived in Europe for economic reasons. Distinctive patterns have emerged in this respect as, once again, the incoming minority interacts with the host society to produce different formulations. Issues that cause a problem in one society do not do so in another—contrasts that more often than not are explained by the strains and tensions of the receiving society, not the minority in question. It is this relationship that forms the crux of the following paragraphs.

The bare bones of the story are clear enough.[14] As the dominant economies of Western Europe, that is Britain, France, West Germany, and the Netherlands, took off in the postwar decades, there was an urgent need for new sources of labor. Unsurprisingly, each of the societies in question looked to a different place in order to meet this need, and wherever possible to their former colonies. Hence in Britain, there were two quite distinct inflows of labor—one from the West Indies and one from the Indian subcontinent. In each case, the implications for the religious life of Britain were different. Afro-Caribbeans were Christians—in many ways more "formed" in their Christianity than the British—but also more exuberant, leading to tensions with the churches of the host society. Whether for racial or liturgical reasons, these new arrivals found themselves increasingly excluded from the religious mainstream, forming in consequence Afro-Caribbean churches for Afro-Caribbean people—churches that have subsequently become vibrant and active Christian communities, the envy of the religious mainstream. Incomers from South Asia were entirely different. Muslims from Pakistan and Bangladesh came together with Hindus and Sikhs from India, bringing with them the religious tensions all too present in the subcontinent in the years following partition. Populations that had been separated on the other side of the world found themselves side by side in British cities. Interfaith issues are an inevitable part of this story and do not mean simply relationships with the predominantly Christian host society.

A similar process took place across the Channel, bringing into metropolitan France a rather more homogeneous population from North Africa (from the Maghreb). In France, the words *Arab* and *Muslim* are (rightly or not) used interchangeably in popular parlance to describe these communities. This could not happen in Britain, where Muslims are rarely Arabs and represent a huge variety of nationalities, ethnicities, and languages. West Germany looked in a different direction to meet the need for labor in the postwar economy—this time to Turkey and the former Yugoslavia, but in each case creating a distinctive Muslim constituency. Post-1989, the influx of cheap labor from the East has brought a new dynamic and new tensions to the German situation. The Netherlands finally encouraged immigration from colonial territories, notably Surinam, but also from Turkey and more recently from Morocco; the overall numbers in the Netherlands are smaller, but then so is the country—markedly so, leading to very specific resentments. One further fact is important: in each of the cases set out above, the incoming populations are now in their third generation, enabling longitudinal as well as comparative studies. Each generation, moreover, presents particular issues—specific combinations of assimilation and difference. A particularly interesting set of studies concerns third-generation women—that is, younger women who are discovering what it is to be a Muslim once the specifically religious identity is detached from, say, the heavily patriarchal Pakistani culture which brought it to the West in the first place.

In the last decade of the twentieth century, an additional factor needs to be taken into account. European countries that traditionally have been places of emigration—notably Spain, Italy, and Greece—now house significant minorities; so too do the Nordic societies. Once again an expanding economy and falling birthrates have generated a need for labor, but particularly in the north of Europe, a comprehensive welfare state is clearly a pull factor for some, including a growing number of asylum seekers. Distinguishing the genuine from the less genuine among the latter has become a hot political issue in societies where the host population is inclined to overestimate the total number of immigrants, and within them asylum seekers, by a considerable figure.

Demographic shifts are important in this connection; they are also complex. In most Western European societies, there is a growing awareness that the ratio between the working and the dependent sections of the population is shifting to the extent that the former is no longer able to support the latter, not least a growing number of retired people. Where, then, are new sources of labor to be found? This, moreover, is as true in the countries of southern Europe as it is in the north—one reason for the influx of labor in this part of Europe as well as the countries further north. Interesting patterns emerge in this respect, in which gender becomes an important element. In north Italy, for example, Italian women are liberated from their domestic tasks by Filipino or Albanian women, who then leave a gap in the family at home.[15] Interestingly, (Catholic) Filipino populations are more easily absorbed into Italy than are (Muslim) Albanian ones, despite the smallness of the Albanian population overall.

But what will happen when those who work today in order that Europeans may enjoy either professional careers or a relatively prolonged retirement become themselves dependent in one way or another on the welfare system? It is at this point that the tensions begin to show, just as they did in Britain, France,

West Germany, and the Netherlands, as the 1960s merged into the rather less prosperous decade that followed. In terms of the latter, two things happened at once. On the one hand, it became increasingly clear that groups of people who were initially viewed as migrant workers—people who came and went as the economy required—were becoming, along with their families, a permanent feature of European societies. At precisely the same moment, however, the economic indicators turned downward, unemployment rose, and the competition for jobs, houses, and schools became increasingly acute. Unsurprisingly, those Europeans whose economic positions were most vulnerable resented the newly arrived populations, leading in both the 1970s and 1980s to extensive urban unrest in which racial and ethnic tensions played a significant role.

Once again the story has been told many times and is not in itself central to this essay. Here the emphasis will lie on the religious dimensions of the problem, paying attention not only to the religious communities themselves, but to the wider questions that they raise for the understanding of religion in modern Europe—not least the challenge that they bring to the notion of privatization. The focus will lie on the British case, using France and the Netherlands as points of comparison—all three countries have had a moderately long-term experience of other faith communities but have come to terms with these changes in different ways.

Each case revolves around a particular episode which became a catalyst. Two of these date from the late 1980s and, at least in their earlier stages, were covered in the appropriate chapter of *Religion in Modern Europe*.[16] These are the Rushdie controversy in Britain and the *affaire du foulard* in France. To an extent, the former has been partially resolved, though the points at issue still resonate, and the *fatwa* is still formally in place. The latter has proved rather more intractable, revealing exactly the same points as the discussion of new religious movements—that is, that we learn as much about France from this episode as we do about Islam and that the understandings of religion set in place by the 1905 law still resonate some hundred years later. The problem lies in the largely unanticipated circumstances of the twenty-first century. The Dutch case is rather different. Here the spark can be found in two very violent episodes— the murders of Pim Fortuyn and Theo van Gogh in 2002 and 2004 respectively. A country for which tolerance is a primary virtue has been thrown into disarray by these events.

Britain

First then the British case. The facts can be summarized in a sentence or two: *The Satanic Verses*, a novel by Salman Rushdie, was published in 1988; Muslim protests followed quickly, including public book burnings. In February 1989, the Ayatollah Khomeini proclaimed a *fatwa* (declaring the author guilty of blasphemy), and Rushdie was forced into hiding. In December 1990 Rushdie claimed to have embraced Islam—a key moment in the chain of events and one that was not reciprocated by the religious authorities in Iran, who reaffirmed the *fatwa*. Lives were lost in violent episodes outside Britain, including the stabbing to death of the translator of the Japanese edition. In short, this is an episode which appears to violate almost every assumption of a modern, liberal, and supposedly tolerant society. The fact that Rushdie was himself of Indian and Islamic origin simply makes the whole episode more bizarre.

What then lies beneath these events, and how should we understand them some fifteen years after the novel was published? Here I return to the paragraphs that I wrote some seven years ago—the essential points have not changed.[17] First, it is important to grasp why *The Satanic Verses* was so deeply offensive to Muslims. Why, in other words, was it so important to the Muslim community to ban the publication of a "blasphemous" book which no one had to read unless they wanted to? It is these questions that the average Briton (or European) finds almost impossible to answer. In order to grasp the issues at stake, a huge imaginative leap is required by the European mind—not only to master a different set of assumptions but to empathize with the emotional impact that *The Satanic Verses* made on an already vulnerable community. It is at this point that the logic of the Enlightenment imposes itself. Europeans think in ways that separate subject from object and have difficulty with a worldview that cannot make the same distinction. This is as true for Christians as it is for nonbelievers. Christians nurtured in a post-Enlightenment climate may not like works of art or literature that mock or make light of Christianity, but have nonetheless the capacity to distance not only themselves but their beliefs from such onslaughts. For most (not quite all) Christian believers, such episodes may lack both taste and discretion; they do not, however, damage faith itself.[18] For the believing Muslim, this distinction is altogether more difficult— hence a rather different understanding of blasphemy. For many Europeans this concept is barely relevant at the turn of the millennium; for Muslims it is central to daily living.

Indeed the most crucial point in the whole affair came two years or so after its inception when Rushdie claimed to have embraced Islam. With every appearance of sincerity, he declared himself a Muslim, apologizing to his core-ligionists for the problems caused by the book and acknowledging that some passages were offensive to believers (an admission of blasphemy). Financial contributions from the book's royalties would be made to those who had suffered injury as a result of protests; in other words, reparations would be made. The attempt to build bridges seemed genuine enough and brought some comfort to the Muslim community. In so doing, however, the gesture provoked an equally potent reaction from the opposing camp, an interesting counter-point to the whole affair. The outrage of the secular liberals at this point could hardly be contained, revealing an alarming illogicality at the heart of their campaign. Muslims should be tolerant of offensive books, but liberals cannot tolerate the writer who becomes a Muslim. Tolerance was quite clearly a social construct, to be applied in some cases but not in others. The resonance with Beckford's work could hardly be clearer.

Rushdie's embrace of Islam turned out to be a temporary phenomenon; before the end of 1991 he was once again displaying a critical view of Islam (in, for example, an attack on the Archbishop of Canterbury's plea for greater understanding of the Muslim position).[19] The flirtation with religion was clearly a mistake, openly acknowledged as such as the controversy began to die down: "There were times when I attempted to compromise, when I said things that weren't true. I'm not a religious person and I shouldn't have rediscovered religion."[20] Mistake or not, the second about-turn was bound to wound the Muslim community almost as deeply as the original insult. They were now twice betrayed. While few Muslims in Britain had any interest in the *fatwa*, they were understandably mistrustful of a writer who had humiliated both them and their religion for a second time. Salman Rushdie's attitudes epitomize the European who has difficulty in taking religion seriously.

Rushdie no longer dominates the headlines; the underlying issues, however, still remain. An interesting postscript, for example, can be found in a combination of events that came together at the end of 2004—both in many ways are quintessentially British. In December, Birmingham's Repertory Theatre put on a play entitled *Behzti*, meaning "Dishonor," written by a Sikh playwright (a woman) and concerned with the abuse of power in the name of religion. The Sikh community was disturbed by particular scenes within the play which depicted sex and violence in a Sikh temple. Peaceful protests and requests for minor changes in the text turned into more violent expressions of disapproval, leading eventually to the play being taken off, primarily for safety reasons, and renewed public discussion about freedom of speech in a multicultural society. Sikhs are rarely involved in this kind of controversy: they are a respected community in Britain, and the turban totally accommodated—even in those professions (the police, for example) where uniform is required. The point at issue remains, however, exactly the same as it was a decade or so earlier: to what extent can a minority prevent the publication or depiction of material in a democratic society if that material is deemed offensive to their religion? Conversely, can the majority afford simply to ignore the feelings of small, but nonetheless significant groups, whose religious views are different from the mainstream? Both views if pushed to the extreme are not only intolerant but nonviable. And neither will be resolved by superficial recourse to the privatization thesis, if the faith of the minority has no concept of the public/private distinction in the first place.

Enter, somewhat surprisingly, the Queen who—coincidentally with the Sikh unrest—made religious tolerance in the United Kingdom the central theme of her 2004 Christmas broadcast.[21] Immediately acclaimed by the faith communities in Britain, the speech endorsed not only the presence of different religions in this country, but the positive values associated with religious diversity (this was clearly a normative statement). Religious diversity is something which enriches a society; it should be seen as a strength, not a threat; the broadcast moreover was accompanied by shots of the Queen visiting a Sikh temple and a Muslim center. It is important to put these remarks in context. The affirmation of diversity as such is not a new idea in British society; what is new is the gradual recognition that religious differences should be foregrounded in these affirmations. Paradoxically, a bastion of privilege such as the monarchy turns out to be a key and very positive opinion former in this particular debate.

So too certain members of the House of Lords. The following quotations exemplify the point perfectly; they are taken from a speech by Baroness Uddin, who—among many other honors—was the first Muslim in Britain to enter the House of Lords and who remains the only Muslim *woman* in Parliament. The extracts speak for themselves:

> The almost total denial for decades of our identity based on our faith has been devastating psychologically, socially and culturally and its economic impact has been well demonstrated. For years Britain's 2 million or so Muslims . . . have been totally bypassed even by the best-intentioned community and race relations initiatives because they have failed to take on board the fact that a major component of their identity is their faith.
>
> Such an identity demanded more than just the stereotypical and lazy imposition of simple cultural labels based on race categorisations. British Muslims, consisting of 56 nationalities and speaking more than 1000 languages, have never been and shall never be happy about an existence and understanding that rarely goes beyond samosas, Bollywood and bhangra.[22]

Progress is slow, but the essential point has been made. Less democratic than most institutions, both the monarchy and (a half-reformed) House of Lords appear to be effective advocates of religious toleration.[23]

They are both, of course, intimately connected to the established church, a significant player in its own right. Here the crucial point lies in appreciating the difference between a historically strong state church, which almost by definition becomes excluding and exclusive, and its modern, somewhat weaker equivalent. A weakened state church is in a different position, frequently using its still considerable *influence* to include rather than exclude, becoming de facto the umbrella body of all faith communities in Britain. This gradual shift from exclusion to inclusion should be read against the changing nature of both society as a whole and the religious communities now present within it. Multiple realignments have taken place (as ever in a pragmatic and piecemeal manner), leading to a growing, if gradual, divergence between those with faith and those without, but equally to a convergence between different people of faith, accompanied by a recognition that faith *communities* (i.e., collectivities) are and must remain an integral part of a tolerant society. Such communities are recognized within the newly created (May 2006) Department for Communities and Local Government.

France

The situation in France could hardly be more different. Here the *affaire du foulard* provides the catalyst, played out in a series of incidents that once again begins in the late 1980s, when three girls attending a state school in a suburb to the north of Paris were sent home from school for wearing the Muslim headscarf. The explanation lies in the history already outlined in the section of this essay concerned with new religious movements—notably the emergence in France of both a secular ideology (laïcité) and a set of institutions (the state and the school) through which this ideology is created, sustained, and transmitted— hence the problem with the Muslim headscarf, which is seen as a religious artifact (similar in fact to a nun's habit). More difficult is the question of why, for most of the postwar period, Christian and Jewish artifacts (the cross and the yarmulke) have de facto been tolerated. Why is the Muslim headscarf regarded as qualitatively different, and why has this provoked not only a series of ex- pulsions, deliberations, ministerial decrees, commissions, and legislation, but a heated and continuing public controversy?

Clear accounts of this sequence of events and of the ideologies that lie behind these can now be found in English as well as French.[24] Such accounts include a real attempt to grasp the principles of laïcité (not easy for Anglo- Saxons), together with a careful listing of the chronology from 1989 onward: the expulsion of the Muslim girls from school, the various and not always con- sistent attempts to find a solution to the problem, the evident difficulty in establishing what constituted an "ostentatious" religious symbol, the estab- lishment of the Stasi Commission in July 2003, its deliberations and report at the end of the year, and finally the promulgation (by a huge majority) of the new law in March 2004, which unequivocally proscribes religious symbols from the state school system: "In public elementary schools, collèges and lycées [senior schools], students are prohibited from wearing signs or attire through which they exhibit conspicuously a religious affiliation."[25] The law, moreover, has the support of the French population—in approving this piece of legisla- tion, France is acting with admirable internal consistency, enforcing codes that are entirely understandable within the logic of the French democratic system. Exactly the same consistency was seen in the reactions to extensive urban unrest in France in autumn 2005, within which the discontent of the Muslim community was clearly a central factor.

Conveying the seriousness of the affaire du foulard to British students has, until recently, been difficult—the more so when at least some in the group have spent large parts of their school lives in a classroom alongside Muslim girls wearing the headscarf. Wherein, therefore, is the problem? The answer lies in the evident tensions between pluralism, tolerance, and democracy. Both constitutionally and institutionally France is undoubtedly the more democratic society—no monarchy, half-reformed House of Lords, or state church here. The political philosophies underlying this democracy, moreover, strongly en- courage assimilation into French culture, with the entirely positive goal that all citizens should enjoy similar rights—hence a mistrust of alternative loyalties, whether to religion or to anything else. In France, it follows, communautarisme is a pejorative word, implying a less than full commitment to the nation em- bodied in the French state. In Britain, the equivalent word (together with the idea that it represents) is viewed positively; in other words, group identities, including religious ones, are affirmed. The result is a less democratic system (in any formal sense), but a markedly more tolerant one, *if by tolerance is meant the acceptance of group as well as individual differences* and the right to display symbols of that group membership in public as well as private life.

Will such tolerance endure following the tragic episodes in London in summer 2005, the alleged attempts to blow up planes just one year later and the intense attention paid to the Muslim community as a result, including their style of dress? At the time of writing, it is still too soon to say. What is clear is that the bombings and their aftermath have sharpened yet further the debate about faith and faith communities in British society. The question is now urgent. On the negative side, the incidents undoubtedly provoked a marked rise in the level of harassment, if not violence, experienced by the Muslim communities in Britain at least in the short term. More positively, there have been repeated and well-informed attempts by almost all public figures involved in this debate (Muslim and other) to draw a sharp line between the violence of these attacks and the teachings of Islam and between the attitudes of the perpetrators and the peaceful intentions of the vast majority of Muslim people. A BBC poll conducted in August 2005 provides a more quantitative basis for comment. Its findings affirm widespread support for multiculturalism—more precisely, that 62% of the population believe that "multiculturalism makes Britain a better place to live."[26] The longer term, however, is more difficult to predict. A great deal will depend on whether these incidents turn out to be an isolated attack or the first of many atrocities.

French riots and British bombings have caught the attention of the global media—and rightly so. In terms of the argument of this essay, however, it is equally important to grasp the two very different ways of thinking that lie beneath these events. Essentially, the British are seeking a solution to a problem—a situation in which pragmatism and compromise are far more likely than an argument based on first principles, the predilection of the French—hence two rather different reactions. In Britain the help of the religious minorities was both sought and given in discovering the identities of the bombers and in calming the public response. In France the interventions of local religious leaders after the car burnings were much more problematic insofar as questions of public order are the preserve of the strictly secular state. Taken seriously, moreover, the principle of secularity renders even the collection of statistics regarding the size and provenance of religious minorities an ideological issue. Interestingly in Marseilles, a city in which the separation of church and state has been applied rather more flexibly, there was markedly less urban unrest in autumn 2005, despite a noticeably large North African population.[27] Why is an interesting question.

The Netherlands

The Dutch case is different again. This time the chain of events was sparked by two more recent and very violent episodes, the murder first of a prominent politician and second of a rather less well-known film producer. Both incidents occurred in broad daylight in public places; the latter was particularly brutal. Such events would be shocking in any democratic society, but particularly so in the Netherlands, a point that becomes clear as soon as the background is put in place. Dutch society, like its neighbor Belgium, dealt with pluralism in a particular way—by constructing pillars in which different sections of the population lived from the cradle to the grave.[28] In the Dutch case, there were Catholic, Reformed (including Re-reformed), and secular pillars, divisions that pervaded education, politics, social services, medical care, journalism, leisure activities, and so on. This system persisted well into the postwar period, resisting for longer than most European societies the pressures of secularization. The obvious parallel in North America is Québec. But when secularization came to the Netherlands, it came fast. Regular churchgoing collapsed along with the pillars, leading among other things to new political alignments. The crucial decades in this respect are the 1970s and 1980s—that is, precisely the moment when new forms of religious life (not least Islam) were beginning to embed themselves in Dutch society.

The second point to grasp is the long-established tradition of tolerance in Dutch society, a sensitivity epitomized in, for example, the Anne Frank Museum in Amsterdam in the 1990s. Not only is this a poignant memorial to a remarkable young woman and her family; it offers a de facto seminar in tolerance, primarily related to the gay issue. Dutch people have been at the forefront of change in this respect, as they have in the legalization of soft drugs and in their attitudes toward a wide range of ethical issues (notably euthanasia). The acceptance of difference is considered a primary virtue for Dutch people.

Pim Fortuyn's position is complex from this point of view. In 2002 this flamboyant, controversial, and sociologically trained politician burst on to the public stage. Gay himself, he defended Dutch acceptance of his lifestyle. Much more controversial were the means to the end, that is, the suggestion that those opposed to this view (notably the growing Muslim population) should be excluded from Dutch society. Such views shocked certain people, but by no means all: despite the country's celebrated reputation for liberalism and religious tolerance, Fortuyn's anti-Muslim views, his calls for an end to all immigration, and his promises to crack down hard on crime quite clearly struck a chord with the electorate—hence the creation of a new political party and considerable interest as the election approached. The dénouement was dramatic: ten days before the election, Fortuyn was shot as he left a radio station by an animal rights activist, an act that bewildered the Dutch.

In terms of this essay, the essential point is the following: to what extent can you defend liberal values with illiberalism, that is, by excluding from society those who do not share the views of the majority?—hence the rather specific and very Dutch combination of acceptance and exclusion, distinguishing Fortuyn from other right-wing popularists. Both in his person and in his views, he is different, for example, from Jean-Marie Le Pen in France or Jörg Haider in Austria. His goal was the re-creation of a Dutch consensus: stable (in population), ethically permissive, accepting of less conventional

lifestyles—but excluding those whose values contravene the majority. Fortuyn's immigration philosophy derived precisely from the socially tolerant
nature of the Netherlands, a quality he valued and wanted to preserve. It is
equally clear that this position resonated with a significant proportion of the
Dutch electorate: condemned by the conventional political class, Fortuyn was
riding high in the preelection polls.

His sudden and violent death complicated the issue: shocking in itself, it
turned Fortuyn into a martyr. It also unleashed currents of opinion in the
Netherlands that had been suppressed for decades. Indeed some of the most
interesting work being done at present in the Netherlands concerns the present
state of opinion, both religious and political, in a society where the conventional
carriers or constraints (the pillars) have collapsed. It is true that the Netherlands have secularized, late and very fast; it is less true that this has produced a
nation of secular rationalists.[29] What emerges is rather more complex, within
which a new pillar is clearly emerging: that of Islam itself. Paradoxically the
system itself has encouraged what the Dutch find so difficult: the independent
existence of a growing Muslim community, itself the victim of growing discrimination. It is this juxtaposition of de- and repillarization that needs to be
grasped by those trying to comprehend Dutch society in the first decade of the
twenty-first century.

Just over two years later a yet more violent murder took place, in which the
clash between liberalism and multiculturalism was even clearer—devastatingly
so. Theo van Gogh, a film producer known, at least among aficionados, for his
ferociously anti-Muslim (and indeed anti-Semitic) views, was stabbed, shot
dead, and beheaded in broad daylight in an Amsterdam street—this time by a
young Dutch-born Moroccan Muslim. The trigger was strikingly similar to the
Rushdie controversy: van Gogh had produced a film which portrayed violence
against women in Muslim societies. Some scenes were considered insulting to
Islam, a point that called for the same imaginative leap for Europeans as had
been required with *The Satanic Verses*. But the outcome this time was even
more shocking. And quite apart from the episode itself, Dutch people were left
coming to terms with the fact that the assassin had been brought up in the
Netherlands, but had failed—manifestly—to absorb the essentially tolerant
values of Dutch society. Something, it seems, had gone very wrong.

What then is to be done? How is it possible to accommodate within modern
European democracies populations whose values are, apparently, so very different from the mainstream? The Dutch reaction has been sharp and not
always indicative of tolerance. Two policies have emerged: the first is expressed
in the enforced repatriation of asylum seekers (even those that have been in the
Netherlands for some time); the second can be found in the renewed emphases
on the need to instill Dutch values in the immigrant populations that remain.
Very little has been said about how Dutch society might accommodate itself to a
more diverse population, a lacuna which is revealing, given the messages quite
clearly "given off" (in Goffman's sense) in the Anne Frank Museum. Unsurprisingly, this is a debate in which stereotype and hyperbole predominate; it is

not one in which Beckford's careful articulation of nuance is allowed much space.

Conclusion

Each of the case studies outlined above, whether these be of new religious movements or of the growing number of other faith communities now present in the West, has underlined a core theme: that the current situation cannot be understood without a detailed knowledge of the past and the pressures that this brings to bear not only on the religious mainstream, but also on the newly arrived religious communities. European societies have particular histories which color their reception of new religious constituencies, just as the different parts of the Islamic world welcome Westerners differently. It follows that one person's mainstream is not simply another person's margin; in any given place the mainstream continues to fashion the religious discourse taken as a whole. It is more sensible to work within these parameters than to pretend or assume that they no longer exist. Or to put the same point in a different way, in European society, the religious playing field is not level, nor is it likely to become so in the foreseeable future.

A second point is equally important. Both the increasing mobility of labor and the even more rapid exchange of information have profoundly altered the situation within which debates about religion take place. It is simply not possible for European societies and the Muslim communities within them to live in isolation from events that are taking place in other parts of the world. Concepts such as pluralism, tolerance, and democracy should be considered in this light. The cataclysmic shock of September 11, 2001, and the subsequent bombings in Bali (twice), Madrid, and London have altered our lives forever, and with them our understandings of the concepts in question. The war in Iraq has had a similar effect. Sadly, it is not only the Muslim communities in Europe that have suffered as a result; anyone "not white" or "not Christian" has been at the receiving end of prejudice and at times of physical violence. Post-9/11, it has become harder rather than easier to assume goodwill in our attempts to build an accepting and mutually considerate society.

These are huge issues claiming the attention of many disciplines. In a rather more modest conclusion to this essay, two sets of ideas deserve particular attention, one being effectively a subset of the other. First, religion has become an increasingly salient factor in public debate, both in the West and elsewhere. That is abundantly clear. Whether this is considered a good or a bad thing depends a good deal on the point of view of the observer. For the social scientist, however, it is a fact to be observed and documented with some care. It must also be explained—a shift that makes considerable demands on a profession unused to thinking in such terms. The second set of ideas follows from this. The salience of religion in public as well as private life has undermined a long-standing Western assumption—the distinction between the public and the private. Many of those now arriving in the West, not least the growing and frequently vulnerable Muslim populations, do not operate in these terms—hence, in many respects, the difficulty in finding a resolution to all three episodes outlined above. Had it been possible to separate the public and private, the Rushdie controversy would have had little or no resonance, young Muslim women in France would simply wear their veil sometimes but not at others, and the depictions of Islam in Theo van Gogh's films could have been safely ignored by those who found them distasteful. Such was not the case.

Who will give way to whom in these problematic debates becomes a difficult question to answer. On the one hand, there are those who take the "when in Rome do as the Romans do" approach. Muslims, or indeed members of a new religious movement, who want to live in Europe must behave as Europeans. This is fine in theory, but pushed too far, it effectively means that such people can no longer practice their faith in any meaningful way. At the other extreme, a few (very few) religious enthusiasts want, it seems, to hold European societies to ransom in demanding special privileges for themselves and the communities that they represent. Here there is a whole spectrum of possibilities, at one end of which can be found acts of physical violence. Most people, of course, lie somewhere between the two, though exactly where will vary from place to place, group to group, and person to person. Finding a way through these dilemmas in terms of policy making has become an urgent and very demanding political task. It is more likely to be successful if careful attention is given to the concepts underpinning the debate and if the communities most closely involved are heard with respect and on their own terms (the discussion must be about religion, not about something else). In short, issues involving religious identities become more, not less, difficult to solve if religion is proscribed as a category in public life.

NOTES

1. James Beckford, *Social Theory and Religion* (Cambridge: Cambridge University Press, 2002).

2. Ibid., 1.

3. James Beckford, *Religion and Advanced Industrial Society* (London: Unwin Hyman, 1989).

4. Beckford, *Social Theory and Religion*, 3.

5. Danièle Hervieu-Léger, *Vers un nouveau christianisme* (Paris: Cerf, 1986).

6. That is not to say that work in this field has disappeared in Britain and the United States, but it has certainly diminished, relatively speaking.

7. See James Beckford, *Cult Controversies: The Societal Response to New Religious Movements* (London: Tavistock, 1985); and David Martin, *A General Theory of Secularization* (Oxford: Blackwell, 1978).

8. A more detailed account can be found in Grace Davie, "Religious Minorities in France: A Protestant Perspective," in *Challenging Religion*, ed. James Beckford and J. Richardson (London: Routledge, 2003), 159–69.

9. The centenary of this event in 2005 led to a series of commemorative events and publications. Information can be found at http://www.laicite-laligue.org/laligue/laicite-laligue/index.html.

10. Danièle Hervieu-Léger, *La religion en miettes ou la question des sectes* (Paris: Calmann-Lévy, 2001); and idem, "France's Obsession with the 'Sectarian Threat,'" *Nova religio* 4.3 (2001): 249–57.

11. New religious movements are still for the most part known as "sects" in the French case.

12. Hervieu-Léger, "France's Obsession with the 'Sectarian Threat,'" 254.

13. See, for example, the case studies brought together in James T. Richardson, ed., *Regulating Religion: Case Studies from around the Globe* (New York: Kluwer/Plenum, 2004).

14. More detailed accounts can be found in Jørgen Nielsen, *Muslims in West Europe* (Edinburgh: Edinburgh University Press, 2004); Brigitte Maréchal, Stefano Allievi, Felice Dassetto, and Jørgen Nielsen, eds., *Muslims in the Enlarged Europe* (Leiden: Brill, 2003); Jocelyne Cesari and Sean McLoughlin (eds.), *European Muslims and the Secular State* (London: Ashgate, 2005); and Jytte Klausen, *The Islamic Challenge: Politics and Religion in Western Europe* (Oxford: Oxford University Press, 2005).

15. This was a principal finding of the Welfare and Religion in a European Perspective study; see http://www.student.teol.uu.se/wrep/.

16. Grace Davie, *Religion in Modern Europe* (Oxford: Oxford University Press, 2000).

17. Ibid., 126–30.

18. The screening of *Gerry Springer: The Opera* on mainstream television in Britain did prompt protests led by evangelical Christians. The theater production was less controversial.

19. See the Morrell address on religious toleration given by the Archbishop of Canterbury in the University of York, November 22, 1991.

20. Suzanne Goldenberg, "Eyewitness to the Taliban," *Guardian*, Sept. 26, 1998.

21. The Queen's Christmas Day broadcast is an important marker of the Christmas holiday for significant numbers of British people. It is planned a long time in advance, and its content will be carefully scrutinized by the press. It is also worth noting the extensive work of Prince Charles as an advocate of Islam.

22. See "Multi-ethnicity and Multi-culturalism," *Hansard*, House of Lords, March 20, 2002, 1432.

23. The point is discussed further in Grace Davie, "Religious Representation in a Revised House of Lords," *International Journal on Multicultural Societies* 1. 2 (1999).

24. See, for example, Jane Freedman, "Secularism as a Barrier to Integration? The French Dilemma," *International Migration* 42.3 (2004): 4–27; and Sharif Gemie, "Stasi's Republic: The School and the 'Veil,' December 2003–March 2004," *Modern and Contemporary France* 12.3 (2004): 387–98.

25. "Dans les écoles, les collèges and les lycées publics, le port de signes ou de tenues par lesques les élèves manifestent ostensiblement une appartenance religieuse est interdit" (law 2004-228, March 15, 2004).

26. Interestingly, the Muslim minority is more affirming of the basic tolerance of British society than the population as a whole. Polling data available through the BBC at http://www.bbc.co.uk/pressoffice/pressreleases/stories/2005/08_august/10/poll.shtml.

27. See Andrew Higgins, "Marseille Seeks Calm by Blurring Church-State Line," *Wall Street Journal*, Nov. 21, 2005.

28. Johan Goudsblom, *Dutch Society* (New York: Random, 1967); and Martin, *General Theory of Secularization*.

29. In this connection it is interesting to note an innovative set of studies emerging through a new and very pertinent research initiative: "The Future of the

Religious Past: Elements and Forms for the 21st century," funded by the Netherlands Organization for Scientific Research; see http://nwo.nl/future.

BIBLIOGRAPHY

Beckford, James. *Cult Controversies: The Societal Response to New Religious Movements.* London: Tavistock, 1985.
———. *Religion and Advanced Industrial Society.* London: Unwin Hyman, 1989.
———. *Social Theory and Religion.* Cambridge: Cambridge University Press, 2002.
Cesari, Jocelyne, and Sean McLoughlin, eds. *European Muslims and the Secular State.* London: Ashgate, 2005.
Davie, Grace. *Religion in Modern Europe.* Oxford: Oxford University Press, 2000.
———. "Religious Minorities in France: A Protestant Perspective." In *Challenging Religion*, 159–69. Edited by James Beckford and J. Richardson. London: Routledge, 2003.
———. "Religious Representation in a Revised House of Lords." *International Journal on Multicultural Societies* 1.2 (1999). http://www.unesco.org/shs/ijms.
Freedman, Jane. "Secularism as a Barrier to Integration? The French Dilemma." *International Migration* 42.3 (2004): 4–27.
"The Future of the Religious Past: Elements and Forms for the 21st century." Funded by the Netherlands Organization for Scientific Research. http://nwo.nl/future.
Gemie, Sharif. "Stasi's Republic: The School and the 'Veil,' December 2003–March 2004." *Modern and Contemporary France* 12.3 (2004): 387–98.
Goudsblom, Johan. *Dutch Society.* New York: Random, 1967.
Hervieu-Léger, Danièle. "France's Obsession with the 'Sectarian Threat.'" *Nova religio* 4.2 (2001): 249–57.
———. *La religion en miettes ou la question des sectes.* Paris: Calmann-Lévy, 2001.
———. *Vers un nouveau christianisme.* Paris: Cerf, 1986.
Klausen, Jytte. *The Islamic Challenge: Politics and Religion in Western Europe.* Oxford: Oxford University Press, 2005.
Maréchal, Brigitte, Stefano Allievi, Felice Dassetto, and Jørgen Nielsen, eds. *Muslims in the Enlarged Europe.* Leiden: Brill, 2003.
Martin, David. *A General Theory of Secularization.* Oxford: Blackwell, 1978.
Nielsen, Jørgen. *Muslims in West Europe.* Edinburgh: Edinburgh University Press, 2004.
The Politics of Toleration. Morrell Memorial Address. Edinburgh: Edinburgh University Press, 1999.
Richardson, James T. ed., *Regulating Religion: Case Studies from around the Globe.* New York: Kluwer/Plenum, 2004.

12

American Religious Pluralism: Civic and Theological Discourse

Diana L. Eck

In the past forty years, since the passage of the 1965 Immigration and Nationalities Act, new immigrants have arrived in the United States from all over the world, the largest groups coming from various parts of Asia and Latin America. They have brought not only their economic ambitions and dreams, but their Bhagavad Gitas and Qur'ans and their devotion to the Bodhisattva Kuan-yin and the Virgin of Guadalupe. Over the past forty years, they have built mosques and Islamic centers, Hindu, Jain, and Buddhist temples, Sikh gurdwaras, Hispanic and Vietnamese churches. They have given us a new and more complex religious America, in which the issues of religious pluralism are more important than ever, especially as they relate to our constitutional democracy.

These immigrants have negotiated new and multiple identities in the American context. They have discovered the leverage of religion and religious organizations in American civil society and have begun to create their own organizational infrastructure to exercise their influence. And some of these immigrants, to be sure, would also describe themselves as thoroughly secular. Some have had quite enough of the dominance, even the oppression, of religion in their home countries; they are relieved to be in a society that recognizes not only the freedom of religion, but the freedom not to be religious, should they so choose. These new immigrants have made America's ethnic and racial composition more complex and varied, even as they have magnified the reality of America's religious diversity.

The Contours of Religious Diversity

Religious diversity has always been an American reality. There was a vast, textured pluralism already here in the multiform lifeways of the Native Peoples, even before the European settlers came to these shores. Those who came across the Atlantic had diverse religious traditions—Spanish and French Catholics, British Anglicans and Quakers, Sephardic Jews, and Dutch Reform Christians. This diversity broadened over the course of three hundred years of settlement. The nonestablishment of religion in the American Constitution made religious communities voluntaristic groups without state support, and this, in turn, gave rise to an entrepreneurial religious energy that produced American denominationalism, with its dozens of forms of Baptists and Presbyterians. As for early evidence of Islam in America, it is estimated that of the Africans captives brought to these shores from West Africa with the slave trade in the eighteenth and nineteenth centuries well over 10% were Muslims.[1] The Chinese and Japanese who came to seek their fortune in the mines and fields of the west in the nineteenth century brought Buddhist, Taoist, and Confucian traditions with them. Eastern European Jews and Irish and Italian Catholics also arrived in force in the nineteenth century, and both Christian and Muslim immigrants came from the Middle East. Punjabis from northwest India came in the first decade of the twentieth century, most of them Sikhs who eventually settled in the Imperial and Central Valleys of California. So religious diversity is not new to America, but the scope and extent of this diversity has expanded considerably in the past forty years.

The Pluralism Project, based at Harvard University, has been documenting this new religious America for over a decade now. The transformation of the religious landscape has been gradual and in many ways invisible. The work of the Pluralism Project has been to cast the light of study and attention on many communities that have scarcely been noticed in their own cities and towns. The Hindu temple might be in a former convenience store in Sunnyvale, California, or in a former church at the corner of Polk and Pine in Minneapolis. The mosque might be in a former U-Haul office in Pawtucket, Rhode Island, in a gymnasium in Oklahoma City, in a transformed bowling alley in Hartford, in a former Super Eight Motel in Flower Mound, Texas, or in a former computer repair company in Colchester, Vermont. For the most part, one could drive right by these centers and not notice anything new at all. A two-car garage in Claremont, California, became a Vietnamese Buddhist temple. The simple home looks like every other house on the street, at least until Sundays when hundreds of people gather in the driveway and the garage door goes up, revealing an elaborate altar with its images of the Buddha.

While much of the transformation is invisible, these communities are also expanding their visible presence, both through their religious centers and through their participation in public affairs. Like many immigrant communities in the past, new immigrants have placed a symbolic value on creating the kind of landmark centers that enunciate their presence. Here we might look to the first major Hindu temples, built in the late 1970s in Pittsburgh and in Flushing, Queens. The subsequent decades have seen the rise of new and spectacular Hindu temples in such places as Lanham, Maryland, Atlanta, and Nashville. The new Buddhist landscape includes huge temple complexes, such as the Hsi Lai Temple in Hacienda Heights, California, the Chuang Yen Monastery north of New York City, Vietnamese temples in Orange County, Cambodian monasteries in rural Minnesota and suburban Maryland, and Thai temples in Phoenix and North Hollywood. While surveying the new Muslim landscape, we would see landmark mosques in such places as Cleveland and Toledo, Houston and Dallas, Miami and Seattle. Sikhs have built striking gold-domed gurdwaras from Fremont, California, to Durham, North Carolina. All of these new building projects have, year upon year for some thirty years now, added a cumulative complexity to America's religious landscape and raised the profile of non-Judeo-Christian traditions in America. Documenting their presence—by the thousands—and recording their histories has been part of the work of the Pluralism Project. When the first-ever Hindu temple is built from the ground up in the state of Delaware, this is of some significance both for the history of Delaware and the history of Hinduism. Someone in the world of scholarship should be paying attention, and in many cases that somebody has been a Pluralism Project student researcher.

Engaging Diversity: Religious Pluralism

Diversity and pluralism are not synonyms, and pluralism is not just the recognition of diversity. Pluralism is a response to diversity, an engagement with diversity. There are certainly other responses to diversity. Exclusion is another response, and indeed exclusion was the intent and purpose of American legislation regarding immigration from Asia, beginning with the 1882 Chinese Exclusion Act and continuing deep into the twentieth century. Exclusion signals an inability or unwillingness to recognize or engage the religious or cultural other at all. Inclusion is another response to diversity: wanting the religious or cultural other to be included under the umbrella of one's own world, on one's own terms, in one's own language, in the structures already made—by us. Being inclusive has much merit, but it stops short of effective agency for the included. Syncretism is also a way of dealing with diversity, seeking to fuse difference into a new creation. Pluralism, however, is not about melting or reducing differences or fusing them into a syncretism. Pluralism is about the integrity and the encounter of diversity and difference. Pluralism does not require the shedding of distinctive cultural, religious, or political differences, but is the effort to create a society in and out of all these differences. Thus, the analysis of the progress of real pluralism needs to go beyond mapping the new contours of our religious life, beyond the study of particular centers and the communities they represent, to investigating the ways in which new religious communities have been actively engaged in the processes of American society.

The development of instruments of participation in public life is certainly one gauge of an emerging pluralism. During the 1990s, American Muslims developed multiple organizations, aimed at facilitating their involvement with American society. The Islamic Society of North America is a broad nationwide network based in Plainfield, Indiana, with annual conferences of some forty thousand participants, including programs for men and women, youth and students, educators and activists. The Muslim Public Affairs Council describes its mission as "working for the civil rights of American Muslims, for the integration of Islam into American pluralism, and for a positive, constructive relationship between American Muslims and their representatives." The Council on American Islamic Relations (CAIR) is the leading force responding to issues of discrimination and civil rights violations of Muslims and raising a voice on continuing issues of racial and religious profiling.

The emergence of CAIR is an example of the circumstances that shape organizational histories. It was a relatively new Muslim watchdog organization, when the bombing of the Murrah Federal Building in Oklahoma City took place on April 19, 1995. For more than a decade, American Muslims, including those who founded CAIR, had worked hard to dispel the stereotypes associating them, one and all, with broad-stroke images of violence. Yet those images were put into play almost immediately after the Oklahoma City bombing, due, in part, to the assumption that the bombing was linked to "Middle Eastern–looking" men seen in the vicinity. Muslim communities in Oklahoma and all over America felt a backlash of harassment—threatening phone calls, broken windows, drive-by shootings, and telephoned bomb threats. Muslim students were assaulted on campus, a fake bomb was thrown at a Muslim daycare facility, and individual Muslims reported a great increase in harassment by coworkers and in public. Many Muslim women were afraid to appear in public wearing Islamic dress.

In May 1995, CAIR released a report, detailing more than two hundred incidents of anti-Muslim threats, harassment, and property damage, reported in the immediate wake of the Oklahoma City bombing.[2] It was the first of what became periodic and now-annual CAIR reports.

The aftermath of September 11, 2001, dramatically amplified the importance of CAIR as a national watchdog organization for Muslim well-being. Its web-based resources provide a way of reporting incidents of harassment or violence and suggest action responses on major issues. Its advocacy network joins with many other civil rights groups in reporting civil rights abuses. The CAIR report released in July 2003 documented a 43% increase in complaints during 2002:

> These incidents included the termination or denial of employment because of religious appearance; the refusal to accommodate religious practices in the workplace, schools, and prisons; the singling out of individuals at airports because of their distinct names, appearances, and travel destination; the detention or interrogation of Muslims by federal and local authorities based on profiling criteria; and the denial

of services or access to public accommodation facilities because of religious or ethnic identity. All of these experiences have common elements of setting religious and ethnic features of Muslim life or Muslim religious and political views apart from what is considered normal and acceptable.[3]

The executive summary of CAIR's findings states a wider point clearly and soberly:

Data gathered for this report demonstrate that Muslims in the United States are more apprehensive than ever about discrimination and intolerance. U.S. government actions after September 11, 2001, alone impacted more than 60,000 individuals. Muslims have charged that the government's actions violated the First and Fourth Amendments to the U.S. Constitution because they included ethnically and religiously-based interrogations, detentions, raids, and closures of charities.[4]

The Sikh community has also been about the business of education and advocacy throughout the 1990s. In middecade the Sikh Mediawatch and Resources Taskforce was formed to correct mistaken and derogatory images of Sikhs in the media and to provide resources to the Sikh community and the press. In 2004 the group changed its name and broadened its mandate to legal defense. Under its new name—the Sikh American Legal Defense and Education Fund—it has become a comprehensive source for Sikh advocacy in the United States and has attempted to bring its identity and agenda into line with other such advocacy organizations in the United States.

Especially since 9/11, Sikh advocacy groups have gained prominence and urgency. The number of Sikhs harassed and subjected to various forms of discrimination escalated with the popular conflation of the turban-wearing Sikhs with the turban-wearing Osama bin Laden. In the days immediately following 9/11, a Sikh was murdered in Mesa, Arizona, while planting flowers around his Chevron Station. The Sikh Coalition was formed, first in the New York area, to take up the growing numbers of issues related to Sikh civil rights. In the past three years, the group has served as an advocate for Sikhs who have been harassed and beaten. It has assembled a team of lawyers who help Sikhs who have faced discrimination in the workplace. They have taken up cases, such as the long-standing controversy of a Sikh who has sought permission to wear his turban as an officer of the New York Transit Authority. In the 2003–4 report of the Sikh Coalition, the achievements the group has highlighted indicate a level of engagement with American society and processes that constitute real pluralism: working with schools to enable Sikh students to attend wearing the *kirpan* and turban, working with employers to allow a Sikh woman to wear her turban at work, engaging with the New York Police Department over the question of turbaned officers, and running educational programs for law enforcement officers and bias officers in cities across the country:

These are just the first steps in the long journey for the Sikh community to be recognized as a vibrant part of American life. We dream of a world where no Sikh child is bullied; the *saroop* [Sikh dress] is recognized and respected as the proud identity of a distinct religious group; our friends and family are free from name calling, insults, and violence driven by prejudice; government agencies support and encourage the rights of Sikhs; and no member of society can claim ignorance of who is a Sikh and what values we hold dear.[5]

During the 2004 election, Pluralism Project researchers also studied the emergence of more widespread political participation on the part of new religious communities.[6] In 2004 the Muslim American Taskforce on Civil Rights and Elections was formed to coordinate the work of many national Muslim organizations, to hold town-hall meetings on the issues in the election, and to mobilize over four million Muslim voters in the United States. The previous year, the Institute for Social Policy and Understanding, based in Detroit, conducted a study of Detroit Muslims with astonishing conclusions: 93% responded that it is important to be involved in community and political affairs, 87% said they participated in the political process, and 68% said they were registered to vote. In the end, in the election of 2004, a much higher percentage of Muslims voted for John Kerry or perhaps, more precisely, voted against George Bush, whom they perceived as having made overtures toward the Muslim community and then having betrayed the community, by the promulgation of what were viewed as oppressive and overtly discriminatory measures in the U.S. Patriot Act, following 9/11.[7]

South Asian Americans were also active in the 2004 election, with organized caucuses for both presidential candidates and extensive debates in the pages of South Asian newspapers, such as *India Abroad*. The Sikh Coalition held an "Every Vote Counts" drive to bring Sikhs to the polls. Bobby Jindal, a Republican from Louisiana, was elected the first South Asian Congressman since Dilip Singh Saund was elected to Congress from California in 1957. On September 2004 the Pluralism Project gathered at the National Press Club representatives of national women's organizations, both religious and secular, that were actively involved in electoral education. They included representatives of Protestant, Catholic, and Jewish organizations, as well as the Muslim Women's League and the Sikh Coalition. At the end of the day, Sammie Moshenberg summed up some of the concerns of the membership of the National Council of Jewish Women and saw them present in the agendas of other women's groups as well: "Childcare, work-family issues, domestic violence, school prayer and vouchers, abortion rights, gun control, peace in the Middle East, international family planning, judicial nominations, among others: these are the issues that Jewish women care about. And it's striking that these are these issues that Sikh women care about, that Muslim women care about, Christian women care about, Buddhist women care about."[8] The major women's organizations of the Christian right were also invited, but none elected to come. This was suggestive of a significant divide in the American electorate, not between the Christian right and an emerging Christian left, but between the Christian right and an emerging multifaith opposition, whether it can accurately be described as "left" or not. While the dominant news on the religion front following the 2004 election was the clout of evangelical Christians, it may well be that the long-lasting significance of the 2004 election year was the entry into active voter participation of many religious groups that had not been heard from previously.

Along with political participation, service is also a gauge of involvement in the larger project of pluralism. The tsunami disaster that struck in late December 2004 provided a lens through which to view the energies of America's newest immigrants, directed outward in public service. Asian religious communities in the United States were among the first to respond. America's first landmark Hindu temple, the Sri Venkateswara Temple in Pittsburgh, immediately held a prayer service, where Hindus drew upon the comfort of the Bhagavad Gita at a time of mourning. They worked with the Tamil Nadu Foundation of western Pennsylvania, collected tens of thousands of dollars, and immediately sent a delegation from the temple to the towns in Tamil Nadu they knew best. Everywhere Hindu temples sprang into action, from Middletown, Connecticut, to Atlanta. Wisconsin's biggest Hindu temple, in Milwaukee, held a fundraiser, with special prayers by Muslims, Buddhists, and Christians. And so, too, a Hindu temple in Omaha held a prayer service that gathered people of all faiths to pray for the living and the dead. In that shopping-center-turned-temple in Sunnyvale, California, Hindus held a fundraiser that brought the four quarters of India together—Punjabis, Gujaratis, Tamils, and Bengalis. In New York's Ganesha Temple in Flushing, the Hindu youth of the temple pulled together a coalition of Flushing youth groups of every religious tradition for a benefit arts performance.

Buddhist response was extensive, and not only among Thai and Sri Lankan immigrants whose home countries were most immediately affected. The huge Chinese Hsi Lai Buddhist temple in Hacienda Heights, California, sponsored an interfaith service in the pounding rain. It was attended by many hundreds of people and some $100,000 was raised in a day. The Buddhist temple in Crystal Lake, Illinois, sent its Sri Lankan monk home with $30,000 in local donations for his hometown in Sri Lanka. A group of Sri Lankan families in Minnesota pledged to build twenty-five new homes, a medical clinic, a school, and an orphanage in a single town in Sri Lanka.

Muslims were very much part of the response as well. The Muslim community in Salt Lake City joined with the Mormons to send a cargo plane filled with seventy tons of relief supplies from Utah to Indonesia. One of the mosques in Columbia, South Carolina, sent donations to the International Red Crescent. Thirteen mosques in Palm Beach, Broward, and Miami-Dade counties in Florida collected $102,000. On New Hampshire Avenue in Silver Spring, legendary for its lineup of diverse religious communities, the Muslim Community Center gathered its many neighbors for an interfaith prayer service. Saffron-robed Buddhist monks from the Cambodian temple down the street offered chants. Gujaratis, neighbors on the other side, offered Hindu prayers. Jews, Protestant Christians, Vietnamese Catholics, and Ukrainian Orthodox joined as well. As the director of the Muslim Community Center put it, "When tragedy strikes, it doesn't discriminate with certain kinds of faith." The Ukrainian Orthodox priest said, "We should not only wait for troubled times to come together."

I sketch this portrait of institutions and organizations, activism, political participation, and social service in what may seem a blizzard of specifics, because, for the most part, all this goes unnoticed in mainstream media. The texture of America's religious pluralism is local. It is visible, but usually not beyond its own locale. Gathering it together in a patchwork of hundreds of local pieces gives us a wider, more detailed, and more complex picture of the emerging forms of religious pluralism in America. Part of the work of the Pluralism Project has been to do targeted searches of local, regional, and ethnic news sources and to compile an edited record of "Religious Diversity News." Here one can see patterns not observable through the sole instrument of large city newspapers. An interfaith group springs up in Salt Lake City at the time of the Olympics and becomes a major ongoing force in interreligious relations; a new interfaith initiative is launched in Memphis in the weeks following 9/11; an interfaith Habitat for Humanity project is sponsored by the Interfaith Council of Central Ohio; an interfaith blood drive takes place in Plano, Texas. All these are individual stories, but multiplied by a hundred, they indicate a spirit of bridge building one might not otherwise see. It is local. As one of the Plano planners put it, "We may not be able to bring peace to the Middle East, but we sure can make a difference in Plano if we work together."[9]

Many people in America have not come to terms with all this diversity. Normative Christian consciousness is still strong, and, after all, the United States is more than 80% Christian by self-identification. Most estimates have Muslims and Jews about tied as the second-largest religious tradition, each having about six million people.[10] This means there are now more Muslims than Episcopalians or members of the Presbyterian Church in the USA. In addition, there are American Bahais, Zoroastrians, Jains, and Sikhs, whose numbers are not large but whose presence is significant. There are hundreds of Native tribal cultures and lifeways, as the most ancient part of this diverse landscape. While it is true that the Christian majority may flex its evangelical strength in the elections, it is also true that religious diversity presents a larger challenge to its force than that of numbers. It presents a constitutional challenge, for the Bill of Rights is framed precisely to protect the welfare of the smallest of minorities, even and perhaps especially, those who do not win elections.

Who Are We?

Coping with all this diversity and wrestling with the engagements of pluralism has taken place on many fronts in the past decades: debates in state boards of education over the shape of a so-called multicultural curriculum; disputes over the public observance of Christmas with carols in the public schools or crèches on the courthouse lawns; zoning controversies over the building of Muslim schools or the esthetic compliance of gold-domed gurdwaras; public disputations over Muslim or Buddhist prayers in state legislatures. All in all, America has been going through something of an identity crisis. Speaking to this matter, Samuel Huntington recently wrote a book with the title *Who Are We? Challenges to American National Identity*. He argues that America has been decisively shaped and defined by its core Anglo-Protestant identity and that we Americans must embrace that core identity and its values lest we begin to disintegrate into a conglomerate nation, more like Europe than ourselves. In his view, it is only the Anglo-Protestant identity that "transcends our sub-national ethnic, religious, and racial identities."[11]

What Huntington calls "the American Creed" of liberty, equality, democracy, civil rights, nondiscrimination, and the rule of law is, in his view, "English in origin, and at its heart Protestant." He argues: "The Creed is unlikely to retain its salience if Americans abandon the Anglo-Protestant culture in which it has been rooted. A multicultural America will, in time, become a multicreedal America, with groups with different cultures espousing distinctive political values and principles rooted in their particular cultures."[12] The book is filled with polls and statistics that support Huntington's concern about immigration. He is convinced, finally, that the very diversity that "we the people" now represent and the very religious minorities that the Pluralism Project studies are a threat to the American polity. Not surprisingly, I disagree with his prognosis for a "multicreedal America." But a more important concern is his understanding of diversity itself, which he understands to be more an "agenda" than a reality. He writes of the recent decades: "Many elite Americans were no longer confident of the virtue of their mainstream culture and instead preached a doctrine of diversity and the equal validity of all cultures in America."[13] He speaks of what he calls the "cults of diversity and multiculturalism."[14]

For those of us whose work takes us into the streets of Queens and Detroit and into the suburbs of Chicago and Los Angeles, it is very clear that diversity is not an ideology, nor a cult of liberal academia, but a very real, challenging fact of our national life. Multiculturalism is not a doctrine preached, but a reality lived—lived in all the places where we come together on the common ground of our civic life, from public schools and hospitals to city councils and zoning boards. Grappling with the meanings of this significant new reality and the possibilities for shaping a vibrant democratic society from all this diversity is surely one of the most important challenges of our time. Pluralism does not mean abandoning the American commitment to liberty, equality, democracy, civil rights, nondiscrimination, and the rule of law, but rather making good on this commitment in the more complex society that is now ours.

For all I may wish to dispute what lies between the covers, the title of Huntington's book is immensely important: *Who Are We?* The "we" question is even more important to issues of identity than the "I" question. All of us use that powerful two-letter word—"we." But whom do we mean when we say "we"? Obviously we mean many groups, large and small, overlapping and distinct—churches and political parties, families, clubs, and educational

institutions. All position us in different "we" groups. Do we mean we Christians, we Jews, we Muslims? Do we mean we at Harvard University or Georgetown University? Do we mean we scholars who work on issues of complex identities? Do we mean "we Americans," "we the people"? And who is included,
excluded, elided in the "we" that we use. In a multireligious society, we need to
begin to watch our use of "we"—especially in civic and religious settings.

Living more closely in the presence of one another poses new questions for
us all—about religion, about religious truth claims, about our relationship as
people of faith, about our relationship as citizens of a common society. Religious diversity is not simply a fact observed, but a fact interpreted. Let us
consider two rhetorical contexts, related and yet distinct, in which we interpret
all this religious difference and give voice to "we" questions. On one hand, we
Americans interpret difference in a civic context and in a civic voice. On the
other hand, we, as people of one faith or another, or even as nonreligious people, interpret religious difference with a religious or value-framed ethical voice.
We need to distinguish what I would call a "civic" and a "theological" voice. We
need to know which is which. Increasingly, the controversies of the public
sphere give evidence of our inability—or unwillingness—to distinguish between the ways in which we voice our views as people of faith and as citizens.
The new religious diversity of America has revealed presumptions and normative elements, long unmarked in the relation of religion and public life.

Engaging religious diversity is a civic and political question in many nations today. New and old multireligious nations such as Malaysia, Indonesia,
India, Britain, France, and Germany have different constitutional bases on
which to adjudicate issues of religious difference. Yet in one way or another,
they have to answer the question of how people of various traditions of faith
will relate to each other as co-citizens of a common nation. Is one tradition
dominant, perhaps even established, as Christianity in the United Kingdom or
Islam in Malaysia? Is the state officially secular, with no established religion,
and perhaps militantly so, as in France, where headscarves, yarmulkes, and
turbans in the public sphere are seen to be an affront to the secular state? What
about secular America, where a teacher who tried to send a child home from
school for wearing a headscarf would be reprimanded or fired?

However, the interpretation of religious diversity is not only a civic and
political question; it is also a question of faith, a theological question. It is an
old question, but one which has become ever more persistent and important
for people of every religious tradition. Given the fact that there are obviously
many religious traditions, many ways of being religious, how do "we" understand, interpret, and value the religious other? Crudely put, are other religions
also true? Is our religion alone true? Is no religion true? The way in which I
have posed this question also makes clear that even those who are ardent
atheists and have no religious affiliation also have an ideological interpretation
of religion and the diversity of religious traditions.

Distinguishing between the rhetorical and social contexts of our theological and civic language, between the spheres in which "we" engage questions
of concern, either as citizens or as people of faith, is essential. It is not that

religious discourse is private, whereas civic discourse is public. Rather, both religious and civic speech can be very public, but they are different. They are directed to different audiences; they employ a different rhetoric of persuasion; they are substantiated with different "footnotes" and appeals to authority. Both are preeminently concerned with ethics; both increasingly require engagement across the lines of religious difference. The "we" an American president speaks about, inside St. John's Episcopal Church across the park from the White House, cannot be the same "we" he brings to the public arena, when he addresses the nation as president of all the people, even those who may disagree with his religious views.

The speech of public officials and candidates for public office in a pluralistic democracy must be "bridging speech," not spoken in the particular dialect of a single religious tradition. Public speech is not and should not be the kind of speech that one would use in a place of worship with its particular community-oriented symbolic forms, but the speech that enables communication with people whose religious presuppositions may be quite different and in a context in which all are equally citizens. The references and the "footnotes," so to speak, of civic rhetoric should not be to the Bible, the Guru Granth Sahib, the Qur'an, or the Levitical codes, but to the covenants of citizenship that are represented by state and federal laws and constitutions. This does not mean that public officials do not employ religious speech, but when they do, they should explicitly position themselves within the religious context: "Speaking as a Christian, I would say. . . . Yet, as an elected public official, I am pledged to serve a constituency of many religions, and not one faith alone." When we or our elected representatives move from one voice to another, from a religious to a civic register, we must be certain to use the "turn signals" that position us in a new context.

Religious Pluralism: Theological Perspectives

America is famous for its overt religiosity, at least when viewed from a European perspective: 80% of Americans identify themselves as Christians, and 60% identify themselves as members of a church or synagogue. Many scholars attribute the energetic religiosity of Americans to the voluntarism that was necessitated by the disestablishment of religion. One of the first observers to express this view was the Frenchman Alexis de Tocqueville, who toured America in the 1820s and discovered, to his surprise, that severing the ties between church and state actually seemed to make religion stronger, rather than weaker. The spirit of voluntarism inspired intense competition in religion and the creation of the throng of denominations that have become a distinctive feature of American religion. He wrote: "There is no country in the world where the Christian religion retains a greater influence over the souls of men than in America; and there can be no greater proof of its utility and of its conformity to human nature than that its influence is powerfully felt over the most enlightened and free nation of the earth."[15]

Protestant Christians, while supporting the ideal of religious freedom, continued to shape the vision of a "Christian America" as an ethos, even though not an established religion. It was through the voluntary energies of the churches that a presumptively Christian ethos would be established. As Washington Gladden wrote in 1905, "And while we have no desire to see the establishment of any form of religion by law in this land, most of us would be willing to see the nation in its purposes and policies and ruling aims becoming essentially Christian. . . . It must be, in spirit and purpose and character, a Christian nation."[16]

Today that presumption of a Christian or Judeo-Christian America has been challenged by the presence of many religious minorities who are not simply "neighbors around the world," encountered in the reports of hometown missionaries, but literally neighbors across the street. A block down the street from a United Church of Christ congregation in Garden Grove, California, is the Lien Hoa Buddhist Temple, the home of several Vietnamese Buddhist monks and a thriving congregation of Buddhist laity. Right next door to the Atonement Lutheran Church in San Diego is the city's largest Islamic center. In Fremont in the East Bay, a Methodist Church and an Islamic center bought property together, negotiated easements, put in a frontage road, and built a new church and a new mosque. This very proximity raises questions of theological interpretation. From both sides, people ask how they should understand their neighbors, their worship, and their ways. These questions require people of each faith to mine the depths of their own religious traditions and to investigate deep-seated attitudes toward and interpretations of religious difference. How do "we" who are Christian, Jewish, Hindu, or Muslim think about the religious other? It is a question that often shades into and colors civic contexts of encounter. We often do not recognize it as a theological question and mistake it for a civic question.

In May 2001, for example, a Minnesota state representative protested and dissented from the visit of the Dalai Lama to the state legislature on the grounds that Buddhism is "incompatible with Christian principles." This is a theological point deserving of discussion and dialogue, but one that has little to do with the Dalai Lama's address to the Minnesota state legislature. In a similar vein, on March 3, 2003, two Washington state legislators walked out of the House chamber in Olympia, when an imam was introduced to offer the invocation of the day. Whatever their own theological understanding of Islam, the imam's invocation certainly would have more to do with their civic understanding of the custom of legislative invocations in the State of Washington. Finally, consider the slippage between religious and civic contexts in the controversy over the National Day of Prayer in Troy, Michigan. In March 2005 the local planners of the National Day of Prayer received a request from a Hindu woman to participate. After all, Troy has one of the major Detroit area Hindu temples, the Bharatiya Temple. She was refused. It became evident that the sponsor of the National Day of Prayer was a conservative Christian group, though it had garnered the approval of the mayor of Troy and the event was to take place at city hall. "Although [the National Day of Prayer is] open for all to come, we coordinate our own speakers, just like any other group would do," said Lori Wagner, one of the planners. She added, "We are there to pray, not to make a politically correct display of diversity."[17] Again, her remarks are most appropriately seen within the context of Christian theological expression. And the Christian-sponsored National Day of Prayer might be more appropriately called the National Christian Day of Prayer. If President Bush had not endorsed the nationwide observance and if the sponsoring group had not asked the mayor for a public venue, all would be well. When the Hindu was refused participation, the mayor withdrew her support.

In Chaim Potok's novel *A Book of Lights*, his main character, a New York rabbi, serving as a chaplain in Korea during the Korean War, takes a brief holiday to Japan and finds himself at a Buddhist shrine. He watches a man standing there before the altar, hands pressed together, eyes closed, in what he can describe only as prayer. He turns to his companion and asks, "Do you think our God is listening?" Scarcely waiting for a response, he goes on, "If not, why not? If so, well, what are *we* all about?"

This, in simple language, is the nature of theological questioning. It probes not only the issue of how we think about God, but also how we regard the person and the faith of another. Is the one whom Jews or Christians call "God," the maker of all that is in heaven and on earth, listening to the pleas of this man who seems to be deeply at prayer? If not, why not? What kind of God would that be? If so, then, what are *we* all about, we who have claimed such a special relationship with God? As with every good theological question, it interrogates more than our understanding of God. It also reveals our understanding of the "we." Who are we? What are we all about?

In February 2005 I received an email from one of my Muslim students, a woman who had grown up in the Muslim community in St. Louis, who was going to Mecca on the hajj. "May I offer a prayer for you when I am there?" she asked. I was moved and responded that I would be deeply honored to be prayed for there and that I would also offer prayers for the success of her pilgrimage. What kind of theological understanding undergirds this exchange? On the other hand, what kind of theological understanding undergirds the reprimand of a Missouri Synod Lutheran pastor for offering a prayer at Yankee Stadium on the same platform with Jews, Muslims, and Hindus? What theological views underlie the statement of a prominent former attorney general and member of the Assemblies of God Church that "Islam is a religion where you send your son to die for God, but Christianity is a faith where God sends his son to die for you."[18]

In theological terms, there are many ways of thinking about difference. For the exclusivist, our religious tradition is true, exclusive of others. Our God simply does not regard the prayer offered in another voice. For the inclusivist, our religion is true, inclusive of others. Of course, God listens to the prayers of others, but it is "our God" who does the listening. For the pluralist, there is no such God as "our God." We may presume that the one we call God is listening, but we do not presume that our understanding of God is complete or encircles the reality of God. We need to listen carefully to the distinctive voice of the religious other, which is not simply an echo of our own. The challenge is to encounter the faith of the other without first erecting walls against them.

If we want to engage theological questions of religious difference, we, whomever we are, must do so in the context of our tradition of faith and its own distinctive language. This is a useful task, and it poses important questions, even the most seemingly simple of them: Is our God listening? Does it make sense to speak of God as ours at all? How do we understand those Buddhist neighbors who speak of the Buddha's realization, but do not use any God language? How do we think about our own faith as we come into deeper relationship with people of other faiths and as we gain a clearer sense of the character of their religious lives? It goes without saying that all of these are not civic, but theological questions.

There are exclusivists and pluralists in many religious traditions. We know the exclusive voices all too well. Their insistence on claiming God's favor, claiming God's land, knowing God's will, or knowing the sole way to heaven is often persuasive with its certainty and clarity. For many exclusivists, religious difference is a threat—not only difference among traditions, but difference within their own tradition. Exclusivists are, for the most part, not dialogically engaged with those who differ from them. They often reject the multisidedness and moral ambiguity of difficult ethical choices.

But there are also those in every tradition who see religious difference as an opportunity to expand and deepen their faith and for whom the theological exploration of religious pluralism is an urgent calling. Here are three examples, each a theologian and writer, whose voice is widely heard and whose books are popularly read. On the Christian side, Marcus Borg sees a new, emerging paradigm of Christianity that both accepts and explores the mystery of God's presence in many religious traditions. Borg, like many Christian theologians today, wrestles with what it means to be a Christian in an age of increasing awareness of religious diversity. He asks: "When we think about the claim that Christianity is the only way of salvation, it's a pretty strange notion. Does it make sense that 'the More' whom we speak of as creator of the whole universe has chosen to be known in only one religious tradition, which just fortunately happens to be our own?"[19] Christian faith, for Borg, is deeply grounded in its particularity, without being closed to the faith and witness of those deeply grounded in other traditions.

Rabbi Jonathan Sacks, chief rabbi of the United Kingdom, a strong advocate of dialogue in and through religious differences, writes of what he calls the "dignity of difference." In addressing the challenges of globalization from a religious perspective, he writes:

Can we find, in the human other, a trace of the Divine other? Can we recognize God's image in one who is not in my image? There are times when God meets us in the face of the stranger. The global age has turned our world into a society of strangers. That is not a threat to faith but a call to a faith larger and more demanding than we had sometimes supposed it to be. Can I, a Jew, hear the echoes of God's voice in that of a Hindu or Sikh or Christian or Muslim? Can I do so, and not feel diminished, but enlarged?[20]

Tariq Ramadan, a Swiss-born Muslim theologian of Egyptian ancestry, writes of the challenges of pluralism at the outset of his book *Western Muslims and the Future of Islam*: "In my view, the issue is to find out how the Islamic universal accepts and respects pluralism and the belief of the Other: it is one thing to relativize what I believe and another to respect fully the convictions of the Other." "The post-modernist spirit would like to lead us unconsciously to confuse the second proposition with the first. I refuse: It is in the very name of the universality of my principles that my conscience is summoned to respect diversity."[21] In addressing religious pluralism, he turns to his own theological starting point in the Muslim doctrine of *tawhid*, the oneness of God:

> It is the principle on which the whole of Islamic teaching rests and is the axis and point of reference on which Muslims rely in dialogue. The intimate awareness of *tawhid* forms the perception of the believer, who understands that plurality has been chosen by the One, that He is the God of all beings, and that He requires that each be respected.... It is out of this conviction that Muslims engage in dialogue, and this is assumed in forming relations with the other.[22]

I mention such thinkers here simply to underline the fact that thinking about religious pluralism is one of the great theological questions of our time. It is a fundamental question that shapes the consideration of many other questions. It is not simply that there might be a plurality of religious views on abortion, environmental degradation, or stem cell research. It is the deeper question of how we regard the validity of other religious views and the integrity of other religious voices.

Each religious tradition is embedded in a particular "we," with its distinctive presuppositions, vocabularies, forms of reasoning, and perspectives. Those of us who are Christians exercise that particular "we" when we affirm our faith in the words of the Nicene Creed: "We believe in One God the Father Almighty, Maker of heaven and earth, and of all things visible and invisible." But that is not the same "we" that we as citizens use when we read the opening words of the U.S. Constitution: "We the people of the United States."

To summarize the difference in the issues that are addressed in theological and civic contexts, let us turn to two cases involving the Hindu community in the United States in 1999 and 2000. First, in 1999 the Southern Baptist Convention published a prayer guide to enable Christians to pray for Hindus during their fall festival of lights, called Diwali. It spoke of the nine hundred million Hindus who are "lost in the hopeless darkness of Hinduism . . . who worship gods which are not God."[23] The Christians responsible for this prayer guide seem to have no trouble at all speaking of "our God" in Christian exclusivist terms. The problem with such a response, however, is that, from a

Hindu standpoint, it misunderstood both Hindu worship and Hindu understandings of God.

The Southern Baptists in Houston at Second Baptist Church were no doubt surprised to find protesters and picketers outside their church, when the Diwali came around that fall. Perhaps many did not fully realize that these lost souls of whom they were speaking were their neighbors in Houston, not simply imagined, oppressed, poverty-ridden Hindu villagers halfway around the world. And the American Hindus who carried placards protesting the Southern Baptist prayer guide did so not because they were averse to being the focus of Christian prayers, but because the characterization of their religious tradition was so ill informed and ignorant. It was hurtful, and it made them angry.

Several Hindus were so outraged by the Baptist publication that they protested to Janet Reno and the Department of Justice and only gradually came to realize that it was not against the law for Southern Baptists to believe and to say what they did about the Hindu faith. To the Hindus it was religious slander, to the Baptists it was religious belief. The Hindu-Christian theological discussion, at least in America, is still in its infancy, yet it is to the venue of interreligious dialogue that the question of whether Hindus or Baptists have seen the light more clearly must be referred. The Department of Justice can be of no help.

While the theological ideas of Baptists and Hindus are not governed by our Constitution, their mutual commitment to the free exercise of religion is. No matter what Baptists may think of Hindu gods and no matter what Hindus may think of Baptist bigotry, both are co-citizens of a state that should ideally treat them equally.

In fall 2000, a Hindu was invited, for the first time in American history, to offer the invocation in Congress.[24] The occasion was a state visit of the prime minister of India, and the priest was from the Shiva-Vishnu Temple in Parma, Ohio, a suburb of Cleveland. A Christian group vociferously protested. The Family Research Council issued the alarm, calling the Hindu invocation a move toward "ethical chaos" and saying it was "one more indication that our nation is drifting from its Judeo-Christian roots." The next day, however, the group issued a clarification: "We affirm the truth of Christianity, but it is not our position that America's Constitution forbids representatives of religions other than Christianity from praying before Congress."[25] This time they got it right.

In these two instances, Hindus and Christians both encountered the distinction between civic and theological views. No matter how we think about and evaluate religions that are different from our own, no matter how we think about religion as a whole, if we are atheists or wholehearted secularists, the covenants of citizenship to which we adhere place us on common ground. As for religious beliefs, Thomas Jefferson put it this way: "The legitimate powers of government extend to such acts only as are injurious to others. But it does me no injury for my neighbor to say there are twenty gods, or no God. It neither picks my pocket nor breaks my leg."[26]

Religious Pluralism: Civic Perspectives

Taking a civic perspective on religious pluralism leads us, first and foremost, to the Constitution. Religious diversity in America is a concomitant of America's constitutional commitment to religious freedom. While most of the "founding fathers" were Christians, some with strong deist leanings, they deliberately created a civic space that would not be dominated by their own faith or any other. God is not mentioned in the Constitution. Given the nuance of constitutional discussion of religious matters, this can be no oversight.

Time and again in debates about religious establishment, the likes of Jefferson and Madison argued against state support for religion and did so in what we might call theological language and out of religious conviction. They were not "secular," a term that would be an inaccurate anachronism. They were guided by deep religious sensibilities to argue for a civic space that is not shaped by religion. In his 1785 "Memorial and Remonstrance," Madison argued that the state is not a competent judge of religious truth and has no business interfering in matters of religion: "Whilst we assert for ourselves a freedom to embrace, to profess, and to observe the religion which we believe to be of divine origin, we cannot deny an equal freedom to those whose minds have not yet yielded to the evidence which has convinced us."[27]

In the two-year debate over religious freedom in Virginia, Thomas Jefferson argued that the Act for Establishing Religious Freedom in Virginia "meant to comprehend, within the mantle of its protection, the Jew and the Gentile, the Christian and the Mahometan, the Hindoo and infidel of every denomination."[28] The point was one that he made in principle: religious freedom has to mean freedom for all religious traditions. The 1786 Virginia Act, which in many ways modeled the Bill of Rights, insisted "that our civil rights have no dependence on our religious opinions."[29]

The first freedom of the Bill of Rights, drafted in 1791, was freedom of religion coupled with the nonestablishment of religion: "Congress shall make no law respecting an establishment of religion or prohibiting the free exercise thereof." Those who signed the Constitution could not have fully imagined the religious diversity of America today, yet, over the course of more than two centuries, the sturdy principles of free exercise of religion and the nonestablishment of religion have stood the test of time. America's religious diversity has broadened to include substantial and increasingly vocal groups like those Jefferson only imagined: Hindu, Sikh, Jain, Muslim, and Buddhist communities. Religious freedom is, to be sure, the fountainhead of this diversity. And, of course, America's secular humanist traditions are also part of the diversity and are protected by the freedom of conscience built into the constitutional foundations. Freedom of religion is also freedom *from* religion of any sort. Jefferson's intention in Virginia, as he put it, was to protect not only the variety of believers, but also the many forms of nonbelievers, the "infidels" of every faith.

Surveying the results of uncoupling church and state in the 1820s, Tocqueville was surprised to find that, in America, freedom and religion seemed to march in the same direction, rather than freedom sparking the abandonment of religion, as had been significantly the case in France. He spoke of religion in America as the "first of political institutions," astutely discerning that even though the churches of America were not supported by the government and were not directly involved in politics as such, they were nonetheless extremely influential in the political sphere.

There would soon be a few activists, however, like the conservative evangelicals who started the National Reform Association in 1864, who wished to bring the religious and civic "we" together more firmly. They worked, in their words, "to secure such an amendment of the Constitution of the United States as will indicate that this is a Christian nation, and will place all the Christian laws, institutions and usages of our government on an undeniable legal basis in the fundamental law of the land."[30] They did not succeed in their bid to rewrite the Constitution, but they kept on trying. Various efforts to insert an acknowledgment of "Lord Jesus Christ as Governor among the Nations" into the U.S. Constitution were pursued until the middle of the twentieth century. This effort to revise the Constitution away from the nonestablishment of religion has taken many forms, and it is far from defunct. In the same decades that have witnessed the exponential growth of non-Christian religious communities in America, the Christian right has grown in strength and in determination to have a role in shaping public policy. Attacks on the independence or so-called activism of the judiciary today might well be seen as today's alternative efforts to alter the Constitution.

In the public context of a democratic, multireligious nation, how should we recognize religious diversity? Some would like to argue for no recognition of religion or religious diversity at all. Others would see recognition as the nod toward religious minorities that a powerful, normative majority can well afford. For the pluralist, the freedom, the initiative, and the independent voice of minorities is truly the test of the well-being of society. Each person can and should be able to speak for himself or herself, because the right to do so is constitutionally granted, not granted by the toleration of the majority. The rhetoric of inclusion has made significant advances in the past decade, but the engagement of genuine pluralism is still incipient. It is one thing for the president to congratulate the Muslim community on the observance of Eid and quite another to seat a Muslim on the National Commission on Terrorism.[31]

One of the increasingly common forms of public rhetoric that gestures toward the new religious diversity is the speech of inclusion and recognition. In the 1990s, public officials began to use locutions, such as "churches, synagogues, and mosques." In his 2005 inaugural address, President George W. Bush gave rhetorical recognition to the Abrahamic faiths when he spoke of America's edifice of character as "sustained in our national life by the truths of Sinai, the Sermon on the Mount, the words of the Koran, and the varied faiths of our people."[32] This is the speech of inclusion. It is but a gesture in the direction of religious pluralism, but there is no question that it is important.

Throughout the past decade, city councils, state legislatures, and governors began to issue the usual holiday congratulatory proclamations for a new set of holidays. The governor of Kansas released a proclamation in honor of the month of Ramadan in 1997. The Board of Supervisors in Fairfax County, Virginia, proclaimed Durga Temple Appreciation Week in honor of the consecration of a new temple to the Hindu goddess Durga in 1999. The governor of Arizona issued a proclamation for the Buddha's birthday in 2000. The State of Michigan formally honored the four hundredth anniversary of the Guru Granth Sahib in 2003. These marks of recognition are instigated, to be sure, by the communities themselves, but in these cases and hundreds of others, the public notice of the presence and contribution of Buddhists and Sikhs expands the public field of vision.

Invocations in city councils, state legislatures, and the U.S. Congress also have become public forms of recognition. Here members of a minority community speak in their own voice in a public space. The wider issue of whether religious invocations are appropriate in governmental bodies notwithstanding, the increasing diversity of such ceremonial prayers can be tracked through the 1990s. The first time a Muslim offered the invocation in the U.S. House of Representatives was in 1991, when Siraj Wahaj, an African American Muslim leader from Brooklyn, led the prayer. In fall 2000 a Hindu priest gave the invocation before a joint session of Congress. Jain nuns opened a session of the Ohio legislature in 2001, shortly after 9/11. Sikhs were invited to deliver the invocation before a session of the Massachusetts state legislature in 2004. In Montana, the default invocation at the outset of the state legislative session has become the ritual voice of the Native Americans, with drumming and chanting in the capitol rotunda. All this, many times over, constitutes the cumulative evidence of the presence of new voices, however ceremonial such occasions may be. As we have seen from the objections to Muslim prayers in the Washington legislature, this gradual shift from an older Protestant, Catholic, Jewish pattern has not been without its controversies. One of the most significant cases under dispute involved a Wiccan priestess who asked to be included among clergy who offer invocations at the Chesterfield County Board of Supervisors in Richmond, Virginia. She was refused, and the case was taken up by the American Civil Liberties Union. The U.S. District Court ruled that the exclusion of the Wiccan was unconstitutional, but the Fourth Circuit Court of Appeals reversed the decision on appeal. In 2005 the U.S. Supreme Court let stand the Appeals Court ruling and did not accept the case.[33]

The 1990s saw a particularly striking growth in America's public awareness of Islam and in the public recognition of Islam as an American religion. By the mid-1990s, public officials from the mayor of Columbus, Ohio, to the governor of Kansas and the president of the United States were issuing greetings on the observance of the month of Ramadan and the celebration of Eid al Fitr. The word *iftar* entered the public lexicon, as Muslims reached out to the wider community, inviting mayors, school superintendents, professors, and office coworkers to break the Ramadan fast with them and enjoy a meal together. Hosting *iftar* meals for the Muslim community also became a common practice among public officials. In Houston, for example, it has become the custom of some four years' standing for the mayor to host an *iftar* for area Muslims by the City of Houston's Reflecting Pool. At the federal level, there have been increasingly visible *iftar* observances for Muslim and non-Muslim employees on Capitol Hill, in congressional office buildings, and in the Pentagon. At a 2003 gathering hosted by Representative John Conyers of Michigan, along with four other congressmen in the House Judiciary Committee Hearing Room, Representative Conyers remarked: "By partaking in this religious tradition, we hope to promote the toleration, understanding, and acceptance of all religions and religious cultures and to celebrate religious diversity, one of the many great principles that our country was founded upon."[34] In 1998 Madeleine Albright presided over an *iftar* dinner at the State Department, a tradition that continued under Secretary Colin Powell. Addressing the State Department *iftar* in 2003, Powell noted with appreciation the long tradition of Muslim hospitality represented by the *iftar*: "As the *iftar* welcomes all in a spirit of brotherhood, so America has been open to welcoming all—as we can see in the diverse and thriving Muslim community in America today."[35]

In assessing the climate of religious pluralism in America, tracking these small, single, but cumulative official acts of positive recognition is as important as tracking the small, single, but cumulative incidents of hatred and harassment. It is in this composite public record that we begin to assemble a more comprehensive picture of who "we" now are. When Muslims were welcomed for the first time to the White House on the occasion of Eid in 1996, when the first Muslim chaplain was appointed to the New York City Police Department in 1999, when both the 2000 Republican and Democratic national conventions included a Muslim prayer, new photographs were added, so to speak, to the American family album. As Hillary Clinton put it on that Eid day in 1996: "This celebration is an American event. We are a nation of immigrants who have long drawn on our diverse religious traditions and faiths for the strength and courage that make America great."[36]

There are, to be sure, some Americans for whom this public recognition of religious diversity is not welcome. There are others for whom such gestures of inclusion do not go far enough. When President Clinton issued a proclamation on the birthday of the Sikh teacher-founder, Guru Nanak, he said: "Religious pluralism in our nation is bringing us together in new and powerful ways."[37] But for many, the controversies that arise with the new religious diversity are not bringing us together but threatening to tear us apart. As our religious diversity grows, are we seeing the emergence of new common ground or a new battle ground?

Two of the most significant symbolic issues in the battle are the Pledge of Allegiance and the Ten Commandments. Both have made their way to the U.S. Supreme Court. The case to declare the words "under God" in the Pledge of Allegiance unconstitutional was brought by a California atheist on behalf of his daughter who was required to recite the pledge in school.[38] The case ultimately failed before the Supreme Court in 2004 for reasons that had to do with Michael Newdow's standing in bringing the case.[39] What may be most interesting from the standpoint of America's religious pluralism, however, is the *amicus* brief filed by American Buddhists stating their dilemma: as Buddhists they should not be forced to choose between their country and their religion. They should not be made to feel outsiders in the American project, either by saying the pledge or remaining silent.[40] In asking Buddhist schoolchildren to recite the pledge, "they are asked to articulate a religious concept irreconcilable with the teachings of their religion and the supreme wisdom, the awakening, that is their goal."[41]

The Ten Commandments Battle

A visitor or worshiper entering many synagogues in America may well find stone tablets carved with Hebrew letters standing for the Ten Commandments, prominently visible in the stone pediment above the exterior door. The tablets might be repeated in the interior iconography of the synagogue, and, of course, the focal point of the synagogue is the ark of the covenant containing the scrolls of Torah, where the text of the Ten Commandments may be found.

We expect to be reminded of the Ten Commandments on entering a synagogue. And we might not be surprised to be reminded of the Ten Commandments on entering a Christian church as well, although I am not aware of Christian churches where posting the Ten Commandments at the doorway or on the lawn is practiced. But should the Ten Commandments be in the foyer of the city hall or the courthouse? Or on the lawn of the state capitol building? In a multireligious nation founded on the nonestablishment of religion, would this not be precisely the endorsement of a particular religious tradition or, indeed, of state religion in general that the U.S. Constitution proscribes?

In March 2005 the U.S. Supreme Court heard two cases on the public display of the Ten Commandments: *Van Orden v. Perry* from Texas and *McCreary County v. ACLU* from Kentucky. The Supreme Court had not taken up the issue in twenty-four years. Since then, there had been an escalating drumbeat of controversy, as tablets of the Ten Commandments in public places across the country from Elkhart, Indiana, to Grand Junction, Colorado, were challenged by those who argued that the display is an unconstitutional endorsement of religion. Lower courts had ruled both ways on the issue. Four federal appeals courts had ruled the Ten Commandments displays constitutional, while three had ruled they are not.

The display of the Ten Commandments in public, government buildings is a strategic drama seemingly staged for the preservation of a Christian or Judeo-Christian America. Jews, however, have not joined in the fray, except on the nonestablishment side through major Jewish church-state watchdog groups. It is the Christian right that framed this issue as critical for their cause, even though there are few Christian churches that display the Ten Commandments on their own lawns or vestibules. Judge Roy Moore, Chief Justice of the Alabama Supreme Court, set the stage for the most public enactment of the saga in August 2001, when he installed a two-and-a-half ton monument of the Ten Commandments in the federal courthouse in Birmingham. As we know, a constitutional battle ensued to remove the monument from the hall of the Alabama courthouse. "It's about the acknowledgement of the God upon which this nation and our laws are founded.... It's time for Christians to take a stand," said Judge Moore.[42] In the end, Justice Moore not only lost his cause, but also lost his job. The monument was removed, but not before weeks of demonstrations, in which Christian activists came from far and near to encircle the tablets and to kneel and pray by the monument in ways that certainly would have evoked the condemnation of Moses himself.

Judge Moore proclaimed, "We need to reclaim our Biblical heritage." His very language suggests our problem: what "we" is he talking about? Many among "we," the people in the United States, do indeed claim a biblical heritage, and yet, even in Alabama, many do not. Judge Moore's "we" does not include the array of Americans, many of them new citizens, for whom the moral compass is set in other ways. In addition, that "we" does not include Americans new and old who think of themselves as secular. Are they outsiders to the American project?

In November 2003 Judge Moore was removed from his seat on the Alabama Supreme Court, and an appeal to reinstate him failed. But the controversy continued. A rural judge in Alabama took to wearing a robe, which he had embroidered with the Ten Commandments at his own expense. In October 2003 hundreds of Christians rallied in Washington to save the Ten Commandments. Some of them had come with a five-day "Save the Commandments Caravan" that had started its five-state journey in Montgomery, Alabama. They ended their pilgrimage on the steps of the U.S. Supreme Court with chanting and prayer. "We are not here for a political issue, we are here for the very future and survival of our nation," said the Rev. Patrick J. Mahoney, director of the Christian Defense Coalition. "In Montgomery, a fire was lit, and we are taking it to the nation. The church of Jesus Christ is arising."[43]

The overtly religious rhetoric framing this symbolic issue is alarming for those concerned with the establishment clause of the Bill of Rights. In the two cases before the Supreme Court in 2005, a multitude of conservative Christian organizations associated themselves with the proponents of the public display of the Ten Commandments, as did the Bush administration. There were also prominent Christian, Jewish, and interfaith groups that filed briefs, urging the Court to strike down the public display. One brief in particular, however, signals the new era of religious pluralism that is the American reality, an *amicus* brief signed by nine groups representing Hindus, Jains, and Buddhists in the United States and submitted on the Texas case.

In Texas, the six-foot-high stone monument bearing the Ten Commandments is situated on the lawn of the state capitol building and maintained with state support. The brief cites the growth of Hindu, Jain, and Buddhist communities in Texas over the recent decades. It notes that the Fifth Circuit, in upholding the constitutionality of the monument, had argued that no one had contested its presence for forty years. The *amici* point out the clear fact that

America has changed in these forty years, and the reality of Hindu, Jain, and Buddhist presence is part of that change. They note that the first major Hindu temple in the United States was built only in the late 1970s, and that today in Texas alone there are some forty Hindu temples, five Jain temples, and over one hundred Buddhist temples.

The Hindus, Buddhists, and Jains also dispute the Fifth Circuit's statement that the Ten Commandments Monument is "nonsectarian," pointing out that they clearly meant only that it displayed a "nonsectarian version of the text." It did not consider seriously the fact that the Ten Commandments themselves are not nonsectarian but very much part of a Judeo-Christian religious world: "The setting of the Monument inherently, inescapably, signals to the religious minority of those practicing non-Judeo-Christian religions, often recent immigrants, that they are not merely religious outsiders, but unwelcome strangers to the political community as well."[44]

Astonishingly, the District Court that first heard the case, began its opinion with an 1892 quotation from Rudyard Kipling: "Ship me somewhere east of Suez, where the best is like the worst. Where there a'n't no Ten Commandments, an' a man can raise a thirst." Hindu, Jain, and Buddhist *amici* may well have been deeply affronted by the use of such images of their cultures "east of Suez." But in the brief, they turn the words of insult to their own purposes:

> The District Court failed to recognize that the world is smaller now,
> and there are many people in the Western District of Texas—and
> millions in the United States—for whom "there a'n't no Ten Com-
> mandments." The District Court also failed to recognize that allowing
> the Ten Commandments Monument to stand on the Texas Capitol
> grounds, affects those people in ways that the majority, for whom the
> Ten Commandments are powerful (or at least inoffensive) symbols of
> religious faith, will never experience.[45]

The Hindus, Buddhists, and Jains clearly state their respect for the ethical principles of the Ten Commandments. That is not the issue. However, the source of the Ten Commandments, the exclusive view of God, the repudiation of the imaging of God, and the prescription of a particular Sabbath—all run against the grain of Hindu theologies. As for Buddhists and Jains, the very conception of a creator god who ordains commandments as a king might hand down rules for his subjects is not only alien, but is seen as an obstacle to enlightenment. The document states: "The primary effect of the Monument, taking into account the perspective of the *Amici*, is to put the weight of the state behind an image underscoring the otherness of the *Amici*."[46]

The issues at stake in the Ten Commandments cases were not primarily about religion versus nonreligion or religion versus secularism, although this debate and others have spurred a jump in membership of both atheist organizations and those committed to civil liberties. The larger issue, however, was whether a particular religious view will be endorsed and what constitutes endorsement. This strategic perception was shared both by those who framed the Ten Commandments debate on the Christian right and those of non-Christian traditions who called attention to their own experience of exclusion. What values will our government, the collective "we," express in the public space we all share? From the standpoint of the Christian right, it is about protecting the Ten Commandments. From the standpoint of their opponents, the protection of the Ten Commandments is the business of churches and synagogues. The issue is, rather, protecting the Constitution at a time when it is being undermined as never before.

In June 2005 the Supreme Court decided the two cases. In the case of the Kentucky display of the Ten Commandments inside the courthouse, the court ruled the display unconstitutional. In the Texas case, however, the history of the monument, placed as many others had been by the Order of the Eagles, was seen in its historical context as one of some twenty monuments on the capitol grounds. It was not deemed an "establishment" and was therefore ruled constitutional. In both cases, the judges were split five to four. Justice Stevens in his dissenting opinion on the Texas case was the only one to reference the Hindu American Foundation *amicus* brief, in a footnote to the following opinion: "Even if, however, the message of the monument, despite the inscribed text, fairly could be said to represent the belief system of all Judeo-Christians, it would still run afoul of the Establishment Clause by prescribing a compelled code of conduct from one God, namely a Judeo-Christian God, that is rejected by prominent polytheistic sects, such as Hinduism, as well as non-theistic religions, such as Buddhism."[47]

Conclusion

The global movements and events of the past decade have augmented the importance of being able to describe the changing reality of our time, to recognize it as a completely new context, and to take stock of how we will deal with the new diversity of our society. Recently, I took note of a sign on a student bulletin board at Harvard Divinity School. "Diversity is Excellence," it said. Is this really so? I think that diversity alone is not excellence. Diversity is just a fact. We may deal with it in excellent or impoverished ways. We may ignore those who differ from us, isolate ourselves from them, or engage with them as fellow citizens, as people of other faiths.

Pluralism is not an ideology, not a new universal theology, and not a free-form theological relativism. Rather, pluralism is the dynamic process through which we engage with one another in and through our very deepest differences. For some that engagement will be in the religious or theological register, and for others it will be in the civic register. For many if not most of us, it will be both. Pluralism is not just another word for diversity, but is engagement with that diversity. It does not displace or eliminate deep religious commitments. It is, rather, the encounter of commitments, in both the religious and the civic sphere. Pluralism does not mean abandoning differences, but holding our deepest differences, even our religious differences, not in isolation, but in relationship to one another. The language of pluralism is that of dialogue and encounter, give and take, criticism and self-criticism. In the world as it is today, it is a language we all will need to learn.

NOTES

1. Allen A. Austin, *African Muslims in the New World: A Sourcebook for Cultural Historians* (Boston: Garland, 1981); idem, *African Muslims in Antebellum America: A Sourcebook* (Boston: Garland, 1984); and Sylviane A. Diouf, *Servants of Allah: African Muslims Enslaved in the Americas* (New York: New York University Press, 1998).

2. The first CAIR report was published in *The Minaret* (June 1995): 43, a monthly magazine of the Islamic Center of Southern California. This figure compares with a total of 119 such incidents reported during all of 1991, the year of the Gulf War.

3. See the CAIR website: http://www.cair-net.org/civilrights2002/.

4. Ibid.

5. Sikh Coalition, "2003–4 Annual Report: Introduction," www.sikhcoalition.org.

6. See "Religion in the 2004 Election" on the Pluralism Project website: http://www.pluralism.org.

7. It is well known that a coalition of Muslim organization supported George Bush in 2000, persuaded, in part, by his willingness to meet with them and by his statement in the second presidential debate opposing secret evidence along with racial or religious profiling. In the 2000 election, the use of secret evidence to detain a Muslim suspected of supporting terrorism, without making public either the specific charges or the evidence, was on the top of the list of Muslim political priorities. In the wake of 9/11 the use of secret evidence has been little challenged.

8. See http://www.pluralism.org/womenvote/index.php.

9. *Dallas Morning News*, March 22, 2004.

10. The question of Muslim numbers in the United States is hotly contested, and there is no question on religion in the U.S. census. In 2000 the Mosque Study Project of CAIR in cooperation with the Hartford Institute for Religious Research estimated there are more than 1,200 American mosques with a combined active membership of at least two million. Adjusting for the numbers of Muslims not affiliated with a mosque, the study estimated the Muslim population at between 6 million and 7 million, about 30% of whom are African American. That same year, the *Encyclopedia Britannica* put its estimate at 4.1 million Muslims, based on the demographic research of David Barrett, the religious demographer of the *World Christian Encyclopedia*. The 2001 American Religious Identification Survey of the City University of New York, based on fifty thousand telephone calls, placed the number at 1.1 and 2.2 million adults, or about 2.8 million Muslims, when adjusted for children. The lowest estimate is that of the Chicago-based General Social Survey of the National Opinion Research Council, which estimated the figure at 1.89 million. Critics say the General Social Survey may well be low because of the many non-English-speaking people among first-generation immigrants.

11. Samuel Huntington, *Who Are We? Challenges to American National Identity* (New York: Simon & Schuster, 2004), 9.

12. Ibid., 340.

13. Ibid., 200.

14. Ibid., 144.

15. Alexis de Tocqueville, *Democracy in America* (New York: Vintage, 1990), 1.303–4.

16. Cited in Isaac Kramnick and R. Laurence Moore, *The Godless Constitution* (New York: Norton, 1997), 146.

17. "Council to Revisit Decision on Day of Prayer Request," *Troy Eccentric*, March 31, 2005.

18. See the website of the Arab American Institute: http://www.aaiusa.org/pr/release02-08-02.htm; and articles in *St. Louis Today*, Feb. 12, 2002; and *Washington Post*, Feb. 20, 2002.

19. Marcus Borg, *The Heart of Christianity* (San Francisco: Harper, 2003), 220.

20. Jonathan Sacks, *The Dignity of Difference: How to Avoid the Clash of Civilizations* (London: Continuum, 2002), 17–18.

21. Tariq Ramadan, *Western Muslims and the Future of Islam* (New York: Oxford University Press, 2003), 5–6.

22. Ibid., 203.

23. *Divali: Festival of Lights Prayer for Hindus* (Richmond: International Mission Board of the Southern Baptist Convention, 1999).

24. Some might wonder why there are legislative invocations at all, but the ceremonial precedent is well established and not considered an "establishment" of religion. Increasingly, however, these legislative prayers have included the recognition of Muslims, Hindus, Buddhists, Jains, Sikhs, and Native peoples.

25. Stephen Koff, "Criticism of Hindu Plucked from the Web," *Cleveland Plain Dealer*, Sept. 23, 2000.

26. Thomas Jefferson, "Notes on the State of Virginia (1782)," in *Thomas Jefferson: Writings*, ed. Merrill D. Peterson (New York: Library Classics, 1984), 123–326.

27. James Madison, "Memorial and Remonstrance," in *Letters and Other Writings of James Madison* (Philadelphia, 1867), 1.162–169.

28. Cited in Susan Jacoby, *Freethinkers: A History of American Secularism* (New York: Holt, 2004), 19.

29. Thomas Jefferson, "An Act for Establishing Religious Liberty," in *The Life of Thomas Jefferson*, ed. Henry S. Randall (New York: Derby & Jackson, 1858), 1.219–20.

30. Robert Handy, *A Christian America* (New York: Oxford University Press, 1971), 100.

31. Salam Al-Marayati of the Muslim Public Affairs Council was nominated for the National Commission on Terrorism in 1999, but his nomination was revoked in a storm of protests from the Zionist Organization of America and other Jewish groups.

32. See http://www.whitehouse.gov/news/releases/2005/01/20050120-1.html.

33. Simpson v. Chesterfield Co. (VA). See related documents and news stories at http://www.pluralism.org/news/simpsonvchesterfield.php.

34. See the CAIR website: http://www.cair-net.org (Nov. 13, 2003).

35. Remarks by Secretary of State Colin L. Powell at the Sixth Annual State Department Iftar Dinner, November 4, 2004, Benjamin Franklin Room, Washington, DC.

36. "Muslims Join Clintons to Celebrate Eid-ul-Fitr," *The Minaret*, March 1996.

37. *San Diego Union Tribune*, Nov. 13, 1998.

38. No. 02-1624, Elk Grove Unified School District and David W. Gordon, Superintendent, Petitioners v. Michael A. Newdow, Respondent.

39. As a divorced father, he did not have standing to bring the case on behalf of his daughter because he did not have custody of her.

40. Huntington's view of this matter is that Newdow, his fellow atheists, and presumably the Buddhists too really *are* outsiders in American culture. He goes on to say that the Muslims or Buddhists who protest the placement of a cross on public land in Boise, Idaho, because it makes them feel like strangers in their own city *should* feel

like strangers, because they are. This was a land founded and peopled, for the most part, by Christians. See Huntington, *Who Are We?* 83.

41. Brief Amicus Curiae of Buddhist Temples, Centers, and Organizations representing over 300,000 Buddhist Americans in Support of Respondents, Kenneth R. Pierce, Counsel of Record. The summary of argument begins: "When children from Buddhist homes across the United States recite the Pledge of Allegiance, they utter a phrase that is inconsistent and incompatible with the religious beliefs and ethical principles they are taught by their parents, by other adults in their communities, and by their teachers at after school religious programs and at Sunday Dharma school. That phrase is that this is a nation 'under God.' Although these children may wish to say the Pledge, express their patriotism, and state aloud their commitment to this 'indivisible' country and the values of 'liberty and justice for all' represented by the flag, they can only do so by referring to a deity and a particular religious paradigm that is at odds with their Buddhist beliefs."

42. See the Pluralism Project website: http://www.pluralism.org/news/index .php?xref=Alabama+10+Commandments+Controversy&sort=DESC#headline4623.

43. See the CNSN News website: http://www.cnsnews.com/Culture/Archive/ 200310/CUL20031006b.html (Oct. 10, 2003).

44. Brief for the Hindu American Foundation and Others Representing the Interests of Hindus, Buddhists, and Jains, as Amicus Curiae in Support of Reversal. No. 03-1500 in the Supreme Court of the Unites States: Thomas Van Orden v. Rick Perry, Governor of Texas and Chairman, State Preservation Board, et al., 14.

45. Ibid., 3–4.

46. Ibid., 22.

47. No. 03-1500 in the Supreme Court of the Unites States: Thomas Van Orden v. Rick Perry, Governor of Texas and Chairman, State Preservation Board, et al., Justice Stevens, dissenting, 13 (decided June 27, 2005).

BIBLIOGRAPHY

Arab American Institute. *African Muslims in Antebellum America: A Sourcebook*. Boston: Garland, 1984.

Austin, Allen A. *African Muslims in the New World: A Sourcebook for Cultural Historians*. Boston: Garland, 1981.

Borg, Marcus. *The Heart of Christianity*. San Francisco: Harper, 2003.

de Tocqueville, Alexis. *Democracy in America*, vol. 1. New York: Vintage, 1990.

Diouf, Sylviane A. *Servants of Allah: African Muslims Enslaved in the Americas*. New York: New York University Press, 1998.

Divali: Festival of Lights Prayer for Hindus. Richmond, VA: International Mission Board of the Southern Baptist Convention, 1999.

Handy, Robert. *A Christian America*. New York: Oxford University Press, 1971.

Huntington, Samuel. *Who Are We? Challenges to American National Identity*. New York: Simon & Schuster, 2004.

Jacoby, Susan. *Freethinkers: A History of American Secularism*. New York: Holt, 2004.

Jefferson, Thomas. "An Act for Establishing Religious Liberty." In *The Life of Thomas Jefferson*. Edited by Henry S. Randall. New York: Derby & Jackson, 1858.

———. "Notes on the State of Virginia (1782)." In *Thomas Jefferson: Writings*, 123–326. Edited by Merrill D. Peterson. New York: Library Classics, 1984.

Kramnick, Isaac, and R. Laurence Moore. *The Godless Constitution*. New York: Norton, 1997.

Madison, James. "Memorial and Remonstrance." In *Letters and Other Writings of James Madison*, 1.162–169. Philadelphia, 1867.

Pluralism Project. "Religion and Politics 2004: Women's Votes, Women's Voices." http://www.pluralism.org/womenvote/index.php.

———. "Religion in the 2004 Election." http://www.pluralism.org.

Ramadan, Tariq. *Western Muslims and the Future of Islam*. New York: Oxford University Press, 2003.

Sacks, Jonathan. *The Dignity of Difference: How to Avoid the Clash of Civilizations*. London: Continuum, 2002.

Sikh Coalition. "2003–4 Annual Report: Introduction." www.sikhcoalition.org.

13

A Voice of One's Own: Public Faith in a Pluralistic World

Miroslav Volf

Flourishing Religions

The world has always been a very religious place, and, by all appearances, it will continue to be so in the foreseeable future. That is not what some of the great figures of European modernity expected, though. They thought that religion would, in one way or another, "wither away," to use a phrase that the Marxist tradition most commonly employed to describe the expected disappearance of religion from private and public spheres. Religion is irrational, the thinking went. It will take flight in the face of reason, just as the night's darkness takes flight before the dawn of a new day. Religion is epiphenomenal. Ultimately, it causes nothing and explains nothing; in fact, other things (such as poverty, weakness, and oppression) cause and explain religion. Once people, armed with knowledge and technological prowess, take their destinies into their own hands, religion will disappear. This is, very roughly, the basic content of the so-called secularization thesis.

The secularization thesis has proven wrong, however. Or rather, it has proven only partially right—and only in a very circumscribed set of societies, those of Western Europe, and at a particular time in history. Even in these societies, religion has not quite withered away, though its influence there is significantly less now than it was a century ago, for instance. But contrary to all expectations, the rest of the world does not seem to be following a Western European pattern. As Charles Taylor rightly notes, it is now obvious that we can no longer speak of a single modernity that started in Europe and spread to the rest of the world. There are many non-Western ways to modernize, what Taylor calls "multiple modernities."[1] In most of these, economic progress, technological advances, and the increase and spread of knowledge sit quite comfortably alongside a thriving religion.

Worldwide, the fastest-growing overarching perspective on life is not secular humanism. If half a century ago secular humanism seemed to be the wave of the future, it is because in many places it was imposed from above by authoritarian and totalitarian governments—in the Soviet Union and Eastern European countries, in China and some Southeast Asian countries. There, secular humanism functioned like a parody of its originally imagined self: in the name of freedom—freedom from ignorance and oppression—secular humanism was imposed as an unquestioned ideology to legitimize oppression on a scale larger than history has ever seen.

In fact, the fastest-growing worldviews today are religious[2]—Islam and Christianity. And for the most part, they are propagated not by being imposed from above but by a groundswell of enthusiasm to pass the faith on and a thirst to receive it. Behind the spread of Christianity—behind the fact that Christianity is now predominantly a non-Western religion with over two billion adherents and growing mainly through conversion—is neither the power of states nor the power of economic centers nor the power of media or knowledge elites. Experts on world Christianity seem unanimous that the masses of believers are themselves the chief agents of its spread.

As the mention of Christianity and Islam signals, the world is not just a religious place. It is a religiously *diverse* place. In addition to these two largest and fastest-growing religions, there are many smaller religions that continue to thrive. Moreover, within Christianity and Islam, there are many varied, sometimes even widely discordant, movements. Finally, secular humanism itself in its diverse forms is also part of the world's religious diversity in that it does share with other religions one important feature: it comprises an overarching perspective on life, or, at least, some of its influential forms, like Marxism, function as worldviews.

Religious Diversity

An important social shift is underfoot in Western societies in regard to religion. Until recently, Western societies were relatively religiously homogenous. For centuries, they were by far predominantly Christian. Of course, there was always a small but significant presence of Jews, with whom relations ranged from overt and sometimes deadly hostility (as in Nazi Germany) to tolerance and friendliness (as in post–World War II United States). And for centuries, Western Christianity itself was divided or, in sociological speak, internally differentiated. Catholics and Protestants—Lutherans, Reformed, Anabaptists, Episcopalians, Methodists, Baptists, Pentecostals, and Seventh Day Adventists—coexisted with one another, often in competition for membership and social influence. And yet with the exception of Jews, a shared religious culture united them.

Slowly, but steadily, the swath of that common religious culture is diminishing. Take the United States as an example, with a robust Christian presence uncharacteristic of the rest of the Western world. Christianity is still by far the predominant religion here, but others have significant presence, too. In addition to about 6 million Jews and about 3.5 million atheists, there are about 6 million Muslims, perhaps 3 million Buddhists, and 1.2 million Hindus, to name just the most populous faiths. In Europe too, religions other than Christianity are growing, especially Islam. In the Western world, in the foreseeable future non-Christian religions will continue to increase in both absolute and relative terms.

And these numbers are not significant only as indicators of the vitality of religions. They are also indicators of their potential political influence. Muslims, for instance, are numerous enough to be a significant political force, both in the United States and in Europe. Moreover, they and other religious groups have both the social power and will to make their voices heard and their interests taken seriously. In the West, religiously pluralistic social spaces are likely to give rise to increasingly religiously pluralistic political bases and actors.

The workplace is a good site to observe the growing significance of religious plurality. In terms of religious diversity, it is a nearly exact though somewhat smaller replica of the wider culture. But it is not just that diverse religions are represented. Believers are also increasingly willing to bring their religious concerns into the office space or onto the factory floor. It used to be that workers hung their religion on a coatrack alongside their coats. At home, their religion mattered; at work, it was idle. This is no longer the case. For many people, religion has something to say about all aspects of life, work included. Indeed, some of them are excellent workers precisely because they are devoutly religious. But if religion is allowed into an office or factory, many religions will come—possibly as many as are represented in the workforce. This leads to interesting questions, like how to configure a work space that is equally friendly to all religions. Religious diversity in the workplace is emerging as a significant issue analogous to racial or gender diversity.

The religious diversity of Western countries increasingly mirrors religious diversity in the world as a whole. At the level of individual nations, religious diversity is, of course, not a Western phenomenon. In a sense, it is a latecomer to the West. Some non-Western countries, like India, have lived for centuries with religious pluralism. Others are likely to become increasingly pluralistic, with various religions—foremost Christianity and Islam—competing for members and vying for social power and political influence. Globally and nationally, religious diversity will continue to be an important issue in the years to come. A modernist longing for a secular world is bound to be disappointed, just as the nostalgia for a "Christian Europe" or a "Christian America" is bound to remain just that: an unfulfilled nostalgia.

Religion in Liberal Democracy

Liberal democracy emerged in the West as an attempt to accommodate diverse religious perspectives on life within a single polity. It is democracy because governance is ultimately vested in adult citizens, all of whom have equal voice. It is liberal because its two key ideas, in addition to equal protection before the law, are (1) freedom for each person to live in accordance with his or her own interpretation of life (or lack of it) and (2) the state's neutrality with respect to all such perspectives on life.

In an essay entitled "The Role of Religion in Decision and Discussion of Political Issues," Nicholas Wolterstorff notes one pervasive, though not defining, feature of liberal democracies. In debates and decisions concerning political issues, citizens are not to base their positions on religious convictions derived from explicit divine revelation (so-called positive revelation). Instead, when it comes to such activities, they are to allow their religious convictions to idle. They are to base their political decisions and their political debate in the public space on the principles yielded by some source *independent of* any and all of the religious perspectives to be found in society.[3]

Wolterstorff also notes that those who advocate such idling of religious convictions in public matters often interpret the state's neutrality with respect to all religions as the *separation* of church and state—the famous "wall of separation"! But for many religious people, it is part and parcel of their religious commitment to base their convictions about public maters on religious reasons—on Torah, on teachings of the Old and New Testament, or on the Qur'an, for instance! How can they be free to live the way they see fit when they are not allowed to bring religious reasons into public debates and decisions? For these people, liberalism, conceived in this way, is illiberal. It hinders them from living out their lives as the faith they embrace urges them to do.

When religion leaves the public square—or is driven from it—the public square does not remain empty. Instead, it becomes filled with a diffuse phenomenon called secularism. Today in the West (unlike in the Soviet Union of the past century), secularism is not, strictly speaking, an ideology but rather a set of related values and truth claims partly inherited selectively from the tradition, partly generated by the marketplace, and partly drawn from the hard sciences. The marketplace enthrones personal preference as the paramount value, and the hard sciences offer explanations using inner-worldly causalities as the only truth. With religions absent from the public square, secularism of this sort becomes the overarching perspective. My point here is not that secularism is not admissible and respectable as such. It is rather that, by barring religious reason from public decision-making and enforcing separation of church and state, secularism ends up as the *favored* overarching perspective— which is clearly unfair toward religious folks.

As an alternative, Wolterstorff suggests a form of liberal democracy he describes as "consocial." It has two main features. First, "it repudiates the quest for an independent source and it places no moral restraint on the use of religious reason. And second, it interprets the neutrality requirement, that the state be neutral with respect to the religious and other comprehensive perspectives present in society, as requiring *impartiality* rather than *separation*."[4] "What unites these two themes," Wolterstorff continues, "is that, at both points, the person embracing the consocial position wishes to grant citizens, no matter what their religion or irreligion, as much liberty as possible to live out their lives as they see fit."

What also unites these two themes is advocacy of "a politics of multiple communities."[5] The liberal who bars religious reasons from public debate and advocates separation of church and state is clinging to "a politics of a community with shared perspective." But Western nations are no longer such communities, if they ever truly were. They are communities made up of adherents of multiple religions and perspectives on life. In a polity that calls itself liberal, each of these should have a right to speak in the public square in a voice of its own.

Will religious communities support a polity in which they can speak in their own religious voices in the public arena and the state relates to all communities impartially? Unless they are simply power hungry, they will. And unless they are secularized, most of them are likely to support such a polity more readily than one that is implicitly secular and therefore favors a perspective on life other than theirs. To be sure, some religions will strive to be favored by the state. But when they do, they are in principle no different than secularism is now or than secularism would continue to be under the consocial proposal. There are legal checks against favoring one perspective on life over others, and all players will have to face the moral demands of fairness and partiality.

Liberal democracy, the kind that sought to take convictions of particular religions out of public life, emerged in the wake of the European religious wars of the seventeenth century. People clashed partly because they had differing perspectives on life. To remove the cause of conflict, liberal democracy said the protagonists' religious perspectives should no longer be part of their public encounters. But if we are to live with a politics of multiple communities that bring their religious perspectives to the common table, as Wolterstorff suggests, will not violent clashes return? Under these conditions, is there a way of avoiding the return of religious conflict, even religious wars?

No Common Core

One way to avoid clashes triggered by particular religious perspectives would be to suggest that all religions are fundamentally the same. On the surface, the differences among them are obvious—from dress codes to arcane points of doctrine. But in this view, all differences are an external husk containing the same kernel. Alternatively, all of them are media, conditioned by the particularities of indigenous cultures that communicate the same basic content. "Lamps are different, but the light is the same," said an old Muslim sage, giving poetic expression to this account of the relations among religions. Its contemporary proponents have christened it "pluralist."

The pluralist account of relations among religions fits rather nicely into the role assigned to religion by liberal democracy. Just as liberal democracy relegates particular religious perspectives to the private sphere, so the pluralist account of relations among religions relegates them to being accidental features of a given culture. In both cases, particularity is rendered idle—in the case of liberal democracy, by leaving it behind in favor of a universally accessible "independent source," and in the case of pluralism, by seeing through religious particularities to the "common light" contained in all of them. More precisely, in both cases religious particularities can be acceptable to the degree that they are an instantiation of something more encompassing—public reason, in liberal democracy, and the heart of religious faith, in the pluralist account.

But the pluralist account of relations among religions is incoherent. I do not mean here that it never ends up making good on its promise of including everyone on equal terms, although this is true, too. Some religious group always ends up excluded, mainly because the teachings and practices of concrete religions are not only different but sometimes outright contradictory and stubbornly refuse to let themselves be interpreted as instances of an underlying sameness. We can expand the circle of the included, but we cannot avoid excluding—unless we declare every religion to be acceptable in advance. From my perspective, this is as it ought to be; otherwise we would end up having to indiscriminately affirm anything and everything. Pluralists should not pretend, however, to have overcome religious exclusivism.

The main trouble with the pluralist account of the relations among religions is that it tries to reduce religious diversity—that is, diversity that is acceptable on its own terms—to an underlying sameness. It offers a framework more overarching than any other in which each religion and all of them together are situated and of which they are made culturally specific instantiations. But such frameworks always squeeze particular religions into a preassigned mold, which is all the more troubling because, for most religious folks, their religion is itself the most encompassing framework for life and thought. Attempts to reduce what is important in different religions to the same common core are bound to be experienced as disrespecting each religion in its particularity.

Religions simply do not have a common core—a crucial claim that I must leave undefended here. Each is comprised of a set of loosely related rituals, practices, and metaphysical, historical, and moral claims to truth. Among different religions, these rituals, practices, and claims partly overlap (for instance, Muslims and Christians believe in one God) and partly differ (Muslims engage in ritual washings before prayers, for instance, and Christians do not) and are also partly mutually contradictory (Muslims object to the Christian claim that Jesus is the Son of God).

Moreover, there is no reason to think that the overlaps, differences, and disagreements in the future will be the same as they were in the past. Religions are dynamic, not static. They develop not only by interfacing with other domains of life, such as economic conditions or technological advances, but they also develop in mutual interaction with one another. To continue with the example of Christianity and Islam, we can trace the history of their encounters as a history of their shifting convergences and divergences. There is a give-and-take between them, sometimes triggered by hostilities and sometimes facilitated by the friendliness of their adherents.

The dynamic character of each religion and the overlaps between them give some reason to hope that the perspectives of various people of faith need not always clash or need not always clash fruitlessly and that, when they clash, the people who hold them need not be mired in endless violence. But that is a hope; that is a possibility. What would it take to make it a reality? What would it take for religions not only to preserve their differences but to bring the wisdom of their own traditions to bear on public decisions and debates? What would it look like to do this and yet live in peace within a single democratic framework in which the law of the land treated members of all religions equally and the state related to all religious communities impartially?

Speaking in One's Own Voice

Each person should speak in the public arena in his or her own religious voice, I have suggested. But what does it mean to speak in one's own voice? The answer has two components, one that is common to all religions and one that is specific to each.

If we think that all religions are basically the same, then what truly matters in each will be the same in all. To speak authentically as a religious person would mean to express that which is common to all religious people. Disagreements that remain between people would be a function of something other than religion. But I have already noted that such an account of the relations among religions is implausible. Religions are irreducibly distinct.

An alternative view about what it means to speak in one's own religious voice takes an opposite tack and seizes on religious differences. What is important in each tradition is the way it differs from others. According to this view, to speak in a Christian voice would be to highlight what is specific to Christianity and leave out what is shared with other religions as comparatively unimportant. Whenever people of different religions enter public debate, their views, if they were religiously informed, would clash. But I have already suggested that religions do not just differ among themselves. They also agree, and they agree on some important issues. Both approaches are wrongheaded because *they abstract from the concrete character of the religions themselves*, the one by zeroing in on what is the same in all religions and the other by zeroing in on what is different. They miss precisely what is most important about a religion, which is *the particular configuration of its elements*, which may overlap with, differ from, or contradict some elements of other religions. If one affirmed one's religion in this kind of particularity, what would it mean to speak in one's own voice?

To speak in a Muslim voice, for instance, would be neither to give a variation on a theme common to all religions nor to make exclusively Muslim claims in distinction from all other religions; it would give voice to Muslim faith in its concreteness, whether what it said overlapped with, differed from, or contradicted what people speaking in a Jewish or Christian or any other voice were saying. Since truth matters and since a false pluralism of approving pats on the back is cheap and short-lived, adherents of various religions will rejoice in overlaps and engage each other on differences and incompatibilities.

But if differences and incompatibilities remain in spite of significant agreements, then what will prevent clashes? Will not religious people, if they bring their differing and diverging perspectives into a public arena, plunge the political community into violence? For some, even to raise this question is to suggest that religious voices should be muted in the public domain and that some form of secularism should be embraced. But secularism will not help. It is just another perspective on life that is not above the clashes but participates in them as one player. Moreover, when it comes to violence, the track record of secularism is no better than that of religions. Most violence perpetrated in the twentieth century—the most violent century in humanity's history—was done in the name of secular causes.

The only way to attend to the problem of violent clashes among differing perspectives on life—whether religious or secular—is to concentrate on the internal resources of each for fostering a culture of peace. For each, these resources would be different, though again they may significantly overlap.

In regard to the Christian faith—the faith I embrace and study and the faith that is a good contender for having a legacy as violent as any other—developing its resources for fostering a culture of peace would mean at least two things. The first concerns the *center* of faith. From the very start, at the center of Christian faith was some version of the claim that God loved the sinful world (John 3.16) and that Christ died for the ungodly (Romans 5.6) and that Christ's followers must love their enemies no less than they love themselves. Love does not mean agreement and approval; it means benevolence and beneficence, possible disagreement and disapproval notwithstanding. A combination of moral clarity that does not shy away from calling evildoers by their proper name and of deep compassion toward them that is willing to sacrifice one's own life on their behalf was one of the extraordinary features of early Christianity. It should also be the central characteristic of contemporary Christianity.

The second consideration about speaking in a Christian voice follows from the first, and it concerns the nature of *identity*. Every discrete identity is marked by boundaries. Some things are in, others are out; if all things were in or all things out, nothing particular would exist, which is to say that nothing finite would exist at all. No boundaries, no identity, and no finite existence. The same holds true with religions. Though necessary, boundaries need not be impermeable. In encounter with others, boundaries are always crossed, even if only minimally. People and communities with dynamic identities will have firm but permeable boundaries. With such boundaries, encounters with others do not serve only to assert our position and claim our territory; they are also occasions to learn and to teach, to be enriched and to enrich, to come to new agreements and maybe to reinforce the old ones, and to dream up new possibilities and explore new paths. This kind of permeability of the self when engaging another presupposes a basically positive attitude toward the other—an attitude in sync with the command to love the neighbor and, perhaps especially, to love the enemy.

To speak in one's own religious voice is to speak out of the center of one's faith. To speak in a Christian voice is to speak out of these two fundamental convictions: that God loves all people, especially the transgressors, and that religious identity is circumscribed by permeable boundaries. Everything else that is said about every topic should be said out of these two convictions. When that happens, the voice that speaks will be properly Christian but will contain nonetheless the echoes of many other voices, and many other voices will resonate with it. Of course, sometimes the voice will find no resonances, only contestation. That is what the stuff of good arguments is made of, in personal encounters as well as in the public sphere.

Exchanging Gifts

In 1779 Gotthold Ephraim Lessing published a small book entitled *Nathan the Wise*. The book was an instant success. It is a play set in twelfth-century Jerusalem about the relationships among the three Abrahamic faiths—Judaism, Christianity, and Islam. But its main theme is gift giving. The Muslim ruler of Jerusalem, Sultan Saladin, pardons a young Knight Templar who then rescues Resha, a daughter of a wealthy Jew by the name of Nathan who himself had adopted Resha when she was an orphaned Christian baby. All this giving—and much more—has one purpose: to underscore that it takes *generosity* for Jews, Christians, and Muslims to live in peace with one another.

In fact, Lessing made two points about relations among Abrahamic faiths, one negative and one positive. The negative one is that we can safely put aside debates about the truth claims of religions. Adherents of each religion believe that their religion is true. But when it comes to comparing them, we cannot know which one is true and which one is not. And if religions' truth cannot be told apart from their falsehood, only pride can lead adherents of a religion to believe that "only their God is the true God" and to try to force the "better God upon the whole world for its own good."[6]

What should they do instead of trying to persuade each other of the superiority of their religion? Here is how Lessing put his positive point. It comes in the form of a statement addressed to the representatives of Judaism, Christianity, and Islam: "Let each of you rival the others only in uncorrupted love, free from prejudice. Let each of you strive to show the power of [his or her religion]. Come to the aid of this power in gentleness, with heartfelt tolerance, in charity, with sincerest submission to God."[7] To Lessing, religions—or at least, the Abrahamic faiths—are enablers of uncorrupted love. The test of their truth is the ability to generate such love, and that is where gift giving comes in. Believers' concern should be to give what others need and delight in and leave the question of truth open—to be decided by an impartial judge on the basis of each religion's track record in fostering love.

A child of the age of Enlightenment—one of the *fathers* of the Enlightenment!—Lessing thought he could neatly separate the practice of love from the question of truth. Truth claims are disputed, he felt, but we all agree on what is a loving thing to do. Moreover, he also believed that being a Jew, a Christian, or a Muslim is a dispensable addition to a more basic, generic humanness stripped of all the particularities of culture and religion. Like truth, cultural and religious particularities divide; like love, generic humanness unites. For a noble person, it would not matter that he or she is a Jew, a Christian, or a Muslim; it would be "enough . . . to be called a human being."[8]

The problem is that there are no generic human beings and there is no generic love. We know neither what love is nor what it means to be a human being outside of the traditions—mainly religious—in which we were raised and in which we live. There are Jewish ways of being human and of loving; there are Christian ways of being human and of loving; there are Muslim ways of being human and of loving; and so on. These various ways of being human and of loving are not identical, though they may significantly overlap. Put differently, Jewishness and Christianness, for instance, are not garments of humanity and love that can be taken off; they are the stuff of a particular humanity and a particular love. And that brings us back to the question of truth. It is the overarching perspectives on life, with their metaphysical and moral claims to truth, that give concrete content to what we think "love" or "being human" means.

On its own, Lessing's exchange of gifts in the practice of "uncorrupted love" is important but insufficient. It needs to be supplemented by the exchange of gifts in search of truth and mutual understanding. At the most basic level, the truth claims of many religions—notably those of the Abrahamic faiths—are contained in their sacred texts. People of faith should practice "hermeneutical hospitality" in regard to each other's sacred texts and exchange gifts as they do so. Each should enter sympathetically into others' efforts to interpret their sacred texts as well as listen to how others perceive them as readers of their own sacred texts. Such hospitality will not necessarily lead to agreement in the interpretation of respective scriptures. And it will certainly not lead to agreement among different religious communities for the simple reason that they hold distinct—even if, in some cases, partly overlapping—texts as authoritative. But such hermeneutical exchange of gifts will help people of faith to better understand their own and others' sacred texts, to better see each other as companions rather than combatants in the struggle for truth—and to better respect each other's humanness and to practice beneficence.

In Praise of Disagreement

The two forms of gift exchange—Lessing's beneficence and my hermeneutical hospitality—will not remove all disagreements and all conflict among various religious communities. In fact, removal of disagreements and conflict may not be even desirable. Public life without disagreement and conflict is a utopian dream whose realization under the nonutopian conditions of this world would do more harm than good. But this kind of gift exchange makes it possible to negotiate disagreement and conflict in mutual respect, and it even contributes to a significant measure of convergence and agreement. Religious communities will continue to disagree and argue. The point is to help them argue productively as friends rather than destructively as enemies.

Ongoing arguments are, of course, no substitute for action. There is no exit from acting. Even as we argue, we act. In a democratic polity, one important way in which we act is by voting. We argue, and then we vote, and then we argue again—or at least that is what citizens of well-functioning democracies do. There is no reason to think that members of different religious communities could not do the same without having to leave their religion locked up in their hearts, homes, and sanctuaries.

NOTES

1. Charles Taylor, *Modern Social Imaginaries* (Durham: Duke University Press, 2004), 1.

2. I am somewhat hesitant to designate any of the world's faiths as "religions" because the very notion of religion is a product of modernity; it represents the reduction of a living and encompassing faith to a sphere—a religious one—within the larger secular society.

3. Nicholas Wolterstorff, "The Role of Religion in Decision and Discussion of Political Issues," in *Religion in the Public Square: The Place of Religious Convictions in Political Debate*, by Robert Audi and Nicholas Wolterstorff (Lanham, MD: Rowman & Littlefield, 1997), 73.

4. Ibid., 115.

5. Ibid., 109.

6. Gotthold Ephraim Lessing, *Nathan the Wise*, trans. Ronald Schechter (Boston: Bedford/St. Martin's, 2004), 56.

7. Ibid., 76.

8. Ibid., 57.

BIBLIOGRAPHY

Lessing, Gotthold Ephraim. *Nathan the Wise*. Translated by Ronald Schechter. Boston: Bedford/St. Martin's, 2004.
Taylor, Charles. *Modern Social Imaginaries*. Durham: Duke University Press, 2004.
Wolterstorff, Nicholas. "The Role of Religion in Decision and Discussion of Political Issues." In *Religion in the Public Square: The Place of Religious Convictions in Political Debate*, by Robert Audi and Nicholas Wolterstorff. Lanham, MD: Rowman & Littlefield, 1997.

14

The End of Religious Pluralism: A Tribute to David Burrell

Stanley Hauerwas

Why Religious Pluralism Does Not Exist

Some years ago I was lecturing at Hendrix College in Conway, Arkansas. I no longer remember the lecture I gave, but I assume it was one of my attempts to suggest why Christians, if we are to be Christians, owe it to ourselves and our neighbors to quit fudging our belief that God matters.[1] When I finished my lecture, one of the professors in the religion department at Hendrix had clearly had enough of me. He had been educated by John Cobb and, therefore, represented that peculiar mixture of Protestant liberalism and process theology.

He reacted to my lecture by observing that my stress on the centrality of Christian convictions provided no theory that would enable Christians to talk with Buddhists. By "theory" people often mean the necessity of a third language to mediate between two traditions. Such a language is often said to be necessary in pluralist societies in order to mediate differences in the public square. Calls for a third language fail to consider, however, that such languages are anything but neutral. Moreover, the assumption that traditions are airtight closed systems is a gross oversimplification. Significant traditions are amalgams of many influences that provide often surprising connection with other traditions. Before assuming the inability to communicate, you have to listen and look. Those concerned with public theology claim that a third language is necessary for the public business. Yet I suspect that calls for a third language, for example, rights, are attempting to underwrite the superiority of those who represent the third language in contrast to traditions that do not see the need for such translations. Those representatives of the public with "all humility" assume they are superior to other traditions because they can appreciate other traditions in a manner that other traditions cannot appreciate themselves.

I, however, apologized for being deficient of such theory, but asked, "How many Buddhists do you have here in Conway? Moreover if you want to talk with them, what good will a theory do you? I assume that if you want to talk with Buddhists, you would just go talk with them. You might begin by asking, for example, 'What in the world are you guys doing in Conway?'" I then suggested that I suspected that the real challenge in Conway was not talking with Buddhists, but trying to talk with Christian fundamentalists.

I relate this story because the response I gave in Conway is more or less the same response I will give to my current subject: "The New Religious Pluralism and Democracy." I am well aware that my response may be understood by many to be irresponsible, but then I am quite suspicious of attempts to have Christians take on the burdens of running the world in the name of being responsible. I am, after all, a pacifist. I, of course, do not like the description "pacifism," not only because such a description suggests a far too passive response to violence, but more important, pacifism names for many a position regarding war and violence that can be abstracted from the christological convictions that I believe are necessary to make the stance of nonviolence intelligible.[2]

John Howard Yoder, the great representative of christological pacifism, rightly challenged Reinhold Niebuhr's accusation that the pacifism of "the sects" was a coherent but irresponsible position.[3] Yoder pointed out that Niebuhr's appeal to responsibility was a disguised legitimation of "the necessity" to accept a Weberian understanding of politics. According to Yoder, appeals to responsibility are used to imply that Christians have an inherent duty to take charge of the social order in the interest of its survival or its amelioration by the use of means dictated, not by love, but by the social order itself. This social order being sinful, the methods necessary to administer it will also be sinful. Responsibility thus becomes an autonomous moral absolute, sinful society is accepted as normative for ethics, and when society calls for violence the law of love is no longer decisive (except in the discriminate function of preferring the less nasty sorts of violence). Of course, according to pacifist belief, there exists a real responsibility for social order, but that responsibility is a derivative of Christian love, not a contradictory and self-defining ethical norm.[4]

At this point you may wonder if I have forgotten that my subject is not pacifism. It will be, however, the burden of my remarks to show that the Christian response to the challenge of the new religious pluralism has everything to do with Christian nonviolence. Just as Yoder had to challenge the claim that Christian pacifists were irresponsible, so I must challenge the very terms used to describe the challenge before us. From my perspective, pluralism is the ideology used by Protestant liberals to give themselves the illusion they are still in control of, or at least have responsibility for, the future of America. Religion is the designation created to privatize strong convictions in order to render them harmless so that alleged democracies can continue to have the illusion they flourish on difference. Indeed, if there is anything new about the current situation, it is that we are coming to the end of Protestant hegemony in America.

This is a strange claim, to be sure, given the rise of the so-called religious right represented by the Bush administration. Indeed I suspect that some may associate my robust theological perspective with the aggressive Christianity associated with the religious right. As far as I know, however, no representative of the religious right has claimed me for an ally. That they have not so claimed me is certainly appropriate because I regard the religious right as representatives of a truncated, if not idolatrous, form of Christianity. Indeed I think the religious right is a desperate attempt of Protestantism to make sense of itself as a form of civil religion for America.[5] That is why the Christianity represented by the religious right is at once so strident and pathetic.

In his book *The First and the Last: The Claim of Jesus Christ and the Claims of Other Religious Traditions*, a book that very helpfully suggests how the Christian understanding of the final primacy of Christ does not close off an appreciative understanding of other traditions, George Sumner observes that the existence of other religious traditions became and has become "a problem for the Christian tradition at the very time that Christianity became a problem to itself."[6] Christians have always known that other religious traditions exist. Why has the knowledge that there are other religious traditions become such a problem?[7] Sumner suggests that the challenge of other religions is but part of the more general Enlightenment challenge to religious particularism in the name of universal reason.[8] I have no doubt that Sumner is right that the very terms of how the challenge of other religions is now understood by Christians is largely the result of the critiques of Christianity by Enlightenment thinkers. But it is very important to remember that what is now understood to be the Protestant right is as much the creature of Enlightenment developments as is Protestant liberalism.[9]

Sumner rightly reminds us of the decisive importance to developments in Protestant theology for understanding the issue of religious pluralism, but the politics of these developments cannot be overlooked if we are to understand the context in which these questions are raised. William Cavanaugh provides an account of the fate of Christianity in modernity that is crucial if we are to understand why the very terms of analysis of the relation of Christianity to democratic societies betray how Christians should think about our faith. According to Cavanaugh the story of the modern state is a soteriological story in which the state is assumed necessary to save us from contentious religious factions spawned by the Reformation. The modern state is alleged to be necessary to stop Catholics and Protestants from killing one another in the name of doctrinal loyalties. The "privatization of religion," indeed the very creation of the notion of religion as more basic than any particularistic practice of a faith, was a necessary correlative of the development of the modern, secular state, whose task was to keep peace among warring religious factions.[10]

This story of the development of the modern state is a staple in modern political theory. Cavanaugh, for example, calls attention to Judith Shklar's account in her book *Ordinary Vices*:

> Liberalism . . . was born out of the cruelties of the religious wars, which forever rendered the claims of Christian charity a rebuke to all religious institutions and parties. If the faith was to survive at all, it would do so privately. The alternative then set, and still before us, is not one between classical virtue and liberal self-indulgence, but between cruel military and moral repression and violence, and self-restraining tolerance that fences in the powerful to protect the freedom and safety of every Christian.[11]

This story of how the modern state saved us from religious anarchy and violence has been repeated so often it is assumed to have canonical status. There is only one problem with the story. It is not true. Drawing on the work of Quentin Skinner, Charles Tilly, and Richard Dunn, Cavanaugh argues that the so-called wars of religion were not the events that gave birth to the modern state, but rather were the birth pangs of the creation of such states.[12] Protestants killed Protestants and Catholics killed Catholics in the interest of the new power configurations developing after the demise of the medieval order. What was crucial for the development of state power was the redescription of Protestantism and Catholicism as religion. Religion, moreover, is now understood as beliefs, personal convictions, which can exist separately from one's public loyalty to the state: "The creation of religion, and thus the privatization of the Church, is correlative to the rise of the state."[13]

It may be objected that Cavanaugh is making far too much of the description "religion." After all, that description is but an attempt to make sense of the diversity of human behavior that seems to deal with, in Christian Smith's words, "superempirical orders."[14] However, such definitions of religion cannot help but die the death of infinite qualifications. For example, it is very hard to make sense of Christianity as a "superempirical order" given the Christian belief in the incarnation. Moreover, anyone familiar with attempts to make sense of religion by religious studies departments in contemporary universities cannot help but be aware that at best religion is understood as an inexact term to describe diverse subject matters that have very little in common.[15] Put more polemically, the creation of religious studies departments can be understood as the ongoing development of universities to provide legitimating knowledges for state power.[16]

The problematic character of the concept of religion, however, is but a reflection of any attempt to make sense of pluralism. I suggested above that pluralism is the ideology of people in power to comfort themselves with the presumption that they are in control of the world in which they find themselves. For example, John Milbank argues that the very terms of discourse which provide the privileged categories for encounters between significant traditions as well as the criteria for the acceptable limits of the pluralist embrace, that is, terms such as *dialogue* and *pluralism*, are themselves embedded in a wider Western discourse that presumes global dominance. As a result the celebration of other cultures and traditions is at the same time the "obliteration of other cultures by western norms and categories, with their freight of Christian influence."[17]

Some may find Milbank's argument exaggerated, but Milbank's argument that pluralism is a rhetoric to avoid difference is not peculiar to him or his work. For example, Ken Surin, drawing on the work of anthropologist Bernard McGrane, argues that the transition from the Christian attempt to understand the non-European other, through the Enlightenment understanding of the other as "unenlightened," to our current attempt to see the other as culturally different has been an ongoing project of cultural imperialism. What Surin calls the "democratization" of "difference" is the exemplification of that imperialism. Such democratization seems like an advance because the non-European other is no longer understood to be in the depths of some petrified past, but "with this radical democratization of difference he or she is thus now our contemporary. . . . Non-European others are still different of course, but now they are *merely* different."[18]

According to Surin this celebration of difference in the name of pluralism underwrites the universalistic ideology of the American way of life in a manner that mimics how McDonald's hamburger has become the first universal food. As a result, Surin argues, the dominant ideology of the new world order declares nations, cultures, and religions obsolete if they maintain their old forms as fixed in intractable particularities.[19] This new world reality and ideological concomitants, that is, that which makes McDonald's into a universal food and sustains the world ecumenism advocated by exponents of religious pluralism, creates the *episteme* or paradigm which renders both sets of phenomena intelligible. To resist the cultural encroachment represented by the McDonald's hamburger, therefore, is of a piece with resisting the similar depredation constituted by this world ecumenism. It is to seek to resist the worldview which makes both possible. The question is: How do we theorize relationships between Hindus, Buddhists, Sikhs, Jews, Christians, and Muslims without underwriting this *episteme*? How can such people talk to each other without endorsing, even if only tacitly, the presumptions embodied in the formulations of the Kraemers, Rahners, Cantwell Smiths, and Hicks of this world? What is needed here, I am trying to suggest, can ultimately be nothing less than the displacement of a whole mode of discourse.[20]

Kraemer, Rahner, Cantwell Smith, and Hick are those Christians identified by Joseph Dinoia as inclusivist, that is, they are Christians who "espouse some version of the view that all religious communities implicitly aim at salvation that the Christian community most adequately commends, or at least that salvation is a present possibility for the members of non-Christian communities."[21] According to Dinoia pluralists are but a variation of the inclusivist type who believe that all religious communities aim at salvation but do so under a variety of scheme-specific descriptions. Yet Surin, rightly I think, has no use for either of these types, believing that even the attempt to develop such typologies betrays ideological presumptions.

Yet if I agree with Cavanaugh, Milbank, and Surin that religion and pluralism are mystifications that hide from us their ideological functions, where does that leave me? Should I try to supply a "whole mode of discourse" as Surin suggests we need? It would seem that that is exactly what we need if we are democratically to find a way to negotiate our religious differences. If I fail to provide such an account it would seem only to confirm Jeffrey Stout's assessment of my work as decidedly antidemocratic.[22] I cannot, however, supply the discourse Surin thinks we need to engage other traditions. I certainly do not have the intellectual power for that task, but even more I cannot be a representative of the "we" that thinks such a task necessary. Nor do I have any moral or policy recommendations to make to suggest how religious differences might be negotiated in this allegedly democratic society. However, by drawing on the work of John Howard Yoder I will at least try to suggest how Yoder's understanding of a non-Constantinian Christianity provides an alternative, at least for Christians, when confronted by the religious other.

The Disavowal of Constantine: John Howard Yoder's Understanding of Interfaith Dialogue

In 1976 John Howard Yoder was on sabbatical at the Ecumenical Institute for Advanced Theological Studies at Tantur/Jerusalem where he delivered a lecture entitled "The Disavowal of Constantine: An Alternative Perspective on Interfaith Dialogue."[23] That Yoder was in Jerusalem—the site of conflict between Judaism, Christianity, and Islam—influenced how Yoder approached his task. But it is also the case that Yoder used this occasion to explore the difference his understanding of a non-Constantinian form of Christianity might make for interfaith relations. Yoder took as his task to "ask what difference it makes or would make for interfaith dialogue,[24] if instead of every 'religion' as represented by its most powerful 'establishment,' the disavowal of the establishment of religion were restored as part of a specifically Christian witness."[25]

According to Yoder, Christianity had been transformed by what he called "the Constantinian shift." Yoder's understanding of the significance of that shift did not entail speculation concerning Constantine's sincerity, but rather Yoder was much more interested in the christological and ecclesiological implications of the church becoming the legitimating institution for empire. For example, prior to establishment, Yoder observes, Christians were confident that God was present in the church, but they had to believe that God was also active in the world. After establishment, given the mixed character of the church, Christians were confident that God was active in the world, but they had to believe that God was present in the church. In particular, when Theodosius made it a civil offense not to be a Christian, Christianity was fundamentally transformed from a nonviolent faith, that is, prior to Theodosius you could become a Christian only through conversion. After Theodosius to become a Christian could not help but be coercive.

The nonviolent character of Christian conversion for Yoder is a correlate of his Christology, for at the heart of Yoder's understanding of Christianity is a "concern for the particular, historical, and therefore Jewish quality and substance of New Testament faith in Jesus."[26] Yoder is, therefore, an uncompromising "particularist" which means, in George Lindbeck's terms, that Yoder is a "Christological maximalist," that is, he assumes that every possible importance should be ascribed to Jesus that is not inconsistent with the rule that there is only one God, the God of Abraham, Isaac, Jacob, and Jesus.[27] Yoder, I think, would also be in agreement with Sumner who, as I suggested above, argues that Christian approaches to interfaith dialogue must be governed by a pattern he describes as the "final primacy" of Jesus Christ. That is, as Christians confront "alien claims" and communities they must do so in confidence that "Christ is the One toward whom the narratives run and from whom their truth (to the extent that they are true) derives. He is at once the *final legis* (the end of the law) and the *prima veritas* (the first truth)."[28]

Accordingly Christians cannot avoid being in mission to witness to what they believe God has done in Christ. Yoder notes that the word *mission* has become a negative word for many because of its colonial history, but the very grammar of the Christian faith requires that Christians be heralds. Christians must be heralds because they announce an event that can be known only through its announcement. Moreover they believe that what they announce is true. Yoder observes:

> If it were not true the herald would not be raising his or her voice. Yet, no one is forced to believe. What the herald reports is not permanent, timeless logical insights but contingent, particular events. If those events are true, and if others join the herald to carry the word along, they will with time develop a doctrinal system, to help distinguish between more or less adequate ways of proclaiming; but that system, those formulae, will not become what they proclaim.[29]

Yoder's christological maximalism requires, therefore, that the herald, the witness, must remain noncoercive if it is to be true to that which it is a witness. You never have to believe it because (1) the message concerns a contingent event with the challengeable relativity of historical reporting, and (2) the herald cannot have the power to force you to believe it. The herald cannot be in a position to make anyone who refuses to believe to be destroyed or persecuted. It is the herald who must be vulnerable: "What makes the herald renounce coercion is not doubt or being unsettled by the tug of older views. The herald believes in accepting weakness, because the message is about a Suffering Servant whose meekness it is that brings justice to the nations."[30]

For Yoder, therefore, for Christians to disavow Constantine requires communal repentance. The Constantinian assumption of the indefectibility of the church must be challenged. But that challenge cannot take the form of saying, "We still think we are right, but you may be right, too" or "Yes, that is a wrong idea, but this is what we really meant." Such responses generate notions (like Rahner's account of other people as "anonymous Christians") which for their goodwill are but attempts to maintain Constantinian power in a tolerant mode.[31] Rather, Christians must say, "We were wrong. The picture you have been given of Jesus by the Empire, by the Crusades, by struggles over the holy sites, and by wars in the name of the 'Christian West' is not only something to forget but something to forgive."[32]

Such forgiveness cannot simply be remorse for the wrongs of the past, but requires *metanoia*. The discovery of a new way to be Christian may well come through being reminded by outsiders of our past failures, but "at least for Christians, the continuing pertinence of the historical memory of Jesus, via the New Testament, as a lever for continuing critique, is part of the message itself. The capacity for, or in fact the demand for, self-critique is part of what must be shared with people of other faiths and ideologies."[33]

Yoder, therefore, does not try to develop or recommend a general theory or strategy for Christian conversations with other faiths or traditions. He cannot because such theories or strategies would only reproduce Constantinian habits. "By the nature of the case," he observes, "it is not possible to establish, either speculatively or from historical samples, a consistent anti-Constantinian model. The prophetic denunciation of paganization must always be missionary and ad hoc; it will be in language as local and as timely as the abuses it critiques."[34] The way forward must be fragmentary and occasional, for the "affirmative alternative underlying the critique of paganization is the concreteness of the visible community created by the renewed message. The alternative to hierarchical definition is local definition."[35]

Yoder's "localism" is not some strategy to avoid conversation with other traditions.[36] Rather it is an attempt to shift the focus from questions about the truth content or validity of the ideas or experiences of other religions as systems or performances in order to attend to "the uncoercible dignity of the interlocutor as person and one's solidarity (civil, social, economic) with him or her as neighbor . . . [and this] must (and can) be defined first."[37] For Yoder to ask in the abstract the status of, for example, Buddhism vis-à-vis the Christian faith is a Constantinian question. I certainly do not think he would object to the kind of close study of other traditions represented by Paul Griffiths, Joseph Dinoia, and George Sumner.[38] Indeed Yoder would have every reason to encourage the close reading of other tradition's texts. Yet that kind of scholarship can never replace the concrete encounter with the neighbor who is different than me.

At the heart of Yoder's account is his understanding of the story of the tower of Babel in Genesis 11. From Yoder's perspective, too often God's destruction of the tower of Babel is interpreted as punishment. But such a reading, according to Yoder, fails to appreciate that the first meaning of Babel was the effort of a human community to absolutize itself. Those who built the tower were attempting to resist God's will that there be a diversity of cultures. Rebellious humanity sought to replace their dependence on God by creating their own heaven: "They were the first foundationalists, seeking by purposeful focusing of their own cultural power to overcome historically developing diversity."[39]

God's scattering of the people from Babel was therefore a benevolent act. At least that is the way Paul saw what happened at Babel as reported by Luke in the book of Acts (14.16–17; 17.26–27). The "confusion" of Babel is such only when measured against the simplicity of an imperially enforced uniformity. Babel is, therefore, a gracious intervention by God to continue the process of dispersion and diversification through which we are forced to learn to respect the other and learn humility: "Thus the 'confusion of tongues' is not a punishment or a tragedy but the gift of new beginnings, liberation from a blind alley."[40]

For Yoder, therefore, the existence of other significant traditions is not a problem for Christians, but rather a gift. That is why Christian missionaries who went and continue to go to make Christ present to those they assumed did not know Christ so often return confessing they discovered Christ in those they went to serve. The great missionary effort of the nineteenth century was no doubt sometimes sponsored by a Western arrogance, but it may well turn out to be one of the ways God used to humble that same arrogance.[41] At the very least the missions served to remind Christians that we rightly are a minority religion. The result Yoder would think providential.

In summary Yoder does not recommend that Christians disavow Constantine

> Because we enjoy concern with either our guilt or our innocence, and still less out of denominational self-righteousness, but because all that we ultimately have to contribute to interfaith dialogue is our capacity to get out of the way so that instead of, or beyond, us or our ancestors, us or our language systems, us or our strengths or weaknesses, the people we converse with might see Jesus. It is that simple: but that is not simple. It will not happen without repentance. If we mean that Jesus of history, the Jewish Jesus of the New Testament, then even here in the land of his birth—to say nothing of Benares or Peking or Timbuktu—there is no alternative but painstakingly, feebly, repentantly, patiently, locally, to disentangle that Jesus from the Christ of Byzantium and of Torquemada. The disavowal of Constantine is then not a distraction but the condition of the historical seriousness of the confession that Jesus Christ who is Lord.[42]

A Tribute to David Burrell

I am sure that my account of Yoder's understanding of what implications might follow from the Christian disavowal of Constantine for interfaith dialogue will seem to some an attempt to avoid the subject before us. Yoder's criticism of Constantinianism may seem interesting, but not relevant to the challenge that the new religious pluralism presents to the American society. At best Yoder represents an inner-Christian debate, but that debate does not translate into implications for broader public policy. More important, however, is to understand why, if Yoder is right about what it means to disavow Constantine, I cannot meet the expectations to articulate a public policy in response to the increasing religious diversity of America.

I suppose one of the ways to try to make my analysis relevant would be to work all the harder for the disestablishment of Christianity politically and socially in America. The First Amendment gives American Christians the presumption that Christianity is not established in law, but in fact Christianity still enjoys a cultural establishment that makes legal establishment unnecessary. If, as some maintain, America is becoming culturally a more secular society that (at least if Yoder is right) is not necessarily bad news for a Christian recovery of what contribution we might have for interfaith interactions.[43]

I do believe that Christians even in America can make a contribution for better interfaith understanding once we are free from the presumption that we have a peculiar role or special position in America. That contribution is quite simply people who are committed to having their lives exposed to other faiths. In particular I have in mind my friend and former colleague David Burrell. David Burrell was chair of the department of theology when I taught at Notre Dame University from 1970 to 1984. He is a distinguished philosophical theologian who has written groundbreaking books on Aquinas. In particular he is often credited as being among the first to offer fresh readings of Aquinas and in particular how Aquinas's understanding of analogy made possible Wittgenstein.[44]

During Burrell's tenure as department chair, money was given to establish a chair in Judaica. The temptation presented by such a chair was to make Judaism an exotic other. However, Burrell was determined to avoid such a development because he had come to understand, an understanding schooled by colleagues such as Joe Blenkinsopp and Robert Wilken, that for reasons internal to Christian theology Judaism could not be relegated to the role of being an antecedent to Christianity.[45] Accordingly, the position in Judaica was structured into the curriculum in a manner that made clear the work done by our colleague in Judaica was crucial for Christian theology.

During this time Burrell was also involved with helping Father Hesburgh, the president of Notre Dame, set up the Ecumenical Center in Jerusalem. Father Hesburgh had been asked by Pope Paul VI to establish the center in the hope that Catholic, Protestant, and Orthodox scholars would be able to study and interact in Israel, where (as Paul VI put it) "we were all once one." As a result Burrell was a frequent visitor to Jerusalem and even served, after finishing his term as chair of theology at Notre Dame, as the director of the center. Once there, he found himself increasingly immersed in the lives of Jews, but also sympathetic with the plight of the Palestinians.[46]

Given Burrell's scholarly excellence you can almost forget that he is first and foremost a priest. The university, while important to him, was not always the most conducive context for the expression of his priesthood. As a result, in 1975 he responded eagerly to his provincial superior's request to teach in the seminary in Bangladesh where his congregation had been present for more than a century. There he encountered Muslims with whose way of life he could not help but be impressed. As a result he wanted to read the Qur'an. But he realized he could not read the Qur'an without learning Arabic. Accordingly, once he had taken up residence in Israel, his practice of saying Mass in Hebrew gave him the opportunity to study Arabic.

Burrell, of course, could not forget that he was an Aquinas scholar. Aquinas, moreover, was a student of Ibn-Sina and Maimonides. It is not surprising, therefore, that Burrell drew on his increasing knowledge of Judaism and Islam to write *Knowing the Unknowable God: Ibn-Sina, Maimonides, Aquinas.*[47] In this book Burrell explored how these thinkers, each in their distinctive way, maintained the crucial distinction between essence and existence in the order of finite beings as crucial for maintaining the difference that creation makes. Without trying to force these traditions "to learn from one another," Burrell was able to show that some of Aquinas's most fundamental moves came from Jewish and Islamic scholars.

However, as a student of Aristotle and Aquinas, Burrell never forgets that metaphysical questions are in service to friendship and, in particular, friendship with God—thus his wonderful chapter in *Friendship and Ways to Truth* entitled "Friendship with God in al-Ghazali and Aquinas."[48] In this chapter Burrell shows how both theologians draw on their respective scriptures to display that as creatures we are necessarily related to our creator in a manner that makes possible the living of our lives as gift. In this essay we begin to see Burrell becoming so internal to Islamic theology that he is able to suggest that al-Ghazali's proposal of a mutual love between Muslims and the one God challenges those stereotypes of Islam overdetermined by the translation of Islam as "submission." Burrell's investment in Islam now even extends to translating al-Ghazali's *Ninety-nine Beautiful Names of God.*

Burrell is obviously a remarkable mind and spirit, but I do not think he is exceptional. Rather I think his life has been made possible because he exemplifies the opportunity opened by the disavowal of Constantine. A strange claim, perhaps, given that Burrell is a Roman Catholic priest. What could be more Constantinian than being a Roman Catholic priest, particularly one who has spent a lifetime teaching at the University of Notre Dame? Yet as Burrell reminds us in *Friendship and Ways to Truth*, it was Karl Rahner (the same Rahner of "anonymous Christianity") who argued that the real point of Vatican II was to sound the end of nineteen centuries of "Western European Christianity" in order to present Christianity vis-à-vis other faiths in a fashion quite different from anything in history since Christianity had parted ways with Judaism.[49]

That David Burrell has been drawn into the lives of Jews and Muslims is not because he is a cosmopolitan. Rather he has been drawn into the lives of Jews and Muslims because he is a Catholic. He exemplifies Yoder's contention that the closer we are drawn to Jesus the closer we must be drawn to those who do not pray as Christians do to the Father, Son, and Holy Spirit. But Burrell has learned that Jews and Muslims recognize in Christians who pray something of their own lives. In that recognition, moreover, is any hope we have that we are not doomed to reject one another from fear.

As a Christian I have no theory or policy to solve the problem of the new religious pluralism. But I do have something to give. I give you the example of David Burrell. Some may not think that sufficient to resolve the challenge before democracies. But I am equally confident that if people like David Burrell do not exist, appeals to democracy will be of no help.

NOTES

1. The heading for this opening section is meant to echo Stanley Fish's short but incisive essay, "Liberalism Doesn't Exist," which now appears in his book *There's No Such Thing as Free Speech and It's a Good Thing Too* (New York: Oxford University Press, 1994), 134–38. Fish argues that the liberal attempt to claim to represent a "rationality" free from beliefs about the world in order to secure a place free from "politics" is not a position anyone can inhabit. I will argue that in a similar fashion no place exists from which anyone might be able to describe religious pluralism in such a way that does not imply a normative position.

2. I do not mean to denigrate forms of pacifism which are not christologically determined. Rather I am simply indicating what I take to be the most defensible understanding of Christian nonviolence. For a wonderful account of the possibilities and limits of other forms of pacifism, see John Howard Yoder, *Nevertheless: The Varieties and Shortcomings of Religious Pacifism*, rev. ed. (Scottdale, PA: Herald, 1992).

3. Niebuhr's brilliant critique of pacifism was largely directed at liberal pacifism associated with mainstream Protestantism after World War I. He respected what he called "religious absolutism" in its apocalyptic or ascetic forms. The former he identified with the left wing of the Reformation who, like Jesus, set "the absolute principles of the coming Kingdom of God, principles of uncompromising love and nonresistance, in sharp juxtaposition to the relativities of the economic and political order and assumes no responsibilities for the latter." Ascetics such as Francis and Tolstoy, according to Niebuhr, sharpen individual ideals of the spirit in contrast to a whole range of physical necessities. Niebuhr respected these alternatives as long as they acknowledged they must "withdraw from politics." See Reinhold Niebuhr, *Love and Justice*, ed. D. B. Robinson (New York: World, 1967), 261.

4. John Howard Yoder, *Reinhold Niebuhr and Christian Pacifism: A Church Peace Mission Pamphlet* (Scottdale, PA: Herald, 1968), 18.

5. In his *Democracy Matters: Winning the Fight against Imperialism* (New York: Penguin, 2004), Cornel West rightly criticizes "conservative Christians" for their Constantinianism, but he praises Walter Rauschenbusch as a representative of prophetic Christianity (146–55). I also am a great admirer of Rauschenbusch, but Rauschenbusch was in his day as implicated in the Constantinian project as the religious right is today. Christopher Evans suggests that toward the latter part of his life Rauschenbusch modified his call to "Christianizing the social order" but the project continued to assume the establishment of Protestant Christianity as necessary for the reform of America; see *The Kingdom Is Always But Coming: A Life of Walter Rauschenbusch* (Grand Rapids: Eerdmans, 2004). What West fails to see is that the religious left is no less Constantinian than the right. For example, in his recent book, *The World Calling: The Church's Witness in Politics and Society* (Louisville: Westminster John Knox, 2004), Tom Ogletree notes that the challenge before Christian social ethics is "to discover constructive ways of relating distinctively Christian social ideas to the civilizational ethic resident in a given social order. The underlying claim is that normative social teachings, Christian or otherwise, cannot become socially effective unless they can be rendered compatible with the organizational principles that structure particular societies. What is possible in one setting may be wholly unrealistic in another. The attainment of such compatibility requires a 'cultural synthesis,' that is, a creative combination of distinctively Christian values with core elements in a reigning 'civilizational ethic.' In the American context, for example, the question for a viable synthesis necessarily involves giving privileged standing to the 'blessing of liberty' celebrated in

the Preamble to the U.S. Constitution" (4). I cannot imagine a clearer account of
cultural Christianity on behalf of the left. The Catholic right in an interesting way
shares much with Ogletree's concerns. For example, in a recent article, "The Deist
Minimum," *First Things* 149 (Jan. 2005): 25–30, Avery Cardinal Dulles defends
the minimal consensus that deism represented because he doubts that, if pluralism
goes unchecked, the nation will lack a corporate vision and collective purpose that have
marked the American past.

6. George Sumner, *The First and the Last: The Claim of Jesus Christ and the Claims
of Other Religious Traditions* (Grand Rapids: Eerdmans, 2004), 3.

7. For some reason, Christians in our time seem to think that the existence of
other traditions presents a decisive challenge to the truth and intelligibility of the
Christian faith. I confess I simply do not understand why they seem to assume that
what we believe is problematic unless everyone believes what we believe. As far as I
can see there is no biblical reason for such a view. Indeed, as I will suggest below,
Christian scripture, and in particular the tower of Babel, implies that we should expect
difference.

8. Sumner employs Alasdair MacIntyre's account of traditioned, determined rationality and the possibility that traditions can create as well as recognize epistemological crisis as a way to display how religious traditions might be able to discover
similarities as well as differences. Sumner rightly points to the logically odd and
anomalous aspect of his use of MacIntyre, namely, he is "marshalling the philosophical proposal of MacIntyre in defense of understanding the thread of pluralism in
a context-specific way, and, in what follows, in support of arguments located in a
manner developed from the Christian theological tradition" (*First and the Last*, 6). In
other words "there is inherently an irony in defenses of the specificity and uniqueness
of traditions that appeal to general observation about the nature of human knowing
(e.g., that it is tradition-specific) or human community (e.g., about practices embedded
in a unique form of life")" (10–11). Sumner sees quite clearly that the only thing a
Christian theologian in response to this tension can do is display how particular
Christian convictions do or do not relate to different communities. I have long thought
the tension Sumner identifies as inherent in his project to be a tension in MacIntyre's
attempt to maintain a too strict distinction between philosophy and theology.

9. For an account of the common roots of Protestant liberalism and fundamentalism, see my *Unleashing the Scripture: Freeing the Bible from Captivity to America*
(Nashville: Abingdon, 1993).

10. William Cavanaugh, *Theopolitical Imagination: Discovering the Liturgy as a
Political Act in an Age of Global Consumerism* (New York: Clark, 2002), 20–21.

11. Ibid., 21.

12. Ibid., 22.

13. Ibid., 31. In their extraordinary book, *Blood Sacrifice and the Nation* (Cambridge: Cambridge University Press, 1999), Carolyn Marvin and David Ingle observe
"in the religiously plural society of the United States, sectarian faith is optional for
citizens, as everyone knows. Americans have rarely bled, sacrificed or died for Christianity or any other sectarian faith. Americans have often bled, sacrificed and died for
their country. This fact is an important clue to its [the country's] religious power.
Though denominations are permitted to exist in the United States, they are not permitted to kill, for their beliefs are not officially true. What is really true in any society is
what is worth killing for, and what citizens may be compelled to sacrifice their lives for"
(9). I take this to be the outworking of the process of state formation Cavanaugh
describes. The result is perhaps most apparent in expressions often heard such as,

"I believe that Jesus Christ redeemed the world, but that is just my personal opinion."
You can be sure that people formed to express such drivel lack the capacity to resist
state power.

14. Christian Smith, *Moral, Believing Animals: Human Personhood and Culture*
(New York: Oxford University Press, 2003), 98.

15. For an excellent discussion of the difficulty of coming to any agreement for
how religion can be understood, see Paul Griffiths, *Problems of Religious Diversity*
(Oxford: Blackwell, 2001), 12–16. Griffiths argues that even if there are natural kinds in
religions, we are not in a position to know what they are or where their boundaries lie,
which means that if we persist in sorting religions into kinds, such sorting ought to be
viewed as useful fictions.

16. For the development of this claim, see Timothy Fitzgerald, *The Ideology of
Religious Studies* (New York: Oxford University Press, 2000). It would, of course, be a
mistake to single out religious studies as the discipline in the modern university
peculiarly in service to state interest. It is hard to find any discipline in the university
not so determined.

17. John Milbank, "The End of Dialogue," in *Christian Uniqueness Reconsidered:
The Myth of a Pluralistic Theology of Religions*, ed. Gavin D'Costa (Maryknoll, NY: Orbis,
1990), 175.

18. Kenneth Surin, "A 'Politics of Speech': Religious Pluralism in the Age of the
McDonald Hamburger," in *Christian Uniqueness Reconsidered: The Myth of a Pluralistic
Theology of Religions*, ed. Gavin D'Costa (Maryknoll, NY: Orbis, 1990), 198.

19. Cavanaugh makes a similar point about the power of the universal in service
to the state. He notes that "globalization does not signal the demise of the nation-state
but is in fact a hyperextension of the nation-state's project of subsuming the local
under the universal. The rise of the modern state is marked by the triumph of the
universal over the local in the sovereign state's usurpation of power from the Church,
the nobility, guilds, clans, and towns" (*Theopolitical Imagination*, 99).

20. Surin, "Politics of Speech," 201.

21. Joseph Dinoia, *The Diversity of Religions* (Washington, DC: Catholic University
Press of America, 1992), 37.

22. Jeffrey Stout, *Democracy and Tradition* (Princeton: Princeton University Press,
2004), 140–61. For my initial response to Stout, see my *Performing the Faith: Bonhoeffer
and the Practice of Nonviolence* (Grand Rapids: Brazos, 2004), 215–41.

23. John Howard Yoder, "The Disavowal of Constantine: An Alternative Perspective on Interfaith Dialogue," in *The Royal Priesthood: Essays Ecclesiological and
Ecumenical*, ed. Michael Cartwright (Grand Rapids: Eerdmans, 1994), 242–61. The
above information is provided by Cartwright's introduction to this essay. We are indebted to Cartwright for putting these essays of Yoder's between two covers, as well as
for writing one of the best introductory essays we have on Yoder.

24. I am aware that Yoder's use of the word *dialogue* is open to Milbank's critique.
I can only ask the reader to be patient before making that association, for I hope to
show that given Yoder's understanding of the conditions necessary for dialogue, the
hegemonic implications that Milbank associates with the word *dialogue* do not apply.

25. Yoder, "Disavowal of Constantine," 247.

26. Ibid.

27. George Lindbeck, *The Nature of Doctrine: Religion and Theology in a Postliberal
Age* (Philadelphia: Westminster, 1984), 94.

28. Sumner, *First and the Last*, 6–17. Yoder observes that Christians are often
tempted to jettison the particular, the local, the specific biblical content in an attempt to

correct the Christian imperialism associated with Christian Europe. Universality and commonality with other traditions is sought at the price of specificity. But he notes there is another way: "It would be possible to say that the error in the age of trium-phalism was not that it was tied to Jesus but that it denied him, precisely in its power and disrespect for the neighbor. Then the corrective would be not to search for a new consensus but to critique the old one. Its error was not that it propagated Chris-tianity around the world but that what it propagated was not Christian enough. Then the adjustment to Christendom's loss of elan and credibility is not to talk less about Jesus and more about religion but the contrary" ("Disavowal of Constantine," 257).

29. Yoder, "Disavowal of Constantine," 256. For Yoder's understanding of the word *doctrine*, see his *Preface to Theology* (Grand Rapids: Brazos, 2002). Yoder's chris-tological center does not entail a strong distinction between reason and revelation. Indeed I suspect that Yoder would have no reason to deny Denys Turner's recent attempt to defend the possibility of a natural theology. In defense of Aquinas, Turner observes "that to prove the existence of God is to prove the existence of a mystery, that to show God to exist is to show how, in the end, the human mind loses its grip on the meaning of 'exists'; such a demonstration is therefore designed to show that within creation itself, with our deepest human experience of the world, the mystery of unknowable existence is somehow always present with the world simply in its character of being created"; *Faith, Reason, and the Existence of God* (Cambridge: Cambridge Uni-versity Press, 2004), xiv. What is remarkable about Turner's defense of natural theol-ogy is how he understands such a defense of reason is made imperative by christo-logical commitments. If I had had Turner's book when I wrote *With the Grain of the Universe: The Church's Witness and Natural Theology* (Grand Rapids: Brazos, 2001), I would have been able better to show how Pope John Paul II's reclaiming of the chris-tological center for Catholic theology is not irrelevant to the argument of *Fides et Ratio*.

30. Yoder, "Disavowal of Constantine," 256.

31. Paul Knitter certainly represents the best attempt from a Rahnerian point of view to do justice to religious difference; see his *No Other Name: A Critical Survey of Christian Attitudes toward the World Religions* (Maryknoll, NY: Orbis, 2003).

32. Yoder, "Disavowal of Constantine," 250.

33. Ibid., 251.

34. Ibid., 250.

35. Ibid., 253.

36. Yoder was particularly concerned to renew the conversation between Chris-tianity and Judaism; see his *The Jewish-Christian Schism Revisited*, ed. Michael Cart-wright and Peter Ochs (Grand Rapids: Eerdmans, 2003).

37. Yoder, "Disavowal of Constantine," 256.

38. I suspect, however, that Yoder might well prefer Paul Griffiths's *Religious Reading: The Place of Reading in the Practice of Religion* (New York: Oxford University Press, 1999) to Griffiths's *Problems of Religious Diversity*. Yoder would, I think, be attracted to Griffiths's attention to the actual practice of reading in the former book. Yoder would also be quite sympathetic with the attempt to discover how religious claims might come into conflict. I suspect, however, he would have found that William Christian's *Oppositions of Religious Doctrines: A Study in the Logic of Dialogue among Religions* (New York: Herder & Herder, 1972) isolated beliefs from practices in a way that failed to do justice to the complexity of a tradition. In a letter responding to this essay, Paul Griffiths reminds me that this criticism of isolating beliefs from practices does not mean that what people believe can be, as near as possible, stated with pre-cision and critically engaged.

39. John Howard Yoder, *For the Nations: Essays Public and Evangelical* (Grand Rapids: Eerdmans, 1997), 63.

40. Ibid., 63. Lamin Sanneh argues quite persuasively that the missionary enterprise, without necessarily intended to do so, had the effect often of strengthening indigenous cultures through a revitalization of the mother tongue made necessary for the translation of the Bible; see his *Whose Religion Is Christianity? The Gospel beyond the West* (Grand Rapids: Eerdmans, 2003), 24–25. On Yoder's grounds, Christians must always desire conversation with those that are not Christian, but we cannot assume that those to whom we wish to talk will want to talk with us. Our first task as Christians is to live faithfully to what makes us Christians in the hope that others will want to know more about what makes us tick.

41. Sanneh provides an interesting account of the new reality of world Christianity in his *Whose Religion Is Christianity?* It would be extremely interesting to know what Yoder would make of his suggestion that the world church is subject to persecution, but that the response should not take the form of state protection. But churches should, when confronted as they often are with low public confidence in state institutions, break with the tradition of religious privatization in order to have an impact in public ethics (29). I suspect Yoder might find Sanneh's understanding of public ethics problematic, but that does not mean he would reject Sanneh's suggestion about the church's public role in the world. Yoder would simply want to know more. For a fascinating study of how Catholicism provided some resistance to colonialism, see Damian Costello, *Black Elk: Colonialism and Lakota Catholicism* (Maryknoll, NY: Orbis, 2005). Costello convincingly argues that John Neihardt's famous account of Black Elk excluded Black Elk's Catholicism.

42. Yoder, "Disavowal of Constantine," 261.

43. I have no intention to enter the debates about secularization. Stout, I think, does a good job of clarifying the different accounts of the secularization thesis in *Democracy and Tradition*, 92–117.

44. Burrell's first book on Aquinas was *Analogy and Philosophical Language* (New Haven: Yale University Press, 1973), but his *Aquinas: God and Action* (London: Routledge & Kegan Paul, 1979) is regarded as his most important book on Aquinas. For the best book on the relationship between Wittgenstein and Aquinas, see Jeffrey Stout and Robert MacSwain, eds., *Grammar and Grace: Reformulations of Aquinas and Wittgenstein* (London: SCM, 2004).

45. The Catholic character of Notre Dame had everything to do with Burrell's way of understanding Judaism. Catholics understood that they often became for Protestants the Jews, that is, Catholics had been surpassed. Nowhere was this more apparent than in the scholarly guilds surrounding the study of scripture in which Second Temple Judaism became the dead priest-ridden religion that the charismatic Christianity of the New Testament replaced. Protestant biblical scholarship simply reproduced that story with their triumph in the Reformation.

46. Burrell is very sympathetic with the position developed by Jonathan Sacks in his book *The Dignity of Difference: How to Avoid the Clash of Civilizations* (London: Continuum, 2002).

47. David Burrell, *Knowing the Unknowable God: Ibn-Sina, Maimonides, Aquinas* (Notre Dame: University of Notre Dame Press, 1986).

48. David Burrell, *Friendship and Ways to Truth* (Notre Dame: University of Notre Dame, 2000), 67–86.

49. Ibid., 38.

BIBLIOGRAPHY

Burrell, David. *Analogy and Philosophical Language*. New Haven: Yale University Press, 1973.

———. *Aquinas: God and Action*. London: Routledge & Kegan Paul, 1979.

———. *Friendship and Ways to Truth*. Notre Dame: University of Notre Dame, 2000.

———. *Knowing the Unknowable God: Ibn-Sina, Maimonides, Aquinas*. Notre Dame: University of Notre Dame Press, 1986.

Cavanaugh, William. *Theopolitical Imagination: Discovering the Liturgy as a Political Act in an Age of Global Consumerism*. New York: Clark, 2002.

Christian, William. *Oppositions of Religious Doctrines: A Study in the Logic of Dialogue among Religions*. New York: Herder & Herder, 1972.

Costello, Damian. *Black Elk: Colonialism and Lakota Catholicism*. Maryknoll, NY: Orbis, 2005.

Dinoia, Joseph. *The Diversity of Religions*. Washington, DC: Catholic University Press of America, 1992.

Dulles, Avery. "The Deist Minimum." *First Things* 149 (Jan. 2005): 25–30.

Evans, Christopher. *The Kingdom Is Always But Coming: A Life of Walter Rauschenbusch*. Grand Rapids: Eerdmans, 2004.

Fish, Stanley. "Liberalism Doesn't Exist." In *There's No Such Thing as Free Speech and It's a Good Thing Too*. New York: Oxford University Press, 1994.

Fitzgerald, Timothy. *The Ideology of Religious Studies*. New York: Oxford University Press, 2000.

Griffiths, Paul. *Problems of Religious Diversity*. Oxford: Blackwell, 2001.

———. *Religious Reading: The Place of Reading in the Practice of Religion*. New York: Oxford University Press, 1999.

Hauerwas, Stanley. *Performing the Faith: Bonhoeffer and the Practice of Nonviolence*. Grand Rapids: Brazos, 2004.

———. *Unleashing the Scripture: Freeing the Bible from Captivity to America*. Nashville: Abingdon, 1993.

———. *With the Grain of the Universe: The Church's Witness and Natural Theology*. Grand Rapids: Brazos, 2001.

Knitter, Paul. *No Other Name: A Critical Survey of Christian Attitudes toward the World Religions*. Maryknoll, NY: Orbis, 2003.

Lindbeck, George. *The Nature of Doctrine: Religion and Theology in a Postliberal Age*. Philadelphia: Westminster, 1984.

Marvin, Carolyn, and David Ingle. *Blood Sacrifice and the Nation*. Cambridge: Cambridge University Press, 1999.

Milbank, John. "The End of Dialogue." In *Christian Uniqueness Reconsidered: The Myth of a Pluralistic Theology of Religions*. Edited by Gavin D'Costa. Maryknoll, NY: Orbis, 1990.

Niebuhr, Reinhold. *Love and Justice*. Edited by D. B. Robinson. New York: World, 1967.

Ogletree, Tom. *The World Calling: The Church's Witness in Politics and Society*. Louisville: Westminster John Knox, 2004.

Sacks, Jonathan. *The Dignity of Difference: How to Avoid the Clash of Civilizations*. London: Continuum, 2002.

Sanneh, Lamin. *Whose Religion Is Christianity? The Gospel beyond the West*. Grand Rapids: Eerdmans, 2003.

Smith, Christian. *Moral, Believing Animals: Human Personhood and Culture*. New York: Oxford University Press, 2003.

Stout, Jeffrey. *Democracy and Tradition*. Princeton: Princeton University Press, 2004.

Stout, Jeffrey, and Robert MacSwain, eds. *Grammar and Grace: Reformulations of Aquinas and Wittgenstein*. London: SCM, 2004.

Sumner, George. *The First and the Last: The Claim of Jesus Christ and the Claims of Other Religious Traditions*. Grand Rapids: Eerdmans, 2004.

Surin, Kenneth. "A 'Politics of Speech': Religious Pluralism in the Age of the McDonald Hamburger." In *Christian Uniqueness Reconsidered: The Myth of a Pluralistic Theology of Religions*. Maryknoll, NY: Orbis, 1990.

Turner, Denys. *Faith, Reason, and the Existence of God*. Cambridge: Cambridge University Press, 2004.

West, Cornel. *Democracy Matters: Winning the Fight against Imperialism*. New York: Penguin, 2004.

Yoder, John Howard. "The Disavowal of Constantine: An Alternative Perspective on Interfaith Dialogue." In *The Royal Priesthood: Essays Ecclesiological and Ecumenical*. Edited by Michael Cartwright. Grand Rapids: Eerdmans, 1994.

———. *For the Nations: Essays Public and Evangelical*. Grand Rapids: Eerdmans, 1997.

———. *The Jewish-Christian Schism Revisited*. Edited by Michael Cartwright and Peter Ochs. Grand Rapids: Eerdmans, 2003.

———. *Nevertheless: The Varieties and Shortcomings of Religious Pacifism*. Revised edition. Scottdale, PA: Herald, 1992.

———. *Preface to Theology*. Grand Rapids: Brazos, 2002.

———. *Reinhold Niebuhr and Christian Pacifism: A Church Peace Mission Pamphlet*. Scottdale, PA: Herald, 1968.

15

Stem Cell Politics, Religious and Secular: The United States and France Compared

Thomas Banchoff

The politics of science provides a window on the new religious pluralism. The rapid pace of discovery, particularly in the life sciences,
has compelled people within and outside religious communities
to rethink old ethical questions in a new context. At the same time,
greater religious diversity in Atlantic democracies has generated a
more varied public debate about scientific and technological progress,
its promise, and its limits. The politics of human embryonic stem
cell research illustrates this dynamic.[1] The cloning of Dolly the sheep,
made public in 1997, and the successful isolation of stem cells
from human embryos, announced the following year, placed the
governance of science on the political agenda in Europe and the
United States. Over the subsequent decade citizens and politicians
of diverse religious and secular backgrounds grappled with the
same questions: When does human life truly begin and deserve
protection? And how should the moral status of the embryo
be weighed against the potential for lifesaving stem cell therapies?
A variety of national legislative and regulatory responses ensued.[2]

  The salience of religious arguments in these controversies has
raised concerns about faith-based claims driving discord and division
in democratic politics. At first glance, stem cell politics might seem
to fit squarely into a "culture wars" prism that opposes Catholic and
evangelical conservatives to a proscience and secular left. The media
and leading intellectuals often point to such a polarization. On both
sides of the Atlantic, newspapers and television typically array believers
committed to the sanctity of human life against researchers and
secular apologists committed to free inquiry and biomedical progress.
Jürgen Habermas, a leading contemporary philosopher in the rationalist
Enlightenment tradition, contrasts scientists "who attack obscurantism"

with churches who condemn "naturalism destructive of morality."[3] And Roger Pedersen, a leading stem cell researcher based in the United Kingdom, criticizes "the seductive appeal of religious fundamentalism"—a sentiment shared by many of his colleagues in the scientific community and beyond.[4]

There is something to this culture wars prism. The Roman Catholic Church remains a principled and active opponent of all embryo research, and research proponents often single out the Vatican and its allies as their main adversaries. The most striking political development of the last decade, however, has been a diversification of religious and secular voices on *both sides* of the issue. After 1997–98 Christian churches grew increasingly divided. Once-predominant views about absolute protection for embryos began to compete with an "ethic of healing," centered on hoped-for medical therapies, even within Catholic circles and in the antiabortion movement. Most Jewish and Islamic authorities, more active in the stem cell controversy than in previous embryo research debates, welcomed new research avenues, while others urged caution. There was also a diverse range of secular perspectives on the issue. While most nonreligious groups strongly supported an ambitious research agenda after 1997–98, secular arguments *against* research as a violation of human dignity or a possible precursor to genetic engineering remained prominent, especially in Germany. In the context of this religious pluralism and religious-secular interaction, cross-cutting coalitions drove diverse legislative and regulatory outcomes. Religious arguments did not generate a hopelessly polarized debate.

The United States and France represent two very divergent cases of the intersection of scientific progress, religious pluralism, and democratic politics. In both countries the 1997–98 breakthroughs gave rise to heated debates about the governance of science—what kinds of research to permit, fund, or outlaw. In the United States, President George Bush opted in August 2001 to support federal funds for research only with stem cell lines already in existence, and Congress deadlocked over therapeutic cloning—the creation of embryos to derive genetically matched stem cells for therapies—over subsequent years. In France, the bioethics law of July 2004 maintained criminal bans on therapeutic cloning and made the creation of embryos for research a criminal offense, even as it allowed research with embryos left over from in vitro fertilization (IVF) treatments under exceptional circumstances. In both countries, the politics driving these policies involved a range of arguments about science, religion, and medicine. In the United States, with its more religious political culture, a powerful Catholic-evangelical coalition opposed to all embryo research frayed under the impact of scientific breakthroughs. In France, where religion is much less prominent in the public sphere, a powerful antiresearch coalition, grounded on secular arguments, weakened over the same period. The U.S.-French comparison sheds light on shifting coalitions and changing patterns of religious-secular interaction in Atlantic democracies. It suggests the emergence of a more fluid and plural political landscape that defies any simple religious-secular opposition.

This essay proceeds in three parts. It first grapples with a methodological problem—how to describe and compare the evolution of national controversies.

While theorists have long debated the appropriateness of religious and secular arguments in the public sphere, we lack strong tools for parsing and analyzing both kinds of arguments in particular cases. A method for distinguishing religious from secular arguments, however imperfect, is necessary to compare and contrast patterns of religious-secular interaction in practice. The second section compares the evolution of embryo politics in the United States and France in the two decades before the stem cell and cloning breakthroughs. It traces the emergence of powerful religious (in the United States) and secular (in France) coalitions opposed to research. The third section shows how the promise of stem cell and cloning research undermined these coalitions and generated a more open debate marked by more diverse religious and secular voices in favor of liberal research regimes. The conclusion places the French and United States cases in their broader Atlantic and global contexts.

Religious and Secular Arguments

Normative controversy over religious language in democratic politics has deep historical roots. Against the backdrop of the European religious wars, prominent early modern and Enlightenment thinkers extolled the virtues of religious tolerance and the dangers of religious conflict in the political sphere. Since John Locke's *Letter concerning Toleration*, first published in 1689, the relationship between religious liberty and political liberty—and between religious tolerance and political stability—has been the continuous object of analysis and debate. Contemporary claims for and against religious arguments in the public sphere are outlined by Miroslav Volf and Diana Eck in this volume. Eck maintains that public policy arguments based on religion involve absolute truth claims, are therefore divisive, and should be avoided. Civic, rather than theological, discourse should dominate public policy controversy. Volf insists that religious arguments are no less valid than nonreligious ones and are protected by free speech. Banning or discouraging religious discourse in the public sphere disenfranchises religious citizens and promotes a particular worldview—a secular one. This running argument, which cuts across familiar left-right dichotomies, has spawned a growing contemporary literature.[5]

Most established work in this area explores particular empirical examples in order to buttress a normative argument about the role religion should or should not play in democratic politics. Empirical analysis of religious and secular arguments and their interaction has received much less attention. Any such analysis is extremely difficult, given the ambiguity inherent in the terms *religious* and *secular* and their shifting meanings across time and place.[6] In order to make the task more manageable, the definitions and distinctions developed here are limited to value-driven issues—public policy controversies that turn on clashing understandings of right conduct in a particular domain of state activity. The focus is on arguments that substantiate ethical claims about public policy projects, different answers to the question: Why is this particular pattern of state action the morally right one?[7]

Prominent value-driven issues in Atlantic democracies have included abortion, capital punishment, euthanasia, and same-sex marriage—controversies that raise basic questions about the ethical obligations that bind human beings. None of these issues is solely about values. Each implicates politicians and pressure groups working to maximize power and material resources. But in contrast to major welfare state issues, where economic interests dominate, or to foreign policy, where security is often paramount, value-driven issues center on clashing ethical claims. This creates an opening for arguments grounded in particular religious traditions that have historically addressed questions of life and death; sexuality, family, and community; and suffering, mercy, and justice. In the context of Atlantic democracies, the most influential traditions are Christianity, Judaism, and—increasingly—Islam.

Stem cell research is not exclusively a value-driven issue. It features interest politics involving scientific, biotechnology, and patient advocacy groups, as well as churches and prolife organizations. And it often involves instrumental as well as ethical reasoning—considerations of the best way to distribute national resources, for example, or to be successful in international scientific competition. But one ethical quandary dominates political controversy on both sides of the Atlantic—whether it is right or wrong to create or destroy embryos to further biomedical research with lifesaving potential. Science cannot resolve the issue. The life sciences illuminate the development of human life from conception through implantation and birth, but cannot tell us when it deserves protection and under what circumstances. Moral ambiguity inevitably gives rise to disagreement. Two ethical claims clash in the public sphere: the protection of the embryo and solidarity with the sick. Both claims, the U.S. and French cases will illustrate, can be argued in either a religious or a secular idiom. And dominant patterns of argumentation can shift over time.

In order to chart the interaction of religious and secular arguments in particular cases one must be able to distinguish between them. To count as religious, a policy argument put forward in a political struggle must meet two conditions. First, it must make some reference, direct or indirect, to a particular religious tradition—to beliefs, practices, or institutions linked back to divine revelation or claims about the transcendent. Second, it must be articulated from within a particular religious tradition, by those who identify with that tradition or by authoritative organizations that represent it. Under this two-part definition, the religious person or group that does not use religious language is not making a religious argument. In the context of the abortion debate, for example, to assert a "right to life" is not to make a religious claim. To invoke the commandment "thou shalt not kill" is. It also follows from the definition that someone outside a tradition who invokes religious language is not making a religious argument. The atheist who upholds the "sacred rights of man" is not referring back to a religious tradition. Nor is the secular environmentalist who inadvertently refers to nature as "creation." To count as a religious argument, then, both the speaker and the speech must link back to a religious tradition.

It might be objected that when someone affiliated with a religious tradition invokes concepts such as the "sacred rights of man" or "creation," he or she is not necessarily making a religious argument. For one can try to prove the existence of God or of sacred rights by reason alone. Efforts to ground religious truths in reason have a long history, including the work of Thomas Aquinas and Immanuel Kant. The Catholic natural law tradition remains a resource for those who would ground ideas, such as the sanctity of heterosexual marriage or the immorality of divorce, in rational reflection on the natural order, rather than on divine revelation or church tradition. Such arguments are not explicity religious. But when they reference religious concepts—"sacred," or "God," for example—and are articulated from within a religious tradition, they have an implicit religious dimension. The position of a speaker within a given community tends to lend such arguments greater plausibility for its members than for those outside it.

It might be further objected that when an avowedly secular speaker eschews religious language, he or she may nevertheless be making a quasireligious argument. Claims about the equality of all human beings or the existence of inviolable human rights, for example, are notoriously difficult to ground in rational reflection or empirical observation. They are often simply asserted as foundational or as axiomatic. Still, such arguments, however they might be indebted to deeper historical and religious legacies, should not be considered religious arguments. To point out that secular claims cannot always be grounded in reason and evidence alone, or that they unwittingly incorporate religious residues, is not to demonstrate that they actually have a religious or quasireligious foundation. It is only to show that from a secular, philosophical perspective, there is still work to be done. By the definition put forward here, to be considered religious, an argument must refer back to a *specific* religious tradition. It is not enough for it to defy clear rational or empirical demonstration.

Examples drawn from stem cell politics, elaborated elsewhere in this essay, illustrate some of the definitional complexities. The claim that the embryo is a person or a potential person deserving of legal protection is not, on the face of it, either a religious or a secular argument. From a secular perspective, one can argue that a person is, by definition, any biological organism with a human genome. Or one can define full humanity in terms of sentience or the capacity for autonomous moral action. From a religious perspective, one might equate personhood with the presence of a God-given spirit or soul, but discern that presence at different points in time: at fertilization or implantation, for example, or at 40 or 120 days. In order to determine whether an argument is secular or religious—or a mixture of both—one must examine who articulates it and how. For example, the claim that the early embryo is a "gift from God," articulated by a believer, is a religious argument. Claims about full humanity that rest on concepts such as biological individuality, sentience, or the capacity for autonomous action, and do not reference religious beliefs, practices, or institutions, are secular arguments.

In any given controversy, it may be difficult to distinguish between religious and secular arguments. Ambiguities abound. The same person or organization may combine both kinds of arguments for full effect, making it hard to keep them conceptually distinct. Or the nature of the audience may further muddy analytical distinctions. A secular politician appearing before a religious audience may use religious language. Similarly, a religious politician within a secular public sphere may eschew the use of any religious idiom. By the definitions put forward here, neither one would be making a religious argument—a claim articulated from within a tradition that includes religious language. But an audience might nevertheless perceive them to be invoking religion, directly or indirectly. Whatever the limitations of the definitional distinctions proposed here, they do provide one way to parse religious and secular arguments and to trace their interaction over time in particular cases. The next two sections deploy these distinctions to show how scientific break-throughs spawned a diversity of religious and secular arguments and new patterns of religious-secular interaction in the United States and France.

The Religious and the Secular in Early Embryo Politics

Embryo research moved only slowly onto the political agenda in Atlantic de-mocracies. In 1968, thirty years before the stem cell breakthrough, the British team of Robert Edwards and Patrick Steptoe fertilized the first human embryo in a laboratory. That feat raised issues for the first time that would later become familiar, including the moral status of the embryo and the permissibility of research destructive of embryos designed to advance human health (at the time, problems of infertility were at the center of discussion). Interestingly, political controversy through the 1970s was muted. Regulators wrestled with the safety of IVF procedures—only finally demonstrated with the birth of the first "test-tube baby," Louise Brown, in 1978—while the media tended to focus on the specter of a Brave New World of genetic manipulation. Only as IVF became an established procedure in the early 1980s and freezing technologies allowed for the stockpiling of surplus embryos did research and its regulation move onto the political agenda in the leading Atlantic scientific powers, first in the United States and Britain and then in Germany and France.

Religious Opposition to Embryo Research in the United States

The strong religious inflection of U.S. embryo politics can be traced back to the 1980s, well before the breakthroughs in stem cell research. During the 1970s, churches and religious groups showed limited interest in the topic. In the wake of the first successful laboratory creation of an embryo in 1968 and the birth of Louise Brown a decade later, the Roman Catholic Church centered its criti-cisms on IVF as an artificial reproductive technology. In keeping with the logic of the 1968 encyclical *Humanae Vitae*—a blanket condemnation of all artificial contraception—the Vatican criticized fertilization in the laboratory as an illicit intervention in the natural procreative process. The destruction of embryos in the research necessary to develop IVF techniques received less attention. Only in the early 1980s, when IVF had proven a successful and popular way to treat infertility and the fate of frozen embryos had moved onto the agenda, did the church and its allies in the antiabortion movement take up the issue. The National Conference of Catholic Bishops forcefully articulated the idea of a "culture of life" from fertilization until death—a major theme of John Paul II's papacy from the mid-1980s onward.[8]

In opposing both embryo research and abortion, church leaders advanced both secular and religious arguments. A 1974 statement on abortion had argued from secular, scientific premises that from "the time that the ovum is fertilized, a new life is begun which is neither that of the father nor of the mother; it is rather the life of a new human being with his own growth." The 1987 Vatican instruction Donum Vitae, the first authoritative church response to IVF technology, made a similar argument about the continuity of human biological development. From the moment of fertilization, it asserted, the "biological identity of a new human individual is already constituted." Secular arguments alone, the document recognized, could not move from the reality of the human organism formed with fertilization to the existence of personhood and a right to life. As Donum Vitae put it, "No experimental datum can be in itself sufficient to bring us to the recognition of a spiritual soul." Science provided evidence of personhood—"how could a human individual not be a human person?"—but no conclusive demonstration. In the final analysis, the embryo, like the fetus, was to be treated as a person because human life is a gift from God and therefore inviolable. Donum Vitae is Latin for "the gift of life." God is the giver. The argument against embryo research ultimately rested on religious and not just secular foundations.[9]

By the late 1970s a range of secular arguments in favor of embryo research had emerged within the still relatively new bioethics profession. Supporters of research argued that the embryo at fertilization was not fully human and therefore did not deserve strong legal protections. Two main arguments were advanced in support of this proposition. Research proponents claimed, first, that before the two-week stage when implantation is complete, the embryo has the capacity to twin and therefore cannot be considered a human individual; and, second, that the early embryo has no nervous system and therefore lacks the physical capacity to feel pain. These arguments, based on the criteria of developmental individuality and sentience, were already well established when the first U.S. committee devoted to the problem of federal funding for embryo research, the Department of Health, Education, and Welfare's Ethics Advisory Board, convened in 1978–79. In its final report the board agreed "that the human embryo is entitled to profound respect." At the same time, however, it insisted that "this respect does not necessarily encompass the full legal and moral rights attributed to persons." Embryo research to perfect IVF techniques was deemed permissible in principle. This remained the dominant view among bioethicists, including influential Catholic moral theologians who dissented from the Vatican teaching, sometimes invoking Thomas Aquinas, who had followed Aristotle in dating ensoulment forty days or more after conception.[10]

For more than a decade no administration acted on the board's recommendations, and the embryo research issue had little salience. Sharp opposition between religious and secular arguments fully emerged only in the mid-1990s. On taking office in 1993, President Bill Clinton moved to enable federal research support by forming the Human Embryo Research Panel to look into the issue. In summer 1994 the panel backed research with surplus IVF embryos and, under certain circumstances, the creation of embryos expressly for research purposes. A political firestorm ensued. The National Conference of Catholic Bishops and their allies in the antiabortion movement campaigned vigorously against the Human Embryo Research Panel report. After the Republican sweep in the November 1994 elections, Clinton publicly rejected the panel's recommendations on embryo creation and ignored the rest of the report. The new congressional majority went further in July 1995, legislating a complete ban on federal funds for research involving the destruction of embryos. Research could proceed only in the unregulated private sector or with state funds.

The reasoning on both sides during the 1994–95 controversy evidenced a polarization of secular and religious perspectives. The Human Embryo Research Panel, made up of prominent scientists and bioethicists, took an avowedly utilitarian and pragmatic stance. It "considered the wide range of views held by American citizens on the moral status of preimplantation embryos." But rather than "decide which of these views is correct," it proposed guidelines "that would be acceptable public policy based on reasoning that takes account of generally held public views regarding the beginning and development of human life." Working from this pragmatic and secular premise, the report concluded that "although the preimplantation embryo warrants serious moral consideration as a developing form of human life, it does not have the same moral status as an infant or child." Research under ethical and scientific oversight was permissible. While the panel considered its work "independent of a particular religious or philosophical perspective," it is worth noting that its nineteen members included no principled opponents of embryo research.[11]

In the public hearings that led up to the report and recommendations, Richard Doerflinger, a spokesman for the National Conference of Catholic Bishops, articulated a range of objections to embryo experimentation. Human life, he insisted, was a continuum that began with conception, deserved fundamental protections, and should not be instrumentalized for other goals, however noble: "The human embryo is a living, thriving, developing member of the human species, deserving human respect." While he took pains to argue from philosophical, natural law premises, Doerflinger ultimately grounded his claims within the tradition of the church. His mission, he told panel members, was "to express the Catholic Bishops' concern that government decisions on human experimentation be guided by a clear commitment to the dignity of human life at every stage of existence."[12] Antiabortion groups, such as the National Right to Life Committee, made the sanctity of life from conception the centerpiece of their drive against the panel's recommendations.

There was not a united religious front against embryo research in the United States in the mid-1990s. Prominent Catholic bioethicists, including one member of the Human Embryo Research Panel, continued to dissent from Vatican teaching on the moral status of the early embryo. Jewish bioethicists invoked sacred traditions about the late onset of the full humanity of the embryo/fetus, in support of a more liberal research regime. The Islamic tradition, much less visible in the U.S. debate at the time, was also generally supportive of embryo research in the service of biomedical progress. At the level of politics, however, these more liberal views, articulated within and across religious traditions, had little impact. A powerful conservative front against research persisted through the mid-1990s. Arguments about the sanctity of life united a Catholic, evangelical, and antiabortion coalition opposed to embryo research—one powerful enough to get Clinton to distance himself from the panel's recommendations and to urge Congress to legislate an explicit ban on federal funding for embryo research.[13]

Secular Opposition to Embryo Research in France

The French debate on embryo research through the 1980s was far less heated. French scientists entered the IVF field much later than their counterparts in the United Kingdom and the United States. The first French child by IVF was born only in 1982, and biomedical research with surplus embryos began only slowly thereafter. A further, critical contrast with the United States was the absence of a divisive abortion controversy and the political weakness of the Catholic Church. Within two years of the 1973 Roe v. Wade court decision in the United States, the French Parliament passed liberal abortion legislation that effectively ended the national abortion debate. While most French citizens identified nominally with the Catholic tradition, church attendance fell steadily over the postwar years, and the hierarchy had little political clout. When embryo research moved onto the political agenda in the early 1990s, France's overwhelmingly secular political culture featured little in the way of religious arguments. Interestingly, however, in contrast to the United States, the dominant secular arguments were directed mainly *against* embryo research.

The French debate emerged out of the National Ethics Committee (CCNE), formed by presidential decree in 1983 in the wake of the first IVF birth in the country. While it included one representative from each of the "spiritual families"—then Catholic, Protestant, and Jewish—the CCNE was dominated by scientists and philosophers of a secular bent. In a series of opinions from 1984 onward, the CCNE took up the embryo research issue in a variety of contexts. Ultimately, the problem of bioethics regulation—of moving "From Ethics to Law," as the title of a 1988 government report put it—was for the Parliament to decide. But the CCNE shaped the terms of the debate through philosophical reflection, designed to determine not just what was acceptable or useful to society, but also what was morally due to the embryo.[14]

From the outset, the CCNE adopted a restrictive approach to embryo research, rooted in the Kantian injunction against the instrumentalization of human life. As the committee put it in late 1986 in its first major opinion on the topic: "The foundation of and due respect for the embryo can be based on the rule of reason." It asserted that embryos were "potential human persons" and argued that "such consideration should take precedence over the advantages that might result from using human beings as though they were objects, even though it represents potential for the improvement of medical knowledge and furtherment of science." While the prohibition against the reification and exploitation of human life was central to CCNE thinking, the report suggested that "ethical requirements cannot always be formulated in 'absolute' dogmatic terms." Exceptions to a general prohibition might be made for surplus IVF embryos condemned to perish, "made tolerable by the ethical principle of the lesser of two evils."[15]

This basic secular and philosophical stance shaped the terms of political controversy around the governance of embryo research that began in 1988 and stretched into the new decade. The national bioethics law, finally passed in 1994, was a comprehensive measure that addressed issues of surrogacy, tissue donation, and human subject protections. It included criminal penalties for any research involving the destruction of human embryos, whether in the public or private sector. Exceptions were to be allowed only for research that might benefit the embryo itself—a class of experiments that was practically nonexistent.

In sharp contrast to the United States, religious opposition to embryo research played almost no explicit role in the French national debate. The Cardinal of Paris, Jean-Marie Lustiger, called surplus embryos in French IVF clinics a "phantom population" that should not be sacrificed for science.[16] But within France's secular political culture, leading conservatives who were also practicing Catholics, including Health Minister Jean-François Mattei, eschewed religious arguments. In one of the key debates, Mattei reminded the National Assembly that "we are in a *laïciste* and pluralist republic." In keeping with the CCNE's emphasis on the embryo's capacity to develop into a human person, he called it a "potential patient" deserving of protection. His arguments were consonant with the Catholic tradition—still a point of orientation for many French citizens, however unobservant—but he took pains to couch them more broadly. In the context of the bioethics law as a whole, he noted a "shared recognition" by both the religious and nonreligious of the "sacred character of man in his dignity."[17]

Socialist leaders generally favored a somewhat less restrictive regime—research with surplus embryos under some circumstances. But they, too, did not break with the cautious philosophical consensus within the CCNE. Most rejected the creation of embryos for research as an illicit instrumentalization of human life and joined the conservative leaders in condemning the British legalization of the practice in 1990 as a dangerous excess of "utilitarianism." There were isolated efforts in the proresearch camp to cast the French controversy as reason battling against religion. Socialist Jean-Yves Le Déaut, for example, warned against the "Galileo syndrome" and the specter of "integrist" abuses, a reference to previous clashes within France over the separation of church and state. But leading Catholic politicians, including Mattei, did not play into their hands. Even the most outspoken—antiabortion campaigner Christine Boutin—invoked religious arguments only on the margin. In a two-hour speech, she referred to the embryo as "a miracle" and a "precious gift," but centered her defense of its rights on "our humanist tradition." She referred to the church only once, attacking those who "would like to place me just in the category of Catholics" in order to dismiss her arguments.[18]

The pattern of embryo politics in the United States and France through the mid-1990s was very different, even if the outcome was a similarly restrictive national research regime. The U.S. controversy was marked by sharp religious-secular polarization, with the Catholic Church and its Protestant allies shaping the substance of national policy. In France, a general consensus in favor of a restrictive approach characterized a debate dominated by secular arguments in which the church and its allies played a marginal role. In the years following 1997–98, these patterns of polarization and consensus would give way to a more diverse religious and secular landscape.

Stem Cell Politics: New Religious and Secular Arguments

The stem cell breakthrough of November 1998 changed the dynamics of em-bryo politics in three related ways. First, it raised the prospect of a new era of regenerative medicine, in which tissues grown from embryo cells might treat a variety of diseases. Proresearch arguments that had centered on the implica-tions of research for improving fertility could now invoke a wider range of potential benefits for the ill. Second, the breakthrough cast the issue of embryo creation in a new light. The possibility of therapeutic cloning to derive ge-netically matched cells and tissues increased support for embryo creation for research purposes. The *Washington Post*, for example, came out in opposition to a congressional ban on therapeutic cloning, reversing its earlier position that "the creation of human embryos specifically for research that will destroy them is unconscionable."[19] Third, the promise of stem cell research moved the issue up the political agenda and made it the object of greater media attention. Against this backdrop, a wider variety of religious and secular arguments in favor of embryo research found articulation in the United States, France, and elsewhere.

A Pluralism of Religious Arguments in the United States

The most striking change in the U.S. debate was a proliferation of different kinds of religious arguments on both sides of the controversy. Arguments about the sanctity of life had held together a powerful coalition opposed to federal support for embryo research. Now key segments of that coalition, including some leading prolife senators, embraced the potential of stem cell research. They not only extolled its biomedical promise, but invoked religious reasons—values of compassion and healing in the Christian tradition. The main lines of the U.S. controversy still revolved around religious injunctions of the sanctity of early human life, on the one hand, and utilitarian and pragmatic arguments about the benefits of research, on the other. Charges and countercharges about religious interference and scientific hubris persisted. But the interplay of secular and religious arguments was more complex and less polarized than it had been a decade earlier.

A first skirmish, little noticed at the time, took place in Congress in early 1998 around the therapeutic cloning issue. A year after news of Dolly, a pro-research majority in the Senate successfully blocked an effort to legislate a complete cloning ban. Scientific and industrial groups rallied around the future prospect of the "cloning of human cells" for research, while the prolife lobby decried plans to "clone and kill" embryos. But alongside the polarized terms of the debate were first signs of changes in the conservative Christian camp. Senators long active in the antiabortion movement, including Connie Mack, Strom Thurmond, and Orrin Hatch, called for careful deliberation before any complete cloning ban. "While we can all agree that to replicate a human being is immoral," Thurmond argued, "we need to investigate this issue more thoroughly so that we do not deny our citizens and our loved ones of any possible life saving research." In calling for caution, Hatch cited possible benefits of research and noted the imperative to "advance medical science in a manner that to the greatest extent possible respects the religious and ethical concerns of a diverse population."[20]

The diversification of religious reasoning only fully materialized in the years after the November 1998 stem cell breakthrough. The issue had limited salience during the balance of Clinton's presidency. Controversy within expert circles centered on whether the federal government could fund stem cell research, as long as it did not support the destruction of embryos to derive the cells, but the media paid limited attention. The issue played almost no role in the 2000 election, although George W. Bush did align himself broadly with prolife forces. Catholic and evangelical leaders expected Bush to follow up on his campaign promise to oppose federal funding for any research involving the destruction of embryos. But no immediate policy was forthcoming. As the issue gained in salience and public opinion remained sharply divided, a policy struggle emerged within the administration during the first half of 2001. Tommy Thompson, the new head of the Department of Health and Human Services and a Catholic, had supported stem cell research as governor of Wisconsin. Karl Rove, Bush's top political advisor, was mindful of an electoral base that included many conservative Catholics. According to media reports at the time, Bush was thinking hard about the issue himself.[21]

In the run-up to Bush's stem cell decision in August 2001, religious arguments in favor of research were articulated more forcefully than ever before. A synod of the United Church of Christ asserted, for example, that "Jesus set an example" by his ministry of healing and caring for the sick and disabled.[22] The ethic of healing also dominated Jewish and Islamic perspectives. Orthodox Jewish leaders argued in a letter to Bush in April 2001 that "our Torah tradition places great value upon human life; we are taught in the opening chapters of Genesis that each human was created in God's very image." The authors further insisted that "the potential to save and heal human lives is an integral part of valuing human life from the traditional Jewish perspective." A year earlier, a leading Islamic scholar testified before the National Bioethics Advisory Commission that whatever their specific approaches to Islamic law, Muslims considered research as "an act of faith in the ultimate will of God as the Giver of all life, as long as such an intervention is undertaken with the purpose of improving human health."[23]

Politically most consequential were new divisions in the coalition of Catholic and Protestant leaders opposed to all embryo research. During Bush's audience at the Vatican in July 2001, John Paul II exhorted Bush to protect life "from conception until natural death." In the meantime, however, several key Christian conservatives in Congress with antiabortion credentials had opted for an ethic of healing. Hatch and another Mormon senator, Gordon Smith, were the most important. Smith situated the debate "at the confluence between science and theology" and insisted one should "err on the side of the broadest interpretations to do the greatest amounts of good." Hatch publicly urged Bush and Thompson to allow federal funding of stem cell research. After "countless hours of study, reflection, and prayer," he recalled, "eventually I determined that being prolife means helping the living." Both could draw on the Mormon tradition that preexisting souls enter the body only after implantation in the womb, although they did not articulate such religious reasoning in their public statements. Doerflinger commented that he did not think that Hatch should make "the rest of us" fund research based on his beliefs— somewhat ironic given his own position within a religious tradition.[24]

Facing conflicting political pressures on an ethically sensitive issue, Bush opted for a compromise that would allow federal funding of research with existing stem cell lines. The decision, he told a large television audience, was the product of consultations, reflection, and prayer. In his speech, Bush noted that the issue was "debated within the church, with people of different faiths, even many of the same faith coming to different conclusions." He expressed his belief that "human life is a sacred gift from our Creator" and worried about "a culture that devalues life." At the same time, he did not endorse the view that the embryo was already a person deserving full protection. Each embryo, he said, had "the unique *genetic potential* of an individual human being" (emphasis added). Bush highlighted the capacity of stem cell research to reduce suffering and produce hoped-for cures, even as he insisted that his policy would not destroy any more embryos. He closed his address: "I have made this decision with great care, and I pray it is the right one."[25]

In 2002–4, as the therapeutic cloning issue moved center stage, Bush drew a line at the creation of embryos for research. "Life is a creation, not a commodity," he told supporters at the White House in April 2002. (Before evangelical audiences, he would refer more explicitly to life as a "creation of God.")[26] Bush's support for a complete cloning ban—a measure that passed the House in July 2001 and repeatedly failed in the Senate—and religious rhetoric earned him the ire of leading scientists. "The president unfortunately was brought up by parents who taught him to believe in God," James Watson, codiscoverer of the structure of DNA, quipped: "he's handicapped." Harvard's Douglas Melton asked, "Has the White House adopted the Catholic Church's position that life begins at fertilization?"[27] This view of Bush's stance as an illicit intrusion of religion into politics also surfaced on Capitol Hill. "Our job in Congress is not to pick the most restrictive religious view of science and then impose that view upon Federal law," Zoe Lofgren of California proclaimed: "we live in a Democracy, not a Theocracy."[28]

While there was some evidence of religious/secular polarization, it did not dominate the national politics of the issue. Here the 2004 presidential campaign was emblematic. Bush repeatedly invoked the Catholic notion of a "culture of life," but also expressed sympathy with those, religious or not, who viewed stem cells as a vehicle for hoped-for cures. His opponent, John Kerry, a prochoice Catholic, sought to make support for stem cell research and therapeutic cloning one of the themes of his presidential bid. But he, too, did not cast the issue as one of religion versus science—at least not explicitly. His first line of argument was to acknowledge "ethical issues," but insist that "people of goodwill and good sense can resolve them." As in the past, he told a radio audience in early 2004 that the United States should lead the "world in great medical discoveries, with our breakthroughs and our beliefs going hand-in-hand." At one point Kerry did suggest an opposition between religion and scientific progress; on the third anniversary of Bush's stem cell decision, in August 2004, he insisted that "here in America, we don't sacrifice science for ideology."[29] At the same time, however, while at odds with the Catholic Church for his stance on abortion, Kerry suggested a religious basis for his support for stem cell research. In his second televised debate with Bush, he insisted that it was "respecting life to reach for that cure."[30]

The evolution of the stem cell issue after 1998 illustrates the fragmentation of religious reasoning in the U.S. controversy. The polarized frame of the mid-1990s—Catholic and prolife forces arrayed against the secular proponents of science—gave way to a more nuanced debate. Under the impact of new scientific discoveries, key Christian conservatives drew on religious beliefs to adopt a less restrictive view of embryo research. The existence of religious arguments on both sides of the issue made it easier for Bush to endorse research under some circumstances, even as he held fast to his conception of life as a "creation of God," not to be tampered with in the laboratory. For their part, Kerry and other leading administration critics cast their views as proscience, not against any particular religious tradition, and invoked the promise of research as an alternative way to respect the value of life by mitigating human suffering. Under the impact of scientific discoveries, the U.S. debate saw a wider array of religious perspectives on stem cell research.

The Fragmentation of Secular Antiresearch Forces in France

In France, it was secular, not religious, opposition to embryo research that fragmented over the same period. As in the United States, a greater plurality of views had begun to emerge even before the stem cell breakthrough. In May 1997 the

CCNE presciently explored the future potential of stem cell research and suggested that it might call for less restrictive regulations on work with surplus IVF embryos. Mattei confessed that he was "shocked" by such suggestions. "I believe that one cannot consider the embryo as laboratory material," he told a scientific conference in November 1997; "I prefer their destruction, which at least preserves their dignity and avoids their instrumentalization." While strident, Mattei continued to eschew religious arguments in articulating his position. Unlike in the United States, he noted, the debate in France "leaves the strictly religious domain and enters that of human dignity."[31] He and other supporters of the 1994 bioethics law could take heart in the continued consensus against embryo creation. In keeping with this broad consensus, Axel Kahn, a leading geneticist and CCNE member who favored some work with surplus IVF embryos, flatly rejected the possibility of therapeutic cloning. "The fabrication of an embryo in order to use its cells for therapeutic goals," he wrote in the leading scientific weekly *Nature* in March 1997, violated the maxim that human life "should never be thought of only as a means, but always also as an end."[32]

The November 1998 stem cell breakthrough began to erode this Kantian position within the CCNE—and among party leaders. In the run-up to first parliamentary debates on scheduled revisions of the 1994 law, the committee revisited the embryo issue in detail for the first time in over a decade. Its January 2001 report reiterated the earlier characterization of the embryo as "a potential human person deserving of respect by all." But it now took a more positive stance on the possibility of research with surplus embryos, casting it as morally justifiable in its own right, rather than a lesser of two evils. In a controversial phrase, the CCNE supported research on surplus embryos, as an example of "virtual solidarity between parents, a life that is not to be, and those who might benefit from research." The extension of the value of solidarity to the embryo, however peculiar, provided a way to undercut the Kantian objection to research as instrumentalization. The embryos were deemed to be laying down their lives for the good of others and the Republic. The report also included an indirect assault on religious and secular thinkers who endorsed the inviolability of the embryo as a form of human life. One should not, it asserted, "sacralize it as a fully [*en puissance*] human person."[33]

Impressed by the potential of stem cell research, a narrow majority of the CCNE came out in favor of therapeutic cloning under certain circumstances in the same January 2001 report. In this they echoed then socialist Prime Minister Lionel Jospin, who had endorsed the practice in a November 2000 speech. Jospin referred to stem cells as "cells of hope" and argued that France should hold open the option of creating them through "the transfer of somatic cells." (He avoided the term *cloning*, insisting that it should be used only in the context of reproductive, not therapeutic goals.) The speech developed a utilitarian rationale for stem cell research and criticized deontological approaches, rooted in either philosophical reflection or religious tradition. Jospin asked: "Should reasons derived from philosophical, spiritual, or religious principles lead us to deprive society and the sick of the possibility of therapeutic advances?" This opposition between science, on the one hand, and philosophy

316 DEMOCRATIC RESPONSES TO THE NEW RELIGIOUS PLURALISM

and religion, on the other, marked a new twist in the French debate. Religion was emerging prominently as a theme within what had been an almost exclusively secular public controversy.

Jospin's effort to change the terms of the debate in this direction failed—at least in the short term. In February 2001 Conservative President Jacques Chirac rebuked his prime minister's support for therapeutic cloning. In a major address, he noted that new discoveries gave a "new significance to all questions touching on the meaning of life, man's place in nature, and human dignity." Though a Catholic, Chirac did not invoke religious arguments. He also did not openly oppose research with surplus embryos under certain controlled conditions. But he did distinguish his appeal for a "democratic conscience" to govern science and underscored that "technology has erupted into the sanctuary of life"—a turn of phrase with religious undertones. His opposition to therapeutic cloning, articulated in the dominant Kantian idiom, clashed sharply with Jospin's own philosophical frame. "This debate," he insisted, "cannot let a utilitarian conception of the human being prevail that would challenge even the foundations of our civilization and threaten human dignity."[34]

Religious actors played a more prominent role in the French debate than they had during the previous decade—though nothing akin to their centrality in the United States. On the conservative side, the French bishops, in June 2001, issued a communiqué on stem cells "which certain people refer to as 'cells of hope.'" Their statement was more theological than similar interventions by their American counterparts—it underscored the sanctity of creation by asserting that "God gave the earth to men to cultivate and protect it," even as they worked within the familiar French humanist idiom. "Some practices honor humanity, others injure it," they warned, referring to the embryo as a "weak link in the human chain."[35] Protestant, Jewish, and Muslim leaders, who had played a completely marginal role in earlier controversies, now participated more openly in the debate—generally in favor of a more liberal research regime.

Ultimately, the judicial branch of the state put a temporary end to the cloning discussion. In its June 2001 report on the planned revision of the bioethics law, the Council of State held that the creation of embryos for research would violate the "human dignity" provisions of the 1946 constitution, instituted after the Nazi occupation and formalized as part of French constitutional law in 1994. On publication of the council report, Jospin dropped the therapeutic cloning project.[36] By this point, however, the French debate had been broadened to include an increasing range of secular and religious voices in favor of some liberalization of embryo research.

This became evident after Jospin lost to Chirac in the 2002 presidential elections and the socialists lost their majority in the National Assembly. Mattei again took over as Health Minister and modified his position and that of the government. Under pressure from the scientific community and the Ministry of Research, he abandoned his total opposition to embryo research. "I have long hoped that we would be able to dispense with stem cell research," he told the National Assembly in December 2003, but "the realities of research imperatives, I have been persuaded, makes it necessary to authorize under certain conditions." In good philosophical fashion, Mattei recognized his own "bouleversement ontologique"—an ontological reversal. But he also staked out a harder line than Jospin's. Not only did the bioethics law he shepherded through Parliament criminalize all cloning. It also authorized research on IVF embryos for only a provisional five-year period.[37]

The parliamentary debates that preceded the 2004 legislation were more divisive than they had been a decade earlier. The fragmenting secular consensus was particularly evident in the address by former socialist Minister of Health Roger-Gérard Schwartzenberg. Like most of his party, he advocated both stem cell research and therapeutic cloning, because "the imperative of solidarity" necessitated doing everything possible "to heal the sick and reduce their suffering." He then asserted a sharp opposition between religious and secular lines of argument. "In a *laiciste* Republic," he asked, "can the legislator privilege one philosophical or religious conception over another, at the risk of imposing a valuable but limited perspective on society as a whole?"[38] Given the long predominance of Kantian thinking in the French debate and Schwartzenberg's own utilitarian perspective, the critique of "philosophical" perspectives may appear curious. But the church, however defanged in the French debate, was apparently the intended target. "One cannot confuse an article of faith with an article of law," he insisted.

French stem cell politics saw the fragmentation of a far-reaching secular consensus in favor of embryo protection and the emergence of a utilitarian frame alongside the dominant Kantian one. Some religious reasons animated the debate. Jewish, Islamic, and Protestant leaders weighed in more forcefully than they had a decade earlier, mainly in favor of looser restrictions on embryo and stem cell research. With the exception of the extremist Jean-Marie Le Pen, who articulated a conservative Catholic position, opponents of stem cell research continued to steer clear of religious reasons. Christine Boutin, for example, by now a member of the Pontifical Council for the Family, still made no major reference to church teaching in her legislative interventions. Despite the best efforts of research proponents to cast the French debate in terms of a secular/religious opposition, it was the fragmentation of secular reasoning that was the most striking aspect of the controversy. Some outside religious traditions continued to invoke secular arguments against embryo research, communist philosopher and CCNE member Lucien Sève, for example, for whom "the embryo incontestably represents the potentiality of a human being."[39] But the far-reaching consensus of a decade earlier had fragmented and given way to a greater diversity of religious and secular perspectives and a political constellation more supportive of embryo and stem cell research.

Conclusion

Stem cell politics are often viewed as an arena of religious-secular confrontation. In the United States, France, and elsewhere, one can find evidence to support such a view: churches that invoke the sanctity of life in opposition to all research are arrayed against the secular proponents of maximum scientific freedom in pursuit of biomedical breakthroughs. Over the past decade, however, the debate has grown more complex as religious arguments in favor of research have emerged in the United States and as secular arguments opposed to research have lost ground in France. The evolution of the U.S. debate shows how predominantly Catholic and evangelical views, centered on the sanctity of life from fertilization, fragmented under the impact of biomedical advances and the idea of an ethic of healing—a concept already embedded within the Jewish and Islamic traditions. In the French debate, by contrast, dominant secular arguments that cast embryo research as a violation of human dignity weakened in the face of scientific advances and biomedical hopes, even as anxiety about the influence of the Catholic Church—probably more imagined than real—introduced a new note of polarization into the controversy. Religious arguments evolved in response to scientific developments and changing political conditions. They complicated, but did not derail, democratic efforts to find regulatory solutions.

The French and U.S. stem cell debates are part of a larger running controversy that extends to other Atlantic democracies. Political constellations in other major scientific powers have varied. In the United Kingdom, for example, large political majorities and most of the Anglican hierarchy supported a liberal research regime that included provisions for therapeutic cloning in 2001. In Germany that same year, a cross-party consensus supported by both Catholic and Protestant leaders endorsed a regime stricter than those in either France or the United States. In these cases and others, religious and secular arguments intersect around the same ethical quandary—how to balance the protection of embryonic life against the promise of biomedical breakthroughs. Under these conditions, a key question is not so much whether religion is becoming more or less important in public policy contests—the familiar secularization debate—but instead how religious and secular arguments are changing and interacting under the impact of both scientific and technological progress and greater religious pluralism.

In the context of stem cell politics, that question is taking on an increasingly global character. As advanced life sciences research moves around the world, the question of its governance is posed differently within diverse cultural and religious contexts. In the rising biomedical powers of China, India, and South Korea, for example, national strategic interests exist alongside incipient ethical debates informed by secular, Confucian, Buddhist, and Hindu traditions. In Pakistan, Saudi Arabia, and other Muslim countries, a religious context generally supportive of embryo research is facilitating the expansion of still underdeveloped scientific capacities. The rise of new scientific powers with different democratic and religious traditions complicates prospects for any workable international governance of ethically charged life sciences research. It also points to the importance of extending the analysis of religious pluralism, politics, and the governance of science beyond the transatlantic context.

NOTES

1. Throughout, "stem cell research" is shorthand for "human embryonic stem cell research." Research with adult stem cells and stem cells derived from nonhuman embryos is relatively uncontroversial.

2. Suzanne Holland, Karen Lebacqz, and Laurie Zoloth, eds., *The Human Embryonic Stem Cell Debate: Science, Ethics, and Public Policy* (Cambridge: MIT Press, 2001); Paul Lauritzen, *Cloning and the Future of Human Embryo Research* (Oxford: Oxford University Press, 2001); and Barbara MacKinnon, *Human Cloning: Science, Ethics, and Public Policy* (Urbana: University of Illinois Press, 2000). On the politics of the U.S. case, see Andrea L. Bonnicksen, *Crafting a Cloning Policy: From Dolly to Stem Cells* (Washington, DC: Georgetown University Press, 2002).

3. *Frankfurter Allgemeine Zeitung*, Oct. 15, 2001, 9.

4. Roger Pedersen, "Can't Stem Progress," *Times Higher Education Supplement*, March 26, 2004, 16.

5. For recent overviews of this terrain, see William A. Galston, *Politics, Policy, and Religion in the 21st Century* (Lanham, MD: Rowman & Littlefield, 2005); Jeffrey Stout, *Democracy and Tradition* (Princeton: Princeton University Press, 2003); William E. Connolly, *Why I Am Not a Secularist* (Minneapolis: University of Minnesota Press, 2000); and Robert Audi and Nicholas Wolterstorff, *Religion in the Public Square* (Lanham, MD: Rowman & Littlefield, 1997).

6. For influential approaches to ideas of the religious and the secular, see José Casanova, *Public Religions in the Modern World* (Chicago: University of Chicago Press, 1994), ch. 1; and Talal Asad, "Religion, Nation-State, Secularism," in Peter van der Veer and Hartmut Lehmann, eds., *Nation and Religion: Perspectives on Europe and Asia* (Princeton 1999), 178–196.

7. Thomas Banchoff, "Path Dependence and Value-Driven Issues: The Comparative Politics of Stem Cell Research," *World Politics* 57.2 (Jan. 2005): 200–230. For a related discussion of "morality policy," see Christopher Z. Mooney, ed., *The Public Clash of Private Values: The Politics of Morality Policy* (New York: Chatham, 2001); and Raymond Tatalovich and Byron W. Daynes, eds., *Moral Controversies in American Politics: Cases in Social Regulatory Policy* (Armonk: Sharpe, 1998).

8. This concept was most fully developed in John Paul II's 1995 encyclical *Evangelium Vitae*. Cardinal Joseph Bernardin of Chicago was among the progenitors of the idea; see his *A Moral Vision for America* (Washington, DC: Georgetown University Press, 1998).

9. Congregation for the Doctrine of the Faith, *Declaration on Procured Abortion* (Vatican: Holy See, 1974); and *Instruction on Respect for Human Life in Its Origin and on the Dignity of Procreation: Donum Vitae* (Vatican: Holy See, 1987).

10. "Report of the Ethics Advisory Board," 44 *Federal Register* 35033–58 (June 18, 1979). Richard McCormick, a member of the Department of Health, Education, and Welfare's Ethics Advisory Board, exemplified the liberal Catholic perspective. For an overview of philosophical positions favorable to embryo research, see Peter Singer, ed., *Embryo Experimentation: Ethical, Legal, and Social Issues* (Cambridge: Cambridge University Press, 1990).

11. *Report of the Human Embryo Research Panel* (Bethesda: National Institutes of Health, 1994), ix–xii.

12. "Testimony of Richard M. Doerflinger on behalf of the Committee for Pro-Life Activities, National Conference of Catholic Bishops, before the Senate Appropriations Subcommittee on Labor, Health, and Education Hearing on Embryonic Cell

Research, December 2, 1998," http://www.nccbuscc.org/prolife/issues/bioethic/
1202.htm.

13. For an overview of the Human Embryo Research Panel's work and the fate of
its recommendations, see Ronald M. Green, *The Human Embryo Research Debates:
Bioethics in the Vortex of Controversy* (Oxford: Oxford University Press, 2001).

14. Conseil d'état, *Sciences de la vie: de l'éthique au droit* (Paris: Documentation
Française, 1988).

15. National Consultative Bioethics Committee, "Opinion on Research and Use
of In-vitro Human Embryos for Scientific and Medical Purposes" (Paris: CCNE,
Dec. 15, 1986).

16. Jean-Marie Lustiger, cited in *Le monde*, Jan. 12, 1994. On the marginalization
of the Catholic Church in French politics and society, see Danièle Hervieu-Léger,
Catholicisme: la fin d'un monde (Paris: Bayard, 2003).

17. Assemblée Nationale, *Compte rendu analytique officiel* (Paris: Assemblée
Nationale, 1994), 650, 652 (April 7, 1994).

18. Ibid., 799 (April 14, 1994); 5749 (Nov. 19, 1992).

19. "Embryos: Drawing the Line," *Washington Post*, Oct. 2, 1994.

20. *Congressional Record*, Feb. 11, 1998, S600, S604.

21. "Transition in Washington; Research and Morality," *New York Times*, Jan. 20,
2001.

22. "Synod OKs Federally-Funded Embryonic Stem Cell Research," *United
Church News*, July 11–17, 2001.

23. Institute for Public Affairs, Union of Orthodox Jewish Congregations of
America, "Letter to President Bush Regarding Stem Cell Research," press release,
July 26, 2001; and Abdul Aziz Sachedina, in *Ethical Issues in Human Stem Cell Research*,
vol. 3: *Religious Perspectives* (Rockville: National Bioethics Advisory Commission,
2000), G-6.

24. The Vatican, "Address of Pope John Paul II to the President of the United
States of America, H.H. George Walker Bush," press release, July 23, 2001; Stephen S.
Hall, *Merchants of Immortality: Chasing the Dream of Life Extension* (Boston: Houghton
Mifflin, 2003), 274; James Randerson, "The Battle over Stem Cells," *New Scientist*,
Oct. 9, 2004; and Thomas H. Murray, "Hard Cell," *American Prospect*, Sept. 28, 2001.

25. White House, "Remarks by the President on Stem Cell Research," press
release, Aug. 9, 2001.

26. White House, "President Bush Calls on Senate to Back Human Cloning
Ban," April 10, 2002; and "Remarks via Satellite by the President to the National
Association of Evangelicals Convention," March 11, 2004.

27. "Watson, Other Scientists Celebrate DNA Discovery," *The Mercury News*, Feb.
21, 2003; "Embryos to Be Treated as Human Subjects," *Nature Medicine*, Dec. 2002,
1338.

28. *Congressional Record*, July 31, 2001, H4919.

29. John Kerry, "Democratic Radio Address," campaign press release, July 12,
2004; idem, "Radio Address to the Nation," campaign press release, Aug. 7, 2004.

30. White House, "Remarks by President Bush and Senator Kerry in Second
2004 Presidential Debate," press release, Oct. 9, 2004.

31. Jean François Mattei, "Vers une revision des lois 'bioethique'?" in *Les lois
bioéthiques a l'épreuve des faits*, ed. Briggitte Feuillet-Le Minter (Paris: PUF, 1999), 333.

32. Axel Kahn, "Clone Mammals...Clone Man?" *Nature* 386 (March 13, 1997).

33. National Consultative Bioethics Committee, "Opinion on the Preliminary
Draft Revision of the Laws on Bioethics" (Paris: CCNE, Jan. 18, 2001).

34. "Allocution de M. Jacques Chirac, President de la République," press release, Feb. 8, 2001.

35. "Déclaration du Conseil permanent de la Conférence des évêques de France," press release, June 25, 2001.

36. "Lionel Jospin renonce à légaliser le clonage à visée thérapeutique," *Le monde*, June 16, 2001. See also, Conseil d'état, *Les lois de bioéthique: cinq ans après* (Paris, 1999), 10.

37. Assemblée Nationale, *Compte rendu analytique officiel* (Paris: Assemblée Nationale, 2003), 11994 (Dec. 9, 2003).

38. Ibid., 12012, 12014.

39. Lucien Sève, "L'humain n'est pas une marchandise," *L'humanité*, Feb. 9, 2001.

BIBLIOGRAPHY

Asad, Talal. "Religion, Nation-State, Secularism." In *Nation and Religion: Perspectives on Europe and Asia*. Edited by Peter van der Veer and Hartmut Lehmann. Princeton: Princeton University Press, 178–196.

Audi, Robert, and Nicholas Wolterstorff. *Religion in the Public Square*. Lanham, MD: Rowman & Littlefield 1997.

Banchoff, Thomas. "Path Dependence and Value-Driven Issues: The Comparative Politics of Stem Cell Research." *World Politics* 57.2 (Jan. 2005): 200–230.

Bernardin, Joseph. *A Moral Vision for America*. Washington, DC: Georgetown University Press, 1998.

Bonnicksen, Andrea L. *Crafting a Cloning Policy: From Dolly to Stem Cells*. Washington, DC: Georgetown University Press, 2002.

Casanova, José. *Public Religions in the Modern World*. Chicago: University of Chicago Press, 1994.

Congregation for the Doctrine of the Faith. *Declaration on Procured Abortion*. Vatican: Holy See, 1974.

———. *Instruction on Respect for Human Life in Its Origin and on the Dignity of Procreation: Donum Vitae*. Vatican: Holy See, 1987.

Connolly, William E. *Why I Am Not a Secularist*. Minneapolis: University of Minnesota Press, 2000.

Conseil d'état. *Les lois de bioéthique: cinq ans après*. Paris, 1999.

———. *Sciences de la vie: de l'éthique au droit*. Paris: Documentation Française, 1988.

Doerflinger, Richard M. "Testimony of Richard M. Doerflinger on behalf of the Committee for Pro-Life Activities, National Conference of Catholic Bishops, before the Senate Appropriations Subcommittee on Labor, Health, and Education Hearing on Embryonic Cell Research, December 2, 1998." http://www.nccbuscc .org/prolife/issues/bioethic/1202.htm.

———. Testimony on Behalf of the U.S. Conference of Catholic Bishops before the President's Council on Bioethics, June 13, 2003. http://www.bioethics.gov/ transcripts/jun03/session6.html.

Evangelium Vitae. Encyclical Letter on the Value and Inviolability of Human Life. Pope John Paul II. March 25, 1995.

Ethical Issues in Human Stem Cell Research, vol. 3: *Religious Perspectives*. Rockville: National Bioethics Advisory Commission, 2000.

Galston, William A. *Politics, Policy, and Religion in the 21st Century*. Lanham, MD: Rowman & Littlefield, 2005.

Green, Ronald M. *The Human Embryo Research Debates: Bioethics in the Vortex of Controversy.* Oxford: Oxford University Press, 2001.

Hall, Stephen S. *Merchants of Immortality: Chasing the Dream of Life Extension.* Boston: Houghton Mifflin 2003.

Hervieu-Léger, Danièle. *Catholicisme: la fin d'un monde.* Paris: Bayard, 2003.

Holland, Suzanne, Karen Lebacqz, and Laurie Zoloth, eds. *The Human Embryonic Stem Cell Debate: Science, Ethics, and Public Policy.* Cambridge: MIT Press, 2001.

Lauritzen, Paul. *Cloning and the Future of Human Embryo Research.* Oxford: Oxford University Press, 2001.

MacKinnon, Barbara. *Human Cloning: Science, Ethics, and Public Policy.* Urbana: University of Illinois Press, 2000.

Mattei, Jean Francois. "Vers une revision des lois 'bioethique'?" In *Les lois bioethiques a l'epreuve des faits,* ed. Briggitte Feuillet-Le Minter. Paris: PUF, 1999.

Mooney, Christopher Z., ed. *The Public Clash of Private Values: The Politics of Morality Policy.* New York: Chatham, 2001.

National Consultative Bioethics Committee. "Opinion on Research and Use of In-vitro Human Embryos for Scientific and Medical Purposes." Paris: CCNE, Dec. 15, 1986.

———. "Opinion on the Preliminary Draft Revision of the Laws on Bioethics." Paris: CCNE, Jan. 18, 2001.

Report of the Human Embryo Research Panel. Bethesda: National Institutes of Health, 1994.

Singer, Peter., ed. *Embryo Experimentation: Ethical, Legal, and Social Issues.* Cambridge: Cambridge University Press, 1990.

Stout, Jeffrey. *Democracy and Tradition.* Princeton: Princeton University Press, 2003.

Tatalovich, Raymond, and Byron W. Daynes, eds. *Moral Controversies in American Politics: Cases in Social Regulatory Policy.* Armonk: Sharpe, 1998.

Index

Church and state, separation
of, 274
Church of England, 61
Cicero, 199n26
Citizenship, 115, 204, 253
Muslims and, 205–8
Civic perspectives on pluralism, 259
Civil liberty, 165
Civil religions, 180–86
Civil rights, 189–92
Civil War, 188, 189, 194
Clinton, Bill, 262, 308, 312
Clinton, Hillary, 262
Cloning, 301, 311, 312
bans on, 313–14
"Cloud Gate" (Kapoor), 196
Cobb, John, 283
Comity, 22
Common cores, 275–77
Communautarisme, 234
Communism, fall of, 60, 227
Communist Manifesto (Marx and
Engels), 6
Comte, Auguste, 32, 183
Conflict, 275
Congregationalism, 68, 227
Conseil consultatif des musulmans de
France, 209
Conseil de réflexion sur l'islam en
France, 209
Conseil d'etat, 212
Conseil français du culte musulman,
210–13
Conservative Jews, 91, 93, 98, 100,
101, 102
Constitution, 135, 190, 257, 259,
260, 263
Cosmopolitan memory, 89
Council on American-Islamic Relations
(CAIR), 136, 246–47, 267n10
Crockett, Alasdair, 42
Crusades, 289–90
Curzon, Lord, 201n43
Czech Republic, 62

Dalai Lama, 254
Darwall, Stephen, 197n
Dauber, Michele Landis, 193, 194
Davie, Grace, 11

Declaration of Independence, 190
Declaration of the Rights of
Man, 206
Decolonization, 59–60
Deigh, John, 197n
Democracy, 136
American identity and, 164–66
consocial, 274
liberal, 273–75
Muslims and, 145–46
new religious movements and,
225–28
religious diversity and, 3–4,
139–44
tolerance and, 234–35
Denominationalism
American, 66–70, 244
evils of, 76
Department of Health, Education, and
Welfare's Ethics Advisory Board, 317
Depression, 193–93
Detroit, 248, 251
Dhimmi, 137, 144–45
Dialogue, 286
Diaspora
Islamic, 216–17
Jewish, 86, 88, 90, 94–97, 99, 100,
103, 104
Dignity, 316
Dinoia, Joseph, 287, 290
Diwali, 257
Doerflinger, Richard, 308, 313
Dolly the sheep, 301, 312
Donum Vitae, 307
Dulles, Avery Cardinal, 295n5
Dunn, Richard, 286
Durkheim, Émile, 32

Eastern Europe, 272
Eck, Diana, 12, 303
Economic inequality, 46f, 47
Education, 178
moral, 183
public, 183
Edwards, Robert, 306
Eichmann trial, 98
Eid, 260, 262
Eisenhower administration, 97
11-M, 124–25